Perspectives on American and Texas Politics
A Collection of Essays

SECOND EDITION

Donald S. Lutz
Kent L. Tedin
University of Houston

KENDALL/HUNT PUBLISHING COMPANY
2460 Kerper Boulevard   P.O. Box 539   Dubuque, Iowa 52004-0539

Copyright © 1987, 1989 by Kendall/Hunt Publishing Company

Library of Congress Catalog Card Number: 89-80805

ISBN 0-8403-5463-0

All rights reserved. No part of this publication may be reproduced, stored in a retrieval system, or transmitted, in any form or by any means, electronic, mechanical, photocopying, recording, or otherwise, without the prior written permission of the copyright owner.

Printed in the United States of America
10 9 8 7 6 5

Contents

Introduction v

Chapter 1 The Political Geography of Texas 1
  John Coffman

Chapter 2 Understanding Public Opinion Polls 21
  Kent L. Tedin

Chapter 3 The Ideology of the American Electorate 41
  Kathleen Knight

Chapter 4 The Paradox of Ignorant Voter, but Competent Electorate 57
  James A. Stimson

Chapter 5 The Puzzle of Low Voter Turnout in the United States 71
  Robert S. Erikson

Chapter 6 Institutional Change in Congress 85
  Bruce Oppenheimer

Chapter 7 Presidential Influences on the Federal Courts 97
  Robert A. Carp

Chapter 8 Conservative and Liberal Evaluations of the Reagan Presidency 109
  John W. Sloan

Chapter 9 Administering America: Bureaucracy in Democracy 125
  Ulf Zimmermann

Chapter 10 Democracy, Civil Liberties, and Political Tolerance 147
  James L. Gibson and James P. Wenzel

Chapter 11 The American Poor: Myths and Reality 169
  Harrell Rodgers

Chapter 12 Federal-State Relations: New Federalism in Theory and Practice 183
  Malcolm Goggin

Chapter 13 The Texas Constitution 201
  Donald S. Lutz

Chapter 14   The Transition of Electoral Politics in Texas: Voting for Governor in 1978–1986   221
Kent L. Tedin

Chapter 15   The Politics of Judicial Selection in Texas   239
Richard Murray

Chapter 16   The Politics of Educational Reform in Texas   249
Gregory R. Weiher and the Graduate Student Public Policy Research Group

Chapter 17   City Charters and Their Political Implications   259
Robert Thomas

Chapter 18   Power in the City: Patterns of Political Influence in Houston, Texas   277
Richard Murray

Chapter 19:   The Grand Jury: Texas as a Case Study   295
Robert A. Carp

Chapter 20:   Politics and the Texas Economy: The Market for Texas   315
Alan Stone

Introduction

This book is unusual in several respects. First of all, it is not a book of readings but a collection of essays. Whereas the standard book of readings contains reprints of articles and essays already published elsewhere, each chapter in this volume is an original contribution by someone commissioned to write a piece in their area of expertise. The result is a collection of essays written specifically for this volume. Thus, we were able to have each author write for the same audience, college students in American government courses, rather than assembling various pieces of writing—some of which might be written in a narrow, highly technical fashion for professional journals, and others of which might be written for readers of newspapers. Also, by commissioning each chapter, the editors were able to suggest beforehand the kinds of questions and methods of approach that would be most interesting, and thereby to supplement and improve upon the information often contained in standard textbooks on American politics.

Textbooks must, of necessity, cover a topic comprehensively and in general outline. What gets lost in textbooks is the flavor of politics as a process, the historical background to that process, and an in-depth understanding of how all the various aspects of politics fit together. The editors have here tried to commission chapters which deal with important matters not normally covered in textbooks—chapters which are written in such a way as to present the flavor of politics, some historical background, and a sense of how the pieces fit together. Another way of saying the same thing is that the authors have written chapters which provide a sense of perspective on American politics.

By "perspective" we do not mean the presentation of different views on a topic in the sense of setting up side by side articles that are opposed to each other in their approach and conclusions. Rather, the editors hope to give the student a sense of which questions in politics are important and require further thought, a sense of what the informed citizen must know if he or she is to be a rational participant in the American political system, and a sense of how political institutions and processes change over time—how they got to be the way they are and what may lead to further change in the future.

An important part of that sense of perspective, and an unusual feature of this book, is the provision of chapters on state and local as well as national politics. We provided chapters on state and local governments in part because these governments are close at hand for the students whom we have frankly targeted as our audience. At the same time, each level of government—national, state, and local—is looked upon as a kind of laboratory for examining certain questions, and the basic political process is typical enough for the information to be of interest to students who live in any state or locality.

For example, one chapter follows the history of Houston politics through its experiences with the three major forms of local government—the commission form, the council-manager form, and the council-mayor form. Students learn not only the basics of each type of government, but also how each tends to structure the political process. The basic sense of politics that is thus provided can be applied to any locality in America.

Likewise, the chapters on power in the city, grand juries, the selection of judges, civil liberties, citizen participation, and American ideologies, to name a few, raise issues, describe fundamental political processes, and provide information that is useful anywhere. Our hope is that students of American politics, by using this volume as a supplement to a standard textbook, can come to a much deeper sense of how political institutions and processes interact at different levels of government to produce the remarkable thing we know as the American political system.

Finally, the various chapters serve as exemplars of the different methods of analysis used by members of the discipline. Equally as important, most chapters illustrate the manner in which the study of politics requires a blending of theoretical and empirical concerns—the manner and extent to which political analysis involves a variety of skills and methods mixed together in a blend that is often not only scientific but also artful. Asking the right question in the right way, drawing reasonable inferences from the data, and recognizing when one does not have some of the information required to systematically reach a conclusion, is part of the art of political analysis, and part of the perspective we hope to convey with this volume.

In this second edition we tried to overcome some of the shortcomings that both our students and colleagues saw in the first. We have added a chapter on the political geography of Texas, we have three new chapters that deal directly with the institutional setting of govenrment, we have also added a chapter on the Texas economy. In addition, several other chapters have been completely rewritten and updated.

Donald S. Lutz
Kent L. Tedin
April 1, 1989

1 The Political Geography of Texas

JOHN COFFMAN

Almost everyone on this planet has heard of Texas. However unfounded their impressions, whether of a miraculous giant with generous millionaires and a genteel life for even the poorest; or of a barren, boring land of philistine red-necks and ill-educated oil barons, the people of the world know that Texas is a place unique unto itself.

At least part of Texas' renown is based on substantive fact. Texas is large: its 266,807 square miles may leave the state at second rank after Alaska among the states, but compared to other nations of the world Texas would rank 28th in size (between Zambia and Burma). It is in the upper fifth of the world's nations as ranked by size. In population, Texas' 17 million people (1989) will likely rank second only to California in the 1990 census and 43rd (between Malaysia and Australia), which places it, compared to nations, in the upper quarter. On many other measures, such as petroleum and natural gas production, per capita GNP, or percentage of its population awaiting execution, Texas ranks even higher when compared to the nations of the world (see Table 1). These comparisons of the *state* of Texas with other *nations* of the world is not as odd as it might seem, for Texas was indeed once an independent nation (1836–1845)—the only state in the union that can make that claim.

Table 1 Comparison of the State of Texas to Nations of the World

	Rank of Texas Compared with all Nations (1982)
Size (Square Miles)	28th
Size (Population)	43rd
Gross National (State) Product	12th
Gross National Product per Capita	2nd
Number of Telephones	10th
Oil Production	5th
Salt Production	5th
Gypsum Production	11th
Cotton Production	5th
Rice Production	15th
Corn Production	17th
Wheat Production	23rd
Infant Mortality	10 lowest
Physicians per Capita	41st

Source: *Fiscal Notes* (Office of the Comptroller, Austin, Texas, December, 1984).

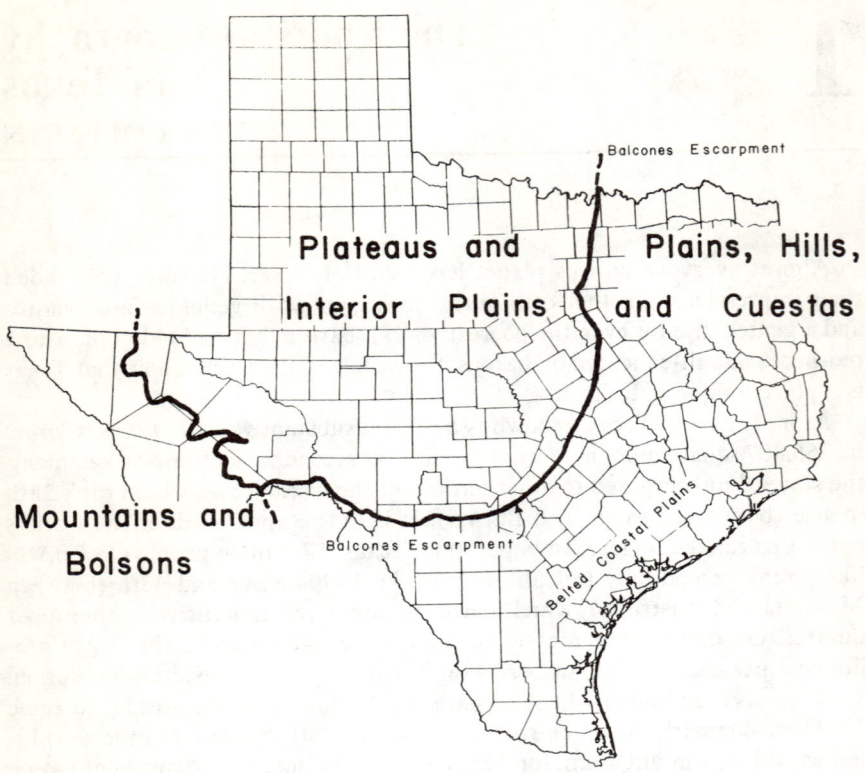

Figure 1.1 Major Physiographic Regions of Texas.

The Natural Environment

Landforms and Soil

The landforms of Texas divide into three large regions (see Figure 1). (1) The coastal plains of east Texas, (2) the west-central plateaus, and (3) the mountains of westernmost Texas. The coastal plains of Texas are part of a vast geographic formation known as Gulf Coastal Plains of the United States. The coastal plains constitute about a third of the land area of Texas and extend in a 200 mile belt from the Red River on the Oklahoma border to the Rio Grande on the Mexican border. The northeastern third of the land is forested East Texas Piney Woods, home to a sizable timber industry. The southwestern third, the South Texas Plains, is ranching country, home of many large estates such as the famous King Ranch, and the citrus and vegetable production of the Rio Grande Valley. The middle third consists of alternating

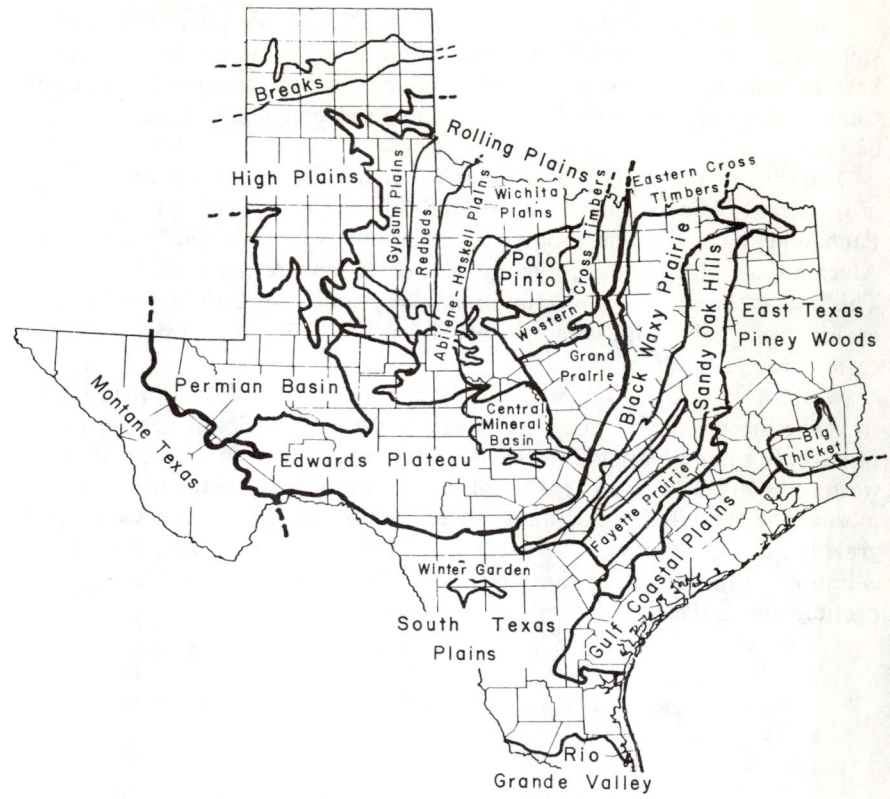

Figure 1.2 Physiographic Regions of Texas.

belts of rich blackland prairie and poor sandy oak/hickory uplands from the Western Cross Timber to the Gulf Coast (see Figure 2). Fort Worth is on the Grand Prairie; Dallas, Waco, Temple, Austin, and San Antonio on the Black Waxy Prairie; and Beaumont, Houston, and Corpus Christi on the Gulf Coast Plains. It was on the Gulf Coastal Plains that oil was first discovered in large quantities.

Between the Balcones Escarpment caused by a fault in the earth's crust (see Figure 1) and the western mountains lie the three great elevated plains (i.e., plateaus). The Rolling Plains region, a southern extension of the American Interior Plains, contains Texas' worst agricultural lands (in the Gypsum Plains and Redbeds) as well as some of its better farm lands (the Abilene Haskell Plain and Wichita Plain).

South of the Rolling Plains is the Edwards Plateau, a massive slab of limestone, often only bare rock at the surface. Only sheep and goats thrive in this barren landscape. The scenic canyons of the eastern Edwards Plateau and Central Mineral Region (see Figure 2) are a retirement and recreation focus of Texas.

The third plateau, the High Plains (or Llano Estacado) is a continuation of the Great Plains of the U. S. The High Plains, covering most of the Texas' Panhandle, have more in common with Kansas, Nebraska, the Dakota's and Alberta than with the stereotype many people have of the Lone Star State. This area is the state's prime crop-producing region—specializing in sorghum grains throughout, with winter wheat to the north focused on Amarillo and cotton around Lubbock.

Westernmost Texas is dominated by mountains which form a line ranging from the Sierra Nevada of northern Mexico to the Rockies of northern New Mexico. Big Bend National Park, one of the true geographical marvels of the western hemisphere, is located in this area. In the higher plateaus that circle most of the West Texas mountain ranges, rich brown steppe soils make cattle grazing quite productive. Otherwise, crop agriculture in mountainous Texas is limited to the broader valleys of irrigated soils along the Rio Grande near Presidio and El Paso (the area's major city).

POPULATION

Texas' population has grown remarkably in the past 100 years:

	Population	*Rank Among the States*
1880	1,591,749	11
1900	3,048,710	6
1920	4,633,288	5
1940	6,414,824	6
1960	9,579,677	6
1980	14,229,191	3
1990	17,500,000	2

Since Texas entered the Union in 1845 its population has increased at least 20 percent between censuses except for 1910–1920 (World War I) and the depression decade (1930–1940). Prior to 1900 most of Texas' growth was created by agricultural in-migrants from the South, who came to take advantage of cheap virgin lands in Texas before and after the Civil War. Since World War II most Texas in–migrants have been attracted by job opportunities related to the petroleum industry. These recent immigrants are, however, much different than those who came prior to WWII. Rather than being from the

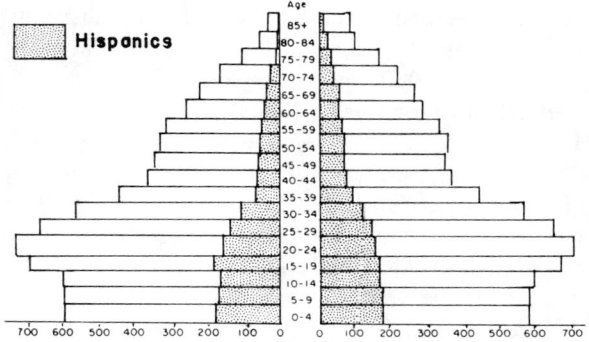

Figure 1.3 Population Pyramid of Texas, 1980 (in thousands).

rural south with little formal education, they tend to be from the midwest and east and often have college degrees.

Surveys show that compared to life-long residents, recent immigrants are younger, better educated and wealthier. About 1/3 have college degrees contrasted to 1/6 of life-long Texans. These newcomers are also considerably more Republican and, interestingly, more liberal as well (particularly on social issues). About 33 percent claim affiliation with the Republican party compared to 20 percent of native Texans. They are also more supportive than natives of the social and political rights of minorities and other unpopular groups.[1]

Texas' population pyramid (see Figure 3) shows the marked influence of the baby boom in the state's population structure. Note that by 1990 this whole structure will have moved upward two levels. By the year 2000, many of the baby boomers will be in their forties and fifties, meaning that a large percentage of the state's population will be at the peak of their earning power.

A significant portion of the white population is beyond child-bearing years while much of the Hispanic population is just approaching puberty. This differential in age distribution as well as higher birth rates among Hispanics has led the Texas Department of Health to make the following projections about the ethnic composition of the Texas population for the years 1990 and 2000.[2]

Ethnic Percentages of the Texas Population

	1980	1990	2000
Anglos	67.0%	60.1%	51.6%
Blacks	11.9	10.3	8.4
Hispanics	21.1	28.6	39.0
Asiatics, Other	1.0	1.0	1.0
	100.0%	100.0%	100.0%

The percentage of the population that is black has consistently declined in the last 100 years. It was 42 percent in 1840, 30 percent in 1870, 12.7 percent in 1950, 11.9 percent in 1980, and is projected to decline to 8.4 percent by the year 2000. Black birth rates are only slightly higher than comparable white birth rates. Higher infant, childhood and teen-age mortality rates among blacks leaves very similar rates of increase for blacks and whites by age 20. In contrast, Hispanics and American Indians have significantly higher birth rates. These higher rates appear to be maintained even with improvements in education and income. The Anglo population of Texas makes up the majority of all counties except for the first two tiers of counties along the Rio Grande, where Hispanics are a clear majority—over 90 percent in Jim Hogg, Maverick, Star and Webb counties.

Distribution

Nineteenth century immigrants into Texas were mainly from two sources: (1) modestly affluent slave-holding English-Methodist planters from the lower south (especially Louisiana, Mississippi, Alabama, and Georgia), Scotch-Irish[3] frontiersmen/farmers of Baptist and other Calvinist groups from Tennessee, Arkansas, and Missouri. The immigrants from the Lower South had significantly smaller families, probably to prevent decimating their estates among numerous children. By contrast, the Scotch-Irish created their farm work force by having children. As a result, the overwhelming majority of the Anglo-American stock and a near majority of Texas and U.S. total population is of Scotch-Irish origin.

Although British groups dominate the European population of Texas, there are several central European groups which have left their mark on Texas, particularly in rural areas. Germans, many originally from Hesse in central Germany, are dominant northwest of Houston from Brenham to Schulenberg, around Yorktown and Cuero in south central Texas, and from New Braunfels to Fredericksburg and Mason. The rather poor agricultural conditions in the German Hill county has left this region undisturbed economically and thus quite distinctly German.

Similarly, Czech migrants, focused originally on Praha near Flatonia, are now dominant in many areas of central and coastal Texas. There are smaller communities of Polish, Swedish, Norwegian, Danish, and Italian groups located mainly in south central Texas.

Although Blacks in 1860 made up a majority of the counties around Houston and in northeast Texas, today no county in Texas has a black majority; Waller country, near Houston, with 42 percent is the highest (see Figure 4). Black populations are largest in Houston (474,000) and Dallas (288,000); however, the much larger Anglo populations in each of these urban counties creates a Black percentage of only about 17.5 percent in both Dallas and Harris counties. The largest rural concentration of Blacks in Texas is in the ante-bellum

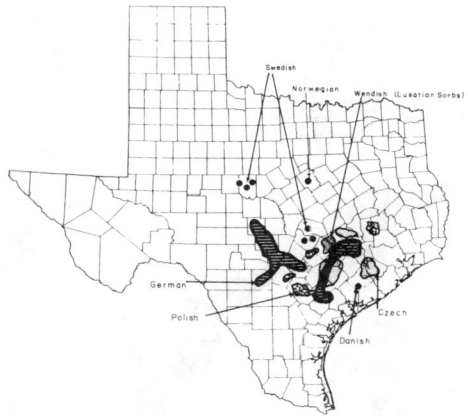

Figure 1.4 Non-British European Settlements in Texas in the 19th Century.

plantation areas along the Brazos and Trinity valleys of south Texas and in northeast Texas around Marshal. Over 80 percent of the rural Black population is in the East Texas Piney Woods. No county west of a line following I-35 south to Austin and thence southeast to Victoria has as much as 10 percent Black population.

The group that has risen to displace blacks as the principal minority group of Texas is the Hispanics. Although there are undoubtedly Hispanics in San Antonio and along the Rio Grande that can trace their heritage to Mexican Texas (1823–1836), there were few Hispanics left in Texas after the bitter U.S./Mexican War (1845–1848). Most of Texas' Hispanics have arrived since the Mexican Revolution of 1910. This migration was triggered by political and economic instability in Mexico coupled with the development of new agricultural areas in the Rio Grande valley (by Californians and Mid-westerners) and in the High Plains. Since there was no quota on migration from the nations of the Western Hemisphere until the 1960's, most of the Hispanic residents of Texas were born here or arrived without any significant legal opposition to their migration. Even after the amnesty program of 1987–88, there continues to be illegal immigration into Texas from Mexico and Central America. Nevertheless, the great bulk of the increase in the Hispanic population in the future will be from their high birth rates.

Since 1920 the Hispanic population has been extending into north and northeast Texas. By 1980, nearly all of the counties south of a line from El Paso through San Antonio to Corpus Christi had a Hispanic majority. Counties with more than 10 percent Hispanic population in 1980 extended northeast to a Brownsville-Austin-Houston line. It is obvious that this line is advancing to the northeast to include the urban counties of north and east Texas.

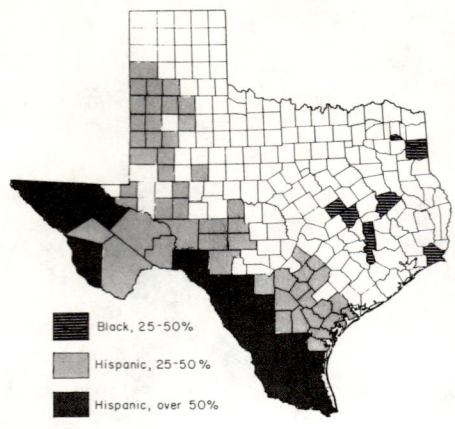

Figure 1.5 Primary Black and Hispanic Areas of Texas.

Texas' oriental population, mainly Vietnamese and Chinese, is concentrated in Houston. The only counties in which orientals account for as much as one percent of the population are small population counties with colleges, military bases, or shrimping activities.

The Texas Economy

The Texas economy is based on two major export products: agricultural goods and petroleum products. Figure 6 shows that about 21 percent of employed Texans are in the export industries. The other 79 percent of the state's workers are providing services. Texas' universities have more than the average number of out-of-state and foreign students, and the Texas Medical Center at Houston clearly serves a national and international clientele.

Agriculture employs only one percent of Texas' labor force, but the $33 billion added by agriculture in 1986 provided many raw materials for Texas' industry and made a major contribution to the service sector.

Although almost the entire non-urban acreage of the state is involved in agriculture, production is very uneven. The first four regions account for over three-quarters of the states production, but these four regions account for less than one-third of the state's land area. Note that the first three are prairie and steppe grasslands with rich black soils. The irrigated oases consist mainly of rich alluvial (river-deposited) soils.

The other agricultural regions of the state occupy two-thirds of the state's land area and account for less than one-fourth of the its agricultural production. Here livestock is extensively raised, although in a relatively unproductive fashion. Crops in these regions are generally isolated in special sandy soils (ideal for sweet potatoes or peanuts) or in irrigated areas.

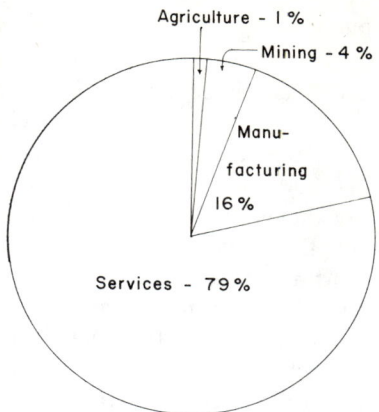

Figure 1.6 Employment Sectors of Texas Labor Force.

Table 2 Agricultural Regions of Texas

Region	Products	Approximate Percent of Farm Production
High Plains		
northern:	wheat, cotton, sorghum	33%
southern:	cotton sorghum	
Interior Prairies		20
grand prairie:	small grains, cotton	
black waxy prairie:	small grains, cotton	
Fayette prairie:	poultry, diary, cotton	
Gulf Coast	cotton, Sorghum, rice	14
Irrigated Oases of South and Motane Texas		10
Rio Grande Valley:	cotton, sorghum, vegetables, fruit	
Winter Garden:	vegetables	
El Paso Area:	cotton, alfalfa, dairy	
E. Texas Piney Woods	poultry, dairy, cotton sweet potatoes	11
Big Thicket:	cattle poultry	
Rolling Plains	cotton, sorghum, wheat	6
South Texas Plains (nonirrigated areas)	cattle, peanuts, cotton, linseed oil	3
Cross Timbers	livestock, dairy peanuts	3
Edwards Plateau	sheep, goats, livestock	2
Montane Texas	cattle, irrigated cotton	1
Permian Basin	cattle, irrigated melons, vegetables	1

Manufacturing and Urban Places

When the nation's first major oil field, Spindletop, came in near Beaumont in 1901, only 17 percent of Texans lived in cities. Rapidly, new salt domes with oil and gas were discovered all along the coastal plains. Houston was the nearest city with modern hotels, refrigerated air, and a modicum of entertainment. Its earlier growth (1848–1900) as a railroad junction had prepared it to be the Texas headquarters of the oil boom. During the 1920's new fields opened in west Texas: the Permian Basin, which continues through the Rolling Plains as the southern leg of the Mid-Continental field, and then the Panhandle field, north of Amarillo, which was rich in natural gas.

During the 1930's, the wildcatter "Dad" Joiner brought in the Kilgore field in a new stratigraphic trap where the major oil companies' experts said there was no oil. The mercantile wealth from 70 years of prime cotton production in the northern Black Waxy Prairie had focused most of the state's banking in Dallas. "Dad" Joiner found money for his dreams in these Dallas banks, and Texas' most productive oilfield was born—the East Texas. The die had been cast: Houston would be the headquarters city for the major oil companies (the Seven Sisters) and the nation's major manufacturer of oil field equipment; Dallas, would becoming the the banking center for the independents—the wildcatters.

Dallas and Fort Worth (see Figure 7) once stood, figuratively, back-to-back with Fort Worth focusing on railroads, cattle, and west Texas; Dallas, on cotton, banking and east Texas. In many ways, Dallas and Fort Worth have grown together. The petroleum industry is still a part of the financial structure of the Metroplex, and its manufacturers produce some important petroleum machinery. Otherwise, Metroplex has become a more diversified manufacturing region, with some focus on aerospace, electronics, and computers.

Houston became the hub of an oil and gas kingdom which extends along the coast from Beaumont and Port Arthur through Victoria to Corpus Christi, with corporate linkages to the producing fields in the Permian Basin, the Panhandle, and east Texas.

Midland (the management town) and Odessa (the blue-collar town) became the regional capitals of the Permian Basin; Abilene and Wichita Falls, for the remainder of the Mid-Continental field; Amarillo, for the Panhandle, and Tyler-Kilgore-Longview-Marshall for the east Texas oil field.

Just before the end of the boom in 1983, 87 percent of Texas' refinery capacity was between Port Arthur and Corpus Christi. It was these oil cities of the Gulf Coast that were hardest hit by the downturn in oil prices after 1983.

Texas' other line-up of cities is along the old Chisholm Trail, now Interstate 35, between San Antonio and Dallas. Only Dallas is significantly involved in the petroleum industry. San Antonio has probably the nation's largest concentration of military bases in a single county. Kileen-Temple-Coperas Cove

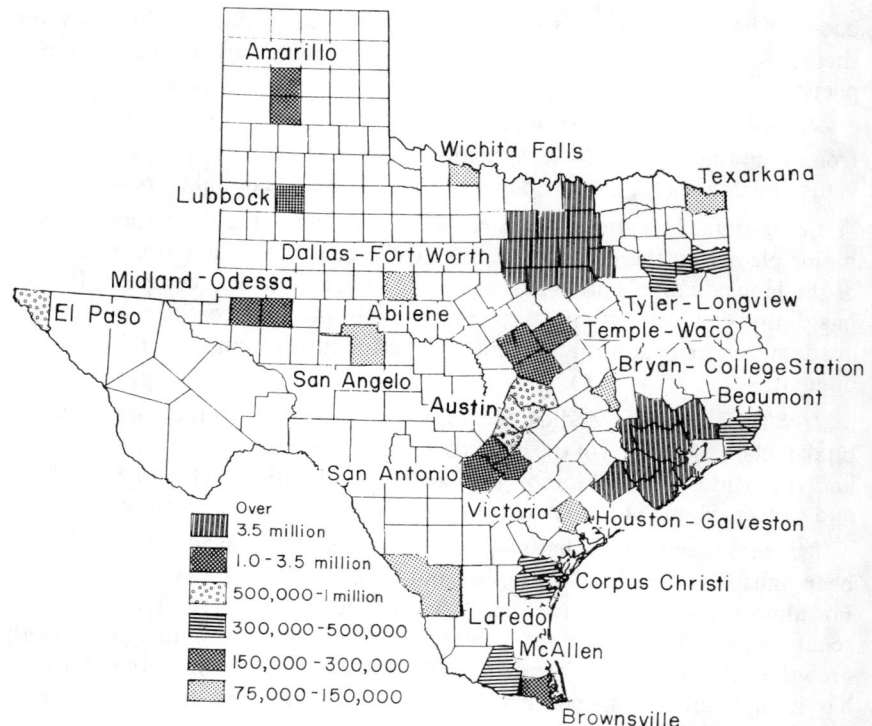

Figure 1.7 Texas Metropolitan Areas.

enjoy similar incomes from Fort Hood, a major Army training base. Waco and Austin both have major universities, with Austin also being the capital of the state, a regional center for the Internal Revenue Service, and a growing computer/electronics focus.

Even the largest of Texas' cities still have some remnants of their agricultural service centers past, but some Texas cities remain specialized only in agribusiness: Bryan/College Station with Texas A&M University, Lubbock with Texas Tech, and the Rio Grande Valley cities from Edinburg and McAllen through Brownsville fall into this category. Finally, Texas has three cities which really specialize in transportation and their gateway function: Texarkana, El Paso, and Laredo.

Although the bursting of the oil bubble had led to much speculation concerning the future economy of the state, local chambers of commerce and other boosters have ranged the spectrum of economic possibilities, but only four themes for the economic future of Texas seem to offer great immediate prospects:

Aerospace. Dallas/Fort Worth has a fifty-year history in aviation, electronics, and aerospace. NASA headquarters southeast of Houston offers obvious advantages for similar developments in the Clear Lake area.

Computers. Houston has joined Dallas in being able to attract and keep major players in the computer industry. Compaq Computer is currently one of the Houston area's prize possessions. Although Austin's computer boomlet has diminished recently in its rate of growth, the I-35 corridor with its rich academic support seems an obvious locale for future computer-related development.

Health. The Texas Medical Center in Houston contains the doctor and hospital of choice for much of the higher socio-economic strata from Latin America and the Middle East. Moreover, in several specialties such as heart disease and cancer, Houston is a specialty medical center for the entire world.

Military. For a state that started with no federally owned land, Texas has been unusually successful in selling and/or giving its land for military bases. For almost a hundred years after Reconstruction, Texas' representatives and senators gained seniority and power that was of no mean advantage in the growth of the military in Texas. Currently, however, the conventional wisdom has it that military spending will diminish as a portion of the government spending, and Texas will do well just to hold its own. In addition, even though a Texan is again Speaker of the House, and Texas' senior senator just ran for Vice-President on the national Democratic ticket, Jim Wright is certainly no Sam Rayburn, and Lloyd Bentsen is probably no Lyndon Johnson.

Electoral Geography

The distribution of the cultural elements of a people are often demonstrated through their voting behavior. One of the most historic votes in Texas' history was that for secession. Germans in Texas voted against secession. A common myth is that they did so because they were impatient with the slave system and because of their European liberal traditions. It should be noted, however, that Comal county, which had a marked German majority, voted strongly for secession. Unlike other German counties, Comal County Germans had acquired good blackland prairies and slaves. Their productive cotton acreage gave the Comal county Germans the same economic interests in secession as their slave-holding Anglo counterparts.

But why then did Germans in general vote against secession? The Scotch-Irish along the Red River were the other major part of Texas to vote against secession. The issue was fear of marauding Indians. In 1861, just west of the settlers in the German Hill country and north of the Red River was Indian country. The frontier settlers believed that all that protected them from plunder, rape, or even murder by their Indian neighbors was the federal troops and forts along their frontier with the Indians. They were afraid that the Confederate government would have neither the will nor the priority funds to continue the protection offered by this string of federal forts. As it turned out their fears seemed well taken, as after secession Indian campfires appeared near Eastertide along the canyons of the Pedernales at Fredericksburg. Re-enactment of these Easter fires has become a tourist attraction in the German Hill country.

After the Civil War, refugees from the Lower South poured westward into Texas' Black Waxy Prairie seeking new and better cotton lands. Successive waves pushed further westward beyond the limits of typical rainfall patterns needed to support cotton production. As the drought years came, crop failures brought poverty and occasional tragedies to the agricultural frontier. To the broken farmers of the frontier, only the railroad seemed to continue to prosper. The Populist Party of Texas grew out of the Western Cross Timbers as it vocalized the frustrations of these farmers against the railroads.

By 1898 Populist majorities had spread through the counties of the state, but the greatest concentrations were in the Western Cross Timbers and in the Sandy Oak Hills. Note that the better-to-do farmers of the best black soil regions were not Populist strongholds. However, by 1900 William Jennings Bryan and the Democratic Party had co-opted the Populist sentiments; the Populist party was history.

In 1954 the juxtaposition of a liberal northern Democrat (Adlai Stevenson) and the economically important tidelands issue broke a long conservative Democratic tradition in Texas. Thereafter, in the ten elections from 1952 to 1988, Texas has voted Republican six times and Democratic four times. Maps of the elections from 1952 to 1988 (Figures 8 through 12) reveal that, although the state's conservative Democratic voting patterns continued at first to dominate most counties, definite regional conservative Republican and liberal Democratic constituencies have developed in particular geographical regions of the state.

The Republican bulwark of Texas is the complex of cities where petroleum dominates the economy: Houston, Dallas, Tyler-Kilgore-Longview, Midland-Odessa, Amarillo, and Abilene. However, this does not include the liberal Democrat blue collar refining cities such as Beaumont-Port Arthur-Orange, Galveston-Texas City, and Corpus Christi, which have high labor union loyalties, high at least for Texas.

The two rural areas with marked Republican preference are the northern High Plains, which are originally settled by Midwestern Republicans and the German Hill country. Slowly, rural East Texas seems to be switching to the Republican party in national elections. Notice the spread through time of the

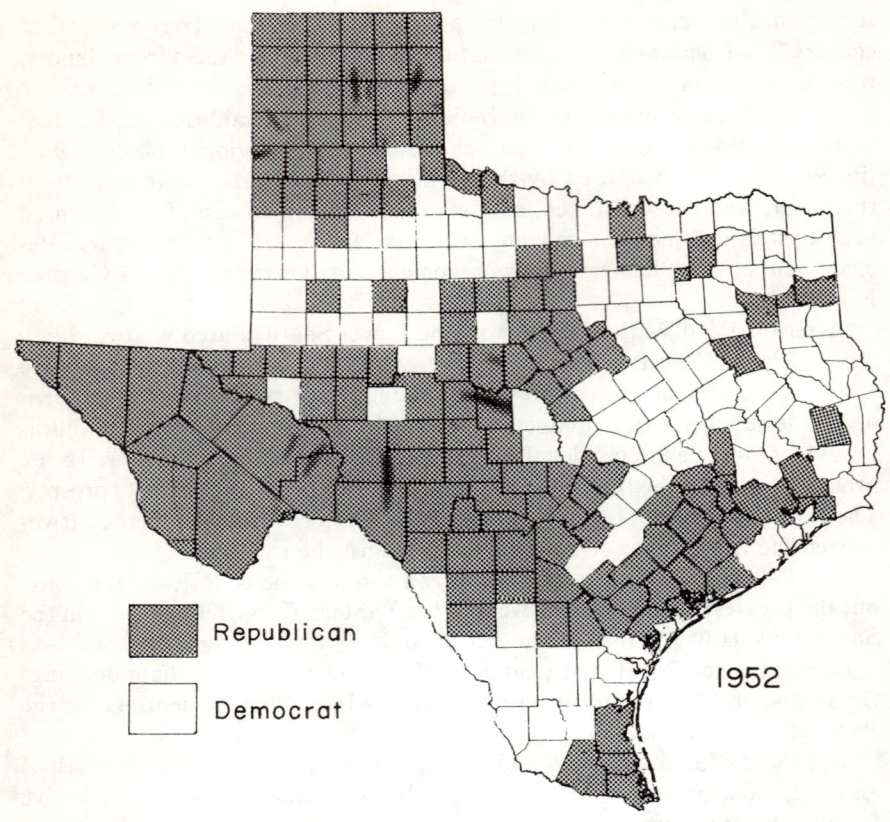

Figure 1.8 Partisan Majorities by County, 1952.

Republican voting strength outward from its base in the petroleum rich Tyler-Kilgore-Longview corridor. By 1988 within the Piney Woods, only the Big Thicket and the traditional rural populations of the Sulphur River bottoms voted Democratic (see figure 11).

The strongest liberal Democratic loyalties are in three areas: (1) the Gypsum Plains, the poorest western fringe of the Rolling Plains, (2) the larger Black populations in the former plantation areas of the Brazos, Trinity, and Sulphur river valleys, and (3) the poor whites of the Big Thicket. Note also the previously described liberal Democratic tradition of Corpus Christi, Galveston-Texas City, and Beaumont-Port Arthur-Orange.

Voting in the South Texas Plains for years was controlled by the Duval County machine—solidly Democratic even in the McGovern debacle of 1972. The other Hispanic areas of Texas are not so reliable. Note that of the election

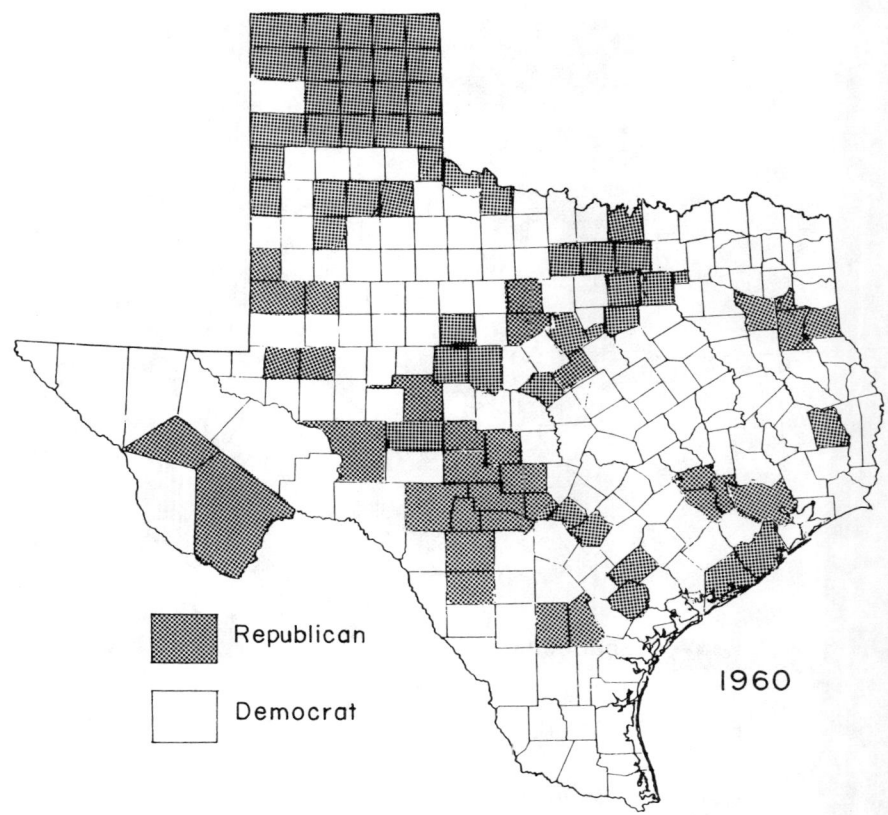

Figure 1.9 Partisan Majorities by County, 1960.

results shown in Figures 8 through 11, Bexar county has voted Republican three times, including 1988; El Paso county, twice. In 1952 Eisenhower (Republican) even carried the Rio Grande valley. Many of the Hispanic counties, including the Rio Grande Valley, have often been carried by conservative Republicans in state-wide elections.

The Future

Predicting the future is a perilous task. A major natural disaster, world war, a Middle East war, worldwide economic depression, any major resource discoveries, or a worldwide deadly viral plague could make the most careful projections and calculations for the future meaningless. Since each of the above items has occurred in the last century, one proceeds cautiously.

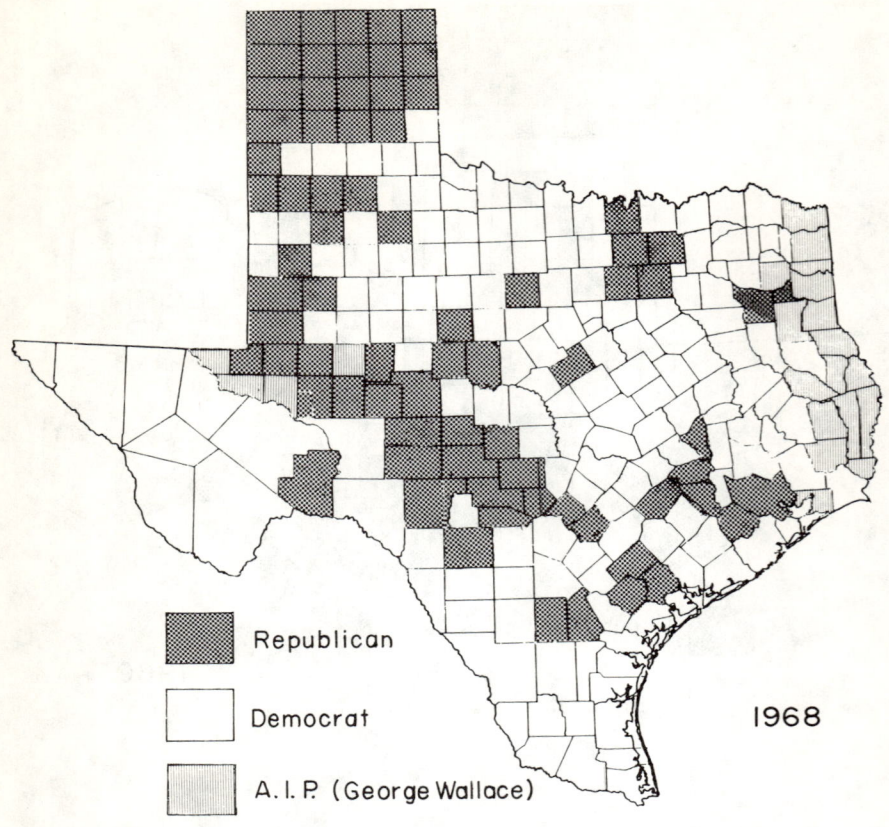

Figure 1.10 Partisan Pluralities by County, 1968.

Natural Environment. The decline of the Ogallala aquifer recharge, unless reversed, will change the High Plains from irrigated agriculture to dry farming, a much less productive system. The pine bark beetle has already damaged the considerable pine acreage in East Texas and changed the forest emphasis to oak and other hardwoods for the future. Also, Texas' chemical industry has left at least its share of polluted sites for the superfund to clean up. Finally, Texas now has operating nuclear power plants which are items of great concern to certain groups. Overall, the massive size of Texas and its resulting lower population densities may protect us from many environmental hazards of the future.

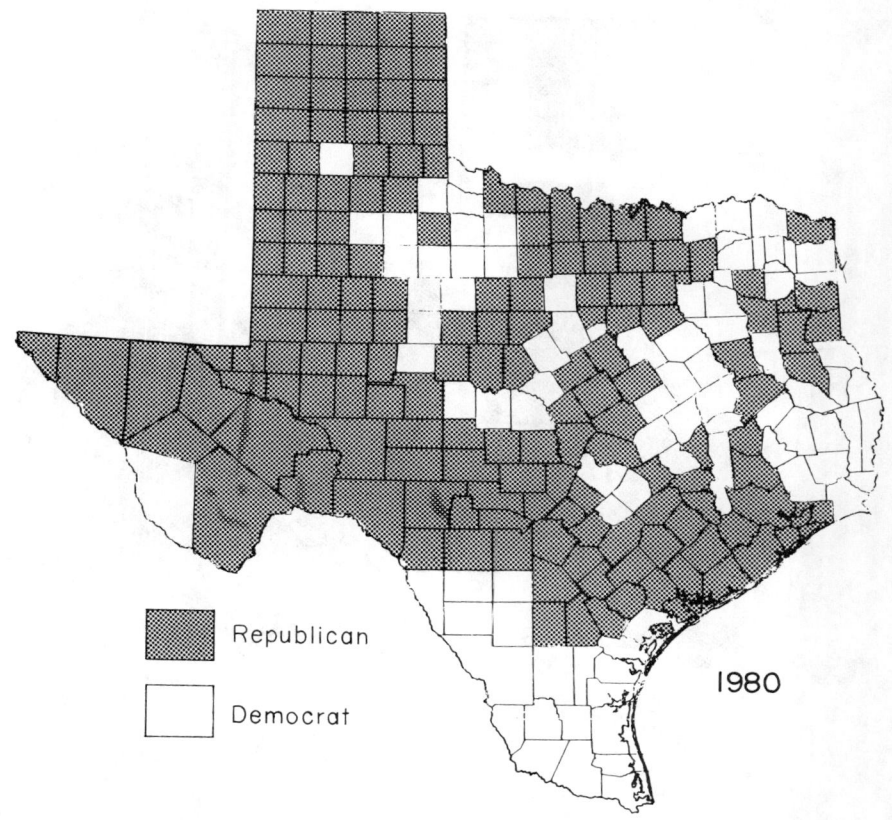

Figure 1.11 Partisan Majorities by County, 1980.

People. If all of the ethnic birth rates remain the same, a Hispanic majority by the year 2010 seems inevitable. Birth rates, however, rarely remain at constant levels through time. Anglos may well again decide to have larger families; more likely, increasing prosperity among Hispanics may encourage them to trade-off large families for lake homes or expensive cars like their Anglo counterparts have done. Nevertheless, marked increases in Hispanic and American Indian populations with parallel declines in Anglo and Black percentages are inevitable. Currently Hispanics vote at much lower rates than Anglos or blacks, thus muting their political strength. However, as they become better assimilated their political participation is likely to approach that of other ethnic groups.

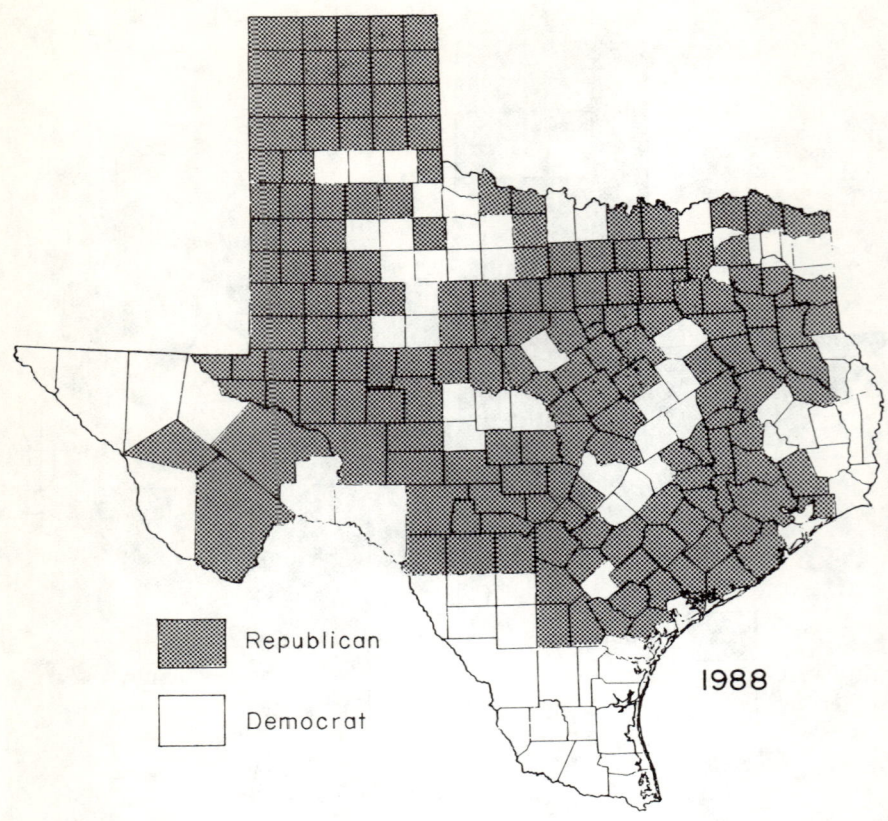

Figure 1.12 Partisan Majorities by County, 1988.

Economy. World demand for agricultural goods almost has to increase in the next decades. Texas' agriculture will profit by producing increasing increments of cotton, sorghum, cattle, and the other specialties of the state.

Coming manufacturing specialties are not so apparent. Lack of a continuing phenomenal boom in the petroleum industry does not necessarily equal a bust. Current petroleum price levels, which may well continue for some time, can continue to support the current leaner, modest petroleum industry of the state. In Houston, Dallas-Fort Worth, and the Chisholm Trail cities, new growth in computers, electronics, aerospace, and research may compensate losses accrued since the glory days (1973–1983) of petroleum. The Waxahatchie supercollider, if funded by the U. S. Congress, could have a significant impact on the Metroplex area.

The continuing growth of housing and industry in exurbia, those areas beyond the usual suburban/rural fringe of our cities will soon complete the Dallas/Fort Worth-San Antonio corridor as a solidly urban axis. Ultimately, similar urban corridors may connect Houston to Dallas (I-45) and to San Antonio (I-10). Since World War II, the boom towns have been along the coast and in the oilfields of west Texas. In the next two decades, the I-35 corridor and the smaller cities and towns of East Texas will likely grow more rapidly. In most cases, the infrastructure (utilities, roads, etc.) of these cities could support a doubling of population without undue stress.

Political. The general political trend of the past 40 years in Texas seems to have favored the Republicans; the Bush-Dukakis contest of 1988 showed surprising Republican strength in East Texas, with Texans running on both the Democratic (Bentsen) and Republican (Bush) tickets. In an ominous sign for the Democrats, the most Republican age group in the electorate is those under 25 and the most Democratic age group is those over 70.

This trend could be easily reversed in the future if the Democratic party could continue the economic promises of welfare, minority opportunity, and the social safety net without offending the very traditional moralistic Hispanic community with issues such as abortion, legalizing drugs, pornography, homosexuality, AIDS, etc. By contrast, the Republicans could similarly become the party of preference among Hispanics if the Republicans' traditional morality were linked to programs of greater economic opportunity and sensitivity to Hispanic interests. In either case, the current population pyramid shows that Hispanics may hold the key for the success of either party and its philosophy in the future of Texas.

Notes

1. *The Texas Poll,* September, 1984.
2. Texas Department of Health, Population Data Systems, Computer Based File.
3. Scotch-Irish refers to Scots who resettled in northern Ireland before coming to the New World, and not Scotch and Irish Intermarriage.

2 Understanding Public Opinion Polls
KENT L. TEDIN

Following the 1980 election, the *Detroit Free Press* ran a headline story "Pollsters Kissed Off by Electorate: Have 1,001 Excuses."[1] Two years later Burns Roper, founder of the Roper Poll, wrote an article entitled "The Polls Malfunction in 1982."[2] Four years later, in 1986, similar complaints were heard. An ABC polling analyst was quoted in the *New York Times* as saying, "I don't think it was a great year for pollsters."[3] According to prominent Democratic pollster Peter Hart, "Polling ranged all over the lot." The *Washington Post*-ABC News polled ten close Senate races in late October. Four of the candidates with leading margins were defeated.[4] These "mispredictions" along with others gave reporters yet another opportunity for a journalistic coup on "What went wrong with the polls."

The analysis of public opinion and elections, using modern survey methods, has now been part of the public landscape for over fifty years. Nevertheless, most popular criticism of public opinion polls seems amazingly ill-informed. Polling certainly deserves a critical look. Many surveys are badly-conceived, poorly executed, and incorrectly interpreted. But few, including those who write about the subject for newspapers and magazines, have an appreciation for why candidates who lead in the final pre-election poll do not always win; why two surveys taken at the same time report different results; or even why Truman beat Dewey when the Gallup Poll poll predicted otherwise.

An understanding of what can and cannot be inferred from political polls has a practical importance that lies beyond the academic world. It is now agreed that a candidate's poor showing in pre-election polls makes fundraising difficult and dampens volunteer enthusiasm. More importantly, democratic governments (as well as others) justify their existence by claiming to respond to "the will of the people." Public opinion surveys have become the commonly accepted tool for uncovering the hopes, fears, wishes, preferences, and values of those whom government serves.

Polls, of course, are not the only way of assessing public sentiment. Prior to the 1930s, party officials, politicians, and leaders of voluntary associations such as labor unions or temperance organizations were able to use as political leverage their claim to understand the political opinions of their constituent members. Today elected officials still claim to have insight into the desires of their constituencies; labor leaders continue to assert that they know and speak for the preferences of the rank and file. However, when faced with contradictory findings from "scientific" opinion surveys, these claims are quickly discounted by the popular press as well as by influential decision makers. In the latter part of the twentieth century, "public opinion" has become that quantity discoverable through of use of modern survey research.[5]

In this chapter we shall outline the major procedures used in conducting public opinion surveys and how they can go awry. Equally as important, however, is that technically correct surveys are often misinterpreted, misunderstood, and sometimes deliberately distorted. We will attempt to provide some guidance which will allow the reader to become an intelligent consumer of the survey product.

Sampling

Most public opinion polls are based on samples. When the *Gallup Poll* reports that 50 percent of adult Americans approve of the way that the President is handling his job, it is obvious that the Gallup organization has not gone out and interviewed 180 million American adults. Instead it has taken a sample. The reasons for sampling are fairly straightforward. First, to interview everyone would be prohibitively expensive. The 1980 census cost well over one billion dollars. Second, to interview the entire population would take a very long time. Months might pass between the first and last interview. Public opinion might, in that period, undergo real change.

Sampling provides a practical alternative to interviewing the whole population—be it national, state, or local. Furthermore, correctly done sampling can provide very accurate estimates of the political opinions of a larger population. The theory of sampling is a branch of the mathematics of probability, and the error involved in going from the sample to the population can be known with precision. However, many surveys of public opinion do not meet the demanding requirements of sampling theory. The attendant result, of course, is a loss in accuracy.

Sampling Theory

The *population* is that unit about which we want information. In most political surveys three different populations are frequently polled: (1) those over 18, (2) those who are registered voters, and (3) those who will (or do) vote in the next election. These are three quite different groups. It is very important that the population be clearly specified. When one sees a poll addressing abortion, presidential popularity, or vote intent in an upcoming election, those reporting the poll should make clear the population about which they speak. It has been shown, for example, that Senator Edward Kennedy is more highly rated among all adults than among registered voters.[6] Evaluations of Kennedy are, in part, determined by how one defines the population.

The *sample* is that part of the population selected for analysis. Usually, the sample is considerably smaller than the population. National political surveys conducted by reputable firms employ samples of about 1500 respondents. State and local surveys by reputable firms may employ as few as 500 cases. But as samples get smaller the probability of error increases. Sample size should always be reported along with the results of a survey. If that information is missing, the alleged findings should not be taken seriously.

When samples accurately mirror the population, they are said to be *representative*. The term *randomness* refers to the only method by which a representative sample can be scientifically drawn. In a random sample each unit of the population has exactly the same chance of being drawn as any other unit. If the population were attorneys in the state of Texas, each attorney would be required to have exactly the same probability of being selected for the sample to be random. Attorneys in big cities could not have a greater likelihood of getting into the sample than those from the Rio Grande Valley or the Panhandle. This situation obviously requires a detailed knowledge of the population. In the case of Texas lawyers, one could get a list from the bar association and then sample from that list. But suppose the population was unemployed, male adults. To specify the population in a fashion to be able to draw a random sample would be very difficult. As a consequence, obtaining a representative sample of the unemployed is not easy.

A probability sample is a variant on the principle of random sampling. Instead of each unit having exactly the same probability of being drawn, some units would be more likely to be drawn than would others. But this would be a *known* probability. For example, if one were sampling voter precincts in a state, it is of consequence that some precincts contain more people than do others. To make the sample of people in those precincts representative, the larger precincts must have a greater likelihood of being selected than smaller ones.

We will use *simple random sampling* (SRS) to illustrate how the principle of probability works in selecting a representative sample. Let us assume our population is a large barrel containing 100,000 marbles, some of which are red and some of which are green. We do not know the percentage of each. Instead of counting them all (a long and tedious job), we will draw a random sample. The question is: How? We could just dip in our hand and take some out, but that would mean that those within our reach would be picked and those close to the bottom would have no chance of being selected. Or we could spin the barrel and take one out after every spin. That would probably work reasonably well, but it still would not be "scientific." Even with a spin those marbles at the bottom might never get close enough to the surface to get picked. If we are insisting on a pure random sample we would have to employ a table of random numbers, and give each marble a numeral between one and 100,000. Random number tables are computer generated digits that are completely unrelated to one another (i.e., random). They can be found in the appendix of virtually any statistics book. Let us assume we sample 600 marbles. Our first random number might be 33,382. We would then find the marble with that number and note if it is red or green. Our next random number might be 13,343. We would again note its color. The process would continue until we drew 600 marbles and recorded the color of each.

Having completed that task, let us say our sample shows 65 percent red marbles. Given the sampling method, we now know some things about the population. Sampling theory (the central limit theorem) tells us that the most likely percentage of red marbles is 65 percent. Of course, it is very unlikely that the real percentage of red marbles is precisely 65 percent. It might be 65.5 or 64.3, for example. The sample will not get the population value exactly correct for the same reason that flipping a coin 100 times will not likely yield exactly 50 heads and 50 tails—although it should be close if the coin is honestly flipped.

We need at this point to introduce the twin concepts of *sampling error* and the *confidence level*. A sample will rarely hit the true population value right on the nose. Sampling error and the confidence level tell us the probability of being off the mark and by how much. The commonly used confidence level is 95 percent. For a sample of 600 the sampling error is four percent. What all this means is that if we took 100 samples from our population, and each of these samples consisted of 600 marbles randomly drawn, then 95 out of 100 times we would be plus or minus four percent of the true population value. Our sample came up 65 percent red. While this figure may not be exactly correct, we at least know that 95 out of 100 times we are going to be within four points—one way or the other—of the true proportion of red marbles in the barrel. This much can been proven mathematically.

Turning to a political example, *The New York Times* reported that during the crisis over the Iranian arms deal President Reagan's popularity plunged from 67 on October 30, 1986 to 46 percent on November 30 of the same year.[7] Since the sample size in the latter survey was 687, we know that if the poll were repeated 100 times, 95 of the 100 repetitions would produce results that are plus or minus four percent of what we would find if we interviewed all adult Americans. Thus Reagan's popularity on November 30, 1986 could have been as high as 50 percent or as low as 41 percent. The "best estimate" (according to the central limit theorem) is 46 percent. Sampling error does decrease slightly as we move away from a 50/50 split, and it increases as the population has more heterogeneous political attitudes. But by far the most important factor is the size of the sample.

This simple truth can be easily demonstrated by flipping a coin. We know an honest coin should come up 50 percent heads. If we were to flip a coin ten times and mark down the percentage heads, then flip it another ten times and mark down the percentage heads, and so on 50 times we would get results that

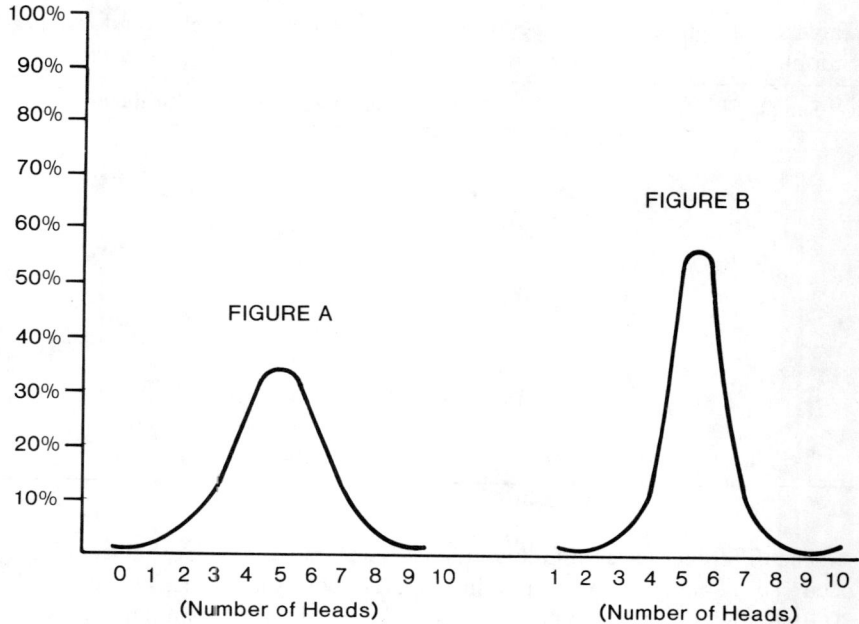

looked like figure A. But if we flipped the coin 100 times instead of simply ten, our 50 repetitions would look like figure B. Clearly there are more "errors" in figure A than in figure B. Error here does not mean mistake; rather it refers to workings of chance. When we talk about mistakes in sampling, we use the term "bias."

Contrary to what might seem common sense, the size of the population is of little consequence for the accuracy of a survey. That is, it does not make any difference if we are surveying the city of Houston or the entire United States. With a sample size of 600, the sampling error would be identical for both the city and the nation—all others things being equal.[8] Presented in Table 1 are the sampling errors associated with specific samples sizes.

Note that when sample size drops to around 150, sampling error gets very large. While one rarely sees a public opinion survey of 150 people, one often sees survey subgroups (men, college educated, blacks, Republicans, etc.) analyzed where the number of respondents fall below 150. For example, a poll done prior to the 1986 election for governor of Texas showed that among voters over 65 years of age, Mark White led Bill Clements by a margin of 52 percent to 46 percent. However, there were only 91 respondents in that subsample. With a sampling error of 10 percent all we know is that for those over 65 somewhere between 42 and 62 percent favored White, and somewhere between 34 and 54 percent favored Clements. To say that White led Clements among this group in the population is not supported by the data.

Table 1 Sampling Error and Sample Size Employing Simple Random Sampling[9]

Sample Size	Sampling Error (plus or minus)
2,400	2.0
1,536	2.5
1,067	3.0
784	3.5
600	4.0
474	4.5
384	5.0
267	6.0
196	7.0
150	8.0
119	9.0
96	10.0
45	15.0

The differences are, in fact, statistically insignificant (i.e., they could have occurred by chance). When reading reports about the politics of those under 30, the gender gap, the politics of the religious right, and similar topics that involve the analysis of subgroups, one should pay special attention to sample size. A difference of five or six percent can be quite *meaningful* in a subsample of 300, and quite *meaningless* in a subsample of 75. If subsamples fall below 100, treat conclusions drawn with great care.

Applied Sampling and Surveys of Public Opinion

Using a large barrel of marbles and a table of random numbers we drew a "perfect" sample. That is, the sampling method fit perfectly with the mathematics of sampling theory. When we sample humans we cannot draw a perfect sample. Although a marble cannot refuse to tell us if it is red or green, a person may refuse to be interviewed. Sampling theory does not allow for refusals. Consequently, surveys of public opinion only approximate the underlying theory of sampling. If these deviations from theory are modest, opinion polls can and do work well. But there are many instances where sampling theory is ignored (or those conducting the polls are ignorant). If the poll simply concerns political opinions (favor/oppose abortion, approve/disapprove of tax reform, keep/abolish the 55 mph speed limit) there is no reality test. The survey may have been done badly and be considerably off the mark, but how would one know?[10] On the other hand, pre-election day surveys have a reality test—election day. In these surveys, sampling mistakes have, in several dramatic cases, cast opinion pollsters in highly unfavorable light.

While we normally think of public opinion polls as being of fairly recent origin, commercial publications were forecasting the outcome of presidential contests as early as 1920. The best known of these publications was the *Literary Digest*. The *Digest* accurately forecast the winner (if not the exact percent) of each presidential election between 1920 and 1932. In 1936, as in previous years, it sent out some 10 million post card ballots "drawn from every telephone book in the United States, from the rosters of clubs and associations, from city directories, lists of registered voters, [and] classified mail order and occupational data. . . ."[11] About 2.2 million returned their postal ballots. The result was 1,293,699 (57%) for Republican Alf Landon and 972,867 (43%) for President Franklin Roosevelt. On election day Roosevelt not only won, but he won by a landslide receiving 62.5 percent of the vote and carrying every state except Maine and Vermont. The *Literary Digest* was not only wrong; it was wrong by 19.5 percent. On November 14, 1936 the *Literary Digest* published the following commentary:

WHAT WENT WRONG WITH THE POLLS?
None of Straw Votes Got Exactly the Right Answer—Why?

In 1920, 1924, 1928 and 1932, the *Literary Digest* Polls were right. Not only right in the sense they showed the winner; they forecast the actual popular vote with such a small percentage of error (less than 1 percent in 1932) that newspapers and individuals everywhere heaped such phrases as "uncannily accurate" and "amazingly right" upon us. . . . Well this year we used precisely the same method that had scored four bull's eyes in four previous tries. And we were far from correct. Why? We ask that question in all sincerity, because *we want to know.*

Why did the poll fare so badly? One reason that can be discounted is sample size. The *Digest* claims to have polled 10 million people. Thus a large sample is no guarantee for accuracy. Rather, their sampling procedure had four fundamental defects. First the sample was drawn in a *biased* fashion. The *Digest* clearly did not use random selection or anything approaching it. Even though questionnaires were sent out to ten million people, a large part of the sample was drawn from telephone directories and lists of automobile owners, during the Depression a decidedly upper-middle class group and one which was predominantly Republican in its political sentiments. In other words, the *Digest* did not correctly specify the population. A second factor contributing to the *Digest's* mistake was time. The questionnaires were sent out in early September, making impossible the detection of any late trend favoring one candidate or the other. Third, 1936 was the year that marked the emergence of the "New Deal Coalition." The *Digest* had picked the winner correctly since 1920 using the same methods as in 1936, but in 1936 voting became polarized along class lines. The working class and the poor voted overwhelmingly Democratic while the more affluent classes voted predominantly Republican. Since the *Literary Digest's* sample was heavily biased in the direction of the more affluent, it is not surprising that their sample tended to favor Landon. Finally, there was the problem of self-selection. The *Digest* sent out its questionnaires by mail. Of the ten million they mailed, only a little over two million responded—about 22 percent. Those people who self-select to respond to mail surveys are often quite different in their political outlooks from those who do not respond. They tend to be better educated, to have higher incomes, and to feel more strongly about the topics dealt with in the questionnaire.[12] So even if the sample of ten million had been drawn in an unbiased fashion, the poll probably still would have been in error due to the self-selection factor. One very fundamental principle of survey sampling is that one *cannot allow the respondents to select themselves into the sample.*

Despite the failure of the *Literary Digest,* several public opinion analysts did pick Franklin Roosevelt as the winner. Among them was George Gallup, Jr. who built his reputation on a correct forecast in 1936. In terms of percentage, Gallup did not get particularly close. He missed by almost seven percent. But he got the winner right, and that is what most people remember. He was, in fact, closer in 1948 (off by five percent) when he made his infamous prediction that Dewey would beat Truman—that too is well remembered.

The technique used by Gallup in 1936 and up until the Dewey-Truman disaster is called *quota sampling.* This technique employs the census to determine the percentage of certain relevant groups in the population. For example, what percentage is male, Catholic, white, and college educated? Within these groups interviewers are then assigned quotas. They must interview a certain percent women, a certain percent with less than high school education, a certain percent black, etc. Once the interviews are completed, the sample is weighted so that it will be representative of the population on those variables. If 15 percent of the population is male, high school educated, and making over $25,000 a year, the sample will be weighted to reflect those proportions. The principle problem with quota sampling is a variation on the problem of self-selection. The interviewer has too much opportunity to determine who is selected for the sample. An interviewer who must get a certain number of "female blacks," may avoid certain areas of town or may get the entire quota from a single block. There is a natural tendency to avoid shabby residences, long flights of stairs, and homes where there are dogs. Experience with quota samples demonstrates that they systematically tend to underrepresent the poor, the less educated and racial minorities. Members of those groups who are interviewed tend not to be "typical." The minorities and poor that found their way into Gallup's quota sample were atypical of those groups. They turned out in larger numbers than anticipated and voted overwhelmingly for Truman. A second factor contributing to Gallup's mistake was that he quit polling two weeks before the election. When significant movement takes place it often occurs just before the election. For example, in 1980 Jimmy Carter and Ronald Reagan were virtually even the weekend before the vote. A strong move toward Reagan over the weekend allowed him to pile up a substantial victory. To capture these changes, Gallup and other survey organizations now poll right up to the day of the election.

Contemporary Sampling Methods

We used simple random sampling (SRS) to illustrate the principles involved in drawing a scientific sample. However, SRS is seldom used in actual public opinion surveys. There is no master list of all Americans that could be sampled. Even if there were, the persons selected would be widely scattered throughout the country making in-person interviews prohibitively expensive. For example, an interviewer might have to travel all the way to Kerrville, Texas, just to talk to one respondent. Rather, polls where respondents are personally interviewed use *multistage cluster samples*.

Modern probability sampling is done by household, not by individual. As an example we shall look at the method used by the Gallup Poll.[13] The first step is to use the census and divide the country into four geographic regions. Within each region, the following population centers of similar size are grouped together:

- Cities of one million or more
- Cities between 250,000 and one million
- Cities between 50,000 and 250,000
- Suburbs of 50,000 or more
- Towns between 2,500 and 50,000
- Villages of less than 2,500

The second step is to draw from these groupings a simple random sample of cities, suburbs, towns, and villages. Each population center is then divided into regions of about equal population size. These are sampled using probability methods (the bigger regions have a greater probability of being drawn). Within these regions, smaller geographical units are selected by probability sampling. These smaller units are called *primary sampling units* (PSUs). About 20 persons are interviewed in each PSU. Once selected, they are often used several years before they are replaced. The reason is economic. Interviewers are expensive to train, but once trained they can be used over and over.

The primary sampling units are divided into city blocks or areas of equivalent population in rural areas. These areas are then randomly sampled. Once again the compact geographic area saves time and money. Most survey organizations then abandon probability methods at the block level and rely on some type of quota. The problem is that specific individuals are hard to locate. Interviewers working for the Gallup Poll are given a randomly drawn starting point and then instructed to stop at every nth household. The interviewer asks to speak to the youngest man over 18. If he is not home, the interviewer asks to speak with the youngest woman. If neither of these is home, or refuses to be interviewed the interviewer goes to the next adjacent dwelling and tries again until successful. Each interviewer has a male/female quota and an age quota, but this is not a *quota sample* because the interviewer cannot choose who gets into the sample.

Multistage cluster samples work well and are an efficient compromise given the expense involved in a simple random sample approach. The drawback is that cluster samples have a greater sampling error than SRS, as would be expected since the respondents are "clustered" into 75 to 100 small geographic areas. A simple random sample of 1000 has three percent sampling error. A typical cluster sample of 1000 would have a four percent sampling error. Gallup reports that its national samples (cluster samples) of 1500 have a three percent error.

In recent years in-person surveys have increasingly been replaced by telephone surveys. The principal advantage of the telephone is its low cost. It also frees one from having to use clusters, as the physical location of a respondent is irrelevant in a phone survey. However, there are disadvantages as well. Nationwide, it is estimated that 20 percent of all phone numbers are unlisted. In some areas, like San Francisco, it is as high as 40 percent.[14] The solution to this problem is to use a random digit dialing scheme. A ten digit phone number is composed of an area code (the first three numbers), an exchange (the next three), a cluster (the next two), and the two final digits. If one knows the geographic assignment of area codes, exchanges and clusters by the phone company (they will usually provide it for a fee), a population can be defined and sampled. In Houston there are approximately 10,000 of these seven digit codes (if we limit ourselves to Houston we can ignore the area code). An example appears below:

(713) 496–78 _____ _____

The first five digits would be randomly sampled from the population of 10,000. Then the last two digits would be chosen from a table of random numbers or with a computer program that generates random digits. These methods allow persons with unlisted numbers to get into the sample. On the negative side we make calls to a large number of nonworking numbers. But the sample is quite representative.

Another problem with telephone surveys, although it applies to in-person surveys as well, is refusal. The telephone, however, particularly lends itself to abuse as persons selling aluminum siding, upholstery, or West Texas real estate will sometimes attempt to gain a respondent's confidence by posing as a pollster. The sales pitch comes later. A study by the Roper organization showed that 27 percent of a national sample had experienced these sales tactics.[15] People, especially in large cities, are becoming wary of those claiming to be taking polls. It is currently estimated that the refusal rate for telephone surveys is 30 percent. However, the refusal rate is only slightly lower for in-person surveys.[16] Refusals are of consequence only if those who decline the interview are systematically different on the *questions of interest* from those who consent to the interview.

Finally, the exact percentage of households with phones is a question open to debate. It is certainly high, but how high? The 1986 census reports that 92 percent of all households have phone service, although in five states the percentage falls below ninety. On the other hand, a study by the U.S. Public Interest Research Group reports that 27 percent of those with incomes under $15,000 do not have telephone service. The principal reason cited was that service costs too much.[17] Those without phones are found among the least affluent segments of society. This "lumpenproletariat" is one population subgroup that rarely finds its way into any survey, regardless of methodology.

Most reputable polls will report their sampling method in a square box embedded with the news story on the poll results. News stories taken from polls often run for several days, but "how poll was done" is often printed only once. Still at some point the news organization has an obligation to inform the reader of the methods used. A good example of this sort of reporting is taken from the *New York Times*-CBS poll.[18]

HOW THE POLL WAS CONDUCTED

The latest *New York Times*-CBS News poll is based on telephone interviews conducted Sunday and Monday with 1,036 adults around the United States, excluding Alaska and Hawaii. The sample of telephone exchanges called was selected by a computer from a complete list of exchanges in the county. The exchanges were chosen so as to insure that each region of the country was represented in proportion to its population. For each exchange, the telephone numbers were formed by random digits, thus permitting access to both listed and unlisted residential numbers.

The results have been weighted to take account of household size and number of residential telephones and to adjust for variations in the sample relating to region, race, sex, age and education.

In theory, in 19 cases out of 20 the results based on such samples will differ by no more than 3 percentage points in either direction from what would have been obtained by interviewing all adult Americans. The error for smaller subgroups is larger. For example, the potential error for liberals is plus or minus 7 percentage points; for moderates and conservatives it is 5 percentage points.

In addition to sampling error, the practical difficulties of conducting and survey of public opinion may introduce other sources of error into the poll.

This statement is extremely informative. It tells the reader the dates of interviewing, the sample size, the method of sample selection, the weighting procedure, and the sampling error for the survey as a whole and for subgroups; and it alerts the reader that this survey, like others involving humans, will not be perfect.

The Misuse of Surveys

The *Literary Digest* poll belongs to a general class of surveys called "straw polls" or the "straw vote." They are nonscientific attempts to measure public opinion, like throwing straw in the air to see which way the wind is blowing. Their principal defect is a biased sample, usually the result of respondents being able to "select themselves" to be counted in the poll. Importantly, there is no way of assessing the sampling error, as the factors by which a person gets into the sample are unknown. One might think that with the advent of modern survey methodology straw polls would have disappeared. Not so. They are in fact alive and well—and most are as unreliable now as they were in the 1930s.

Modern Straw Polls

A natural poll that receives a fair amount of media play consists of letters to the president (the media also sometimes pick up on letters to congressmen). When a national crisis occurs which is generally perceived as presenting the president in a poor light, the White House will frequently report that "the mail" is running 10 to 1, 5 to 1, etc. in favor of the president. When Special Prosecutor Archibald Cox was fired during the Watergate scandal, the Nixon White House reported that the mail was running 5 to 1 in favor of the president's actions. Many senators and congressmen, on the other hand, reported that their mail was running 25 to 1 in opposition to the president's action. More recently the White House claimed that the mail was running 10 to 1 in favor of the president when it was revealed that arms were shipped to Iran in return for aid in hostage releases. However, *New York Time*/CBS news poll showed that the public disapproved of this policy by a 3-1 margin.[19] These letters are basically meaningless as an indication of public sentiment. We know that those who "self-select" to write to public officials overwhelmingly tend to write to those whom they feel are sympathetic. If people like the president and support him in the controversy, they will write the White House. If they are hostile, they will write somewhere else or not at all.

Another common straw poll involves surveys sent out by public officials or various partisan organizations. These are often published by the media in bold headlines as if they constituted a reasonable assessment of public opinion. For example, a story in the *Houston Chronicle* carried the following headlines: "Survey Here Shows Opposition to President's Energy Program." The "survey" turned out to be responses to 200,000 questionnaires mailed out by west side Houston Congressman Bill Archer. There were a total of 43,010 responses to this mailout, or about 22 percent (about the same response to the *Literary Digest* poll). The poll also reported that respondents favored production of the B-1 Bomber and retention of "right to work laws."[20] Suffice it to say a survey of this sort measures absolutely nothing. It is severely contaminated by self-selection. There is no way to compute sampling error, given the bias in the way respondents got into the sample. While the information might be valuable to Congressman Archer as an indication of what his attentive constituents think, it has no value as a measure of public opinion.

In addition to reporting the straw polls of others, newspapers have gotten into the business of conducting their own. These are often found on the editorial page labeled "Tuesday Poll," "Voice of the Reader," and "Readers Poll." There is usually a cut-out ballot which is mailed to the newspaper. The results are reported a few days later. The Ft. Lauderdale (Florida) *Sun-Sentinel*

"Tuesday Poll" asked readers "Should the state conduct an experiment to ban trucks from the passing or median strip lane of I-95?" The Wisconsin *Capital Times* "Readers Poll" recently inquired into one of the pivotal questions facing state citizens: "Are you satisfied with the the job Elroy 'Crazylegs' Hirsch is dong as the University of Wisconsin's athletic director?"[21] As a general rule, those with intense negative feelings are the most likely to "self-select" into these surveys.

A variety of political organizations also attempt to assess public opinion using mail surveys, often combined with highly biased questions. For example, a questionnaire in 1980 from the Republican National Committee with a return deadline of September 29, 1980, included the following items:[22]

1. Recently the Soviet armed forces openly invaded the independent country of Afghanistan. Do you think the U.S. should supply military equipment to the rebel freedom fighters?
2. The Soviets now have a combat brigade in Cuba training Marxist revolutionaries for use in South America and Africa. Do you approve of Mr. Carter's decision to do nothing in response to this direct Soviet/Cuban challenge?
3. Do you believe the U.S. should launch a new program to modernize and increase our Navy in view of the Soviet's massive naval buildup worldwide?

Given the highly loaded questions it should come as no surprise that critics of Mr. Carter would be more likely to complete this questionnaire and return it than those who are undecided or supporters. This survey has many of the same defects as mail surveys that are periodically conducted by *Playboy* and *Penthouse* about sexual habiats. There is a great likelihood that those willing to divulge information about their sex lives differ in important regards from those who are unwilling. Mail surveys are not always meaningless, but they must be conducted with great care by those with specialized training. Most that are done correctly are published in academic journals and rarely show up in the popular media. When one does encounter a popular account, it should be treated with considerable skepticism.

Recently television, including highly regarded network news programs, has been getting into the straw poll business. On October 20, 1980, ABC news asked its viewers to evaluate the Reagan-Carter presidential debate by calling in one telephone number if they thought Reagan won and another if they thought Carter won. This system, called "Dial It" by AT&T, cost each caller 50 cents. Of course, there was no limit on how many times any one person can call—as long as one did not mind paying 50 percent for each call. About 727,000 people called (at a profit of $363,500 to the phone company), with Reagan being perceived the winner by a 2 to 1 margin. Other television straw polls involve Warner-Amex's CUBE system which allows for two way communication for cable TV subscribers. The results of these poll have found their way to NBC News and the Cable News Network.[23]

With regard to the findings on the Carter-Reagan debate many of Carter's supporters were rightly outraged. Carter pollster Patrick Caddell argued that since the poll was conducted in the late evening it oversampled callers from the Western time zone (an area of strong Reagan support) while many of Mr. Carters supporters in the southeast had already gone to bed. Also callers from urban areas (where Carter would be strong) had a more difficult time getting through than callers from nonurban areas because the dense population led to a clogging of the telephone exchanges. One might also speculate that the poor would be less willing to spend a frivolous 50 cents than would the middle class. However, not all "Dial It" polls are frivolous. They have sometimes been used to decide questions of life and death. NBC's Saturday Night Live posed a question to its viewers as to whether "Larry the Lobster" should be boiled alive at the end of a restaurant skit. Over 466,000 viewers called. Larry was spared by a scant 12,000 votes.[24]

The Dial It procedure has been used several times on the ABC late night news program "Nightline," where attitudes on current topics are assessed. Ted Kopple usually introduces these polls with a disclaimer that "we don't pretend the results are scientific, but here's what we found." Viewers should treat that statement as the equivalent of "certain bored people with strong feelings on some subjects are willing to pay 50 cents to register their views in a poll that means nothing. Here are the results."

Interpreting Scientific Surveys

Polls correctly executed do not always "predict" the actual election day winner. Polls taken at the same time will on occasion show conflicting numbers. Sometimes the numbers will swing wildly over a short period of time. These characteristics do not necessarily mean the polls are defective, but they do require explanation.

Pre-Election Surveys

The media tend to attribute more accuracy to pre-election polls as "predictors" of the election day outcome than even the best designed polls can possibly deliver. First an obvious point. Pre-election polls refer to sentiment at the time they are conducted, not on election day. The "horse race" analogy commonly used to discuss elections is, in this case, appropriate. The horse that is ahead going into the stretch is not always the horse (or the candidate) that wins. With the exception of exit polls (election day polls where respondents are interviewed as they leave the voting booth) no one conducts surveys on the day of the election. At least five percent of the electorate (sometimes more) is normally undecided the weekend before the vote. As one approaches the election, there is often a momentum which favors one of the candidates—the undecideds do not split 50/50. This flow of the undecideds was one reason Truman beat Dewey (the last Gallup poll showed that 19 percent of the electorate was undecided). It is also the reason that Richard Nixon squeaked out a win of less than one percent over Hubert Humphrey in 1968 when the polls had shown Nixon with a substantial lead throughout the campaign. And it is the reason Ronald Reagan soundly defeated Jimmy Carter in 1980 when polls showed the contest to be very close.

But there is a more fundamental problem with pre-election polls as election day predictors. It is impossible to properly define the population. Recall that a random sample must be drawn from a finite population. But it is impossible to define the election day population. Less than 55 percent of adult Americans vote in presidential elections. No one has yet determined a method which with any degree of accuracy predicts who will vote, yet it is those election day voters who constitute the population, not adult Americans or even registered voters. In the final 1986 pre-election survey for the *Houston Chronicle* a sample of registered voters were asked if they were "certain to vote" on election day, would "probably vote," or "would not vote." The results:

Certain to Vote	83%
Probably will Vote	14
Will not Vote	03
	100% N = 666

Actual turnout in Texas was 39 percent.

The problem in accurately assessing turnout is linked to social desirability. People want to be good citizens, and so they say they will vote. Even after the election, respondents will tell interviewers they have voted when in fact they have not. In 1972 the Survey Research Center at the University of Michigan did a "vote validation" study in which they checked poll records to see if those who said they voted did in fact vote. Seventy-two percent of their sample claimed to have voted, but the official record showed that only 55 percent had actually cast their ballot.[25] Clearly, then, pollsters must employ "educated guesswork" in place of science to define the population. Turnout patterns are fairly constant from one election to another but they do change, and that change can often spell the difference between victory and defeat (see Chapter 15 on the Clements-White elections as an example).

Without an agreed-on population, pollsters use a cornucopia of methods for estimating likely voters. Most pollsters ask a series of screening questions designed to identify likely voters (such as past voting behavior, strength of candidate preference, etc.), although the Gallup Poll does no screening and reports the preferences for all registered voters. Those polls that do screen employ a distinctive methodology. Generally speaking, no two polls use the same screening questions, and consequently no two polls look at exactly the same population.

Screens are of consequence for poll results. The tougher the screen in terms of weeding out potential nonvoters and those with weak candidate preferences, the greater the support for Republican candidates. For example, both the NBC poll and the Gallup poll did surveys between August 15 and August 17, 1980.

Gallup used all registered voters (an easy screen); NBC interviewed only registered voters who had made up their minds (a tough screen). Gallup showed Reagan with 39 percent; NBC showed him with 48 percent.[26] It is, by the way, the use of screens to define likely voters that allows a pollster working for Democratic candidate Smith to say his client is ahead while the pollster working for Republican candidate Jones says his client is ahead. Neither have "faked" the numbers; rather they disagree on the probable composition of election day voters. The Republican pollster sees a big turnout among affluent whites; the Democratic pollster sees an atypically high minority turnout.

There are also reasons polls may not agree that simply go beyond sampling considerations. Some pollsters ask the undecideds if they "lean" to one candidate or the other. These leaners are then counted as having candidate preferences while other polls may not ask the question and count them as undecideds. In a survey following the 1980 Democratic convention the Gallup, Harris, and Roper polls using the "leaning" question reported only 10 percent undecided when asked to chose between Carter and Reagan. The NBC poll which did not use the "leaner" question reported that 50 percent were undecided.[27]

By far the best strategy in watching pre-election surveys (particularly those conducted early-on) is not to look at the numbers from one specific poll, but at the overall trend. Is one candidate consistently improving or is there no movement? It is the trend that can give insight into progress (or lack thereof) in the campaign.

Volatility in Candidate Choices and Issues Preferences

Example 1: Prior to the 1980 Iowa Caucuses a *New York Times*/CBS poll showed Ronald Reagan ahead of George Bush by a margin of 45 percent to six percent. Two days after the caucuses Reagan led by a margin of only 33–27 percent. Bush had picked up 21 points and Reagan had lost 12 within the span of about a dozen days. Example 2: In the past ten years there has been considerable debate over the Strategic Arms Limitation Treaty (SALT). There have been many attempts to use opinion surveys to determine if Americans favor or oppose it. In early 1979 three surveys taken at the same time showed quite different results. An NBC/AP poll showed 81 percent of the public favored Salt; a CBS/*New York Times* poll showed 63 percent favored it, and a survey by the Roper Organization showed just 40 percent favored SALT.[28]

Both these phenomena are a function of the fact that the mass public has surprisingly little knowledge or interest in politics. Most opinions are not deeply held. In the case of Iowa, Bush was almost completely unknown, and despite his previous run for the presidency Ronald Reagan was in 1980 a fairly dim fixture on the political landscape. George Bush won the Iowa Caucuses, and the media attention he garnered allowed him to make up considerable ground on Reagan in the early going. The same phenomena occurred in 1984 when

Gary Hart unexpectedly won the New Hampshire primary. He moved from virtual obscurity in the polls to draw even with Vice-President Mondale. This sort of movement, however, usually takes place only very early in a presidential campaign. Once the electorate becomes better informed about the personalities, these sharp fluctuations are less and less frequent.

Social desirability also contributes to voter volatility. People believe that good citizens have opinions. Consequently, when polled they will volunteer one even if they have given absolutely no thought whatsoever to the subject. In one relevant study respondents were presented with a fictitious issue (the "Public Affairs Act") and asked: "Some people say that the Public Affairs Act should be repealed. Do you agree or disagree with this idea." Fully one-third of the sample expressed an opinion (16 percent agreed, 18 percent disagreed and 66 percent claimed no opinion).[29]

The explanation for disagreement among the polls over the SALT treaty follows very much the same logic. Most Americans have little information about a highly technical subject like the Strategic Arms Limitation Treaty. In fact only 23 percent could accurately identify the two nations who were negotiating the treaty.[30] As topics recede from a people's immediate day-to-day concerns, the wording of the question can make considerable difference in the response. While the questions were essentially the same, the Roper item noted that Salt was "controversial" which probably cued people to give a less positive response. As topics become more salient, minor variations in question wording have less effect. The abortion issue and attitudes toward the Ayatollah Khomeini would be more likely to generate stable responses than are inquiries about the Salt treaty or the Strategic Defense Initiative (known popularly as "star wars").

The wording of questions can clearly affect the response pattern. One only need page back to those questions used in the survey by the Republican National Committee for an example of items likely to yield distorted results. There are several general principals that are worth noting when looking at questions asked in surveys. Some words are loaded. When the Nicaraguan opponents of the Sandinistas are referred to as "freedom fighters," responses are more positive than when they are called "rebels" or "contras." Clearly, freedom fighter contains a positive cue. People are more likely to agree with statements than disagree with them, favor them than oppose them. Support for continuance of the 55 MPH speed limit will be greater if one is asked to agree or disagree with question A as rather than question B.

Form A: The 55 MPH speed limit should be retained.
Form B: The 55 MPH speed limit should be abolished.

An experiment by the author revealed that with form A 64 percent favored the current speed limit, while with form B only 53 percent were in favor. Sometimes only one option is presented to the respondent: "Do you favor the

55 MPH speed limit?" Note the alternative "oppose" is never mentioned. When looking at questions ask yourself: How could the wording of this item affect the responses? Or given what this question asks, are the results reasonable? A query about freedom fighters in Afghanistan should yield a positive response, and the results must be interpreted in that context.

Conclusion

During the 1930s, 40s and 50s public opinion polls received little attention from the mass media. Reporters saw pollsters as potential competitors—given the technical nature of their subject they might want a byline of their own. Those fears have now subsided. Polls are ubiquitous and commentary on public opinion is fair game for all. There is much to be learned about American democracy from an intelligent examination of polls. Attempts to deliberately mislead occur, but they are not frequent. Rather, the key to understanding polls is a realization that the numbers do not speak for themselves. They require interpretation. While the average American cannot be expected to master the intricacies of modern survey research, an appreciation of the principles laid out in this chapter should allow the reader to do more than simply take at face value the assertions by others about the measurement and meaning of public opinion.

Notes

1. Everett C. Ladd and G. Donald Gerree, "Were the the Pollsters Really Wrong?" *Public Opinion* (December/January, 1981), p. 13.
2. Burns Roper, "The Polls Malfunction in 1982," *Public Opinion* (December/January, 1982), pp. 41–45.
3. Martin Tolchin, "The Pollsters Look Back," *The New York Times,* November 8, 1986, p. 17.
4. *Ibid.*
5. For elaboration on this point see Benjamin Ginsberg, *The Captive Public.* (Basic Books, Inc., 1986), chapter 3.
6. Burns Roper, "Reading the Signals in Today's Political Polls," *Public Opinion* (February/March, 1980), p. 48.
7. Reported in *The Houston Chronicle,* December 2, 1986, page 2.
8. National samples are usually larger than state or local samples because one other factor that effects sampling error is variation, and there is likely to be more variation in the attribute measured nationally, as opposed to those in a geographically smaller area. Also, those conducting national samples are often interested in looking at subgroups (like blacks or women). The larger the sample, the lower the sampling error when one is looking at subgroups.

9. Gerald M. Goldhaber, "A Pollster's Sampler," *Public Opinion* (June/July, 1986), p. 48.
10. One's suspicions are aroused, however, if polls on the same topic at similar times show quite different results.
11. *Literary Digest,* 122 (August 22, 1936), p. 3.
12. Don A. Dillman, *Mail and Telephone Surveys* (New York: Wiley, 1978).
13. The method described here is that used by Gallup Poll. See Paul Perry, "Election Survey Procedures of the Gallup Poll," *Public Opinion Quarterly* 20 (Fall, 1960), pp. 531–541.
14. Robert Groves and Robert Kahn, *Surveys by Telephone* (New York: Academic Press, Inc., 1979), p. 20.
15. Charles Turner and Elizabeth Martin, *Surveying Subjective Phenomena* (New York: Russell Sage, 1984), p. 73.
16. Groves and Kahn, p. 64; Seymour Martin Lipset, "Different Polls, Different Results in 1980 Politics," *Public Opinion* (August/September, 1980), p. 20.
17. Based on a survey of 816 respondents with incomes under $15,000. Reported in "One in Five Low-Income Homes lacks Telephone, Survey Finds," *Houston Chronicle* (Sunday, February 1st, 1987), Section 1, page 3.
18. *The New York Times,* December 10, 1986, p. 9.
19. *Ibid.*
20. The *Houston Chroncile,* Saturday, October 8, 1977, p. 3.
21. Barry Orton, "Phony Polls: The Pollster's Nemesis," *Public Opinion* (June/July, 1982), pp. 56–57.
22. Conducted by Survey Research Center, Republican National Committee, 310 First Street, Washington, D.C., 20003.
23. Orton, pp. 57–58.
24. *Ibid.,* pp. 58–59.
25. Michael Traugoota and John Katosh, "Reponse Validity in Surveys of Voting Behavior," *Public Opinion Quarterly* (Winter, 1979), 359–377.
26. Lipset, p. 20.
27. Roper, p. 48.
28. Michael Wheeler, "Reining in Horserace Journalism," *Public Opinion* (Feb/March, 1982), p. 42.
29. George Bishop, Robert Oldendick, Alfred Tuchfarber and Stephen Bennett, "Pseudo-Opinions on Public Affairs," *Public Opinion Quarterly* (Summer, 1980), p. 201.
30. Wheeler, p. 42.

3 The Ideology of the American Electorate*

KATHLEEN KNIGHT

Introduction

The term "ideology" is used in many different ways in political science. In the most general sense it refers to a "system" of beliefs and values which helps a person make sense of political information and decide how (or whether) to respond to political events. "Beliefs" in the context of this discussion can be defined as bits of information which an individual takes to be true whether or not they can be empirically verified. "Values" refers simply to the positive or negative connotations an individual associates with the belief. An attitude can be defined as the interaction of belief and value which predisposes a person's behavior toward some new information. This "behavior", or action, can be as minimal as paying attention, or as definitive as taking up arms to defend a principle.

An ideology is a "system" of political attitudes which are related to each other such that information triggering one attitude usually calls into play a set of other attitudes which together determine how a person will respond. These sets of attitudes need not be organized in any particular logical fashion, but when they are we can begin to talk about individuals as sharing a common "point of view." In current social psychology this kind of attitude system is frequently called a "schema," and the term political schema will be used interchangably with ideology throughout this chapter.

Obviously, the political schemata possessed by Americans can vary greatly in complexity and salience. Some people pay no attention to politics, others have elaborate and coherent explanations for political events which they can communicate easily and use to persuade others. Still others can be described as "ideologues" in the sense that Napoleon used the term—individuals who have such tightly-woven and committed views of the world that they do not recognize what most other people regard as "reality." Political scientists these days, however, generally uses the term "ideologue" non-pejoratively to refer to individuals who appear to structure their political opinions with respect to an underlying liberal-conservative continuum. This is the definition adopted here.

---

*I wish to express my thanks to Carolyn V. Lewis and Evelyn Bernadette McKinney for their assistance with the data management and analysis.

As we shall see the liberal-conservative continuum is not the only organizing device people use to structure their political opinions, but it has been a particularly important one in the United States over the last fifty years. For those who understand them, the terms "liberal" and "conservative" provide a convenient short-hand for communicating a large amount of political information about a candidate and his/her stands on issues. Even when the terms are only vaguely understood they can provide a sense of political identity—a way of separating "us" from "them" in political conflicts.

This chapter explores the way citizens use the terms "liberal" and "conservative" to identify their political views and to evaluate political objects like candidates and issues. It begins with a discussion of the way in which the terms entered American political discourse and what they are generally understood to mean today. It then traces the course of ideological identification across time in the United States. This is followed by a discussion of the way political scientists have generally defined ideology. We will consider the extent to which the American public can be said to possess a sophisticated sense of ideology and how useful ideologies are in structuring political opinions. Finally we will explore what the terms generally mean to members of the public at large by looking at the kinds of things people say when asked to define the terms "liberal" and "conservative" in their own words.

Liberalism and Conservatism in the American Political Context

There can be no doubt that the term "conservative" is more popular in the United States today than the term "liberal", but this has by no means always been the case. In the critical election of 1932 both Franklin Roosevelt and Herbert Hoover competed to be called "liberal". With Roosevelt's success the term liberal became associated with the programs of the New Deal and with the Democratic Party. In the United States, since Roosevelt, the liberal viewpoint has been one which asserts that the government has a positive role to play in ameliorating the negative consequences to society brought about by economic and technological change.

Liberalism does not oppose individual initiative, but recognizes that a single individual is so small in comparison to a national or multi-national corporations that he/she can rarely succeed alone. Liberalism, then, juxtaposes "big government" against "big business" in an effort to balance the scales in favor of the individual, and to insure that individual rights and human dignity are not sacrificed to "efficiency" and "profit."

Another connotation of liberalism that deserves mentioning because it is so frequently implied in elite discourse is orientation toward change. Liberalism is progressive in its willingness to adapt to, and sometimes even create, change. Because it adapts to new ideas (like environmentalism, or race and gender equality), it is not always easy to define the exact scope of the liberal ideology, and even among those who call themselves "liberal" there are differences in willingness to adopt all of its goals.

When Roosevelt captured the liberal label, the opposition was left with the conservative one by default. This sequence of events essentially replicated the process in England in the 1830s where the Tories adopted the conservative label after the new Liberal Party succeeded in casting the Tory label into disrepute. The term "conservative" was used in the United States to mean the opposite of liberal from the late 1930s, but it did not become a popularly recognized political symbol until the Republican, Barry Goldwater, took up the conservative standard in 1964.

"Conservatism" can be defined as a reaction against "big government," against the big taxes needed to support it, and against the "interference" of government in local and state affairs, and in business. Conservatives argue that government regulations produce inefficiency, and that "free enterprise" will create the greatest good for the greatest number. It is frequently argued that conservatives emphasize liberty, in the sense of the relative absence of governmental interference in private affairs, while liberals emphasize equality. However, this distinction is a little more complicated than it first appears. While generally striving to limit government, conservatives these days generally support extensive government spending programs designed to achieve military superiority. In addition, modern conservatism also contains a moralistic strain demanding a return to "traditional values." This means that conservatives are substantially more likely than liberals to support governmental intrusion into people's private lives to enforce appropriate behavior through laws such as those regulating sexual conduct, or requiring drug testing.

Because the "model" for the proper role of government and the proper behavior of the individual can be found by looking to the past, conservatism is generally regarded as past-oriented rather than progressive. At the same time, most conservatives would not seek to dismantle the programs originally set in motion by the New Deal (e.g., Social Security, unemployment insurance, Security and Exchange regulations, and the like), and many would maintain more recent programs such as environmental regulation, and welfare for the "truly needy." It is frequently argued that the American public is "ideologically conservative" but "operationally liberal." This point is useful to keep in mind when exploring ideological identification across time.

Liberal and Conservative Sentiment in the Public at Large

Opinion polls attempting to determine the liberal and conservative leanings of the public at large can be traced back at least as far as the 1930s. While these polls cannot tell us how deeply the meanings generally associated with the terms penetrate into the public consciousness, they do allow us to track the general trends in ideological sentiment in the United States for an extended period of time.

Figure 3.1 describes the balance of liberal and conservative identification in the American public between 1936 and 1984. Each data point represents

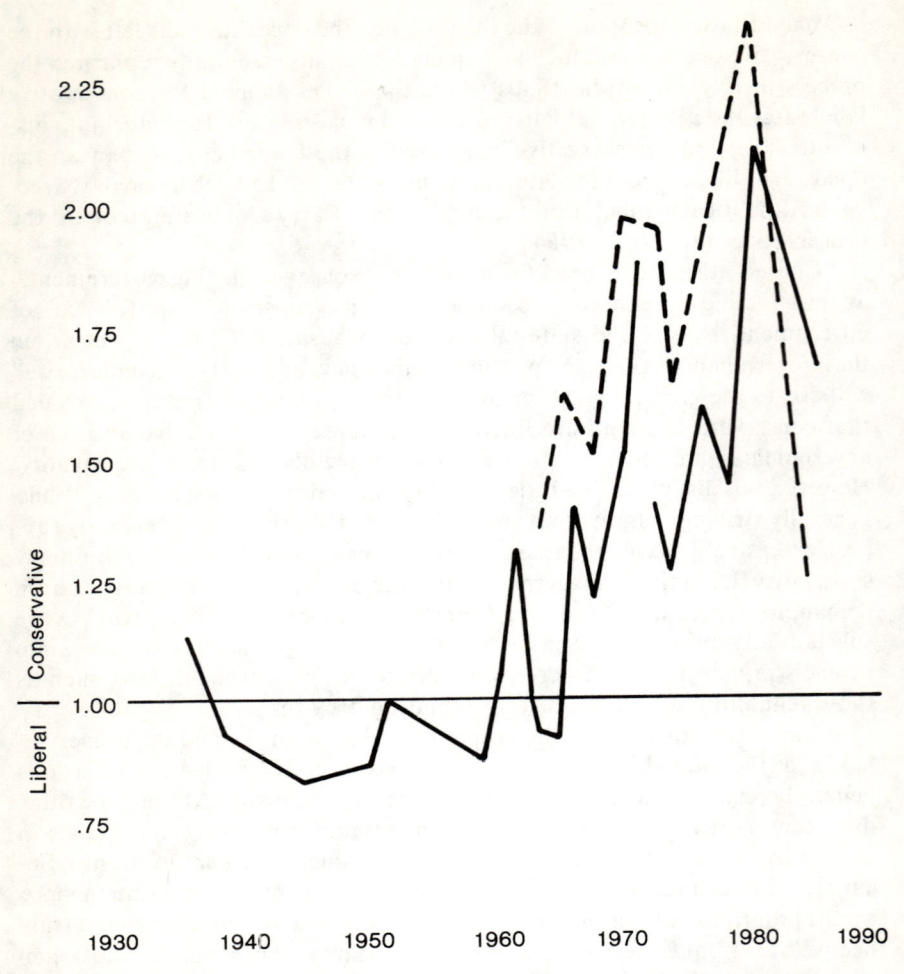

Figure 3.1. Patio of Conservatives to Liberals in the American Public 1936 to 1984.
   ——— Gallup Polls 1936–1971, CPS/NES liberal-conservative scales 1972–1984.
   ---- SRC/CPS/NES liberal-conservative "feeling thermometer" difference 1964–1984.

number of people who said they were conservative divided by the number of people who said they were liberal. Before considering the implications of this graph, it is important to point out that it represents only individuals who were willing to call themselves liberals and conservatives in the survey setting. A substantial part of the public (25–30%) call themselves "moderate" if provided with that alternative in the survey question, and another ten to twenty percent say they don't know, or refuse to take a position.

The Gallup questions (covering the 1930-1970 period) were not always phrased in exactly the same way, and not as many data points are available for the Gallup period, so the picture we see may be somewhat less distinct than that for the later years.

The solid line representing two-year intervals from 1972 to 1984 is taken from the University of Michigan Center for Political Studies/American National Election Studies (CPS/NES) surveys which always included the question "or haven't you thought much about this?" as well as a "moderate" option. Thus these data points represent the ideological positions of a little less than half of the public. The dotted line is taken from a set of survey questions which asked respondents to rate liberals and conservatives on a hundred point "feeling thermometer." In these questions roughly sixty percent of the public in any year expressed a preference for liberals or conservatives (i.e., rated liberals more warmly than conservatives or vice versa). In examining any report of ideological identification in the mass public, it is very important to consider what proportion of the public actually commits itself to the liberal or conservative label. A two to one ratio of conservatives to liberals does not look as impressive when we know that the percentage of the sample not identifying either way is equivalent to the percent conservative (e.g., 20% liberal, 40% conservative, and 40% moderate or "don't know"—roughly the distribution after the 1980 election).

With this qualification in mind Figure 3.1 can be thought to depict an ideological "fever chart" plotting the rise and fall of conservative sentiment over the last fifty years. From the 1940s until the early 1960s ideological sentiment seems to have been fairly evenly balanced with a slight liberal edge. In the mid-sixties conservative sentiment began to rise. From 1964 forward the ratio of conservative to liberal identifiers never drops below 5 to 4. In 1980 there was an abrupt increase in conservative identification, apparently in response to Reagan's election, which pushed the conservative edge to better than two to one. By 1984 (considering the solid line) conservative identification appears to have declined somewhat from its all time high in 1980, but still reflects more than one and a half conservatives for every liberal.

Considering the feeling thermometer ratios (represented by the dotted line in Figure 3.1) completes the fever chart analogy. The feeling thermometer measure tends to classify more people as having liberal or conservative sentiment (roughly 60% on the feeling thermometer vs. 40% on the CPS/NES liberal-conservative scale), and also reveals sentiments which seem to shift more radically with the nature of the times. The ratio of conservative sentiment measured by the feeling thermometer is higher than that measured by the Gallup survey or the CPS/NES from 1964 to 1980.

In fact the 1980 thermometer ratio, obtained from surveys conducted in the two months immediately following President Reagan's election, is well "off the chart" at 2.36 to 1. In 1982 the ratios obtained from the two measures are nearly identical, but by 1984 the feeling thermometer ratio is lower than at any time previously measured. Time will have to tell whether the thermometer ratio is a more sensitive measure which began to reflect a liberal reaction to the Reagan policies even during his landslide re-election, or is simply subject to greater measurement error.

The Relevance of Ideology for Political Evaluations

Political scientists have for some time been concerned with the problem of "non-attitudes" in survey research. Non-attitudes are reflected not only by the number of people who decline to answer the question, but also in some percentage of spur-of-the-moment responses given in order to avoid appearing uninformed. Non-attitude responses are characterized by instability, or a tendency to change sides when asked the same question repeatedly over time. In effect, if the person answering the question has no real opinion he/she may not even remember what answer was given the last time the question was asked.

Since liberalism and conservatism are presumed to be ideologies which help people make sense of the political world, we would generally expect that they would be reflected in stable identification. Yet this is by no means the picture which emerges when the question is put to a test. Whether asked the same question repeatedly over time, or asked different questions designed to measure liberal-conservative identification in the same interview, only a little more than half of the public stays on the same side more often than would be expected by chance. This instability suggests another reason to be cautious in making inferences about the extent of ideological thinking in the public at large based on the results of public opinion polls.

Many political scientists would go farther in expressing doubts about the impact of ideological identification by itself. A number argue that if ideology is really meaningful to a respondent, it should be reflected in the kinds of things he/she tells the interviewer when asked to provide open-ended evaluations of the presidential candidates and their parties. This hypothesis has given rise to a good deal of work examining public "levels of conceptualization" of politics.

In open-ended survey items respondents are not provided with any pre-established categories for answering a question. Rather, a set of general questions is asked and the interviewer writes down whatever the respondent says. In the case of the SRC/CPS/NES data available from 1956 to 1984 the questions were simply phrased: "What do you like about _____ (the Democratic candidate for president)? Is there anything in particular that would make you vote for him or against him?/ What do you dislike about _____ (the same person)?" Interviewers are instructed to ask "What else?" until the respondent has nothing more to say. The interviewer then moves on to ask the same questions about the other candidate and each of the two major parties. This series of questions yields a set of eight open-ended responses in which people have been allowed to say as much, or as little, as they want about the major "political objects" in each presidential election, and to say it in their own words.

Table 1. Distribution of the Public in the Levels of Conceptualization: 1956–1984.

	1956	1960	1964	1968	1972	1976	1980	1984
Ideologues	12%	19%	27%	26%	22%	21%	21%	19%
Group Benefit	42	31	27	24	27	26	31	26
Nature of the Times	24	26	20	29	34	30	30	35
No Issue Content	22	23	26	21	17	24	19	19
Sample n	1740	1741	1431	1319	1372	2870	1612	2257

Source: University of Michigan Survey Research Center/Center for Political Studies National Election Studies (Pierce/Hagner coding of the levels of conceptualization) ICPSR Study Number 8151.

The "levels of conceptualization" measure is based on reading and coding the responses to the eight open-ended questions. Four categories of respondents are distinguished in the levels of conceptualization. Individuals who fall into the first category are called "ideologues" because they use terms like "liberal" and "conservative" in their verbal evaluations, and provide coherent detailed rationalizations for their "likes and dislikes." Individuals in the other levels of conceptualization respond with non-ideological evaluations. People in the "group benefit" category evaluate the candidates and parties with reference to the kinds of groups (e.g., businesses/unions, rich/poor, old/young, racial, regional, and religious groups) which will be helped or hurt by the election of one candidate or the other. Those in the "nature of the times" category generally respond in terms of the performance of the past presidential administration with respect to the economy and to international security. Individuals in the "no issue content" category rarely say very much at all, and generally confine their evaluations to party labels and vague personal characteristics.

Table 1 presents the distribution of the public in the levels of conceptualization for each presidential election year since 1956. The incidence of spontaneous use of the ideological terms (reflected in the ideologue category) has always been quite limited. It appears that Goldwater's campaign and the activism of the sixties stimulated an increased awareness and use of ideological terminology. Surprisingly, however, ideological rhetoric in the public at large was not sustained into the Nixon/McGovern election, and the active use of an ideological dimension of evaluation continued to decline slightly even during the Reagan elections.

For most of the public the salient dimensions of evaluation are group benefits and nature of the times concerns. The schemata from which such evaluations arise are certainly relevant to politics, but they lack any explicitly ideological component. Only about a fifth of the public spontaneously employs ideological language when asked to make open-ended evaluations of the presidential candidates and major parties. For this twenty percent ideological considerations clearly play an important role in processing political information, but for the rest of the public ideological awareness seems more minimal.

The Liberal-Conservative Continuum as an Organizing Device

According to the theories of many researchers in the area, one of the main advantages of possessing an ideological view of the world is that it allows a great deal of information about politics to be organized coherently and communicated effectively. These researchers hypothesize that citizens who know where they stand with respect to the liberal-conservative continuum will be likely to take consistent positions on a large number of the issues that make up the terms of the political debate in any presidential election. Common sense and experience with political discussions also lead to the general expectation that certain positions on various issues "go together," not so much because they may bear some direct logical relationship to each other as because the beliefs and values which they reflect are understood to be part of the liberal or conservative points of view. Indeed, when someone tells us they are a liberal or a conservative we can usually begin to make accurate guesses about where they stand on some, if not all, of the political issues of the day.

Table 2 suggests, however, that the expectation of ideologically based coherence in issue positions is somewhat better supported by common sense than by the data. This table displays the correlations between people's preferences for a variety of issues of public policy asked about in the 1984 survey. These issues (defense spending, spending on government services, government provision of health insurance, jobs, aid to minorities, attitude toward women's role in society and toward cooperation with Russia) would seem to provide a fair sample of the issues raised in the 1984 campaign, and to reflect a number of the dimensions of liberal and conservative ideologies detailed at the beginning of the chapter.

The correlation provides a simple measure of the degree to which each issue position is related to the others and to the respondent's position on the liberal-conservative scale. A correlation of 1.0 would indicate a perfect relationship between one issue and another, but because of the response format used for these questions and measurement error we would always expect that the correlations in these data would be something less than one. The items have been arranged so that the liberal and conservative positions always occupy the same end of the scale. For example, the liberal position on defense spending would be for less of it, while the liberal position on government services spending is generally understood to favor more; conservatives are generally understood to favor a tougher stand in bargaining with Russia, and because of their support for "traditional values" to be less favorable toward an equal role for women. Thus, a positive correlation indicates that the relationship between the issues is what would be expected of people whose issue positions have some ideological coherence.

Table 2 allows us to examine the degree of issue organization among individuals classified in each level of conceptualization. Ideologues, as might be expected, display the highest degree of issue consistency. The correlations between issues range from a low of .14, suggesting that there is essentially no

Table 2. Issue Constraint: Correlation between Issue Scales, and between Issues and Liberal/Conservative Position by Level of Conceptualization, 1984.

Ideologues

	v375	v1058	v382	v408	v250	v414	L/C
v395 defense spending	.38	.28	.42	.54	.25	.42	.56
v375 services spending		.50	.43	.40	.16	.60	.50
v1058 health insurance			.21	.14	.21	.53	.30
v382 minority aid				.34	.30	.41	.42
v408 "detente"					.25	.39	.43
v250 women's role						.16	.26
v414 job guarantee							.51

Group Benefit

	v375	v1058	v382	v408	v250	v414	L/C
v395 defense spending	.14*	.10	.36	.28	.18	.14	.24
v375 services spending		.16	.16	.08	.03*	.32	.09
v1058 health insurance			.11*	−.04*	.03*	.30	.20
v382 minority aid				.17*	.14	.36	.25
v408 "detente"					.16	.15	.30
v250 women's role						.21	.16	.23
v414 job guarantee							.25

Nature of the Times

	v375	v1058	v382	v408	v250	v414	L/C
v395 defense spending	.04*	−.03*	.18	.37	.05*	.18	.13
v375 services spending		.29	.26	.24	.08	.31	.17
v1058 health insurance			.03*	.18	.01*	.07*	.03*
v382 minority aid				.27	.14	.40	.16
v408 "detente"					.06*	.16	.16
v250 women's role						.10	.19
v414 job guarantee							.19

No Issue Content

	v375	v1058	v382	v408	v250	v414	L/C
v395 defense spending	.04*	−.01*	.11*	.31	.21	.18	.08*
v375 services spending		.18	.19	.12	.02*	.24	.01*
v1058 health insurance			.09*	.13*	−.07*	−.14*	−.13*
v382 minority aid				.28	.10*	.31	.02*
v408 "detente"					.14	.17	.03*
v250 women's role						−.04*	.16
v414 job guarantee							−.06*

* not significant, p. > .05.
variable numbers are from the 1984 NES traditional time-series data set (ICPSR Study Number 8298).
L/C = liberal/conservative scale identification.

relationship between the positions that ideologues take on seeking accomodation with Russia and their positions on government provision of medical insurance, to .60, suggesting that there is a fairly strong likelihood that an ideologue who favors government guarantee of jobs will favor more government spending on services. The column labelled "L/C" allows us to consider the relationship between positions on each of the issue scales and a respondent's identification as a liberal or conservative. The high correlations for government services and defense spending, and government guarantee of jobs, can be interpreted to mean that among ideologues these issues are fairly strongly connected to a person's underlying ideological predispositions. In 1984 conservative ideologues favored increased defense spending, and opposed services spending and job guarantees; liberal ideologues opposed defense spending and favored services spending and job guarantees. On the other hand, the relationships between ideological identification and attitudes toward women's roles in society and government provision of medical insurance are not very strong even among ideologues.

People in the other levels of conceptualization manifest substantially less issue consistency than the ideologues. A few moderate-sized correlations are apparent among group benefit respondents and those in the nature of the times categories. For example, in both groups favoring accommodation with Russia (detente) is associated with preferring less defense spending, and favoring government guarantee of jobs is associated with favoring more government spending on domestic services. However, in all cases these correlations are substantially smaller than the ones obtained for ideologues. Also, among group benefit respondents there are some modest associations between a few issues (detente, minority aid, government guaranteed jobs) and general liberal-conservative identification. Once below the group benefit category even these weak relationships fade out.

The evidence presented in Table 2 suggests that individuals who spontaneously evaluate the candidates and parties in ideological terms tend to structure their issue preferences with respect to some more general sense of their liberal-conservative leanings. For this fraction of the public (roughly one fifth) knowing the person's ideological identification allows us to make some fair guesses about the kinds of position he/she will take on a number of political issues. In the rest of the public we would have much less success predicting issue attitudes from liberal-conservative identification. In fact, except to a small extent among group benefit respondents, political issues do not seem to have much relevance for liberal-conservative identification.

The foregoing provides some reasons to be skeptical about the degree to which ideological considerations have an impact on people's political thinking. While roughly sixty percent of the public seems to have some sense of ideological identification, only about a third of these citizens actually use ideological terminology when asked to provide political evaluations in their own words. On closer examination only these "ideologues" seem to structure their issue opinions in a way which suggests that they hold the kinds of coherent liberal and conservative ideologies described at the beginning of the chapter.

Public Understanding of the Ideological Terms

A number of political scientists have argued that the difficulty with "issue consistency" as an indicator of ideological thinking is that most of the public is not issue- oriented. Thus the lack of structure in the issue opinions of the non-ideologues should be attributed to their lack of attention to issues rather than to a lack of ideological awareness. For example, they argue that the "non-ideological" use of ideological labels may help citizens structure their preferences in the political world even though a sophisticated understanding of the terms is lacking.

Some research has found that although people may understand that "liberal" is the opposite of "conservative," the meanings associated with the continuum are different for liberals as opposed to conservatives. While liberalism and conservatism can be defined in terms of opposing views toward the various intellectual components of the liberal-conservative continuum, there are also fundamental differences in the importance liberals and conservatives attach to these components. Thus conservatives can be mobilized to support some kinds of political initiatives without necessarily arousing opposition among liberals, and vice versa. For example, the fact that liberals emphasize race and gender equality does not necessarily mean that conservatives are racist and sexist. Nor does the fact that conservatives emphasize support for "traditional values" mean that liberals necessarily favor sex and drugs.

This phenomenon can be illustrated by looking at the way citizens themselves define the terms. Starting in 1978 respondents in the National Election Study surveys were asked what sorts of things they had in mind when they said someone's views were liberal or conservative. These open-ended responses allow consideration of the extent to which people raise the kinds of concerns generally associated with the definitions of liberal and conservative ideologies when given an opportunity to define the terms in their own words.

The data in Table 3 are arranged so that it is also possible to see if there are differences in the way self-identified liberals and conservatives define the terms. Even if the definitions offered are not very sophisticated, the fact that there are differences in the kinds of things important to liberals and conservatives may provide some reason to believe that the terms are meaningful to the general public. The categories of content reflected in Table 3 are those thought relevant to ideological debate by a number of previous analysts.

The percentages reflected in each column of Table 3 represent the percentage of all liberals or all conservatives in that year who mentioned each specific element of content in that category. This means that the table only

Table 3. Percent of Liberals and Conservatives Mentioning Each Element of the Definitions of the Ideological Terms. (Columns total more than 100% because some respondents mentioned more than one aspect of the definition.)

	1978 Lib.	1978 Con.	1980 Lib.	1980 Con.	1984 Lib.	1984 Con.
Fiscal principles	13.6	21.3*	14.6	20.7*	12.2	21.9*
Spend/Save	16.5	49.8*	16.5	37.8*	20.1	37.4*
Econ/Issues	13.3	25.3*	17.2	25.3*	22.0	32.3*
Econ/Groups	9.3	5.5*	21.7	6.8*	20.5	9.3*
Groups/Gen	7.0	4.7	11.2	4.5*	10.6	9.3
Race	10.4	10.0	9.0	6.4	5.1	6.0
Change	56.8	31.9*	36.7	18.9*	34.6	22.5*
Personal	16.7	17.6	15.7	17.5	21.3	13.8*
Social Values	18.3	6.6*	31.1	16.7*	25.6	16.8*
Government	7.5	11.8*	9.0	13.8*	5.1	9.9*
Philosophy, other	4.1	3.9	2.2	1.1	4.3	2.7
Issues, non-econ.	3.2	3.5	1.5	2.1	5.1	6.0
Issues/New	17.2	14.0	9.7	11.0	9.4	14.4*
Foreign Policy	5.9	12.4*	14.2	12.1	13.4	14.4
Labels	2.9	4.8	3.4	5.1	1.2	2.4
	(442)	(620)	(267)	(629)	(254)	(334)

*difference in proportions significant at the .05 level.

considers the roughly sixty percent of respondents who called themselves liberals or conservatives. The percents in each column sum to more than 100% because some respondents provided more than one definition. Categories marked with asterisks are those in which there was a significant difference between the proportion of liberals and conservatives defining the ideological terms in that fashion.

The first four categories of definitions considered in Table 3 reflect economic concerns. These have been found in previous studies to make up a large part of the content of citizens' ideological definitions. The references to fiscal principles and symbols are the kind that we might expect to find in a relatively sophisticated discussion of the economic aspects of ideology. Individuals in this category defined the ideological differences with phrases like "free enterprise" and "capitalism," or indicated in some fashion that the differences in ideology are to be found in government approaches to handling the economy. Looking across the row labelled "fiscal principles," one sees that these kinds of responses were not offered by a very large number of respondents. More importantly, conservatives were significantly more likely to mention fiscal principles than liberals.

The single most common element of shared meaning among conservatives in each of the years examined is the "spend/save" distinction. The idea that liberals generally favor spending money while conservatives are for saving is quite common in American political discourse, but it is generally not regarded as a very sophisticated understanding of the distinction. The next most common element for conservatives is also "economic," but is articulated in terms of specific issues like welfare, taxation, and employment policy. Both the spend/save distinction and specific economic issues are significantly more important to conservatives than to liberals. In general, then, economic concerns dominate the definitions of the ideological terms offered by conservatives. When liberals mention economic concerns, thay are much more likely to cast the differences in terms of economic benefits to specific groups, or divisions in society with economic foundations such as poor vs. rich, or workers and unions vs. owners and managers. Interestingly, in contrast with its importance in intellectual definitions of the conservative point of view, remarks about the scope of government involvement in non-economic concerns are not obtained from a very large number of conservatives. However, they are significantly more likely to be mentioned by conservatives than liberals.

Among liberals the most common element of shared meaning revolves around the definition of the liberal-conservative continuum in terms of orientation toward change. In 1978 over half of all liberals who defined the terms did so by saying in some fashion that liberals favored change while conservatives oppose it. Conservatives, particularly in 1978, were also quite sensitive to this element of the definition. However, in each of the three years examined liberals were significantly more likely to mention change than conservatives. Over the same period liberals appear to pay increasing attention to general social values (equality, caring about others, and human dignity) as an element of the liberal-conservative distinction.

A final point concerning the distribution of the definitional elements over the last few years is worthy of some discussion. While conservatives remain fairly united around economic definitions of the ideological terms, liberals display greater and greater variety in their definitions. By 1984 six separate definitions of the terms are mentioned by at least 20% of liberal identifiers. Two of these increasingly mentioned definitional elements refer to components generally more important to conservatives (spend/save and economic issues). Looking at these responses in more detail, it appears that liberals are adopting the elements salient to conservatives and attempting to refute them—arguing, for example, that conservatives are unwilling to spend money even when it is needed, or that liberals defend social security and unemployment programs. Interestingly, over time, liberals also pay increasing attention to personal characteristics (thoughtfulness vs. rashness, realism vs. idealism, and the like).

Considering the definitions of the ideological terms obtained in the respondents' own words provides a somewhat more comprehensive picture of ideological thinking in the public at large. Differences in the way liberals and conservatives define the terms provides evidence that the labels represent generally meaningful and different points of view, even if the definitions are not very sophisticated. Of course these observations apply only to the roughly 50% of the public that identifies as liberal or conservative and provides some definition of the terms. Still this estimate of the extent of ideological thinking is somewhat larger than that obtained using other methods.

Summary and Conclusions

In this chapter ideology in the American public has been explored from several different perspectives. We have not considered the deeper intellectual roots of the ideological viewpoints, nor the arguments about meaning that politically sophisticated individuals may sometimes entertain. Rather, we have concentrated on the common meanings generally associated with the terms in an attempt to determine how far ideological considerations penetrate into the political thinking of the public at large.

The most important thing to emphasize in summarizing the results of this excursion is that ideological thinking is far from universal. In considering any poll purporting to measure ideological identification it is important to keep in mind that at least 40% of the public will not take sides if given the opportunity to remain neutral. Beyond this it is important to consider just how important ideological distinctions really are in the evaluative processes of most citizens. Only about a fifth of the public can truly be called ideologically sophisticated. Among this limited part of the public ideology is an important dimension for evaluating political candidates and parties. In addition, only among ideologues does knowing a person's ideological identification help much in predicting positions on the kind of policy issues that make up the usual presidential campaign.

At the same time, most of the people who are willing to call themselves liberal or conservative have at least some minimal understanding of the terms. Moreover, there is a different consensus among liberals and conservatives about the importance of various elements of the definitions of the terms. In this respect liberalism and conservatism can be said to represent different points of view, or frames of reference for viewing the political world. It is not simply the case that liberals and conservatives propose different solutions for the same problems; rather liberals and conservatives appear to pay attention to different problems.

It is this "dualistic" characteristic of ideology in the American public that makes it particularly useful for political communication. To some extent, astute politicians can tailor their appeals in a manner which will mobilize one ideological side without necessarily arousing opposition in the other. In the recent past, for example, both Carter and Reagan have been able to use opposition to "wasteful" government spending to mobilize underlying conservative sentiment in the public. However, because the implications of ideological sentiments do not penetrate very far into the public, the fact that the federal deficit doubled during Reagan's first term did not have any negative impact on Reagan's bid for re-election in 1984.

In thinking about ideology in the general public it is important to keep in mind that many of the assumptions made about ideology by journalists and intellectuals simply do not apply to the public at large. This is particularly clear when looking at the degree to which ideological considerations structure preferences for various kinds of public policies. In this respect, it is better to consider ideology a matter of public mood rather than policy mandate. These considerations do not mean, however, that ideology is meaningless. Roughly half of the public at the present time possesses some measurable degree of ideological sentiment. Among this half of the public the possession of such sentiment appears to be associated with differences in ideological schemata. To get a true idea of the impact of ideology in America it is important to keep in mind that many people pay little attention to politics at all, and that only about half of eligible adults even vote. Ideology penetrates the electoral process because the half of the public which can be said to possess even a minimal ideological point of view is generally the half that votes.

Bibliography

Campbell, Angus, Phillip E. Converse, Warren E. Miller and Donald A. Stokes. (1960) *The American Voter.* New York: Wiley.

Converse, Phillip E. (1964) "The Nature of Belief Systems in Mass Publics," in D.E. Apter, (ed). *Ideology and Discontent.* New York: Free Press.

Helms, Jesse. (1976) *Where Free Men Shall Stand.* Grand Rapids, Mi: Zondervan Publishing House.

Kerlinger, Fred N. (1984) *Liberalism and Conservatism.* Hilldale, N.J.: Earlbaum Press.

Minar, David. (1961) "Ideology and Political Behavior," *Midwest Journal of Political Science,* 5: 317–331.

Putnam, Robert. (1973) *The Beliefs of Politicians.* New Haven, N.J.: Yale University Press.

Rotunda, Ronald D. (1986) *The Politics of Language: Liberalism as Word and Symbol.* Iowa City, Ia: University of Iowa Press.

Viguerie, Richard A. (1980) *The New Right: We're Ready to Lead.* Falls Church, Va: The Viguerie Company.

4 The Paradox of Ignorant Voters But Competent Electorate*

JAMES A. STIMSON

After four decades of carefully studying the American voter political scientists continue to be faced with a central paradox—individual Americans seem to pay relatively little attention to politics and consequently appear quite ignorant on the topic, yet taken as a whole the American electorate appears to have accurate perceptions concerning the positions of candidates and parties and thus seems to be well informed. How is it possible that voters could be ignorant as individuals yet collectively informed? That is the question motivating this chapter.

We shall survey some evidence of what the electorate does and does not know, ponder some proposed explanations for the conflicting evidence of ignorance versus knowledge among voters, and suggest a resolution for the apparent paradox based upon the intermediary role of citizen political activists. The model used as the basis for the resolution is derived from communication theory. In the two-step theory of mass communication, a relatively small percentage of the public is tuned into public affairs and is the primary conduit of information to the majority who are not so attuned. In the political sphere this means that those who are more interested in politics convey information about candidates and political parties, and those not attentive to political matters evaluate candidates and party positions on the basis of how they evaluate those among the activists who are conveying such information to them.

Thus, for example, a political "activist" may somehow convey the information that one candidate is in favor of a freeze on the production of nuclear weapons, and express approval for the candidate. Those to whom the information is conveyed will then project onto the candidate the views of the activist, and evaluate the candidate in terms of how they evaluate the activist. If, for some reason, the member of the inattentive public is inclined to evaluate the activist conveying the information in a positive fashion, the inattentive citizen will project onto the candidate a positive reponse, as well as a positive response with respect to the issue. If the inattentive citizen has reason to evaluate the activist conveying the information in a negative light, this negativism will be projected onto the candidate and issue.

This process of political information being conveyed by, and filtered through a cadre of political activists is described by the model of "mediated cognitions." The political knowledge of most citizens is seen as being mediated by political activists. As it turns out, the model of mediated cognitions can be used to account for the apparant paradox of the United States having ignorant voters but an informed electorate.

A Paradox and a Model

Voters repeatedly tell those studying American voting behavior that they don't follow public affairs, have little interest in politics or governmental policies, view government as relatively remote from their lives, and have little concern over which group of public officials is in charge. Yet, taken together as an aggregate, these same voters seem surprisingly well informed about the choices they make. This contradictory set of facts has produced one of the longest running conflicts among political scientists, and the length and bitterness of the conflict seems to indicate there is no easy way out of the paradox. We can deny one or the other set of facts, but after decades of arguments between the "voters don't pay attention" and "voters are not fools" schools of thought, the evidence marshalled on both sides is impressive.

For example, the area of economic policy-making provides a stark contrast between ignorant citizens and informed electorate. Citizen ignorance of the basic facts of economics and government economic policies has been long noted. Even matters as simple as the relationships between government expenditures, revenues, and deficits seem to elude most citizens. But research also demonstrates that electoral support for government economic policy is based upon a relatively sophisticated level of information so that the electorate as a whole will consistently support neither full employment policies nor anti-inflationary policies, but rather support the right policy at the right time given national economic circumstances.

In a similar vein, public officials such as members of the United States Congress repeatedly tell researchers that the public seems wholly unaware of how their representatives behave and what policies they support despite the best efforts of the representatives to inform their respective constituents. At the same time, these members of Congress worry a great deal about the consequences of their actions for reelection. Are members of Congress irrationally fearful and ignorant of the true level of public information, or is there some way in which the general public does not know about a single act by a congressman, such as a vote on a particular bill, yet somehow comes to understand the congressman's general pattern of behavior?

Furthermore, there are many examples in electoral history where voter perceptions on important matters are contrary to the facts, at least as can best be objectively determined, yet the general electorate manages to choose the party or candidate that in fact is closest to voter preferences. For example, in 1972 McGovern was widely, and incorrectly, perceived to be in favor of "acid, amnesty, and abortion," a rather radical agenda, when McGovern in fact had a mixed, and largely private view of the abortion issue, and certainly did not favor the legalization of LSD or illegal drug use in general. However, as inaccurate as those perceptions were, the electorate ended up seeing McGovern accurately as the more congenial of the two major candidates to the counterculture to which these issues were tied.

Even more striking was the widespread belief in 1980, a belief of considerable consequence to the election's outcome, that Jimmy Carter was opposed to increased spending on defense. In fact, Carter instigated perhaps the most impressive peacetime increases since the beginning of the Cold War in the late 1940's. But applied to the choice between Carter and Ronald Reagan, the public's misperception of Carter was the basis of an accurate relative assessment of which candidate would be more likely to spend even more on defense in the future.

Most debates over public policy are very technical, and even the basic alternatives are usually very difficult to communicate for mass consumption. Such debates usually revolve around specific and complicated facts and assumptions. Competing values are also usually involved, but the role of values in public policy debate is often so subtle that only experts following the day-to-day process can sort out their impact. Still, despite the complexities and subtleties, voters frequently make choices in deciding whom to support which accurately reflect their underlying preferences.

If we are to resolve these apparent contradictions and paradoxes, we must begin by abandoning the image of individual citizens as isolated fact-collectors and decision makers. If instead we view the collection of factual information as a social process, including a two-step flow of communication, we can come to understand how millions of inattentive citizens acquire reasonably accurate information about policy positions and policy choices.

We have long known that inattentive citizens are likely to obtain information from the more politically attentive people with whom they have contact, but for some reason political scientists tend to forget this fact when analyzing general voting behavior. Perhaps this fact is often forgotten because democratic theory tends to idealize the citizen as an individualistic, self-contained decision maker. Also, the study of voting behavior in political science is dominated by survey research, which constantly directs our focus to the individual as the unit of analysis, producing a tendency to revert to the psychology of individuals. Whatever the reason, our inclination is usually to view decisions by voters as if they occurred in a social vacuum—the lonely vigil of the individual citizen in front of his or her television set trying to figure things out alone.

Consider the problems of gathering facts about policy choices. The citizen who would express his preference between candidates and parties must know what the choices are, who stands for which choice, how each policy choice is likely to affect himself and others, and so forth. Two major barriers stand in the way of gathering such information. First, the activity is extremely expensive in time and energy. It requires a level of attentiveness to government and politics well beyond what most citizens seem willing to attain. Second, a citizen who pays the high price of attentiveness to public affairs could still end up being wrong—that is, taking a position contrary to what he would support if he had more expert knowledge on the matter. Put another way, even a highly attentive citizen may often not have enough information to make a rational decision.

On the other hand, a citizen might prefer to be inattentive to politics, thereby avoiding the costs of attentiveness, and instead look to someone in his personal environment, someone whose views he knows (often, perhaps, without wishing to). The following pattern of inference is simple, yet accurate enough on average to make it a reasonable guide: Joe Blow supports candidate X, therefore X probably stands for the same things as Joe Blow does. If one fills in television's "Archie Bunker" for Joe Blow, and Richard Nixon for candidate X, one inference that follows, for example, is that Nixon is not warmly disposed toward black Americans.

This sort of inferential reasoning is probably very common. It provides a simple and at times impressively accurate means for making sense out of complicated political alternatives without having to pay the costs of high attentiveness. Indeed, one of the more interesting aspects of this type of political reasoning is that it can proceed without ever having to listen to the candidate at all.

Who would be those of known views in the individual's environment? Citizen political activists, those relatively ordinary people who take the opportunities for political participation that most shun, would seem to be prime candidates. They are the citizens who pay attention to politics when others do not. Their views are public, on display through lawn signs, campaign buttons, and bumper stickers. Sometimes their views have been conveyed directly to those around them, in which case they convey considerable information about the party and candidates they support. Sometimes their views are not know directly, but are advertised along with candidate support. A peace symbol and a McGovern sticker on the same bumper told a story in 1972. Sometimes the association of political support with a subculture or life-style is the basis of inferences about candidate views. If the McGovern sticker appeared on the bumper of an aging Volkswagon van, the symbolic association of the candidate with a cluster of liberal political views might be inferred.

The process of inferring candidate and party issue positions from the views of activist supporters would be most direct and powerful for members of primary groups like families. An activist member of the family would provide information on issue positions as a result of direct conversation over a long period of time. That might be supplemented, in some cases replaced, by figures who are highly visible but not personally known, such as movie stars. A Jane Fonda endorsement in the 1970's and 1980's could tell us a good deal about a politician's set of views. And then, of course, there are the entirely anonymous and impersonal mechanisms such as the bumper sticker. By combining the "cues" we receive from these various sources, it may be possible to develop a reasonably sophisticated picture of what different candidates and parties stand for.

We assume for this analysis that one of the things which distinguishes activists from non-activists is the public expression of political views. Indeed, "talking about politics" is one of the activities used to define activism. If we assume, furthermore, that the visibility of a citizen's views is in rough proportion to his or her activity, a matter of degree rather than of kind, then a method of examining visible party positions suggests itself. Thus, the citizen who reports no activity beyond voting is altogether removed from this public opinion analysis, while the more active are weighted by degree of activism.[1]

Party and Candidate Policy Positions: How Much Does the Electorate Know?

We begin the analysis with evidence of what the public knows using the National Election Series (NES) national surveys. Since 1972 similar information has been obtained in each election about candidate positions. Looking at Table 1, we can see that there is a close fit between how voters perceived a party and the party's actual issue positions.

Not only do voters uniformly perceive the Democrats to be more liberal on most issues in most elections, but these perceptions appear sensitive to variations in party positions from election to election. For example, in cases where a new party position is defined—race in the 1960's and women's rights around 1980—citizen perceptions follow closely. One important feature is that while perceptions follow actual party positions, they tend to exaggerate the differences between parties.

After hearing all the appalling stories about how little citizens know about politics, it should come as some surprise that such essential information about policy choices is perceived with commendable accuracy by the American electorate. Table 1 suggests strongly that American citizens see little confusion or randomness in the political world.

The perceptions of candidate positions shown in Table 2 tell a similar story. Since candidates have much less time than a political party to establish what they stand for, and since there is apt to be considerable variation from candidate to candidate, the ability of the American electorate to sort them out as well as it does is quite impressive. What can be said about both tables is that there is little evidence of a confused or ignorant electorate. Although we find ignorance, confusion, and serious misperception among individual voters, there is none to be seen in the electorate as a whole.

Table 1 The Positions of Party Activists and Perceptions of Party Positions

Issue	Party Activist Positions Democrats	Republicans	Difference	Perceived Party Positions Democrats Liberal	Republicans Liberal	Difference
Women's Role						
1972	52.86	49.86	3.00	30.4	9.6	20.8
1976	52.01	49.22	2.79	34.2	8.2	26.0
1980	58.89	56.04	2.85	60.4	8.6	51.8
1984	53.11	46.58	6.53	59.3	13.2	46.1
Minority Aid[a]						
1956	49.72	49.83	−.11	20.1	22.1	−2.0
1960	51.52	50.28	1.24	22.7	21.4	1.3
1964	52.69	45.10	7.59	60.4	7.3	53.1
1968	53.64	48.29	5.35	51.0	10.8	40.2
1972	53.95	47.97	5.98	53.3	11.3	40.0
1976	51.63	49.24	2.39	53.3	14.5	38.8
1980	52.41	47.63	4.78	76.2	9.4	66.8
1984	52.31	46.52	5.79	63.1	17.7	45.4
Jobs and Standard of Living						
1956	51.32	46.83	4.49	34.8	15.9	18.9
1960	50.38	45.82	4.56	51.2	12.5	38.7
1964	50.93	44.95	5.98	60.8	8.1	52.7
1968	54.06	48.12	3.94	53.0	13.1	39.9
1972	52.92	45.48	7.44	69.6	11.7	57.9
1976	52.84	45.91	6.93	62.8	12.5	50.3
1980	45.43	38.08	7.35	72.5	9.3	63.2
1984	53.09	44.53	8.56	65.8	10.6	55.2
Education Aid						
1956	51.70	48.13	3.57	29.7	14.9	14.8
1960	51.85	44.81	7.04	41.9	13.1	28.8
1964	52.41	43.75	8.66	52.9	11.7	41.2
1968	52.97	45.38	6.59	43.3	15.8	27.5
School Desegregation						
1956	49.61	50.80	−1.19	22.8	25.0	−2.2
1960	50.71	49.88	.93	15.7	20.4	−4.7
1964	52.03	47.70	4.33	56.4	6.9	49.5
1968	52.59	49.44	3.15	51.7	8.7	43.0

a. The item used for 1956 through 1968 refers to "fair treatment in jobs and housing" for minorities.

To recapitulate, research tends to portray individual voters as disinterested, uninvolved, ignorant, unsophisticated, and nonideological; while at the same time portraying the general electorate as aware, knowledgeable, sophisticated, and reasonably ideological. The precise manner in which the paradox can be resolved is yet to be explained, but an important conclusion for democratic theory can already be derived. If the key for developing an informed, effective

Table 2 The Positions of Candidate[a] Activists and Perceptions of Candidate Positions

Issue	Candidate Activist Positions			Perceived Candidate Positions		
	Democrats	Republicans	Difference	Democrat More Lib.	Republican More Lib.	Difference
Liberal/Conservative						
1972	60.62	44.20	16.42	84.0	9.2	74.8
1976	56.92	42.55	14.37	74.7	13.1	61.6
1980	57.32	40.85	16.47	71.1	22.2	48.9
1984	56.65	42.12	14.53	68.9	20.5	48.4
Women's Role						
1972	55.48	51.05	4.43	36.4	12.7	23.7
1976	50.72	49.51	1.21	25.6	16.6	9.0
1980	58.76	54.15	4.61	65.0	10.3	54.7
1984	55.24	46.00	9.24	65.5	14.8	50.7
Defense Spending						
1972	50.18	38.82	11.36			
1976	51.17	46.81	4.36			
1980	47.61	42.48	4.93	77.8	13.5	64.3
1984	56.29	44.80	11.49	82.2	8.5	73.7
Minority Aid						
1972	58.02	47.90	10.12	65.2	11.5	53.7
1976	51.77	46.81	4.96	46.0	16.5	29.5
1980	47.61	42.68	4.93	76.4	12.0	64.4
1984	53.60	46.37	7.23	63.6	17.9	45.7
Jobs and Standard of Living						
1972	55.89	45.55	10.44	79.6	10.8	68.8
1976	54.76	44.59	10.17	58.5	16.5	42.0
1980	47.81	38.08	9.73	71.1	12.9	58.2
1984	54.81	44.26	10.55	69.3	10.0	59.3

a. "Candidate Activists" are party identifiers who report voting for their party's presidential candidate.

electorate is to create an aggregation rather than a mass of individual voters, then the importance of elections becomes obvious since elections are our primary means for creating that aggregated whole. There is thus added empirical support for the utility of representation, and the elections that representation requires, in creating the kind of citizenry that democratic theory assumes. The critical link in all of this is something here termed the "citizen activist." We need to take a closer look at this crucial link.

Citizen Activists: Who, What, and Why?

Citizen activists are in many respects very normal people, but they have the one atypical attribute of being intensely involved with politics. While they are clearly not a cross-section of the electorate, they also have very little in common with professionals in the world of politics. The citizen activists do not hold or seek office, and their involvement in politics, counted in hours or days, is intense only relative to most members of the electorate who do little or nothing.

The literature in political science has little to tell us about the attributes, behavior, or institutional role of citizen activists. The citizen activist falls between the well-studied mass electorate on the one hand and the professional politician on the other.

Public activism is occasional in American politics. Wearing political buttons or ringing doorbells on behalf of candidates are intermittent activities because elections occur only periodically. Furthermore, different citizens become active in diferent campaigns. Each campaign faces anew the problem of recruiting "foot soldiers." Political campaigns need citizens with the personal attributes of good salesmen in order to sell the party or candidates. At the same time, political activism is costly in terms of time, energy, and emotional involvement, with little in the way of compensation other than the sense of being a good citizen, advancing one's personal views, or perhaps the social rewards that come from working with others. Given the high costs and low compensation of activism, it is not surprising that the failure to recruit adequate numbers of workers is a normal attribute of political campaigns. Sometimes a presidential campaign will succeed in inducing widespread political activity, but the normal campaign, whatever the level of politics, usually involves relatively small numbers of people rather than the "armies of volunteers" usually described by media hype.

Activism is occasional in a second sense. The pool of potential activists is much larger than the number of actual activists in any given year. All activists are occasional activists; they are active only periodically. But quite a number participate in some elections but not others. They are occasional in the sense of being active only during elections, and also in the sense of being active only in some elections. Generalizations about activists and activism must therefore be based upon information gathered over many elections if we are to draw a reasonably accurate picture of the "normal" activist.

At the same time we want to examine the variation in activist attributes from election to election. Although activists may have many similar attributes from election to election, different candidates and different issues will bring out activists of a different "coloration, and this tendency of elections to activate people of varying values, ideologies, and commitments is part of what we want to study. In a sense, it is the tendency of a given election to recruit selectively from the vast pool of potential activists that allows the citizen activist to respond so quickly to changes in the political context, and makes the citizen activist the most variable set of actors in the political system. This tendency for selective recruitment also suggests an important role for the citizen activist in any explanation for the dynamics of political change.

Data and Method

The remaining discussion is based upon an analysis of all presidential elections between 1956 and 1984 using data from the National Election Series. The eight elections allow us to identify a pool of over fifteeen thousand citizens interviewed in the studies. Although activists comprise a small percentage of the general electorate, from this very large pool the method used here allows the identification of almost one thousand citizen activists over the eight elections, more than enough for a systematic analysis.

Two overlapping sets of activists can be isolated from the election study samples. The first, and most important for our analysis, are "campaign activists." These are identified by their reports of having engaged in more than one of the following activities; (1) voting;(2) attending political rallies or meetings; (3) wearing a campaign button or displaying a bumper sticker; (4) working for a party or candidate through the formal organization; (5) attempting to influence the opinions of others through conversation; and (6) donating money (not including the one dollar federal income tax checkoff). Anyone who engaged in four or more of these activities was classified as a "citizen activist, which placed them in the most active five or six percent of the electorate.[2]

"Informational activists," the second set of citizen activists, were identified by their reports of having paid attention to the campaign through various media (newspapers, magazines, radio, and television). Not activist at all in a behavioral sense, informational activism measures passive involvement in the world of politics. There was only modest overlap between the two types of citizen activist, and thus we will have little need to pursue analysis of informational activism in this study except for a crucial test at the end. Our ability to clearly distinguish the two types of activism shows that those who actually do something are quite different from those whose involvement is only psychological or intellectual.

Citizen activists, particularly those active in campaigns, have been identified and described. We are now able to pursue the fundamental thesis that mass perceptions of party and candidate issue positions are "driven" by these activists, and that through their efforts ignorant individual citizens are aggregated into a knowledgeable total electorate.[3]

Examining Mediated Perceptions in Two Policy Areas

The model of "mediated perceptions" outlined earlier held that most voters use information provided by citizen activists as the basis for their perceptions of parties and candidates. If an activist attributes a policy position to a party or candidate, those exposed to the activist will likewise attribute that policy position to the party or candidate. A positive assessment of those activists encountered leads to the projection of a positive assessment onto the party, candidate, and policy the activists supported, a negative assessment leads to a negative projection. In this way the perceptions of the general electorate are mediated by that portion of the electorate we have identified as the citizen activist.

If the mass electorate projects party and candidate positions on the basis of information provided by citizen activists, then we should expect to find a correlation between activist positions and the perceptions of the general electorate. As activist positions change from election to election, we should expect mass perceptions to "track" or follow the activists. To test our model we will focus upon two issue areas—policies related to the encouragement of full employment, and policies related to the promotion of minority rights.

These issue areas were chosen for a number of reasons. First of all, they were issues in all eight elections. Second, the election studies asked questions about voter perceptions on these issues so that data are available for our analysis. Third, there turns out to be no substantial regional variation on these issues (even on matters of race). This lack of variation permits us to exclude any possible effects due to geography or regional subculture. Fourth, every issue shows significant variation over time, from election to election, so that we can see whether of not there is indeed "tracking." If there were no variation, we would have no basis for seeing if changes in voter perceptions follow changes in citizen activist positions.

Our first issue area has to do with creating full employment. The degree to which government should intervene in the private economy to secure full employment was one of the central issues of the New Deal. Since 1932 the two major parties can be easily differentiated by their respective stances on this issue. From Figure 4.1 we can see that during the period 1956–1984 the Democrats were perceived as the party more likely to pursue an active federal role. Figure 4.1 also shows that perceptions on this old and stable issue have fluctuated considerably over time. The high points of party differentiation in 1964, 1972, and 1980 correspond with the candidacies of strong ideologues—Barry Goldwater, George McGovern, and Ronald Reagan. In each of these three elections the issue of governmental intervention in the economy was unsettled by the taking of new positions, and the electorate's perception of these changes.

Figure 4.1 also shows graphically the strong relationship between the party activist positions and the perceptions of the general electorate. The relationship is clearly evident in every campaign except that of 1984. The electorate seems to know where the parties stand on the issue of full employment, and this is no trivial matter, but these results by themselves are not as convincing as they might be because Democrats and Republicans have maintained such consistent positions for so long. For half a century the Democrats have been more liberal, activist, and interventionist than the Republicans, and the electorate does not need to have very current information in order to correctly reflect the party positions.

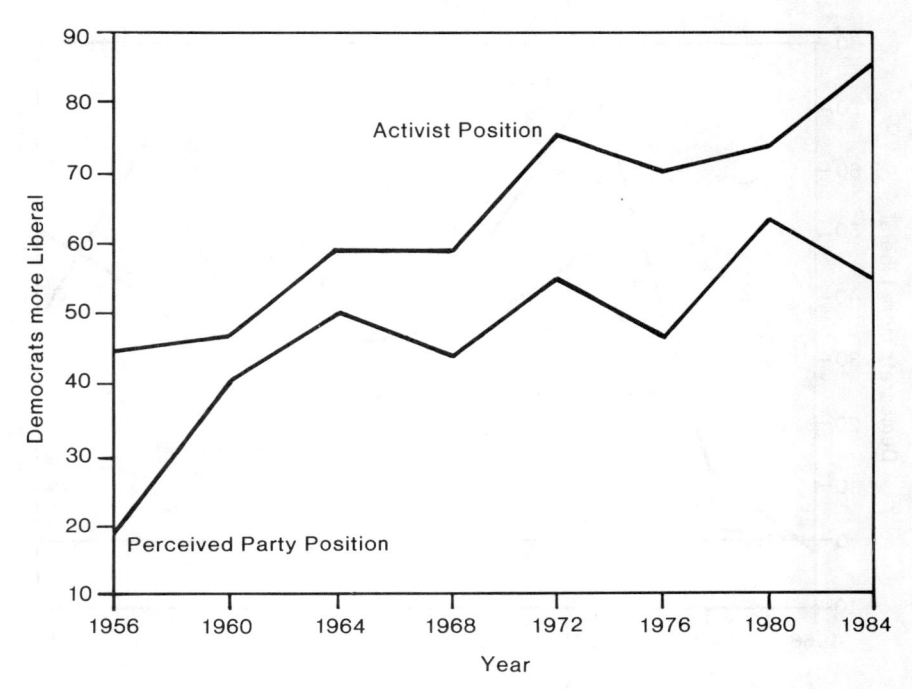

Figure 4.1. Jobs and Standard of Living: Party Images and Activist Positions.

A more demanding, and thus more convincing, kind of evidence would be data which show the electorate accurately perceiving change from election to election. Such knowledge would imply that the electorate is in fact responding to current political debate despite their apparent indifference, and thus significantly strengthen the utility of the mediated cognitions model. It would also imply that the outcome of elections represents more of a mandate to the winning side than is usually credited in the voting behavior literature.

The other policy area we have chosen to examine illustrates the sensitivity of the electorate's perceptions to changes in the activists' positions, which makes mass perceptions of party positions on matters of race more interesting than our first issue area. During the 1950's the Republican Party was on balance slightly more liberal on matters of race than the Democratic Party. Since 1964 there has been a dramatic shift to the left among Democrats so that the Democrats are now much more liberal on race than the Republicans. Although this does not mean Republicans have become less supportive of racial equality than they once were, they have not kept up with the Democratic change, and thus the parties have reversed position on the issue in terms which is more strongly supportive.

Because racial issues present more changes in party positions, and because these changes occur with some rapidity, they present a greater challenge to

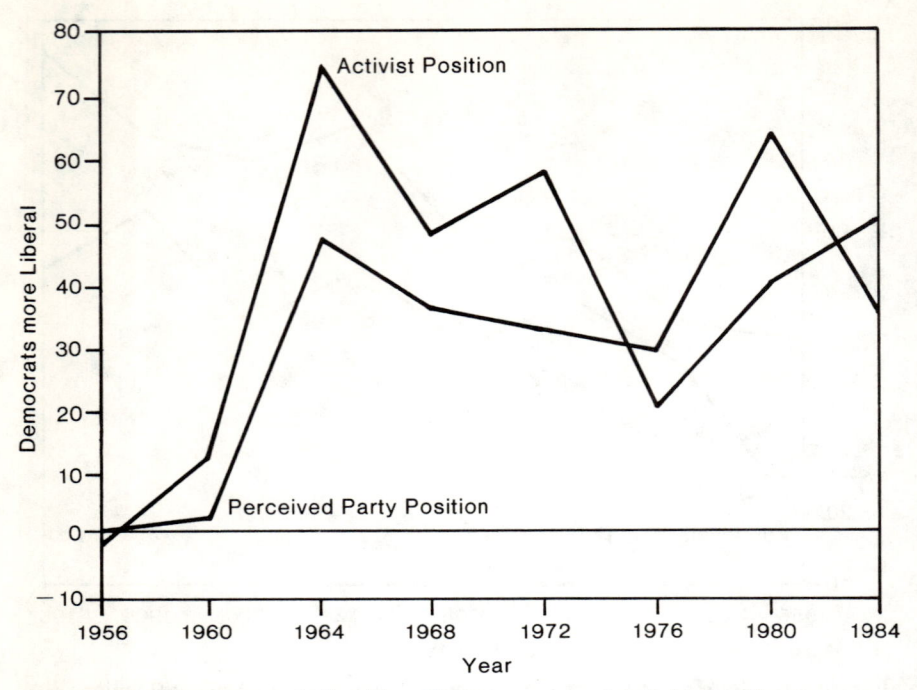

Figure 4.2. Treatment of Minorities: Party Images and Activist Positions.

the mediated cognitions model. Figure 4.2 shows that the model works very well on these issues as well, thus strengthening our confidence in its utility. The prediction of mass perceptions from citizen activist positions is even better than with the issue of full employment. Looking at changes from election to election, the evidence supports the thesis very nicely. When American political parties change their customary policy positions, American voters know it, and supposedly indifferent and ignorant voters appear to learn of these changes from citizen activists. Put another way, mass perceptions track activist positions.

There is always the danger that these results are spurious. That is, the electorate might be tracking the party positions directly through their own efforts rather than by learning from activists. In this case activist positions being close to party positions is irrelevant since the electorate would perceive parties as they do without ever noticing a citizen activist.

We can test for this by using the other kind of activist, the informational activist, as a kind of control group. Informational activists are those who report paying close attention to the campaigns through the media of radio, television, newspapers, and magazines, and therefore should possess a high level of information on their own. They constitute the very part of the electorate that does not rely upon campaign activists for their perceptions. If the mediated cognitions thesis has substance, the informational activists' positions should be as good at predicting the perceptions of the mass electorate as the positions of the citizen activists. As it turns out, the positions of the informational activists, whose positions remain essentially private, do not predict the perceptions of the mass electorate as well as the positions of the citizen activists who engage in public distribution of their views. The results are consistent for both issue areas, although the relationship is clearer on racial issues. In short, the connection between mass electoral perceptions and citizen activist positions is not spurious. The connection appears to be a causal one otherwise the mass electorate would do no better, and probably worse, than the informational activists in matching actual party positions.

The Implications of Mediated Cognitions

What matters most about the thesis of mediated cognitions is that it accounts for the paradox of inattentive voters versus well informed electorates. It means that the presence of many inattentive and ignorant voters does not prevent the American electorate from being well informed and making rational choices among parties and candidates. It suggests that the many studies demonstrating the ignorance of individual voters has less to tell us about how the political system works than it does about how not to go about testing the health of democratic processes. It suggests that electoral mandates are real, not fictions of the overactive imaginations of successful candidates for public office.

The thesis of mediated cognitions also redirects our attention to some basic aspects of democratic theory. Elections, with the opportunity they provide for producing aggregate results, are an effective and efficient way of maintaining popular control of government. Also, it emphasizes once again the importance of political participation for democratic government, although it suggests that not every voter needs to have a high level of participation. In the long run it may be highly rational for most voters to rely on cues from those who are activist as a means of both conserving their time and energy, and as a means of electing the kind of government that they most desire.

Notes

*The author would like to acknowledge the assistance of Carolyn Lewis in undertaking the massive data manipulations that are a necessary part of analysing data from the National Election Study series, and of Mark Hartray who also aided in the task. The chapter has benefited from the critical wisdom of Chris Achen, Lee Epstein, John Ferejohn, James Kuklinski, Carolyn Lewis, Bob Luskin, Paul Sniderman, and Aaron Wildavsky. None will have to bear the consequences, however, of any errors by the author. The data used in this chapter were made available by the Inter-University Consortium for Political and Social Research. The data were collected under a grant from the National Science Foundation.

1. This weighting by visibility technique is borrowed from the work of Converse, Clausen, and Miller.
2. Necessarily excluded by the design of the election studies are the sizable numbers of young people who became activists before attaining the right to vote. This exclusion is no doubt more serious in the years before 1972 when the national eligibility age was lowered to eighteen.
3. For full details on the design, method, and analysis used here see James A. Stimson, "The Process of Perception of Party Issue Position: A Longitudinal and Regional Perspective," a paper presented at the annual meeting of the Midwest Political Science Association in Chicago, 1985.

References

Paul Allen Beck and M. Kent Jennings, "Political Periods and Political Participation," *American Political Science Review,* 73 (1979), pp. 737–750.

Henry E. Brady and Paul M. Sniderman, "Attitude Attribution: A Group Basis for Political Reasoning," *American Political Science Review,* 79 (1985), pp. 1061–1078.

Edward G. Carmines and James A. Stimson, "The Structure and Sequence of Issue Evolution," *American Political Science Review,* forthcoming.

Henry W. Chappell and William R. Keech, "A New View of Political Accountability for Economic Performance," *American Political Science Review,* 79 (1985), pp. 10–27.

Philip E. Converse, Aage R. Clausen, and Warren E. Miller, "Electoral Myth and Reality: The 1964 Election," *American Political Science Review,* 59 (1965), pp. 321–34.

David Nexon, "Asymmetry in the Political System: Occasional Activists in the Republican and Democratic Parties," *American Political Science Review,* 65 (1971), pp. 716–730.

Sidney Verba and Norman H. Nie, *Participation in America* (New York: Harper and Row, 1972).

5 The Puzzle of Low Voter Turnout in the United States
ROBERT S. ERIKSON

The estimate of voter turnout is an election day ritual in the U.S. The morning of each election day, the news media send reporters to various polling places to observe the voter turnout. When the reporters see crowds at the polling places, they report back that turnout seems heavy this year. So as voters drive to the polls later in the day, the election story they hear on their car radios is that a heavy voter turnout is expected. Inevitably, however, this expectation turns out to be incorrect. When the votes are counted, voter turnout is revealed to be down or at best the same as in the last comparable election.

The truth is that a minority of Americans consistently exercise their right to vote. Moreover, the trend shows no improvement. Why do so many people choose not to vote? What could attract these voters to the polls? This chapter addresses these questions.

Essentially, all American citizens 18 years old and older are eligible to vote. (Exceptions include convicted felons and inhabitants of mental institutions) Of eligible American adults, only slightly more than half bother to vote in presidential elections. In midterm elections, held every four years between presidential elections, only slightly over one third of eligible voters vote. And these figures apply only to general elections. In primary elections, turnout rates are lower still.

Low voter turnout is especially puzzling because Americans like to think of their nation as a standard-bearer of democracy, yet voter turnout is lower in the United States than in virtually every other democratic nation. And, again, voter turnout has been declining in the U.S.

Figure 5.1 shows the turnout rates for presidential elections and midterm elections going back to 1868. For each election year, the graph shows the percentage of the eligible voters who actually voted. Of course, the requirements of eligibility change over the years. Before the Nineteenth Amendment passed in 1919, women could not vote. So for the early years of this graph, the eligible population includes only males; for 1920 and thereafter, the eligible population includes men and women. Before the 26th Amendment guaranteed the vote for eighteen year olds in 1971, only people twenty-one years of age or older were generally eligible. So until 1972, the eligible population includes people 21 years old and older; for 1972 and later, the eligible population included people 18 year olds and older.

Figure 5.1 shows four major trends in the voting rate. First, we see a surprisingly high turnout rate in the nineteenth century (1800s), followed by an

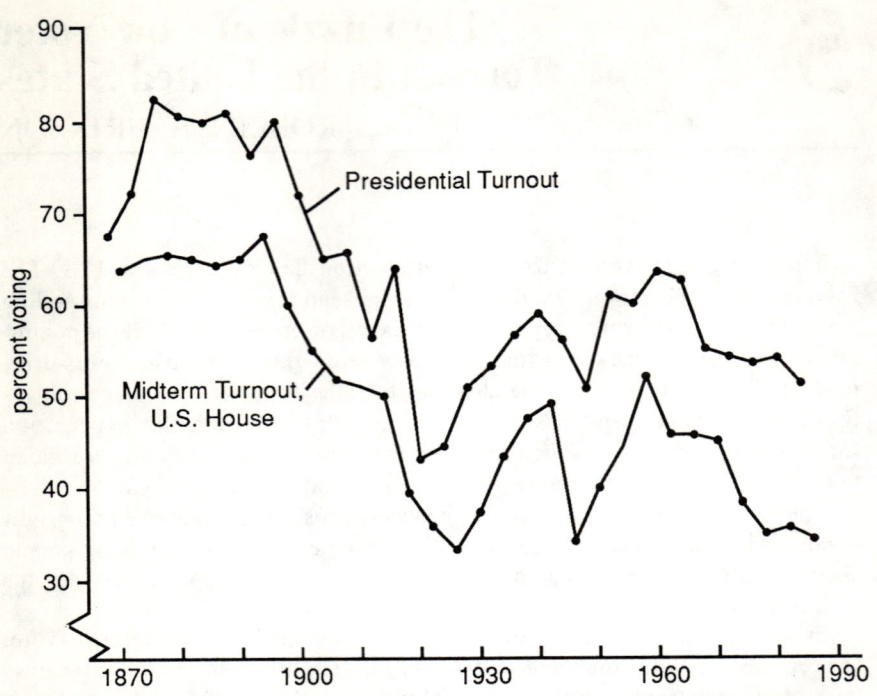

Source: Adapted from William H. Flannigan and Nancy H. Zingale, *Political Behavior of the American Electorate,* 6th Edition (Boston: Allyn and Bacon, 1986), p. 14; *Statistical Abstracts of U.S.*

Figure 5.1. Turnout of Eligible Voters in Presidential and Midterm Years, 1868–1986.

abrupt dropoff in voter turnout around the turn of the century. We will try to account for this drop in the voting rate shortly. Second, we see another abrupt dropoff around 1920, this time followed by a slow recovery. This trend is easy to explain as the result of women becoming eligible to vote in 1920. Newly eligible women voters began to exercise their franchise at a gradual rate, although women now vote as frequently as men. Third, we see a mild downturn in participation during the 1940s, due to the disruption of World War II, followed by another recovery. Fourth and finally, we find ourselves currently in the midst of another downturn in the voting rate that began about 1960. Naturally this recent trend is the most interesting. But as we will see, this recent trend is not easy to explain.

Voter Turnout in the Nineteenth Century

Figure 5.1 shows that voter turnout underwent a major change at about the turn of the century. In presidential elections of the late 1800's, voter turnout typically reached levels of 80 percent of those eligible. By the early 1900's voter turnout had dropped to about 60 percent in presidential elections. The turnout decline in midterm elections was equally strong.

Seemingly, something important must have happened to American politics in the 1890s or thereabouts to create this decline in voter participation. One important part of the decline was effective disenfranchisement of blacks in the American South. Following the Civil War, the presence of northern troops in southern states protected blacks' voting rights, and as a result blacks in the South voted in sufficient numbers to elect several black politicians to important state offices. But when the northern troops left the South in the late 1870s, white state governments began to reinstitute barriers to black voting in the South. By 1900, blacks effectively were barred from voting in much of the South. Not until the Voting Rights Act of 1965 was southern black voting participation restored to its rightful level.

Disenfranchisement of southern blacks contributed to the overall decline in voting participation around the turn of the century, primarily in the South, but even in northern states, the voting rate declined precipitously. To understand this decline, we need to look at the differences between electoral politics in the 1800s and electoral politics now.

One important difference is the role of political parties. Today, political parties are not very important in political campaigns. To be sure, most important elections are partisan, so politicians run with party labels. But whether aspiring for the presidency or some local office, today's politicians rely mainly on their personally based campaign staff rather than their political party organization as the means of getting themselves elected.

This reliance was not so great, however, in the 1800's. Then, the two major political parties were like competing democratic armies. Each party would do its best to get its supporters to the polls, and the fates of individual candidates were tied to the fate of their particular party. Voters too were different. Voters of the 1800s were far more partisan than voters today. Voters of the 1800s almost always went to the polls to vote for one party over the other for all offices. Today's voters are more likely to split their ticket, voting for some Democrats and some Republicans on election day.

How do these historical differences account for a decline in voter turnout? With partisan voters and organized parties, elections of the 1800s were often determined by which party was able to get more of its supporters to the polls. Moreover, the rules of politics facilitated this battle of voter turnout between the parties. It may surprise many to learn that in 1890, people generally did not need to register in order to vote. It may also surprise many to learn that in 1890, voting generally was an open act rather than the casting of a secret ballot. As we will see, voting without registration and without a secret ballot both contributed to high voter turnout. Both practices were generally eliminated, however, by reforms of the 1890s intended to clean up a corrupt electoral system. But the introductions of voter registration and the secret ballot in the 1890s also had the consequence of curbing voter participation.

Let us consider how the electoral practices of the day encouraged higher voter turnout in the 19th century. Back then, citizens generally did not need to register in order to vote. The procedure was more informal than today. Citizens simply showed up at the polling place on election day, pledged that they were local residents, and voted. Obviously, this procedure would encourage some citizens to vote who probably would not have even registered under the current rules. Also, as one might expect, the informality of no voter registration invited some amount of voter fraud. According to political lore, many party organizations would pay armies of supporters to go from polling place to polling place voting many times. The best estimate is that voter fraud inflated the reported turnout rate for the 19th century by a few percentage points. The potential for and the actuality of voter fraud were major reasons for the reform of voter registration.

One reason why parties made such an effort to get out the vote in the nineteenth century was the nature of the balloting process. Voting was an open and public act rather than a secret ballot like today. Also, it was generally the case that the government did not print the ballots. Rather, people would bring their own ballots to the polling place and drop them in the ballot box. Since the government did not print the ballots, entrepreneurs would do so, and these entrepreneurs often turned out to be the political parties themselves. Naturally, the parties would print the ballots already filled out, with either a straight-ticket Republican vote or a straight-ticket Democratic vote. a voter could split his ticket like today, but it was a troublesome task, requiring that the voter make or obtain a ballot that was not already filled in for him.

This inability to split tickets gave the parties an additional set of incentives for mobilizing voters. Not only did they not have to worry about getting their supporters registered to vote; they also could provide the ballots already filled in. Perhaps most important of all, because the ballot was not secret, parties could make sure that the people they corralled got to the polls and actually voted for their party rather than the opposition.

This situation changed with the electoral reforms that swept through the states around the turn of the century. No longer were people able to vote without registering, which reduced voter fraud but also hindered many eligible voters from voting. No longer were the ballots printed by the parties, already filled in. And voting (i.e. filling the ballot) was now done in secret. These reforms lessened the incentive for the parties to get their supporters to the polls, because no longer could the parties guarantee that peoples' ballots would be filled in for the "correct" political party.

Finally, one more important change occurred around the turn of the century in the political aftermath of the "critical" or "realigning" election of 1896. For at least two decades prior to 1896, American elections tended to be very close, at both the national, state or local level. The closeness of American elections was an added encouragement for political parties to get out the vote among their supporters. Also, this closeness signified a strong sense of partisanship within the American electorate and motivated voters themselves to vote, apart from any added encouragement from their particular political party.

The 1896 election, however, changed this atmosphere of partisan competitiveness in the U.S. In that year, the Democrats nominated Congressman William Jennings Bryan for president. The Republicans nominated Ohio's governor, William McKinley. While Bryan's supporters were highly committed to him, McKinley's campaign organizers cleverly presented Bryan to the American public as a dangerous radical. Indeed, Bryan and the Democratic platform called for what many voters saw as major changes.

The result of the 1896 election was a Republican victory for McKinley. But the most important fact about this election was the long-term realignment it created. From 1896 to the 1930s, the Republicans were the dominant party nationally and in most of the nation. The Democrats also became more locally dominant in their areas of strength, mainly in the South and West.

The 1896 presidential election resulted in elections no longer being close in most areas of the country. Not only were parties discouraged by voter registration and the secret ballot, but getting every last supporter to vote for the party would not do that much good anyway. Elections tended to be won by the dominant party, which needed only to slightly exceed the turnout for the weaker party in order to win. In national elections the Republicans dominated in numbers, and Republicans expended much less effort at mobilizing their supporters than they had in the past. The Democrats had little chance at winning, and demoralization reduced their turnout in national elections as well.

Thus, several factors caused a decline in turnout around the turn of this century. First, blacks became effectively disenfranchised in much of the South. But in addition, several factors combined to cause a decline in turnout nationally. These were the reforms of voter registration and the secret (government printed) ballot, plus the lessening of meaningful party competition brought about by the 1896 election. Perhaps regrettably, compared to elections of say, 100 years ago, contemporary elections are rather quiet affairs. While there are far more eligible and practicing voters today than 100 years ago, the turnout rate (the percentage of the eligible who actually vote) is far lower than it was back then.

It is debatable whether the higher turnout rate of the nineteenth century meant that the quality of American democracy was any higher than today. Some scholarly observers look back on the late 19th century as a period when people had greater passion about politics and greater interest in political affairs. But skeptics note the greater amount of obvious corruption in the late 19th century than today. They also raise doubts about whether the citizenry could have been as politically informed as today's electorate in a time before modern mass media such as radio and television, and when newspapers were primitive compared to their modern counterparts. Suppose, however, we could combine the greater voter turnout and involvement of the late 19th century

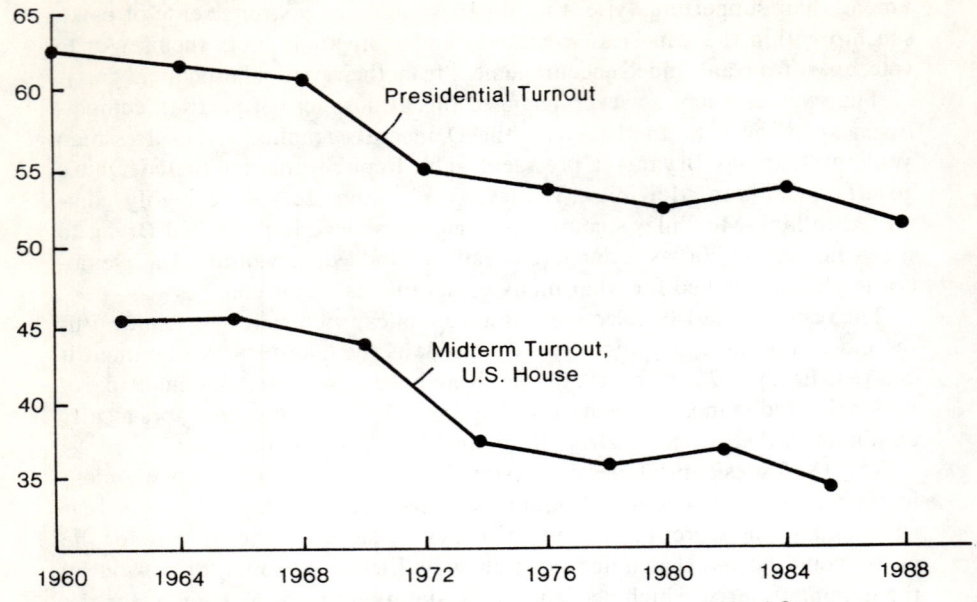

Source: M. Margaret Conway, *Political Participation in the United States*, (Washington, D.C., CQ Press, 1985), p. 6; *Statistical Abstracts of U.S.*

Figure 5.2. Turnout of Eligible Voters in Presidential and Midterm Years, 1960–1986.

with the greater amount of political information available today. That would be an interesting prospect, if difficult to attain.

The Recent Decline In Voter Turnout

The turn-of-the-century decline in voter turnout may seem like ancient history. But the rate of voter turnout has undergone a very recent decline as well, and one that is far less understood. Looking back on Figure 1, the reader can see a steady decline in the turnout rate since the recent peak in 1960 when about 63 percent of American adults voted for president. Since then, turnout rate in presidential elections has steadily deteriorated to about 55 percent. The turnout rate in midterm elections has suffered a similar decline. Figure 5.2 highlights these trends in greater detail.

Looking at Figure 5.2, one can see a slight but unalarming decline in the turnout rate between 1960 and 1964 and then again between 1964 and 1968. But then a major drop occurred between 1968 and 1972. At the time, this drop was attributed to the the 1972 presidential race (Nixon over McGovern) which was widely known in advance not to be close. But the 1976 presidential race (Carter over Ford) was so close that the outcome was genuinely in doubt on election day. Still, the turnout rate did not improve. The outcome of the

1980 presidential race (Reagan over Carter) was also in doubt on election day and the turnout rate did not improve. Although the 1984 presidential outcome (Reagan over Mondale) seemed clear in advance, it was likely that voter turnout would go up for the reelection of a president who was genuinely popular with many voters and intensely disliked by others. Still the turnout rate barely improved in 1984 over the low point in 1984. Then in 1988, turnout declined once again, to barely 50 percent of eligible—the lowest rate for a presidential year since 1924!

In midterm elections turnout is lower because there is no presidential race to dominate the ballot. Thus, for midterm elections, one cannot attribute changes in voter turnout to changes in the closeness of the race, the attractiveness of the choices, or the intensity of feeling about the merits of the candidates. At midterm, voters are motivated only by state and local contests. In any midterm year, many of these contests are close; others are not. Many have a particularly interesting set of candidates who provoke voter passions; others do not. From one midterm year to the next, the overall nature of these individual elections presumably does not change. Changes in midterm voting turnout must be due to something other than change in the nature of the candidate choices available.

Thus, the decline in the midterm voting rate is particularly puzzling and disturbing. American voters are getting turned off from politics to the extent that the midterm voting rate declined by almost a third (from 45 percent to 33 percent) between 1962 and 1986. There is no easy answer for this decline. The most puzzling aspect of the decline in voter participation is that there are at least five reasons why voting turnout should be going up instead of down. Let us look at some of these reasons.

There is only one reason why the turnout rate should be going down. This is the advent of the 18 year old vote nationwide (following the 25th Amendment) in time for the 1972 election. Young voters are notorious for their low voting rate. Therefore, it is not surprising that the newly enfranchised young 18–21 year old voters voted at a less than average rate. Their relatively low voting rate naturally caused an overall decline in the rate of voting participation. This is analogous to what happened when women were first given the franchise in 1920: a greater number of voters but a lower voting rate.

Balancing out the dilution of the voting rate by the 18 year old vote are five readily identifiable factors that should be causing the voting rate to be going up. These are:

- the Voting Rights Act of 1965 (and its extensions)
- state laws that make voter registration easier
- the relaxation of once stringent residency requirements for voting
- the gradual increase in the number of hours that polling places stay open on election day
- the American public's increasing education level.

Let us take a look at these five factors.

The Voting Rights Act

One of the most significant pieces of federal legislation of the 1960s was the 1965 Voting Rights Act. Prior to this legislation, blacks were systematically excluded from voting in many parts of the South. This exclusion was particularly prevalent in much of the rural South where blacks were numerically very strong. Where blacks were a numerical majority or close to it, the opposition by the white establishment to black voting was often strongest.

For decades, most southern members of Congress had fought any meaningful federal legislation to prevent discrimination against black voters. It was a former House and Senate member from Texas, President Lyndon Johnson, who provided the leadership for the 1965 Voting Rights Act. Once this legislation was enacted, blacks quickly began to register and to vote in the South at rates equivalent to the white electorate. With blacks voting in the South in great numbers, southern white politicians no longer could cater to white racism. The nature of southern politics would never be the same.

Because of the 1965 Voting Rights Act, southern blacks now vote at a far greater rate than they did twenty-five years ago. Perhaps because southern states now have a greater degree of party competition, the white voting rate in the South also has not declined since 1960 and may have even gone up slightly. With both black and white turnout going up in the South, the overall decline in the turnout rate is concentrated in the northern states. But as we will see, there are forces encouraging greater turnout in both the North and the South, making the general decline in turnout all the more puzzling.

Easier Registration

For most Americans, the decision to vote is a two step process. The first decision is whether or not to register. Once registered, the second decision is to vote or not to vote in a particular election. Both registering and voting are means toward an end: participating in the collective decision-making of the electoral process. But registering and voting involve some costs as well. In the case of voting, the costs are essentially the time and risk taken getting to and from the polls. Registering involves additional costs, which may be either relatively painless or relatively major, depending on the exact procedure. Obviously, the less costly the registration procedure, the more people are likely to vote. Since most states have made registration easier over the past twenty-five years, we should expect the voting rate to go up.

When states first began to require people to register in order to vote, generally around the turn of the century, they often made registration rather difficult. In the extreme, voters would have to register every year in order to maintain their names on the voter rolls. Registration would often be at one location in every county, typically the county Court House. And the times available to register would be the limited workday times typical of county and state offices. Moreover, the cutoff date for registration would typically be several months before an election. In times past, a voter might have to register every year, and at an inconvenient time and an inconvenient place, long before the voter began to think actively about voting in a particular election.

Currently, states make registration easier. Now, permanent rather than annual registration allows voters to register only once and then stay on the voting rolls permanently. With permanent registration, people are purged from the voting rolls only when they die, move, or perhaps fail to vote in any election over a period of two or more years. Particularly in the past twenty-five years, registration has been made easier in other respects as well. Now in many states people can register by post-card. A few states even have same-day registration. By this procedure, voters can show up at their polling places and both register and vote in one step. Same-day registration removes virtually all the costs of registering.

That registering to vote is easier than before has not been enough to cause the voting rate to go up. But this simplification does not mean that easier registration has not prevented turnout from being even lower than it otherwise would. Later in this chapter we will take another look at making registration easier and its role in determining the turnout rate.

Residency Requirements

At one time, states typically imposed rather harsh residency requirements as a qualification for voting. Residency requirements in some instances included living at the same residence for an entire year or sometimes longer. It took a 1971 Supreme Court decision to prod the states to lower the residency requirement (and the cutoff date for registration) to thirty days before the election. The result was enfranchisement of many voters who previously would have been unable to vote.

Millions of adult Americans move from one residence to another in the months before an election. Before the early 1970s many such Americans were not allowed to vote. These otherwise qualified electors would, however, be included in the base population of theoretically eligible adults for whom the turnout rate is computed. Making these people eligible to vote undoubtedly raised the voter turnout rate of the past decade above what it otherwise would have been.

On the other hand, it is not clear how great a difference this renewal of eligibility made. People new in a community find that high on their list of things to do are activities like getting the utilities turned on and a telephone installed. Perhaps they can be forgiven if they do not also register in time to vote in the next election.

Late Poll Hours

States vary in the hours that they keep the polls open on election day. However we can observe some general trends. Twenty-five years ago, the typical state would keep the polls open from about 7 A.M. to about 5 P.M. Now the typical state will keep the polls open longer, until 7 P.M. (for example, in Texas) or even later. This change obviously makes it easier for working people to vote. Undoubtedly, this change too has made the voting rate higher than it otherwise would be.

Education

A fifth reason why the voting rate should be going up is the American public's increasing education level. The one personal characteristic that most readily separates voters from non-voters is their education level. College graduates typically vote at a rate of 90 percent or above. At the other extreme, people without a high school degree are heavily represented among the chronic non-voters. It stands to reason, then, that as the United States becomes a more educated society (with the proportion of adults who have graduated from college doubling over thirty years) the voting rate should go up. But the voting rate has not gone up, even though increases in education make the turnout rate higher than it otherwise would be.

We have identified five factors that should make the turnout rate go up and only one (the eighteen year old vote) that should make the turnout rate go down. Thus, it is a genuine mystery why the voting rate has gone down. The best guess for the turnout rate decline may be that voters are becoming increasingly disillusioned with politics. Political scientists, however, have yet to convincingly demonstrate empirically that disillusionment is the cause.

We can speculate about the impact of potential reforms that would be intended to improve the turnout rate. To do so, it is helpful to look at American turnout in comparison with turnout rates in other democratic nations.

Voter Turnout in Other Democracies

In the 1930s, the relatively new democracy in the nation of Spain underwent a brutal Civil War. Eventually, the "loyalist" democratic forces lost to Generalissimo Franco's "Falangist" (some say Fascist) movement. For four decades, Spain was without democratic elections. Then, with Franco dead and democracy restored, Spain finally held a parliamentary election in 1977. In this first election in over 40 years, 77 percent of the eligible men and women of Spain went to the polls. Obviously inexperience was no deterrent to high levels of participation in voting.

The example of Spain is not unusual for democracies outside the United States. Figure 5.3 illustrates some examples of voting turnout rates in democracies of the world. The graph shows how turnout is generally higher in the more prosperous democracies, as measured by per capita GNP. The United States stands out as exceptional on this graph. Although the U.S. was the most prosperous of the nations examined, it had one of the lowest voting rates, along with Switzerland and Lebanon. Switzerland's low voting rate may result from national politics taking second stage to local (cantonal) politics. Lebanon's low

Figure 5.3. Voter Turnout of Different Notions by Level of Economic Development.

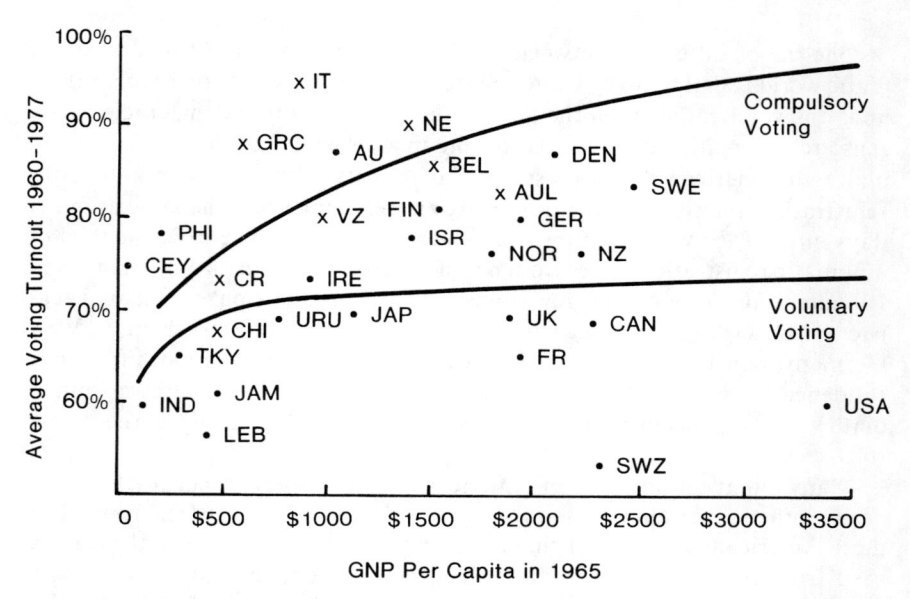

Source: G. Bingham Powell, Jr., "Voting Turnout in Thirty Democracies: Partisan, Legal and Socio-economic Influences," in Herbert Weisberg and Richard Neimi (eds)., *Controversies in Voting Behavior,* 2nd edition (Washington: C.Q. Press, 1984), p. 48.

voting rate (back when Lebanon was a functioning democracy) may have resulted because Lebanese party politics was constitutionally structured to *avoid* the nation's tragically sharp divisions, thereby minimizing the relevance of elections. Is the reason for the low U.S. turnout that American national politics is irrelevant? Although some may argue that irrelevance is the cause, we should also look to other factors, particularly how the United States does not take the steps other nations do to encourage voter participation.

Figure 5.3 gives one good hint how some other nations encourage participation. Some democracies are signified as having "compulsory" rather than "voluntary" voting. And these nations with compulsory voting enjoy some of the highest voting rates—well over 90 percent in the case of Italy. "Compulsory" voting usually means that the nation imposes a gentle penalty in the form of a small fine for those who do not vote. It should not be surprising to find that this small inducement to vote does push voter turnout upward beyond what it would otherwise have been. Americans may react negatively to the foreign idea of compulsory voting. But even those other democracies with "voluntary" voting offer encouragements to vote that we in the United States perhaps should consider.

One major difference between the United States and most of the democratic world is that only the United States puts the burden of voter registration upon the voter rather than the government. In most other democracies, citizens are automatically registered to vote in approximately the same way virtually all American adults possess social security numbers. With automatic registration, the costs of registration are entirely removed—the same as in the days in the U.S. when there was no voter registration. The exact method of automatic registration varies from nation to nation. In Canada and the United Kingdom, for instance, the government sends canvassers out to find and register citizens who are missing from the voting rolls and registers them. In West Germany, registration involves the local police. When people move from one residence to another, they are required to report their new addresses immediately to the police who helpfully add newly arrived residents to the voting rolls.

Many might consider it "Un-American" to require us to report to the police or any other government agency whenever we move to a new residence. But most Americans do not feel threatened when they obtain a Social Security card from the federal government. And young men generally comply with hardly a murmur when they are required by law to register for the draft at age eighteen. Still, adding one more governmental intrusion into our lives—even for the purpose of getting us to vote—would be seen by many as a threat to civil liberties.

The most politically plausible mechanism for automatic (or costless) registration in the United States would probably be the "same day" registration procedure begun in some states, but this solution is not without its drawbacks. A real problem is that new but unregistered voters tend to create additional headaches and bottlenecks at polling places. In one state (Ohio), same day registration proved so unpopular that voters voted to overturn it in a statewide referendum. Paradoxically, new voters who registered on election day and then voted *against* same day registration reportedly accounted for the narrow defeat of same day registration in Ohio.

Another difference between the United States and other democracies is our peculiar habit of generally holding elections on Tuesdays. Tuesday elections make voting inconvenient for working people. The simple alternative in most other democracies is to hold elections on Sundays, when most people do not have work obligations. One final encouragement to voting is to hold elections in a holiday atmosphere that encourages common activity. One reason for Italy's high voting rate for example, is that Italian election day is a holiday when people return to their home town to vote—much like Americans "going home" for Thanksgiving holiday.

Some Americans would object to Sunday voting because it would interfere with their religious activities. However, a compromise might be to hold elections on two days, say a Sunday and a Monday, allowing all to vote. There is no sign, however, of this simple change coming any time soon. And there is also the example of Texas, which holds some elections on Saturdays. There is no evidence that Saturday elections result in any higher turnout than elections held at their more normal Tuesday time.

Would Reforms Matter?

How much would voter turnout increase if voter turnout were made virtually costless or automatic? We do know that the big hurdle is often getting people to register rather than to get the registered to vote. Existing registrants do vote. For instance, 87 percent of all registrants voted in the 1980 presidential election. The problem seems to be that less than two thirds of American adults were registered at the time of the election. Would these nonregistrants also vote at a high rate if we automatically registered them? Or is their failure to register a sign that they would not vote if allowed to do so? Perhaps the answer is somewhere in between these extremes.

Fortunately we need not rely on guesswork alone. Because different states have different election laws, we can make state-to-state comparisons of their effects. One state—North Dakota—even today has no voter registration. The turnout rate in North Dakota is clearly above the national average, but not much above that of neighboring states. Thus, this laboratory state gives inconclusive evidence regarding the consequences of removal of the costs of registration. Other states with same day registration also have relatively high voting rates but not excessively so. The best statistical studies suggest that easing the registration cost does make a measurable difference of several percentage points. So, too, do the reforms of removing residency requirements and adding late polling hours. Since many of these reforms are already widespread, the recent decline in voter turnout becomes all the more baffling.

Any discussion of manipulating voter turnout must also take into account the *political* consequences of adding new voters to the rolls. How does that half of the electorate which does not vote differ from the half that does? Of course nonvoters are relatively uninformed politically, and some people argue that the system is better off without these people participating. The prevalence of this attitude is one impediment to reform. But because nonvoters are relatively poor and relatively uneducated, the relatively poor and uneducated are underrepresented in the political process. It stands to reason that expansion of voter participation would give more power to the poor.

From a partisan standpoint, added participation would help the Democratic party. Because the relatively poor and the relatively uneducated tend to vote Democratic, the Democrats presumably would be helped by greater voting participation. But the added difference would not be large. Another consideration, based on surveys of nonvoters, is that nonvoters seem to be attracted to winners, apart from partisan considerations. Thus, if nonvoters had been forced to vote in 1988, George Bush might have had a larger margin of victory!

In summary, making voter registration easier would probably make voters out of many current nonvoters. This approach would seem to be the fair thing to do, but it is not certain that the increase in voter participation would be dramatic or that it would alter many election outcomes.

References

Brody, Richard A. "The Puzzle of Political Participation in America." *The New American Political System,* Anthony King (ed.) Washington, D.C.: American Enterprise Institute for Policy Research, 1978.

Burnham, Walter Dean. *The Current Crisis in American Politics.* New York: Oxford University Press, 1982.

Conway, M. Margaret. *Political Participation in the United States.* Washington, D.C.: Congressional Quarterly Press, 1985.

Kleppner, Paul. *Who Voted? The Dynamics of Electoral Turnout, 1870–1980.* New York: Praeger, 1972.

Piven, Frances Fox, and Richard A. Cloward. *Why Americans Don't Vote.* New York: Pantheon, 1988.

Wolfinger, Raymond E. and Steven J. Rosenstone. *Who Votes?* New Haven: Yale University Press, 1980.

6

Institutional Change in Congress
BRUCE I. OPPENHEIMER

There is a strong tendency to think of the major institutions of government as stable to the point of being immune to change. Nowhere is this impression as strong as with the Congress of the United States. This view, although incorrect, is not without foundation.

The buildings which hold the House of Representatives and the Senate provide an overwhelming sense of stability. The Capitol Building, especially if one ignores the structural problems with its west face, and the office buildings that are part of the congressional complex convey in their granite and marble stonework an immovable and unchanging presence. The environment is rich in a historical tradition from the heroic figures of Statutory Hall in the Capitol to the traditional desks on the Senate floor to the Speaker's mace in the House, symbols that are noted for citizens on tours of the Capitol. Yet these symbols and the stone that encases them belie the enormous, and nearly continuous, change that has occurred over two centuries of Congress' operation.

The Capitol complex is not the only factor that misleads us about Congress. The Constitution also offers evidence for those who see Congress in a relatively constant state. After all, Article I, which deals with the legislative branch, has undergone only very modest change since 1787. The fourteenth amendment removed the language providing that slaves count as three-fifths of a free person when apportioning for state representation in the House of Representatives. The seventeenth amendment altered the selection process for the Senate, providing for the direct election of senators rather than election by state legislatures. And the twentieth amendment moved the day of the first meeting of Congress. Only the sixteenth amendment, which gave Congress the authority to place taxes on income, directly altered the enumerated powers of the House and the Senate. Thus, a reading of the Constitution offers additional evidence for those who see Congress in an unchanging light.

But beyond the buildings and the formal documents, if one looks at how Congess operates—its organization, its membership, its rules and procedures, the quantity and range of its workload, its interactions with other institutions of government, and the demands placed on it—one will see an institution which has undergone enormous change throughout most of its two centuries of existence. The purpose of this article is to examine institutional change in Congress, to understand what causes it, and, in turn, to build a framework for comprehending changes yet to come. To start we must first ask the question why do institutions change?

Why Do Institutions Change?

Political institutions do not exist in isolation. They operate in the context of a broader social and political environment. Unlike a hermit who may crawl into his cave when the outside world starts to impinge on him, a political institution does not have that luxury. It may be bombarded by a range of forces outside its control to which it must react. And any action, even non-action, is likely to require internal institutional activity and lead to new responses from the outside environment. Of course, many of these activities will not change the character and basic operation of the institution. Some of this activity, however, will produce internal change as well as alter the way the institution interacts with other institutions competing for policy influence. The surrounding social and political environment may place new demands on an institution to act, or may open new avenues for institutional influence, or lead some members with certain characteristics to leave the institution and be replaced by those with different characteristics, or may require that it develop new ways of responding to the challenges with which it is presented. Even institutions that do not adapt to altered environments will find their roles changed by their failure to adapt.

Such abstract comments about congressional change are not difficult to understand, especially if one reviews briefly the political and social environment in which Congress operated during an earlier era and ask how and why it differs from the one faced by Congress today.

Congress in a Swamp

In his brillant account of Washington, D.C. during the first three decades of the nineteenth century, James S. Young provides a clear example of the interaction of social environment with institutional operation. What one finds in Young's description is that Washington was a most unpleasant place to conduct the business of government or anything else. The city, which had no other reason for existing than to conduct of the national government's business, did not provide even the most rudimentary comforts for its time. Its climate was horrid— hot and humid in the summer and cold and damp in the winter. Built on and adjoining marsh and swamp land, it was a haven for mosquitos and disease. Washington's residents tended to be non-permanent and thus took little interest in its improvement. Unlike other cities of its time, it had few, if any, well planned streets. Transportation within the city was hazardous at best. Places were poorly marked or mapped, making finding one's way chancey during the day and dangerous at night, and social activity beyond dining with one's fellow officeholders was non-existent.

If these were not sufficient handicaps, Washington also isolated those who came to conduct the government's business. Although centally located in the new country, means of transportation and communication between the nation's capital and the home of a Member of Congress were cumbersome.

Horseback and carriage over roadway affected by the whims of the weather made for arduous trips and unpredictable mail. Members were cut off from their families and their businesses. The saving grace of this isolation was that it also freed them from constituents, lobbyists (non-existent for all practical purposes), and media coverage of their activities.

The final ingredients in this governing environment were the issues facing the national government. With some exceptions the major concerns of the period, unlike today, were issues of state and local attention. True, the national bank, tariffs, and internal improvements were important, but the national political scene was far from dominant.

One should hardly be surprised by the kind of Congress this environment fostered. It was one with extremely high membership turnover. Service in the House of Representatives and the Senate was viewed as an obligation by many, not as the start of a political career. It was undertaken with the knowledge that it would mean financial hardship at best and perhaps ruin, long periods of separation from family and friends, and personal as well as geographic isolation. And what was to be gained in return? For most members relatively little. The chance to influence decisions of great public concern? No. The opportunity to enrich oneself at the public expense? No. The promise of political fame? No.

Not surprisingly then, members frequently served only a single term, and many resigned before that term was completed. They desired to complete the business of Congress as quickly as possible and return home to the demands of untended farms and small businesses and to the comforts of family. A political career might be built at the state or local level without the costs of banishment to the nation's capital.

What kind of Congress did this environment produce? It was one very different from today's. First, as already mentioned, it was an organization with very high membership turnover. On average almost half the members of the House were serving in their first term, and concern with reelection was not a high priority. Such high turnover made the organization of the Congress very fluid. Seniority in terms of length of membership was not a particularly important criteria for influence. Henry Clay, for example, was elected Speaker during his first term in the House at age 34. And during a remarkable political career Clay resigned his House seat twice (in 1814 and 1820) but was reelected Speaker immediately upon returning. The situation contrasts markedly with current times. The 100th Congress (the one elected in 1986) contained only 50 first term House members. Of the 435 House members in the previous Congress, 393 sought reelection, and 98% of those were successful. And Jim Wright became the new Speaker at age 64. Wright, unlike Clay, had served continuously in the House for 32 years prior to his selection as Speaker.

Second, Congress was rarely in session for more than a few months a year, if that, during the early nineteenth century. Short sessions not only reflected the desire of members to depart Washington as soon as possible, but it also indicated a limited workload. Being a member of the House or the Senate was hardly a full-time occupation and certainly not a career. In contrast, now Congress operates nearly year round. The workload today so outstrips the capacity of the instituiton to deal with all of it that congresses end with much business unfinished. Even some important legislation, such as appropriation bills for major departments of government, remains unpassed (in such cases the departments operate under what are know as continuing resolutions).

For most House members and Senators their service in Congress is a full-time occupation. Congress recognized the growing responsibilities of membership when it adopted new ethics provisions in the 1970s. Among other things those provisions limited the amount of outside "earned" income (derived from another job occupation or career) a member could receive but placed no limit on "unearned" income (derived from investments, property, etc.). Those who argued in favor of limits on earned income did not claim that outside occupations should be limited because of potential conflicts of interest (after all, unearned income can create such conflicts) but because attention to outside occupations detracted from fulltime attention to their legislative jobs.

Third, the House and the Senate were rather simple organizationally in the early nineteenth century. Most legislative business was conducted on the chamber floors. Standing committees did exist for the referral of legislation, but they often had no ongoing agenda. Select committees, formed to work on single legislative items, were relied upon to develop the details of legislation. Referral of legislation to a committee was normally done only once the parent chamber had debated the legislation and decided on the general shape it would take.

There are several reasons why the House and Senate did not rely heavily on standing committees in the early nineteenth century. The membership was considerably smaller than today. Not until the mid 1820s did the House surpass 200 members, and there were fewer than 50 senators until 1835. The small size made meaningful debate possible. Further, the issues were not so complex as to require the bodies to have specialized expertise among the membership. This also fit with the spirit and philosophy of the Enlightenment to which many of the members adhered. They believed that through thoughtful and reasoned debate individuals could deal with even the most complex issues. The idea of referring legislation to a specialized committee was in some ways an affront to a belief in the rationality of man. Finally, the legislative workload was manageable (relatively few bills were introduced) so there was little need for the division of labor that a well developed committee system could offer.

Later in the nineteenth century a full-blown set of standing committees would become operational, and legislation would be referred to them prior to its consideration on the floor. When forced to choose between reliance on expertise from the executive branch or reliance on an internal committee system, there was a willingness to bend the application of enlightenment philosophy.

The membership continued to grow, and especially in the House general debate became increasingly unwieldy. And with the growth in the size of the country and the onset of the industrial revolution, the range of legislative issues facing the national government grew. To handle the workload, Congress needed the division of labor which a committee system afforded.

Today the workload of Congress is such that the Senate and the House need more than just the sixteen and twenty-two standing committees they have respectively. Division of labor and specialization have reached a point where the Senate standing committees now have over 100 subcommittees and the House standing committees have over 130 subcommittees. And these committees and subcommittees require extensive staffing to handle the work and provide the needed expertise to the Congress, independent of that offered by government agencies and interest groups.

These figures suggest just part of the picture of internal complexity. They do not include the development of congressional party organizations. Beyond caucuses used to select the party's presidential candidates, internal congressional party organizations were nearly non-operational in the early nineteenth century. Party floor leadership positions taken for granted today were only formally established in the early part of this century after existing informally at the end of the nineteenth century. The elaborate whip systems operated by both parties in the House got their starts in the post World War II period and have grown and flourished largely in the last decade. And the active role of congressional party policy committees and campaign committees is an even newer phenomenon.

The leadership, especially in the majority party, now has the sizeable task of managing the workload: keeping track of the activities in the various committees and subcommittees, ensuring a timely flow of legislation through the ever more cumbersome processes, and scheduling legislation so that it can be handled on crowded floor agendas in as efficient a fashion as possible. As recently as the first decade of this century the Speaker of the House alone or in conference with a handful of members who served on the Rules Committee, which the Speaker chaired, performed most of these tasks quite easily.

In sum, the Congress of the early nineteenth century was neither highly professionalized nor institutionalized. It was forced to do its business in an inhospitable work environment. It required its members to be cut off from their families and livelihoods. The job entailed significant personal sacrifice without the promise or even the likelihood of future reward. Many had to be drafted to serve and remained no longer than necessary. Leadership and organization were largely informal and simple. And the issues facing the national legislature were frequently neither challenging nor critical.

Since then the constitutional responsibilities of the Congress have not changed substantially. But the institution has. Washington is now a hub of activity and attention. Membership in the Congress is viewed as a major political prize, and extraordinary efforts are made to ensure reelection. The leadership and organization of the House of Representatives and the Senate are highly structured and complex. The workload is unending, and the issues are the key ones facing society.

This leads to the obvious question: what factor or factors caused these changes in Congress?

Causes of Change

Given the many changes that have occurred in Congress since the early nineteenth century, it is impossible to find a single explanation for them or to exhaust the full list of explanations. Nevertheless, it is useful to consider and discuss some of the prime factors which contributed to this transformation and to illustrate their impact with some actual and hypothetical examples.

Technological advances have had a major effect on how Congress operates and particularly on the lives of its members. The development of transportation systems means that members obviously no longer have to rely on horses and dirt roads in getting from their home districts to Washington. The availability of rail, automotive, and air transportation has led to marked improvement in the time and effort involved in these trips.

Of course, the changes did not all occur at once. The interstate highway system and wide ranging commercial air transportation have only become available in the post World War II era; commerical jet traffic came into being around 1960. It was not unusual as late as the 1940s for members, especially those from areas far distant from Washington, to drive to the capital at the start of a session and return home only once the session ended.

The improvement in transportation has also placed some new burdens on members. Because it is easier for members to travel between their homes and Washington, they are expected to do so more often. A 1973 study found that nearly 70% of House members made 24 or more trips home that year. The complement to this travel availability is that it is now easier for constitutents, lobbyists, and district media to descend on Washington. Transportation changes mean that the job of a national legislator is no longer performed in isolation. Personal contact with the home district is available and expected.

Similarly, other forms of communication have evolved. Letters to and from the district have not gone the way of horseback, although responses from the member may now be processed by a computer and not individually written with a quill pen. Reliable long distance telephone service is rapidly becoming an antique when a live television interview can be beamed via satillite from Capitol Hill to the local television station. Not only can the members keep their hands on the pulse of their districts, but interested constituents can monitor their members' activities in Washington. Thus, the problems for members of Congress are no longer social isolation and distance from life back home. Today's congressmen suffer from an almost total loss of privacy.

Technological improvement has greatly altered the desirability of living in the Washington community. Air conditioning has made it possible to tolerate residing and working in Washington even during the summer. A modern mass transit system provides easy mobility. Increasingly, it has become an attractive city in which to live. The transitory population has been replaced by a more permanent one. In turn, the social and cultural life reflects and reinforces these structural changes. Museums, theaters, shops, restaurants, and sports teams (with the noted absence of major league baseball) make Washington a far cry from the city from which nineteenth century politicos sought to escape. It is now the trend that defeated or retiring members of Congress remain in Washington rather than return to Peoria, Pensacola, or Pocatello.

The quantity and substance of the demands placed on the national government are other factors that has affected Congress. In comparison with the early nineteenth century the differences are vast. When there are no airplanes, government does not have to deal with issues of airline safety, noise pollution, hijacking, or construction of aircraft carriers. When there is little public education, Congress does not concern itself with federal involvement in school construction, student loans, or school integration. When corporations do not exist, Congress does not have to debate anti-trust laws, securities trading, or corporate taxation.

True, some national issues of the early nineteenth century no longer present problems for Congress. But if debates over slavery and its extension to the territories and protection against Indian attacks are no longer heard, they have been replaced by many more issues of civil rights and defense.

One need not make additional comparisons to the nineteenth century to grasp the change in the congressional workload. In the past twenty years alone the national government has been called upon to address legislatively an enormous range of new issues. Automobile emissions, energy conservation, abortion, strip mining, strategic defense initiatives, nuclear waste disposal, and affirmative action far from exhaust the list.

Related to the growth in the workload, and a third factor resulting in congressional change, is the growth in the complexity of the issues with which Congress must deal. No one would claim that the debates over slavery or the tariff or the national bank were without complexity. The issues and information available about them were, however, readily comprehensible to the average member. Certainly some factual information was helpful in the writing of legislation, but even that was likely to be fairly straightforward. By comparison, many of today's legislative issues are so complex, and the information surrounding them so difficult for non-experts to understand, that members of Congress cannot expect to deal with the issues by themselves.

Consider, for example, what one may need to know in dealing with just a single current day issue such as automobile emission standards. If the only question Congress had to address on this issue was whether it was in favor of clean air or not, the task of legislating would be easy. But once accepting that automobiles are a major source of air pollution, a range of complex questions need to be answered before placing limits on emissions. What pollutants do automobiles produce? What is the relationship between the existence of these pollutants and respiratory disease? What is the technological capacity to reduce emissions? What is the cost in terms of buyer cost of automobles for reducing emissions? Will increased automobile costs lead to a loss of jobs and if so, how many? Should emission contol devices be inspected? What will the effect of emission control be on gasoline consumption and on automobile performance? What are the health benefits for each increment in emission reduction?

To know what questions to ask, to answer those questions or to get answers to them, to understand what the answers mean, and then to be able to carefully craft legislative language to meet the desired policy goal require a sophisticated level of intelligence and some specialized expertise. But the automobile emissions issue is just one facet of the air pollution problem. Congress also has to deal with pollution from steel mills, electric generating facilities, and chemical plants. It may be necessary to adopt different standards for clean air areas of the country than for "dirty" air areas of the country. One begins to see the magnitude of the problem.

Although it may dwarf the issues of the early nineteenth century in its complexity, the air pollution issue is far from the most taxing one Congress faces. For example, an issue like the Strategic Defense Initiates (star wars) deals not just with the substantive complexities of laser technology, its feasibility, and its cost, but also with elaborate theories of international relations and arms control. To master either the technical side or the negotiating side of the Strategic Defense Initiative issues is no easy task. To become competent in both requires that a member of Congress have the necessary time to devote to the issue as well as the capacity to deal with the complexities.

Is it any wonder that Congress has found it necessary to have an ever more elaborate set of specialized committees and subcommittees? Should we be surprised by the growth in the size of the professional staffs that serve the members, the committees, and the support agencies? Isn't it to be expected that bills being considered by the Congress are far longer and more detailed than ever before? Whether these trends are desirable or not, Congress has little choice. If Congress does not have the internal capacity to meet the complexity of issues with which it must deal, it will have to abdicate responsibility for decision-making to other branches of the government.

In sum, it is easy to see how technology, a growing workload, and ever more complex issues have altered the way in which Congress operates. However, the impact has not been felt by Congress alone. The other institutions of government, which compete with Congress for policy influence, have had to react to this altered environment as well; their reactions in turn have affected the Congress. The President can claim, for example, that many issues are so complex and are so in need of an immediate, coordinated response that Congress should defer to executive leadership on these issues. Supporters of strong presidential government argue that Congress is too parochial, too amateurish, and too sluggish to be involved in setting more than the broad outlines of policy.

Some may claim that Congress and our other national political institutions have already experienced these changes and that we are now in a period of relative stability. Of course, it is ludicrous to think that the social and political environment has been in a constant state of turmoil since the early nineteenth century. Clearly it is subject to ebbs and flows. But it is equally naive to believe that the environment stagnates for very long. Many of the environmental changes, for example, are relatively recent ones.

If the late Speaker of the House Sam Rayburn were magically to return to Congress today, he would find it a very different institution from the one at the time of his death in 1961. Arguably today's Congress and the environment in which it operates might strike him as more changed from the perspective of 1961 than the Congress he first entered in 1913 appears when juxtaposed with 1961. After all, the Washington, D.C. of 1961 was little more than a slow-paced city about which newly-elected President John Kennedy would remark combined features of the North and the South— "southern efficiency and northern charm." There was no subway, no Kennedy Center, and no Air and Space Museum. More importantly, the offices of lobbyists did not line K Street. There were no Departments of Housing and Urban Development, Transportation, and Energy and no Environmental Protection Agency. True, congressional sessions were getting longer, but Congress was adjourning in September not December.

The point of this discussion is a simple one. Although its basic responsibilities may remain the same, Congress is continuously changing. Political and social environments are in a constant state of flux, and sooner or later political institutions must respond. The difficulty comes in using our knowledge about Congress' past responses to changes in its environment to predict the future directions it will take as an institution of American national government.

Can Congress Survive?

Through much of the 1970s and '80s we have witnessed a significant effort by Congress to reassert itself in the national policy arena. The development of subcommittee government was in part an effort to meet a growing and more complex workload. The specialization and division of labor that a committee system first offered was no longer sufficient to meet the policy demands. Subcommittees needed to be fully activated—given jurisdictions, staff, and budgets— if Congress were to stop or at least slow the drain of policy influence to the executive branch. A new budget process was instituted in the hope of giving Congress better control over federal spending. The strengthening of the Congressional Research Service, the General Accounting Office, and the Office of Technological Assessment, plus the establishment of the Congressional Budget Office, were undertaken to strengthen the expertise available to Congress. The War Powers Act had as one of its goals the institutionalization of a larger role for Congress in the design of U.S. foreign policy. And the growing placement of legislative veto provisions in authorizing legislation gave Congress a workable oversight technique to check on executive branch use of legislative authority.

Although these efforts did not fully meet the intended goals (especially in the case of the legislative veto which the Supreme Court ruled unconstitutional in 1983), they represented a strong effort to adapt to changes in the political and social environment. The alternative was to abdicate even more responsibility for the direction of policy to the executive branch.

Yet this resurgence may represent only a pause in the general trend toward greater executive authority. It seems that only when the executive branch clearly oversteps its authority or errs badly in the conduct of policy is there broad public support for congressional resurgence. Vietnam and Watergate offered just such an opportunity. More recently the Iran-Contra affair may serve to slow the renewed flow back to strengthening the executive. But it is entirely possible that the impact in terms of renewed congressional influence will be short-lived.

Part of the responsibility for the decline of Congress in the last half of the twentieth century rests with Congress and its members. Some correctly see the goals of individual members in conflict with those of the institution. In particular, the attention to reelection activities among House members and the presidential ambitions of some senators mean that the House and the Senate may not be organized and operated in an optimal manner for securing institutional policy influence. When members focus on reelection prospects and on future political careers, they may not be willing to make the difficult policy decisions or to devote themselves to the time-consuming chore of legislating.

The institution and its members are far from totally responsible for Congress' declining policy influence. In fact, changes in the social and political environment may be having effects that are outside Congress' ability to respond. In today's society efficiency and quickness of response to issues are highly valued. Nearly every issue is treated as if it were an emergency. Congress with 535 members and a complex organizational structure, despite its adaptations, does not appear to fit these values. The natural strengths that Congress has to offer in the policy-making arena—representativeness, legitimacy, and deliberativeness—are not as highly valued as they once were. These qualities may be important in a republican form of government, but in the late twentieth century they become grounds for denigrating Congress' policy role.

Under these circumstances the survival of Congress as a major policy-making institution is threatened. Although it can improve its organizational efficiency, that can only be achieved with some additional sacrifice of its deliberative qualities. Certainly its members can assert policy influence as critics of presidential and executive branch leadership. The overall outlook, however, is bleak. Unless the American social and political environment again values its basic institutional strengths, Congress will play a diminished role. Some of the underlying principles of government will exist in form but not in substance.

The words of the Constitution may remain unchanged, but we may find that we have traded the messiness of a representative democracy for the efficiency of an administrative state.

References

Bullock, Charles S., III. "House Careerists: Changing Patterns of Longevity and Attrition." *American Political Science Review* 66 (1972): 1295–1305.

Fenno, Richard F., Jr. *Home Style.* Boston: Little, Brown & Co., 1978.

Polsby, Nelson W. "Institutionalization in the U.S. House of Representatives." *American Political Science Review* 63 (1969): 787–807.

Young, James S. *The Washington Community, 1800–1828.* New York: Columbia University Press, 1966.

7 Presidential Influences on the Federal Courts

ROBERT A. CARP

Introduction

In this article we wish to examine the links between the policy values of the elected chief executive and the decisional propensities of federal judges. If in electing one presidential candidate over another the citizenry expresses its policy choices, is there evidence that such choices spill over into the kind of judges presidents appoint and the way those judges decide policy-relevant cases? For instance, if the people decide in an election that they want a president who will reduce the size and powers of the federal bureaucracy, does that president subsequently appoint judges who share that philosophy? And, equally important, when those judges hear cases that give them the opportunity either to expand or reduce the extent of a bureaucrat's power, do they opt for the reduction of authority?

We shall look at this overall query by exploring two separate sets of questions. First, what critical factors must exist for presidents to be able to obtain a judiciary that reflects their own political philosophy? Second, what empirical evidence is there to suggest that judges' decisions to some degree carry the imprint of the presidents who selected them? We shall respond to this second question by specifically examining the voting records of federal district judges appointed by thirteen recent Presidents.

Before we begin our analysis let us put the subject into some historical perspective and define some basic terms. A look at America's political history reveals that presidents have always believed that judges have their own distinct philosophies of public policy. Thus, presidents have weighed the political and philosophical orientations of would-be-appellate and trial judges before making their judicial appointments. Or, as Howard Ball puts it, ". . . presidents since George Washington have on occasion resorted to 'common politics' in the selection of federal judges. . . ."[1] This has usually meant that presidents appoint members of their own political party to fill federal judgeships, even though the chief executive may occasionally cross party lines to fill a judicial vacancy. Henry J. Abraham says that "an old political maxim governs here; namely, that 'there are just as many good Republican (or Democratic, as the case may be) lawyers—so why appoint someone from the enemy camp?"[2]

Richardson and Vines, reviewing data on appointments to the lower federal judiciary as far back as 1884, noted,

> All but three of the thirteen Presidents before Johnson have appointed lower federal judiciary from their own party 90 percent of the time. Two Republican Presidents who fell slightly short of that figure, Taft and Hoover, did so not because of neutrality, but because there were no Southern Republican candidates for the appointments. During the administration of both, there were few Republicans members of the bar in the South and probably fewer still who were sufficiently prominent to merit consideration for judicial appointment.[3]

When the president does cross party lines to fill a judicial vacancy, he usually looks to those who share his basic political values. President Roosevelt's 1941 appointment of the Republican—but liberal—Harlan Fiske Stone as chief justice of the Supreme Court is a case in point.

In short, the historical evidence suggests that presidents consider the credentials of the potential judges as they make judicial appointments: liberal chief executives tend to appoint liberals to the bench just as conservatives tend to seek out persons with right-of-center judicial values.

Before we proceed further, it is probably useful to offer some examples to define the sometimes slippery terms of "liberal" and "conservative." In the realm of civil rights and civil liberties, liberal judges would generally take a broadening position—that is, they would seek in their rulings to extend these freedoms, conservative jurists, by contrast, would prefer to limit such rights. For example, in a case in which a government agency wanted to prevent a controversial person from speaking in a public park or at a state university, a liberal judge would be more inclined than a conservative to uphold the right of the would-be speech giver. Or in a case involving school intergration, a liberal judge would be more likely to take the side of the minority petitioners. In the area of government regulation of the economy, liberal judges would probably uphold legislation that benefited working people or the economic underdog. Thus, if the secretary of labor sought an injunction against an employer for paying less than the minimum wage, a liberal judge would be more disposed toward the labor secretary's arguments, whereas a conservative judge would tend to side with business, especially big business. Another broad category of cases often studied by judicial scholars is that of criminal justice. Liberal judges are, in general, more sympathetic to the motions made by criminal defendants. For instance, in a case in which the accused claimed to have been coerced by the government into an illegal confession, liberal judges would be more likely than their conservative counterparts to agree that the government had acted improperly.

Presidential Capacity to Influence the Political Character of the Federal Courts

What factors determine the degree to which a President is successful in obtaining a federal judiciary that mirrors his own political philosophy? Four general factors have tended to be crucial in this regard.

Presidential Support for Ideologically Based Appointments

One key aspect of the success of chief executives in appointing a federal judiciary that mirrors their own political beliefs is the depth of their commitment to do so. Some presidents may be content merely to fill the federal bench with party loyalists and pay little heed to their nominees' specific ideologies. Some may consider ideological factors when appointing Supreme Court justices but may not regard it as important for trial and appellate judges. Other presidents may discount ideologically grounded appointments because they themselves tend to be nonideological; still others may place factors such as past political loyalty ahead of ideology in selecting judges.

Dwight D. Eisenhower was a chief executive in the first category—that is, an almost apolitical president for whom ideological purity counted little. While his judicial appointees were indeed primarily Republican, upper middle-class types, there is no evidence to indicate that they were picked because their political philosophies matched Eisenhower's. As a result, the Eisenhower judges turned out to be a mixed bag; progressives and strong civil libertarians mingled with jurists of more conservative, law-and-order values.

As a President, Harry Truman had strong political views, but when selecting judges he placed personal loyalty to himself ahead of the candidate's overall political orientation. Truman's interim appointment in 1949 of Carroll O. Switzer, an unsuccessful Democratic candidate for the Iowa governorship in 1948, to fill a vacant judgeship in Iowa's Southern District provides an excellent example. Truman wanted to reward Switzer for sticking with him in the 1948 presidential campaign when so many others had deserted the President, and he couldn't have cared less whether Switzer was a liberal or a conservative. Said Truman, "That guy Switzer backed me when everyone else was running away, and, by God, I'm going to see that he gets a judgeship!" Truman's premium on personal loyalty rather than ideology is generally reflected in the group of men he put on the bench. For example, there was scant linkage between Truman's personal liberal stance on civil rights and equal opportunity and his judicial selections: he appointed no blacks and no women at all, and at least three of his key southern district court appointees have been identified as being very unfriendly toward the cause of civil rights.

If Eisenhower and Truman exemplify presidents who eschewed ideological criteria, Ronald Reagan provides a good example of a chief executive who selected his judicial nominees with a clear eye toward their compatibility with his own conservative philosophy. During the first six years of his administration, Reagan appointed 287 judges to the district and appeals courts. Of these, 95 percent were Republicans, 94 percent were white, and 92 percent were males; the majority were well-off (45 percent had net worths of over $500,000 and more than one in five were millionaires); virtually all had established records as political conservatives and as apostles of judicial self-restraint. Indeed as the Reagan administration's conservative programs began to bog down in the more liberal-minded Congress, the Reagan team looked more and more toward implementing their values through their judicial appointment strategy. As White House communications director Patrick J. Buchanan once put it, "(our conservative appointment strategy) . . . could do more to advance the social agenda—school prayer, anti-pornography, anti-busing, right-to-life and quotas in employment—than anything Congress can accomplish in 20 years."[4] In fairness to President Reagan it should be pointed out, however, that he was not the only modern president to pack the bench with those who shared his political and legal philosophies: both Presidents Johnson and Carter successfully appointed activist liberal judges.

The Number of Vacancies to Be Filled

A second element affecting the capacity of chief executives to establish a policy link between themselves and the judiciary is the number of appointments available to them. Obviously the more judges a president can select, the greater the potential of the White House to put its stamp on the judicial branch. For example, George Washington's influence on the Supreme Court was significant because he was able to nominate ten individuals to the High Court bench. Jimmy Carter's was nil, on the other hand, because no vacancies occurred during his term as president.

The number of appointment opportunities depends, of course, on several factors: how many judges and justices die or resign during the president's term, how long the president serves, and whether or not Congress passes legislation that significantly increases the number of judgeships. Historically the last factor seems to have been the most important in influencing the number of judgeships available, and, as one might expect, politics in its most basic form permeates this whole process. A study of proposals for new-judges bills in thirteen Congresses tested these two hypotheses: (1) "proposals to add new federal judges are more likely to pass if the party controls the Presidency and Congress than if different parties are in power" and (2) "proposals to add new federal judges are more likely to pass during the first two years of the President's term than during the second two years." The author concluded that his "data support both hypotheses—proposals to add new judges are about 5 times more likely to pass if the same party controls the Presidency and Congress than if different parties control, and about 4 times more likely to pass during the first two years of the President's term than during the second two years." He then noted that these findings serve "to remind us that not only is judicial selection a political process, but so is the creation of judicial posts."[5] Here, for instance, is a dramatic account of the impact of a new-judges bill passed during John Kennedy's presidency:

> Promptly upon Kennedy's election, Congress zipped through an omnibus judgeship bill giving the new president—and, of course, the politicians who helped elect him or whose friendship he now needed—an unprecedented store of judicial boodle to distribute. The act created 71 new judgeships. That wasn't all. Because of vacancies the Democratic Senate had not permitted Ike to fill, Kennedy during his first twenty months in office appointed 147 persons to the federal bench. By way of perspective, Harding, Coolidge and Hoover didn't have that many judgeships in their combined terms. In one slam-bang stretch of 47 days, from August 11 through September 27, 1961, 69 judges were nominated or appointed, an average of almost eleven per week. By midsummer 1962 almost 40 percent of federal judges were Kennedy appointees.[6]

Thus the number of vacancies that a president can fill—a function of politics, fate, and the size of the judicial workloads—is another variable that helps determine the impact a chief executive has on the composition of the federal judiciary.

The President's Political Clout

Another factor is the scope and proficiency of presidential skill in overcoming any political obstacles. One such stumbling block is the U.S. Senate. If the Senate is controlled by the president's political party, the White House will find it much easier to secure confirmation than if opposition forces control the Senate. Sometimes, when the opposition is in power in the Senate, presidents are forced into a sort of political horse trading to get their nominees approved. For example, when the Democrats controlled the Senate during the Nixon and Ford administrations, those two presidents had to make a political deal for the district judgeships in California; the state's two Democratic senators were permitted to appoint one of their own for every three Republicans that were put on the bench.

The Senate Judiciary Committee is another roadblock between the will and political savvy of the president and the men and women who sit on the federal bench. Some presidents have been more adept than others in easing their candidates through the jagged rocks of the Judiciary Committee rapids. Both Presidents Kennedy and Johnson, for example, had to deal with the formidable committee chairman James Eastland of Mississippi, but only Johnson seems to have had the political adroitness to get most of his liberal nominees approved. Kennedy lacked this skill, and he was often obliged to appoint some very conservative—often racist—judges to the bench in the South.

The president's personal popularity is another element in the political power formula. Chief executives who are well liked by the public and command the respect of opnion makers in the news media, the rank-and-file of their political party, and the leaders of the nation's major interest groups, are much more likely to prevail over any forces that seek to thwart their judicial nominees.

Personal popularity is not a stable factor and is sometimes hard to gauge, but there is little doubt that presidents' standing with the electorate helps determine the success of their efforts to influence the composition of the American judiciary. For example, in 1930, President Hoover's choice for a seat on the Supreme Court, John J. Parker, was defeated in the Senate by a two-vote margin. It is likely that had the nomination been made a year or so earlier, before the onset of the depression took Hoover's popularity by the throat, Parker might have gotten on the Supreme Court. Likewise, in 1968 President Johnson's low esteem among voters and the powers-that-be may have been partially responsible for Senate rejection of Johnson's candidate for chief justice, Abe Fortas, and also for the Senate's refusal to replace Fortas with Johnson's old pal Homer Thornberry. As one observer commented, "Johnson failed largely because most members of the Senate "had had it" with the lame-duck President's nominations." Conversely, President Eisenhower's success in getting approval for an inordinately large number of nominees dubbed "not qualified" by the ABA (some 13.2) percent) may be attributed, in part at least, to Ike's great popularity and prestige.

The Judicial Climate into Which the New Judges Enter. A final matter affects the capacity of chief executives to secure a federal judiciary that reflects their own political values: the current philosophical orientations of the sitting district and appellate court judges with whom the new appointees must interact. Since federal judges serve lifetime appointments during good behavior, presidents must accept the composition and value structure of the judiciary as it exists when they first come into office. If the existing judiciary already reflects the president's political and legal orientation, the impact of new judicial appointees will be immediate and substantial. On the other hand, if new chief executives face a trial and appellate judiciary whose values are radically different from their own, the impact of their subsequent judicial appointments will be weaker and slower to materialize. New judges must respect the controlling legal precedents and the existing constitutional interpretations that prevail in the judiciary at the time they enter it, lest they risk being overturned by a higher court. Such a reality may limit the capacity of a new set of judges to get in there and do their own thing—at least in the short run. Several examples bring this principle down to earth.

When Franklin Roosevelt became president in 1933, he was confronted with a Supreme Court and a lower federal judiciary that had been solidly packed with conservative Republican jurists by his three GOP predecessors in the White House. A majority of the High Court and most lower-court judges viewed most of Roosevelt's New Deal legislation as uncostitutional, and indeed it was not until 1937 that the Supreme Court began to stop overturning virtually all of FDR's major legislative programs.

To make matters worse, his first opportunity to fill a Supreme Court vacancy did not come until the fall of 1937. Thus, despite the ideological screening that went into the selection of FDR's judges, it seems fair to assume that, at least between 1933 and 1938, Roosevelt's trial and appellate judges had to restrain their liberal propensities in the myriad of cases that came before them. This may explain in part why the voting records of the Roosevelt court appointees is not much more liberal than that of the conservative judges selected by his three Republican predecessors; the Roosevelt team just didn't have much room to move in a judiciary dominated by staunch conservatives.

The decisional patterns of the Eisenhower judges further serve to illustrate this phenomenon. While we will momentarily point out that the Eisenhower appointees were more conservative than those selected by Presidents Truman and Roosevelt, the differences in the rulings they made are pretty small. One major reason was that the Eisenhower jurists entered a realm that from top to bottom was dominated by Roosevelt and Truman appointees, who were for the most part liberals. Ike's generally conservative judges didn't have much more room to maneuver than did Roosevelt's liberal jurists in the face of a conservative-dominated judiciary.

Bringing this line of reasoning up to date, President Reagan's impact on the judicial branch continues to be substantial. By the spring of his last year in office he had appointed an unprecedented 334 federal judges, 45 percent of those on the bench. When he entered the White House, the Supreme Court was already teetering to the right because of Nixon's and Ford's conservative appointments. (Carter had no opportunity to appoint anyone to High Court.) Despite Carter's liberal appointees on the trial and appellate court benches, Reagan still found a good many conservative Nixon and Ford judges on the bench when he took office. Thus he has had and should continue to have a major role in shaping the entire federal judiciary in his own conservative image even though his tenure of president has ended. The Bush judges should likewise have a much easier time making their impact felt since they are entering a judicial realm wherein well over half the judges already partake of conservative, Republican values.

Presidents' Values and Their Appointees' Decisions

We now know the conditions that must be met if presidents are to secure a judiciary in tune with their own policy values and goals. What evidence is there that presidents have in fact been able to do so? Or, to return to our original question, when the people elect a particular president, is there reason to believe that their choice will be expressed in the kinds of judges that are appointed and the kinds of decisions that those judges render? To answer these questions we shall look at an investigation of the liberal-conservative voting patterns of the teams of U.S. district court judges appointed during this century.

Table 1 indicates the percent of liberal decisions rendered by the trial court appointees of Presidents Woodrow Wilson through Ronald Reagan. Fifty-one percent of the decisions of the Wison judges are liberal, which puts these jurists almost on a par with those of Lyndon Johnson and Jimmy Carter for

Table 1 The Percent of Liberal Decisions Rendered by the District Court Appointees of Presidents Wilson through Reagan, 1933–1986

Appointing president	Percent	Number
Woodrow Wilson	51	94
Warren Harding	41	538
Calvin Coolidge	43	630
Herbert Hoover	42	910
Franklin D. Roosevelt	47	2838
Harry S. Truman	40	3273
Dwight D. Eisenhower	37	4401
John F. Kennedy	41	5065
Lyndon B. Johnson	52	7577
Richard Nixon	38	6872
Gerald R. Ford	45	1311
Jimmy Carter	54	3498
Ronald Reagan	36	702

Source: Unpublished data collected by Profs. Robert A. Carp, Ronald Stidham, and C. K. Rowland

having the most liberal voting record. The liberal patterns of the Wilson judges is not surprising: Wilson was one of the staunchest liberal presidents of this century—particularly on economic issues. Moreover, he chose his judges on a highly partisan, ideological basis: 98.6 percent of his appointments to the lower courts were Democrats—still the record for any president in recent memory.

Succeeding Wilson in the White House were the three Republican chief executives of the 1920s, beginning with Harding's "return to normalcy" in 1921 and followed by the equally conservative Coolidge and Hoover. The right-of-center policy values of these three presidents (and the undisputed Republican domination of the Senate during their incumbencies) are mirrored in the decisional patterns of the trial judges they selected. The liberalism score drops by 10 points from Wilson to Harding, 51 to 41 percent, and stays around that same level for the Coolidge and Hoover judicial teams.

With Franklin D. Roosevelt's judges it's back to left-of-center. At 47 percent liberal, the Roosevelt jurists are five points more liberal than those of his immediate predecessor, Herbert Hoover. We have good evidence that FDR used ideological criteria to pick his judges and that he put the full weight of his political skills behind that endeavor. He once instructed his despenser of political patronage, James Farley, in effect to use the judicial appointment power as a weapon against senators and representatives who were balking at New Deal Legislation: "First off, we must hold up judicial appointments in States where the (congressional) delegation is not going along (with our liberal economic proposals). We must make appointments promptly where the delegation is with us. Second, this must apply to other appointments. I'll keep in close contact with the leaders."[8]

At first blush the comparatively conservative voting record of the Truman judges seems a bit strange in view of Truman's personal commitment to liberal economic and social policy goals. Only 40 percent of the Truman judges' decisions were liberal, a full seven points less than Roosevelt's jurists—and even two points below the Hoover nominees. As we noted earlier, however, Truman counted personal loyalty much more heavily than ideological standards when selecting his judges, and as a result many conservatives found their way into the ranks of the Truman judges. Indeed, even Truman's Supreme Court nominees were of a rather nondescript, conservative ilk:

> Harry Truman's first [Supreme] court appointment was a Republican senator from Ohio, Harold Burton—the only Republican ever selected by a Democratic President. His three other nominees were high-ranking Democratic politicians—Chief Justice Fred Vinson had been his Secretary of the Treasury, Tom Clark had served as Attorney General, and Sherman Minton was an Indiana senator. Truman's men generally held to the modest "judicial restraint" defended so brilliantly by Frankfurter, the court's intellectual eminence. Three of Truman's appointees—Vinson, Burton, and Minton—were among eight justices rated as "failures" in the 1971 poll of professors.[9]

Because of Truman's lack of interest in making policy-based appointments, coupled with the president's strong opposition in the Senate and general lack of popular support throughout much of his administration, his personal liberalism was generally not reflected in the policy values of his judges. Eisenhower's judges were more conservative than Truman's, as expected, but the difference is not very great. But we have already noted that Eisenhower paid little attention to purely ideological appointment criteria; in addition, his judges had to work in the company of an overwhelming Democratic majority in the whole federal judiciary. These factors must have mollified many of the conservative inclinations of the Eisenhower jurists.

The 41 percent liberalism score of the Kennedy judges represents a swing to the left. This is to be expected, and at first blush it may appear strange that John Kennedy's team on the bench was not even more left of center. However, we must keep in mind Kennedy's problems in dealing with the conservative, southern-dominated Senate Judiciary Committee; his lack of political clout in the Senate, which often made him a pawn of senatorial courtesy; and his inability to overcome the stranglehold of local Democratic bosses, who often prized partisan loyalty over ideoogical purity—or even competence—when it came to appointing judges.

Lyndon Johnson's judges moved impressively toward the left, and, as we noted his judges were as liberal as Wilson's and much more so than Kennedy's. We can account for this on the basis of the four criteria discussed earlier in this chapter that predict a correspondence between the values of chief executives and the orientation of their judges. Johnson knew well how to bargain with individual senators and was second to none in his ability to manipulate and cajole those who were initially indifferent or hostile to issues (or candidates) he supported; his impressive victories in Congress—for example, the antipoverty legislation and the civil rights acts—are monuments to his skill. Undoubtedly, too, he used his political prowess to secure a judicial team that reflected his liberal policy values. In addition, Johnson was able to fill a large number of vacancies on the bench, and his liberal appointees must have felt right at home ideologically in a judiciary capped by the liberal Warren Court.

If the leftward swing of the Johnson team is dramatic, it is no less so than the shift to the right made by the Nixon judges. Only 38 perent of the decisions of Nixon's jurists were liberal. Nixon, of course, placed enormous emphasis on getting conservatives nominated to judgeships at all levels; he possessed the political clout to secure Senate confirmation for most lower-court appointees—at least until Watergate, when the Nixon wine turned to vinegar; and the rightist policy values of the Nixon judges must have been prodded by a Supreme Court that was growing more and more conservative.

The 45 percent liberalism score of the Ford judges puts them right between the Johnson and Nixon jurists in terms of ideology. That Ford's jurists were less conservative than Nixon's is not hard to explain. First, Ford himself was much less of a political ideologue than his predecessor, as reflected in the way in which he screened his nominees and in the type of individuals he chose (Ford's appointment of the moderate John Paul Stevens to the Supreme Court versus Nixon's selection of the highly conservative William H. Rehnquist illustrate the point). Also, because Ford's circuitous route to the presidency did not enhance his political effectiveness with the Senate, he would not have had the clout to force highly conservative Republican nominees through a liberal, Democratic Senate, even if he had wished to.

With a score of 54 percent, Jimmy Carter holds the record as having appointed judges with the most liberal voting record of all thirteen presidents for whom we have data. Despite Carter's call for an "independent" federal judiciary based on "merit selection," it is clear that his judges were selected with a keen eye toward their potential liberal voting tendencies.[10] That there is a correspondence between the values of President Carter and the liberal decisional patterns of his judges should come as no surprise given our aforementioned criteria. First, Carter was clearly identified with liberal social and political values, and while his economic policies were perhaps more conservative than for recent Democratic presidents, there is little doubt about Carter's commitment to liberal values in the areas of civil rights and liberties and of criminal justice. Carter, too, had ample opportunity to pack the bench: the Omnibus Judgeship Act of 1978 passed by a friendly Democratic Congress created a record 152 new federal judicial openings for Carter to fill. Carter also possessed a fair degree of political clout with a Senate and Judiciary Committee controlled by Democrats. Finally, the Carter judicial team found many friendly liberals (appointed by Presidents Johnson and Kennedy) already sitting on the bench when they first entered the judicial arena.

Reagan's judicial team has the distinction of having the most conservative voting record of all the judicial cohorts in our study. Only 36 percent of their decisions have been tainted with the liberal stain. Again our four criteria shed some understanding of this phenomenon. To begin with, President Reagan's conservative values and his commitment to reshaping the federal judiciary in his own image was a secret to no one. Early in his first presidential campaign Reagan had inveighed against left-leaning activist judges, and he promised a dramatic change. As with his predecessor, Reagan had the opportunity, through attrition and newly-created judgeships, to fill the judiciary with persons of conservative inclinations. (At the end of his second term about half the federal judiciary bore the Reagan label). This phenomenon was aided by Reagan's great personal popularity throughout most of his administration and a Senate that his party controlled during six of his eight years in office. Finally, the Reagan cohort entered the judicial realm with conservative greetings from right-of-center Nixon and Ford judges who already were seated on the federal bench.

Conclusion

Back to our original question: Is there a policy link between the values of the President, the judges he appoints, and the subsequent ideological direction of the judges' decisions? Such a link does indeed appear to exist. Liberal or conservative presidents can expect to see many of their values manifested in the voting patterns of the jurists they select. This is true provided that the Chief Executive is inclined to make ideologically-based appointments, that he has a sufficient number of judicial vacancies to fill, that he possesses ample political clout, and that his appointees enter a judicial system in which they find jurists with like-minded attitudes and values.

Notes

1. Howard Ball, *Courts and Politics* (Englewood Cliffs, N.J.: Prentice-Hall, 1980), p. 168.
2. Henry J. Abraham, *The Judiciary: The Supreme Court in the Governmental Process,* 5th ed. (Boston: Allyn and Bacon, 1980), p. 171.
3. Richard J. Richardson and Kenneth N. Vines, *The Politics of Federal Courts* (Boston: Little, Brown, 1970), pp. 68–70.
4. Jack Nelson, "Courts Main Hope for Reagan Social Stand," *Houston Chronicle,* March 18, 1986, 1:6.
5. Jon R. Bond, "The Politics of Court Structure: The Addition of New Federal Judges," *Law & Policy Quarterly* 2 (1980): 182, 183 and 187.
6. Joseph C. Goulden, *The Benchwarmers: The Private World of the Powerful Federal Judges* (New York: Weybright and Tally, 1974), p. 59.

7. Henry J. Abraham, *The Judicial Process, 3rd ed.* (New York: Oxford University Press, 1975), p. 77.
8. James A. Farley, "Why I Broke with Roosevelt," *Collier's,* June 21, 1947, p. 13.
9. Donald Dale Jackson, *Judges* (New York: Antheneum, 1974), p. 340.
10. Jon Gottschall, "Carter's Judicial Appointments: The Influence of Affirmative Action and Merit Selection on Voting on the U.S. Courts of Appeals, *Judicature* 67 (1983): pp. 165–173.

8

Conservative and Liberal Evaluations of the Reagan Presidency

JOHN W. SLOAN

Introduction

Early evaluation of a president is a hazardous activity; the constantly emerging reevaluations of past presidents should make us cautious about making a definitive judgment regarding a recently retired president and more open to opposing points of view. Because of the Korean War and several domestic scandals, Harry Truman (1945–53) was a very unpopular President in 1952 (as measured by the Gallup Poll), but a few decades later historians judged him to be fairly successful and the American people made him a folk hero. While Dwight Eisenhower (1953–61) was viewed by Richard Neustadt as a political amateur in 1960, by the 1980s the former General was being reinterpreted by Fred Greenstein as a surreptitious Machiavellian.[1] Evaluations change because more evidence comes to light and time allows us to separate durable achievements (Truman's Marshall Plan) from passing phenomena (Truman's scandals).

The problems in evaluating the Reagan Presidency are particularly severe because the partisan and social science interpretations of the 1981–1989 period are so diverse. His supporters talk of the Reagan Revolution; they claim he came to power to change the United States, and he ended up changing the world.[2] His detractors claim that the Reagan Presidency only appears to be a success; the reality is that his policies were and will be detrimental to the long-term interests of the United States. Jesse Jackson evaluated the Reagan legacy in these words:

> The gap between the haves and have-nots has widened. . . . Eight years later, one-third of all black people are in poverty. And it is much the same for Hispanics. We've lost more family farms than at any other time. . . . Our glitter is brighter, but our foundation is weaker. Reagan has left a trail of sleaze, corruption and contemptible acts against the American people and the Congress. And when America sobers up, the nation will see the Reagan years were damaging both economically and socially.[3]

My response to the difficulty of evaluating the Reagan Presidency is tentative and cautious. I offer two contrasting perspectives of the Reagan Administration—a Conservative, positive analysis that stresses the Administration's successes, and a Liberal, negative one that points out its failures.

Ronald Reagan: Personality and Philosophy

To understand Reagan's successes and failures it is necessary to understand his personality and philosophy. Reagan's most important personality characteristic is his optimism. With the notable exception of having an alcoholic father, Reagan has led a charmed life. He was born in Tampico, Illinois in 1911, but raised in Dixon, Illinois. His mother was a devoted member of the Disciples of Christ Church who taught her son how to perform—reciting poetry, acting in plays—at an early age. Reagan graduated from Eureka College, a Disciples of Christ Church school, in 1932. After graduation, in the midst of the Depression, he soon found a job as a radio announcer in Iowa. As a sports announcer, he accompanied the Chicago Cubs to California for spring training in 1937 and was granted a screen test. He was hired by Warner Brothers and subsequently made 54 movies over the next twenty years. Reagan's movie reputation was that of an easy-to-direct actor who quickly learned his lines because of his photographic memory. In Hollywood he married Jane Wyman, became president of the Screen Actors Guild, and was active in politics as a Democrat supporting his hero, Franklin D. Roosevelt, and Harry Truman. Jane Wyman became a bigger star than her husband and divorced him in 1949. Three years later Reagan married Nancy Davis. When Reagan's acting career fizzled, he was hired by General Electric to be the host of its TV series in 1954. He also agreed to travel around the country speaking to GE employees, an experience that developed his skills in political rhetoric. In 1964, after GE cancelled his contract, Reagan delivered a very successful political speech in support of Barry Goldwater's campaign which was broadcast on national TV. A group of California millionaires were so impressed by Reagan's speech that they agreed to finance his 1966 campaign for Governor of California against the Democratic incumbent, Pat Brown. The ultimate goal, however, was the presidency. Reagan defeated Brown in 1966 and was re-elected in 1970. After retiring as Governor in 1974, Reagan ran against President Gerald Ford in 1976 in the Republican primaries and barely lost. Four years later he was elected President. In 1988 another group of California millionaires bought him and Nancy a $2.5 million home in Los Angeles. In brief, life has confirmed Reagan's optimism.

In Reagan's optimistic perspective, there are always solutions, usually simple ones, to problems; he does not think in terms of painful trade-offs. He has faith in his instincts and feels, therefore, that there is no need to search for and agonize over facts. In his world view, good intentions lead to good results. This view is protected by his great ability to block out from his consciousness unpleasant facts that do not confirm his ideological beliefs and expectations. Hence, he is generally a happy and secure person; he does not have the low self-esteem associated with James David Barber's passive-positive personality.

Because of his mother's religious influence, Reagan is also moralistic, but it is an easy-going, feel-good type of morality. Reagan's morality does not call for any sacrifices; nor does it try and make anyone, except liberals, feel guilty.

Reagan talks constantly about religious values, but he does not attend church and is occasionally influenced by astrological considerations.[4] He also believes in heroes. As a boy in Dixon he served as a life-guard during the summers and saved over seventy people from drowning. In the movies he always wanted to play cowboy heroes. As President he enjoyed playing the ultimate hero, who saved the United States from the internal threat of liberal big government and the external threat of the "evil empire" of Communism.

Watching Reagan in the movies, in his role as Governor, or as President, one realizes that Reagan is a persistent performer, who wants to be loved because he is acting in a morally correct way. He is always playing himself. Reagan loves to receive applause and make people laugh; like his father, a shoe salesman, he has memorized hundreds of jokes. As a performing salesman Reagan has sold religion, sports, Hollywood, GE, and the conservative ideology. Success has come to Reagan not because of his hard work, but because of his good looks, his voice, his charm, and especially his ability to mobilize others to work hard for him. While Reagan's opponents have constantly underestimated and ridiculed him for being an actor, he has frequently triumphed precisely because he is an actor who believes in his own performance.

In terms of his political philosophy, Reagan is always classified as a conservative, but he is less conservative in policy behavior than many people believe. Reagan's conservatism can be diluted by his desire to receive applause, by his inattention to detail, and by his management style, with its extensive delegation of authority to subordinates. Reagan himself concedes that, personally, he is a "soft touch." Perhaps that would explain why, in 1988, the President promoted and signed into law the Catastrophic Illness Bill, which would appear to violate Reagan's commitment to stop the growth of the welfare state.

Hugh Heclo claims that Reagan's conservatism consists of three interacting components: anti-government nationalism, communitarian individualism, and free market radicalism. Reagan separates the nation, which is composed of individuals, from its government, which is either a bungling or alien force. Reagan argues that government has been impeding the progress of the nation. Whereas liberals ask what government can do to correct the public problems of the day, Reagan stresses that, "Government is not part of the solution; it is the problem." Consequently, the Reagan Administration's public policies have been ideologically motivated to get government off the backs of the American people by cutting taxes and deregulating the economy. However, the foreign threat of communism requires that the United States government constantly expand its defense efforts because "defense commitments advance, not big government, but American nationhood in a threatening world."[5]

Reagan's communitarian individualism assumes that people will help each other, especially the less fortunate, as they did in Reagan's nostalgic remembrance of life in Dixon, Illinois. In Reagan's America, the nation is filled with heroic good samaritans working in private voluntary associations, who gladly help the poor. Liberal-inspired government programs stifle this charitable impulse while promoting a welfare addiction among those who are helped. If money or food is given to the poor as a social right (entitlement), they have incentives to remain destitute, become dependent, and not develop the ability to help themselves. In Heclo's words, "The presumption of community-based goodwill makes it possible to believe that being negative toward social spending by big government . . . is not the same thing as abandoning helpless people to their fate."[6]

Because the communitarian orientation can be relied on to provide a compassionate society, Reagan is able to endorse free market radicalism without any reservation. According to Heclo, "Reaganism portrays a social realm of individuals in caring association and an economic realm of individuals following their own separate dreams for self-advancement. Taken together these conceptions constitute individualism rightly understood: A nation of neighbors and an economy of rugged individualists. Thus, given its capacity for nurturing individual autonomy—the sources of both community engagement and economic progress—the free market is not just a technically efficient device but also the embodiment of an ethnically superior order."[7] For Reagan, capitalism and technological changes have only positive consequences. Individuals "going for it" will help us all. The Reagan dream foresees an era of boundless private market growth, but it is oblivious to the possible negative side effects, such as damage to the environment. Acid rain does not fall on Reagan's parade. Nor do deregulated banks fail.

In reviewing Reagan's personality and philosophy, the President's supporters emphasize that he is a natural born leader who has demonstrated his skills in college, Hollywood, California, and the Presidency. For his advocates, Reagan rescued the United States from the self-destructive path of liberalism and renewed American strength and morals with conservative values. For Reagan's opponents, he has been an amiable dunce, a tool of business interests and his staff, whose conservatism masked greed and ignorance, and whose political success was based on illusion.

Reagan's Popularity

A few days before the inauguration of George Bush, the *New York Times* reported the results of a poll that indicated that two-thirds of the American people approved of Reagan's performance over the last eight years, the highest rating given any President at the end of his term since World War II. While 68 percent of the public approved of his overall record over eight years, 71 percent supported his handling of foreign policy, particularly with the Soviet Union, and 62 percent commended his economic policies. Reagan was given a positive performance evaluation because solid majorities of the public perceived that his Administration had provided peace and prosperity. Many Americans also liked him personally.[8]

However, Reagan experienced "fluctuating fortunes" in his eight years in office. In 1980, he won an overwhelming electoral college victory over President Carter and John Anderson, yet he received only about 50 percent of the popular vote. When he was inaugurated in January 1981, his approval rating still stood at only 50 percent, the lowest inauguration rating for any modern president. Reagan's popularity went up after the assassination attempt in March 1981, the economic recovery in 1983, the Grenada invasion in October 1983, the Libya bombing in July 1986, and the signing of the INF Treaty with Gorbachev in December 1987. His popularity declined into the low 40 percent range during the 1981–82 recession and after the Iran-Contra scandal was revealed in November 1986.[9] These oscillating evaluations of Reagan suggest that the public appraises a President in terms of conditions (economic and international), performance and persona (is the President compassionate, decisive, etc.).

What was frustrating to the President's adversaries was the fact that Reagan, the man, was more liked than his policies. Reagan, the polished performer, had the benefit of following Jimmy Carter, who gave a particularly inept performance as President. In a manner reminiscent of Franklin Roosevelt's use of Herbert Hoover as a foil, Reagan ran against Carter throughout the decade, contrasting his own optimism with the Democrat's pessimism. Whereas Carter saw complexity and limits, Reagan saw simplicity and unlimited opportunities. Reagan's view was more in conformity with the traditionally optimistic American perspective concerning progress and thus was easier to sell. In Laurence Barett's words, "By 1980 a frustrated, confused America had lost all patience with stagflation at home, impudent adversaries abroad and ambiguity from its leadership. The moment was perfect for a leader who dealt in stark simplicities."[10]

In an age of self-doubt and conflicting trends, Reagan stood out as the most self-assured politician in the United States. He was sure of his facts and his reality, which often were not the facts and reality perceived by many other people. Reagan was a "conviction politician," a leader with a sense of direction. Even those who ridiculed Reagan's convictions often conceded that they were honestly held. Reagan's convictions led to policies that were not impeded by the fear of painful trade-offs. Hence, Reagan could move decisively to break the air traffic controller's strike or send the fleet into the Persian Gulf. But Reagan's Administration was flexible enough that, when his decisiveness backfired, as it did in Beirut in 1983 when 241 marines were blown up, he could quietly withdraw the troops. Reagan was not the rigid ideologue his opponents painted or some of his proponents loved. We were not asked to die for Reagan's beliefs.

Reagan was a moralist without being a prude; he led a happy crusade that did not call for any sacrifices. No President ever looked as comfortable with a greater variety of people and situations than Reagan did. He was "at home" in either Dixon or Los Angeles, Eureka College or Notre Dame; he looked good in either cowboy jeans or a tuxedo; he could communicate with both hard-hats and businessmen, religious fundamentalists and movie stars, young people and old people, Democrats and Republicans. As a former Democrat he was more likely to quote from Franklin Roosevelt than any Republican President. To help explain Reagan's popularity, Ceaser suggests that Reagan had "the knack, as Eisenhower did, not to offend by pomposity, yet never to disgrace by an affected populism."[11] Gary Wills adds, "The geriatric 'juvenile lead' even as President, Ronald Reagan is old and young—an actor, but with only one role. Because he acts himself, we know he is authentic. A professional, he is always the amateur. . . . He is perfectly suited to the most varying scenes of his life, yet his manner never changes. He is the opposite of a chameleon: environments adapt themselves to him."[12]

With so many people identifying with Reagan, the Democrats often hurt themselves by ridiculing him. They generated laughs by characterizing the Reagan era as the "reign of terror," punctuated by such Reagan howlers as, "Trees are the major polluters in the United States," but it was the Reagan Republican who won the presidential elections. What the Democrats did not understand was that, by jeering Reagan, they were alienating many voters and lowering expectations on what such a lazy, ill-informed actor could possibly achieve. No politician ever gained more mileage from just avoiding catastrophe than Ronald Reagan. In retrospect, ridicule was not an effective response to the challenge of Reagan's brand of conservative populism. Heclo explains why.

> Reaganism contains a populist streak that helps shield it from the conventional attack on conservatives as elitist and isolated from the concerns of ordinary people. It can present itself as conservatism for the little man, Reaganism understands the concerns of people who feel bewildered by the machination of public bureaucracy and corporate America, who are attached to local concerns and natavistic worries, who distrust the experts and who know a "traditional value" when they see one without the need for philosophical debate. These localist and subcultural attachments—which the intellectual opponents of Reaganism typically dismiss as unmodernized and aberrational—are an enduring part of the American political scene. The available niches of personal autonomy are likely to become more, not less, important to people as modernization proceeds.[13]

In short, it was a shock for Democrats to realize that much of the public—and especially segments of the working classes—were more estranged from liberal elites (intellectuals, the media) than from the conservative elites which Reagan identified himself with.

The Reagan Presidency: The Case For Political Success

In January 1981 Ronald Reagan became the sixth president to be sworn into office since 1961. During that 20-year period there had been a shift in interpretation of the presidency from the *imperial presidency* that characterized the office under Johnson and Nixon to the *imperiled presidency* model that was used to describe the destruction of the Ford and Carter Administrations. Under Carter the demands and expectations of office appeared to be impossible to satisfy. Under Reagan, judging by two landslide elections, the polls, and the subsequent election of his Vice President as President, the presidency no longer looked like an impossible job.

The Reagan White House was one of the keys to the political success of his Presidency. The chief organizational problem in managing the Reagan administration was conceptualized by Bert Rockman: "How can organizational structures, systems, and strategies be developed for a committed President (to major policy changes) and a detached President?"[14] The solution in the first term was to create a troika of top staff positions: Edwin Meese was named Counselor to the President, James Baker was made Chief of Staff in charge of running the daily operations of the White House, and Michael Deaver was put in charge of taking care of the personal interests of Reagan and his wife Nancy. The original division of labor among these top aides was: Meese would be in charge of developing policy proposals to Reagan concerning *what* should be done; Baker would orchestrate *how* it should be done; and Deaver was concerned with protecting the Reagan's personal image in this process. However, the Chief of Staff controlled the internal paper flow, access to the President, and (in alliance with Deaver) public relations, which meant that Baker dominated the crucial levers of power. Thus, students of public administration were not surprised when Baker's power soon increased at the expense of Meese's.

The Reagan Administration developed the idea of the strategic Presidency in its concept of "hitting the ground running."[15] Without strategic priorities, there is a danger that a presidency will appear to be a fire-fighting brigade rushing to put out one fire after another. Since there are so many "fires," the image of just trying to cope can easily degenerate into the disarray of the imperiled presidency. Unlike Carter's Presidency, the Reagan Presidency was determined to be guided by a clarity of purpose. The Reagan policy agenda was not to be cluttered with competing objectives; its probability of success would be aided by focused efforts. In the first few months of the Reagan Presidency, all resources were mobilized to achieve a limited set of strategic objectives: a tax cut, budget cuts of social expenditures, and a major defense build up. For the most part these objectives were achieved, and, by the summer of 1981, Reagan had established his credentials with both Congress and the public as a winner. Unlike Carter, who had wasted his advantages during the so-called honeymoon period (the first few months of a new Administration), Reagan had taken advantage of this limited window of opportunity. Reagan's early legislative victories may have set a new standard of performance for the American Presidency, replacing FDR's model of the first hundred days.

According to Rockman, "The key to the Reagan Presidency was to have the President fuel the policy agenda—to enunciate his goals and sell them rather than watch over operations or intervene obtrusively in the process of decision making and policy formulation at lower levels."[16] Since this was what he had been doing for much of his adult life, Reagan was very comfortable with this assigned role. He was a true believer, a professional actor, operating from the "bully pulpit" of the presidency, all of which combined to make him the great communicator.

The public relations efforts of the Reagan White House—supported by Republican Party money and organization—were particularly effective. All presidents attempt to manage the news in order to influence public opinion, but Reagan proved to be highly successful at this. While Kennedy had the pleasing personality and Nixon had the public relations techniques, Reagan had both in abundance. His own public relations skills were augmented by those of Michael Deaver, James Baker, David Gergen, Richard Darman, Larry Speakes, and Richard Wirthlin. These advisers had witnessed the debilitating consequences of the credibility gap in the Johnson and Nixon Presidencies and the inept use of communication techniques in the Ford and Carter Administrations. They understood that the chronic dilemma of the contemporary presidency is that its performance cannot match the public's expectations. The public confuses the President's prominence in the media with the President's power to resolve problems. Reagan's media advisors responded to this problem by developing methods that could satisfy many of the public's expectations symbolically rather than substantively. They also believed that the President could not lead the country if he could not communicate with it. In Hertsgaard's words, "Both Deaver and Gergen recognized that to engineer mass consent in the modern media age, the government had to be able to present its version of reality to the public over and over again. Neutralizing the press, by limiting journalists' ability to report politically damaging stories, was necessary but not sufficient. The press had to be turned into a positive instrument of governance, a reliable and essentially non-intrusive transmitter of what the White House wanted the public to know."[17] This objective was attained because the adversarial component of media coverage of the Presidency was softened by Reagan's public relations apparatus.

The public relation techniques used by the Reagan Presidency included: (1) severely reducing the number of regular press conferences; (2) presenting well-planned coordinated themes of the day and/or week to get the President's message simplified and repeated to the public; (3) prepackaging attractive visuals; (4) having members of the Administration speak in one voice; (5) stage-managing Reagan speeches to take advantage of his communication skills. This strategy utilized Reagan's ability as an actor while it camouflaged his lack of knowledge regarding policy.

The Reagan Presidency: The Case Against Political Success

To many of Reagan's critics, the political success of his Presidency was a function of image over substance, illusion over reality. Democrats charge that Reagan and his public relations apparatus fostered "national self-delusion and called it patriotism."[18] But balloons, visuals, and flags cannot fool history. A day of reckoning is looming concerning problems the Reagan Presidency either avoided or actually made worse: the budget deficit, the national debt, the savings and loan crisis, the trade deficit, the corporate merger mania, and the growing inequalities in the United States. When these chickens come home to roost, the evaluations of the Reagan legacy are likely to become more negative. In brief, these critics compare the Reagan Presidency to the apparent success of Calvin Coolidge in the 1920s.

The following members of Reagan's Administration have written books on their experiences: Alexander Haig, David Stockman, Michael Deaver, Larry Speakes and Donald Regan. The portrait of Reagan in these so-called kiss-and-tell books is not flattering. Apparently the promise of making money for their memoirs entices many of those who leave the Reagan team to expose the fantasies of Ronnie and Nancy. Ironically for Reagan, such individual enterprise (Going for it!) is not helping Reagan's historical reputation.

Neither is the legacy of his Administration's so-called sleaze factor. With all of Reagan's rhetoric about morality, he presided over one of the most scandal-racked Administrations in the history of the United States. More than 110 of Reagan's political appointees were accused of criminal activities during his eight years in office. Among those convicted were: Michael Deaver, Lyn Nofziger, Rita Lavelle, and Paul Thayer. Former Secretary of Labor Raymond Donovan was indicted on fraud charges but was eventually acquitted. Attorney General Meese was investigated by an independent counsel for his alleged roles in helping the Wedtech Corporation gain a government contract and in bribing an Israeli official in the Iraqui pipeline affair, but was not indicted; however, he was reprimanded by an internal Department of Justice investigation for violating ethical standards. David Fischer, a former Assistant to the President, pleaded guilty for illegally receiving $20,000 a month to help arrange private meetings between the President and large contributors to the Nicaraguan Contras. At the time of this writing, former National Security aides John Poindexter and Oliver North are under indictment for their roles in the Iran-Contra scandal. Finally, the Pentagon procurement scandal which erupted in the last year of the Reagan Presidency will result in numerous trials and revelations over the next few years.[19] Thus, it is not surprising that the Bush Administration is stressing an emphasis on ethics in public service in order to differentiate itself from the Reagan record in this area.

Reagan's critics also stress that his Presidency was not able to achieve fundamental political changes. Whereas Franklin Roosevelt was able to realign the American electorate and make the Democratic Party the majority party in the United States, Reagan has been much less successful. In 1981 the 97th Congress consisted of 243 Democrats and 192 Republicans in the House of Representatives and 46 Democrats and 54 Republicans in the Senate. Reagan's 1980 electoral victory had helped 13 new Republican Senators win seats and had given the Republicans majority control over the Senate for the first time since the first two years (1953-54) of the Eisenhower Presidency. Republicans hoped to extend their majority to the House in 1982, but the recession stifled that ambition; instead, they lost 26 seats in the 1982 elections. In 1986 the Republicans lost control of the Senate, which set the stage for the Senate rejection of Reagan's Supreme Court nominee, Robert Bork. When Reagan left office in January 1989, George Bush was confronted with a Democratically-controlled Congress: 262 Democrats and 173 Republicans in the House, and 55 Democrats and 45 Republicans in the Senate. Paul Beck concludes, "What we have as the Reagan years draw to a close is an incomplete realignment—some movement toward Republican ascendency, but no consolidation of the movement by Republican successes beyond the presidential level or in enduring partisan loyalties. Temporary conditions have been strongly in its favor (a popular President, a fractioned opposition, no foreign policy catastrophes, and real economic growth), which does not augur well for the future of the GOP."[20]

Regan's Economic Policies: The Case For Success

The strategic priority of the Reagan Presidency was to change the economic direction of the nation with a new set of economic policies. New policies were required because the country was suffering from problems caused by increasing governmental interference in the economy since the New Deal. Such interference inevitably brought about less satisfactory results than if reliance were placed on free and competitive markets. After almost 50 years of Keynesian fine-tuning and governmental regulation of the economy, the United States was confronted with: the highest level of real interest rates in the nation's history; a high and persistent level at unemployment; the lowest rate of personal saving in the post-World War II period; a falling level of labor productivity; a government sector increasing in both its absolute and its relative size; a series of annual federal budget deficits steadily enlarging a massive national debt; and a rising taxpayer's revolt against high taxes.[21]

Reagan stepped into this void with an economic strategy that was based on three components: monetarism, which would prevent inflation by tightening the money supply; market-oriented economies, which would rely on competitive markets to regulate the economy; and supply-side economics, which would stimulate economic growth by providing a massive tax cut. The first two components were traditional, conservative Republican approaches to managing the economy that the GOP had had trouble selling politically because they involved short-term sacrifices for long-term benefits. Reagan's innovation was to add the populist supply-side tax cut, which promised short *and* long-term benefits as well as balanced budgets.

Thus, the key to Reagan's economic policy was the supply-side inspired Kemp-Roth tax cut of 1981. Unlike Keynesian economics, which calls for the government to manipulate aggregate demand with fiscal and monetary policies, the Kemp-Roth bill, renamed the Economic Recovery and Tax Act (ERTA) when introduced by the Reagan Administration in February 1981, was designed to encourage people to work harder, and to save and invest more because, with lower tax rates, they would be able to keep more of their income. The increase in the supply of more efficient labor and capital would assure prosperity. The magic of this strategy, according to Congressman Jack Kemp, was that cuts in the tax rates would actually increase tax revenues and soon balance the budget.

Reagan passed ERTA over the inept opposition of Congressional Democrats in August 1981. According to Peterson and Rom, "Reagan's $162 billion tax cut in 1981 dwarfed any that had occurred in the postwar era. (Ford's $22.2 billion cut in 1975 taking a distant second place) . . . ERTA's major features included a 23 percent reduction in personal income taxes (spread out over three years), a cut in the marginal tax rate from 70 to 50 percent, a cut in the capital gains tax from 28 percent to 20 percent, and major cuts in business taxes, mainly by allowing businesses to speed the depreciation of their assets (e.g., buildings, machinery, and vehicles)."[22] ERTA also indexed the tax brackets to the inflation rate beginning in 1985, which meant that federal revenues would no longer be automatically increased by "bracket creep" (individuals being pushed up into higher tax brackets by inflation even though their real income might not be rising).

Three other major tax bills passed during Reagan's Presidency included sections which raised revenue. Social Security taxes also steadily increased throughout the period. However, the supply-side notion of reducing tax rates was achieved. When Reagan took office the maximum tax rate was 70 percent; Reagan's Tax Reform Act of 1986 reduced the top rate to 28 percent (some will pay 33 percent). Four million poor families no longer pay any income taxes at all.

In terms of budgetary policy, in 1981 Reagan's Office of Management and Budget Director David Stockman was able to get $40 billion in domestic policy cuts and $7 billion in defense expenditure increases accepted by Congress. The domestic reductions, many of which were targeted against the poor rather than against middle class entitlement programs, were particularly difficult to pass through Congress. After 1981 Reagan generally was not successful in reducing these expenditures. The President succeeded in expanding the military budget until 1985 when Congress balked because of the budget deficit, and these expenditures have leveled off at a little less than $300 billion. Reagan's budget legacy is summarized by Martin Tochin: "Most agree that Mr. Reagan has lowered expectations of what the Federal Government can and should do, reordered the nation's priorities and changed the terms of the fiscal debate. . . . (H)is Presidency has made it perilous for any politician to propose new programs without specifying how to pay for them."[23]

Reagan claims that his proudest achievement as President was the economic recovery. When Reagan left office, the United States had experienced 74 straight months of economic growth—the largest peacetime expansion in the history of the nation. In January 1989 unemployment was near a 14-year low; inflation was one-third of its 1981 pace; interest rates were only half as high as they were 8 years ago. Nearly 18 million new jobs had been created since 1982. Reagan has always blamed the Carter Administration for the 1981–82 recession, and he holds the Democratically-controlled House of Representatives responsible for the budget deficits. Additionally he asserts that the trade deficit has steadily improved since 1986.

Reagan's Economic Policies: The Case for Failure

Reagan's critics claim that the President's policies have provided us with a false and immoral prosperity. Reagan used to condemn Democratic policies as being based on the strategy of "tax, spend, and elect;" his critics now claim the President merely substituted a scheme of "borrow, spend, elect." While Reagan's economic policies were a political success, their legacy will burden our future. According to Benjamin Friedman, "The trouble with an economic policy that artificially boosts consumption at the expense of investment, dissipates assets, and runs up debt is simply that each of these outcomes violates the essential trust that has always linked each generation to those that follow. We have enjoyed what appears to be a higher and more stable standard of living by selling our and our children's birthright."[24]

Instead of eliminating the $79 billion budget deficit inherited from President Carter, Reagan allowed deficits to soar from $128 billion in 1982 to a high of $221 billion in 1986. The total national debt accumulated under the nation's first thirty-nine presidents more than doubled under its fortieth, Ronald Reagan. The national debt rose by 170 percent under Reagan, while the national income increased by only 50 percent. When Reagan left office, the national debt he passed on to George Bush was not the $914 billion he inherited from Carter, but $2.6 trillion. During the 1980s annual interest on the national debt has grown from $96 billion to over $150 billion—the latter constituting a higher cost than the combined budgets of nine departments. In brief, under Reagan's leadership we mortgaged our future, borrowing more than $20,000 on behalf of each family of four to finance the illusion of prosperity.

Supply-side economics simply did not work as planned. It produced neither balanced budgets nor increases in the propensity to save. Supply-siders promised their policies would boost the nation's savings rate and make America more productive. Instead, the personal savings rate declined from 7.1 percent in 1980 to about 4 percent in 1988. In Japan and Western Europe, personal savings rates have averaged 15 percent and 7 to 10 percent respectively. Consequently, improvements in United States productivity have been sluggish: "Output per hour increased by 1.6 percent between 1981 and 1987, compared to an average of 2.7 percent per year between 1950 and 1970, and 1.2 percent between 1970 and 1980."[25]

The lack of domestic savings and the budget deficits have had a devastating effect on our ability to compete successfully in international markets. Friedman explains the link between our fiscal deficit and our international trade deficit in these words: "With government borrowing absorbing nearly three-fourths of our private saving, heightened competition among business and individual borrowers for the remainder has raised our interest rates, in relation to inflation, to record levels—and importantly, to levels well above what investors could get in other countries. For half a decade, therefore, the dollar became even more expensive in terms of other countries' currencies, as foreign investors competed among themselves to acquire dollars with which to buy high-interest debt instruments in America. As the dollar rose, the ability of our industries to compete with foreign producers all but collapsed not only in world markets but even here in America.[26] A painful measure of that collapse was the fact that the United States registered a record-breaking 1987 trade deficit of $170.3 billion. Even though the value of the dollar has declined in terms of other currencies since 1985, the United States trade deficit in 1988 was still about $135 billion. Thus, while Reagan began his term as President of the world's largest creditor nation, George Bush is leading the world's largest debtor nation and will have to confront the shift in prestige and influence that this change implies.

Reagan's critics also condemn his economic policies for promoting inequality. During the 1980s the gap between the rich and the poor widened. According to a Census Bureau study of 60,000 households, the share of total income received by the most affluent fifth of American households rose to 46.1 percent in 1986, from 43.3 percent in 1980, while the proportion received by the poorest fifth declined to 3.8 percent, from 4.1 percent. Among the richest one-fifth of families, the average income rose from $70,260 to $76,300 in 1986 (in 1986 dollars). Among the poorest 20 percent of families average income declined from $8,761 to $8,033. Part of this trend is explained by the fact that there has been an increase in female-headed households, which tend to have relatively low incomes, and a simultaneous rise in two-earner married couples, which are likely to have higher incomes. In 1986, perhaps for the first time in our history, the 3.6 million female-headed families accounted for more than half of all poor families.[27] The feminization of poverty was an issue that was almost totally ignored by the Reagan Administration and actually was probably intensified by its budget cuts of domestic welfare programs.

Reagan, using a John F. Kennedy line, had claimed that "a rising tide lifts all boats." But the economic growth of the 1980s has left 32 million people, or 13.5 percent of the American population, submerged in poverty. While the elderly have continued to improve their economic conditions under Reagan, almost 25 percent of the children under the age of six are growing up in poverty; more than half of the black children are. Another disturbing trend is the increase in the number of people who are not covered by health insurance, which has grown from 29 million in 1980 to 37 million in 1988. Finally, as large numbers of low-income housing units have disappeared since 1980 because of market forces and budget cuts, there has been a visible increase in the number of the homeless.[28] In brief, Reagan's policies did not produce the progress toward equality which is as important to the political culture of the United States as liberty is.

Conclusion

This essay has provided contrasting evaluations of the Reagan Presidency. Conservatives have praised the Reagan Administration for promoting a "revolution" that changed the policy direction of the United States. They stress that Reagan's policies have overcome the "malaise" of the Carter period and morally rejuvenated the United States. For Reagan's supporters, the Administration's historic achievements include: the largest tax cut in American history; the longest peacetime period of economic growth; the defense build-up; the Strategic Defense Initiative; the liberation of Grenada; and the withdrawal of Soviet troops from Afghanistan. Conservatives contend that the President could have accomplished more if the pragmatists on his staff (James Baker and Michael Deaver) had allowed "Reagan to be Reagan" and if the Republicans could have gained control over the House of Representatives.

Liberals, on the other hand, credit most of Reagan's apparent political success to his first-rate public-relations staff, incompetent Democratic Party opposition, and luck. Despite Reagan's image, liberals delight in pointing out that he was lazy, uninformed, and not close to his family or religious. Beneath the illusions propagated by Reagan's public relations apparatus were: a series of annual budget deficits which significantly increased the national debt; a continuing trade deficit; a savings and loan crisis; a federal bureaucracy larger than the one Reagan inherited; a legacy of sleaze and bureaucratic corruption; and a more socially unjust society.

These contrasting images become even more complex when one realizes that some conservatives praise Reagan for his first term achievements but condemn his Administration for developing much closer ties with Gorbachev's Soviet Union in the second. Some liberals, begrudgingly, reverse these judgements. In the coming years, historians will obviously be busy trying to make an accurate appraisal of the most controversial presidency since FDR's.

Notes

1. Richard E. Neustadt, *Presidential Power: The Politics of Leadership.* (New York: John Wiley, 1960); Fred I. Greenstein, *The Hidden Hand Presidency: Eisenhower As Leader.* (New York: Basic Books, 1982).

2. Martin Anderson, *Revolution* (New York: Harcourt Brace Jovanovich, 1988).
3. Jesse Jackson, quoted in *Newsweek* (Jan 9, 1989), p. 22.
4. Donald T. Regan, *For The Record* (New York: Harcourt Brace Jovanovich, 1988), pp. 3–5.
5. Hugh Heclo, "Reaganism And The Search For A Public Philosophy," in *Perspectives On The Reagan Years,* edited by John Palmer, (Washington, D.C.: The Urban Institute Press, 1986), p. 44.
6. *Ibid.*, p. 45.
7. *Ibid.*, p. 46.
8. *The New York Times,* Jan. 18, 1989.
9. James W. Ceaser, "The Reagan Presidency and American Public Opinion," in *The Reagan Legacy,* edited by Charles O. Jones (Chatham, New Jersey: Chatham House, 1988) pp. 172–211.
10. Lawrence Barrett, "Going Home A Winner," *Time* (Jan. 23, 1989), p. 15.
11. Ceaser, *op. cit.,* p. 183.
12. Gary Wills, *Reagan's America: Innocents At Home* (Gardner City: Doubleday, 1987), p. 1.
13. Heclo, *op. cit.,* p. 50.
14. Bert Rockman, "The Style and Organization of The Reagan Presidency," in *The Reagan Legacy: Promise and Performance* (Chatham, New Jersey: Chatham House, 1988), p. 8.
15. James P. Pfiffner, *The Strategic Presidency: Hitting the Ground Running* (Chicago: The Dorsey Press, 1988).
16. Rockman, *op. cit.,* p. 9.
17. Mark Hertsgaard, *On Bended Knee: The Press and The Reagan Presidency.*
18. *Ibid.* p. 300.
19. *The New York Times,* May 15, 1987 and June 17, 1988.
20. Paul Allen Beck, "Incomplete Realignments: The Reagan Legacy For Parties and Elections," in Jones, *op., cit.,* p. 168.
21. Bruce W. Kimzey, *Reaganomics* (St. Paul: West Publishing Co., 1983) p. 12.
22. Paul E. Peterson and Mark Rom, "Lower Taxes, More Spending, and Budget Deficits," in Jones, *op., cit.,* pp. 218–219.
23. Martin Tolchin, *The New York Times,* Feb. 16, 1988.
24. Benjamin Friedman, *Day of Reckoning: The Consequences of American Economic Policy Under Reagan And After* (New York: Random House, 1988), p. 5.
25. Emma Rothschild, "The Real Reagan Economy," *The New York Review of Books* (June 30, 1988), p. 51.
26. Friedman, *op., cit.,* p. 10.
27. *The New York Times,* July 31, 1987.
28. Rothschild, *op., cit.,* p. 46.

9 Administering America: Bureaucracy in Democracy
ULF ZIMMERMANN

What do we think of when we hear the word bureaucracy? Probably something negative—something that puts stumbling blocks in our way, ties up our time, and seems indifferent to our concerns. There is the departmentalized hierarchy that keeps us running from pillar to post to get anything done at all, the impersonality of the "faceless bureaucrat" who makes decisions about us without in the slightest considering our personal circumstances, the seemingly endless and needless regulations, the "red tape" that governments entangle us in as over-taxed individuals and overburdened businesses. If we read the newspapers we will time and again be told of the hapless 87-year-old woman who is not getting her social security check because the Social Security Administration has declared her dead—and won't seem to accept her living presence in its branch office as proof to the contrary. We learn of directly contradictory requirements, the Catches-22, government imposes on businesses—OSHA requiring warning sirens whose sound the EPA forbids as noise pollution. We see bureaucracy depicted as "a brontosaurus of unimaginable size, appetite, ubiquity and complexity," "over-staffed, inflexible, unresponsive, and power-hungry," with bureaucrats who are seen as "lazy or snarling, or both . . . bungling or inhumane, or both."[1]

More academically, we hear economists call bureaucracy inefficient because it lacks the incentives provided by competition and profit. Sociologists decry the goal displacement of bureaucrats who put the means of the bureaucracy before its ends, alienating both its clients and its employees. We even find political scientists complaining that while legislative bodies enact new policies, bureaucracies fail to implement them because they do not like change and resist it. With such accusations of failure to perform, repression of people, and abuse of political power, it's a wonder that vast majorities of the people at the receiving end of bureaucratic actions are as satisfied with them as surveys consistently show them to be.[2]

Because these perceptions and accusations of bureaucracy are so common, so nearly all-pervasive in modern society, I will attempt to explain historically why bureaucracy is subject to them and to describe it more realistically, to counter some of those charges and to correct some of those images.

Bureaucracy: Origins of a Word and of Our Worries

The negative stereotype of bureaucracy is, instructively, not a new phenomenon. Nor is bureaucracy a German invention, as one might have expected; it is, in fact, a French coinage. The term was first used by Vincent de Gournay, one of the 18th-century French economists known as physiocrats, the Milton Friedman of his day, who thought that government should not interfere in the economy. He diagnosed a "French illness" in government that he termed "bureaumania."[3] "Mania" is of course the standard word or suffix for illnesses, especially of a psychological nature such as kleptomania. "Bureau" itself is simply a French word referring originally to a writing table, especially one with drawers, a usage one still encounters shopping in antique stores. The word quickly came also to refer to the room where the writing was done, hence the office and, more abstractly in our contemporary governmental usage, a bureau such as the Federal Bureau of Investigation, the Bureau of Indian Affairs, the Bureau of the Census, and so forth. From this etymology it is easy to see the associations with an excess of writing (records and red tape) and of compartmentalization (pigeon-holing) that we perceive in bureaucracy.

De Gournay occasionally also used the ending we use on bureaucracy, and we must ask ourselves what that means because it will explain the underlying reason bureaucracy is so worrisome to people. What other words share that ending? Perhaps the first one to come to mind is "democracy." Perhaps we will also think of aristocracy, and thereafter a host of others. "Cracy," in the original Greek, signified power or strength, and in combination with such words as "demo" and "aristo" it indicated where the power resided: "Aristo" means "the best" so that aristocracy signifies rule by the best; "demo" of course refers to the people, hence rule by the people. That gives us an idea of the real worry of early writers on bureaucracy—and their counterparts today: rule by those in the bureaus, that this secretive record-keeping, scribbling class which held all the government's knowledge would gain totalitarian control over government and unilaterally exercise its whole power.

American worries, however, have some additional origins and grounds. As our French neologist suggests, and as we know from European history, bureaucracy had long been established there and associated with the preordained monarchic governments which had used it as their instrument in nation and empire building from the Renaissance forward. In European countries, therefore, the complete bureaucratic machinery of state was already fully in place when the new democratic forms of government displaced the autocratic regimes of kings and emperors. But in the United States the founding of the new nation itself began with the creation of a new form of government, a democracy, with no long-rooted indigenous bureaucracy in place. Born well after the democracy in America, our bureaucracy has thus always retained a smack of illegitimacy in the American mind, which we will also explain and seek to rectify.

True total bureaucracy in de Gournay's sense was classically portrayed in George Orwell's *1984*. A brief recollection of it will show just how little American administration warrants our worries about such bureaucracy. In Orwell's vast superpower, Oceania, all aspects of life are subordinated to the administration of four central superagencies, monolithic ministries which administer everything from art to war. By contrast, one quick glance at the U.S. Government Manual reveals that, instead of four such superagencies, we have thirteen cabinet level departments alone—plus some three score and more independent agencies, government corporations, and other quasi-governmental organizations, ranging from a multi-branched Department of Defense to the sprawling Smithsonian Institution. And while in Oceania one central "Ministry of Love" is responsible for law and order—for social and personal, moral and legal behavior, and all related internal affairs—here, given the founding premises of this federal nation, most such "police powers" that affect individual citizens are, in fact, administered by the states and by their local governments, precisely so that no remote national bureaucracy could interfere in the daily lives of Americans.

American administration has resisted centralization. It developed and grew not, in fact, as a single bureaucracy but rather as a large and loose collection, often likened to a holding company, of distinctly individual and strongly independent bureaucracies which, rather than submitting to harnessed coordination, vigorously compete in overlapping policy arenas. While we may thus seem to have a large bureaucracy it is a highly decentralized one in which every organization is prominently concerned to defend its turf, and this great proliferation of organizations and their competition have kept us from becoming an Oceanic bureaucracy. The issue of the Houston Ship Channel is an apt topical illustration: The EPA is supporting the U.S. Army Corps of Engineers in its plans to enlarge the channel, while the U.S. Fish and Wildlife Service and the National Marine Fisheries Service are strenuously opposing it.

Not only is our federal bureaucracy organizationally decentralized—and federally, as noted—it is not at all as centrally concentrated as the usage of the term "Washington" would suggest. Only about 12 percent of our civilian bureaucrats work in the Washington metropolitan area.[5] Moreover, while there are indeed some agencies of the federal government that employ thousands in one place, like our own local NASA Johnson Space Center (which employs around 10,000, though only about a third of these are actual government employees), 85 percent of the units of federal administration have fewer than 25 employees and the overall average is 58 employees.[6] And if one is worried about the size and cost of the federal bureaucracy itself, it might be heartening to know that the federal civilian labor force has hardly grown since the early fifties, and its proportionate payroll costs have been steadily declining.

Anatomy of Bureaucracy

While it was in France that bureaucracy and its pathologies had been first diagnosed, it was in Germany, early in this century, that bureaucracy was first dissected. Max Weber, the legally trained social scientist, saw bureaucracy as a distinct subspecies of social organization which he described as consisting of three basic elements: the leader, the administrative staff, and the rank-and-file members. In this typically hierarchical schema, the leader directs and guides the organization in its mission and the rank-and-file carry out the specific duties, delivering the specific goods and services that are the organization's *raison d'être*. In between these directing and delivering agents, the pivotal administrative staff maintains the organization as a coherent and operative body by managing the workers and keeping the leader informed, i.e., communicating directives to the workers and overseeing their execution and communicating information for decisions to the leader.

Power and Authority

To do all this smoothly and effectively, one clearly needs some procedural rules and regulations. These rules and regulations must come from somewhere acceptable, and there must be some equally acceptable reason for following them. Looking at the organizational structure, the pyramid in this case, one can surmise that they come from the top, even from above that in the case of the traditional divine right of kings and of, say, the Vatican.

But apart from a universally accepted divinely ordained will, what is there to make one follow a given set of rules and regulations, to do what the organization requires? Perhaps the most familiar example is doing what one's parents want one to do. Clearly parents or some other party wield a form of superiority that will lead one to follow. In simplest terms there is plain brute force—parents are bigger and stronger, and so is the school bully. But while parents are smarter as well, the school bully probably isn't; hence intelligence is another such form of superiority. These are rudimentary forms of what Weber calls plain "power."

Such power, though, is evanescent—the first person or group to come along with more brawn or brains could usurp it. For power to last and leadership to endure, for them to be institutionalized in other words, something more must therefore be involved. This something more Weber defines as "prestige"—people don't simply just fear the leader's strength or cunning but they also somehow admire and respect it, like that universally acknowledged divine right in which kings cloaked themselves. Without retracing Weber's full explanation, we can say summarily that prestige lends power the "legitimacy" that makes it stable and enduring, and that in turn translates power into "authority."

Now of course we must ask precisely what makes authority work, what makes it acceptable and what makes one follow it. It is here that we get to Weber's famous three types of authority. There is, to begin with, the familiar kind of authority we've been talking about, the kind exercised by the head of the household—and, by extension, chieftains, feudal rulers, kings—all of whose authority depends on long-standing custom and practice and is hence known as "traditional" authority. Secondly, Weber discerned a type of authority that emanates from some individual directly because this individual communicates some characteristic, like a gift of grace, that makes this person stand out and makes other people look up to him or her. This gift is "charisma," hence the charismatic authority that is typical of religious leaders who have no power per se but command vast followings nonetheless. Christ is clearly an archetypal example, while Gandhi and Martin Luther King illustrate charismatic authority in our own time. We also extend the term charismatic to political leaders such as John F. Kennedy, through whom the term entered popular American currency.

Traditional and charismatic authority are thus leadership types of long history. Weber's third type, however, is the most modern and for us the most pertinent. This is his "legal" authority, called that because this type of authority depends on a codified set of rules and regulations.

The Basis of Bureaucratic Authority in Democratic Government

We accept traditional authority because we believe in long-standing customs and certain roles associated with them, and we accept charismatic authority because we believe in a person who represents something transcendent and who has more or less captivated us. But we accept legal authority as legitimate because we believe in a set of socially shared and rationally agreed-upon values; it is thus consent-based. We agree, for example, to obey police officers because we have consented to have police officers enforce a set of rules and regulations that we have, in turn, previously agreed upon. America's most fundamental agreement of this sort is embodied in the Constitution which itself is based on previous models of constitutions going back, via the Mayflower compact, all the way to the Magna Carta. In everyday terms such agreements have their roots in commercial contracts, which first became common with the rise of mercantilism.

Instead of residing in the person or the family, as in the case of traditional authority, or being immanent in a given individual, as in the case of charismatic authority, authority here inheres in the position: Instead of doing what your parents tell you because they are *your* parents, or doing what some individual tells you because you revere that person, you do what the police officer tells you to because she is *a* police officer. You sometimes even do what your teacher tells you to do because he is *a* teacher. You do what they tell you because you believe they are telling you, not as individual persons, but as representatives of a legal order of which you are a consenting, contractually bound member. The teacher and the police officer are only telling you to do what any other person in their positions would tell you to do and, moreover, what they would equally tell any other person in your position.

Weber's Model of Bureaucratic Staff

Such legal administrative systems as those we participate in do not, of course, have to be bureaucracies, but bureaucracies, for Weber, represent them in their purest form. According to Weber, the bureaucratic administrative staff "consists, in the purest type, of individual officials who are appointed and function according to the following criteria":

(1) They are personally free and subject to authority only with respect to their impersonal official obligations.
(2) They are organized in a clearly defined hierarchy of offices.
(3) Each office has a clearly defined sphere of competence in the legal sense.
(4) The office is filled by a free contractual relationship. Thus, in principle, there is free selection.
(5) Candidates are selected on the basis of technical qualifications. In the most rational case, this is tested by examination or guaranteed by diplomas certifying technical training, or both. They are *appointed,* not elected.
(6) They are remunerated by fixed salaries in money, for the most part with a right to pensions. Only under certain circumstances does the employing authority, especially in private organizations, have a right to terminate the appointment, but the official is always free to resign. The salary scale is primarily graded according to rank in the hierarchy; but in addition to this criterion, the responsibility of the position and the requirements of the incumbent's social status may be taken into account.
(7) The office is treated as the sole, or at least the primary, occupation of the incumbent.
(8) It constitutes a career. There is a system of 'promotion' according to seniority or to achievement, or both. Promotion is dependent on the judgment of superiors.
(9) The official works entirely separated from ownership of the means of administration and without appropriation of his position.
(10) He is subject to strict and systematic discipline and control in the conduct of the office.[7]

According to 1, then, when you work in a bureaucracy you deal with people only in your official (clerical, technical, professional, etc.) capacity, treating them as citizens, clients, constituents, criminals, or whatever the case may be; your private feelings, theoretically, stay at home. In 2 we have the vertical division of labor, ranging in, say, a city from the mayor to the director of public works to the manager of the water division down to the meter reader. In addition, there is, 3, the horizontal division of labor, as is the case in that city with its different departments—public works, police, fire, etc., and the departments with their different responsibilities such as traffic, narcotics, vice, burglary, crime prevention in the police, for example.

The core of Weber's legal authority lies in 4: The two parties, employer and employee, agree formally and in writing to have certain things done and to do certain things and only those for the organization and the superiors—and that only within the strict confines of the position—not after work or at home. As implied in this and the preceding three, if you're a typist, you can't be asked to make coffee, technically, since it's not in your "job description"; likewise, if you're a neurosurgeon, you don't do deliveries.

To be that typist, according to 5, you'd have to pass a typing test; to do research for nuclear power deployment, you'd probably have to have a Ph.D. in nuclear physics; for government administration there is the public sector equivalent of the MBA, the MPA—Master of Public Administration. Given these qualifications, once you have demonstrated in a probationary period that you can apply them appropriately, you become a permanent civil servant, 6, like university professors who have "tenure." This, and particularly the pension rights, exist to assure that the government retains the expertise embodied in its employees; they also exist to assure "neutral competence" within the bureaucracy, i.e., both that the bureaucrats work not only for one political party and that they are protected against being fired by the next party to come into office. We might also translate that into assuring loyalty to our constitutional state, and some would add that these securities also exist to compensate for often considerably lower pay than might be found in the corporate world.

Likewise corollary to 1 and 4 you are, according to 7, supposed to devote your working hours to that particular office and its responsibilities and not spend them on your private affairs. There are, for example, limits on what kind and how much consulting professors can do. As technical fields illustrate particularly clearly, you have expertise in a single given field, and that expertise increases with experience so that you tend to stay in a single organization and get promoted within it, as 8 indicates. You may start as a bookkeeper, get an accounting degree and get promoted for that; by seniority you might be made head of accounting; if you acquit yourself well in that management position, your superiors may ask you to direct, say, the whole department of finance. (Of course as we know from the Peter Principle the best accountant is not necessarily the best manager any more than the best defense attorney will necessarily make the most impartial judge.)

Per your purely contractual relationship, according to 9, the office, staff, supplies, and so forth remain the property of the government—or the corporation—you work for. Unlike the hereditary positions in traditional feudal societies, or those at the head of private firms today, these offices also cannot be passed on to your daughter or son. The discipline and control of 10 are exercised both from within the given agency by your own superiors and their superiors and from without, by overhead agencies such as the Office of Management & Budget (OMB), which helps decide how much you get to work with, and the Government Accounting Office (GAO) which oversees what you've done with it; by other interested parties, such as Congress itself, interest groups, clients, constituents, affected citizens, and of course the courts.

The Bureaucratic Machine: Personality, Power, and Politics

In theory, then, government bureaucracy is supposed to be a neutral mechanism that implements unquestioningly the policies formulated by its political superiors who, in democracies, have been elected to represent and enact the will of the people, much as Ronald Reagan referred in his farewell speech to government as a car of which we, the people are the driver. This clear dichotomy of politics and administration has, of course, never truly obtained in practice; it was, at best, an ideal for Woodrow Wilson and a "model" for Weber. Weber's typology of bureaucracy is indeed a model and, like Freud's contemporary model of the workings of the human psyche, depended greatly on the mechanistic conception of the world emanating from this "machine age." Yet the bureaucracy does not function like a machine, for it is not composed of a machine's almost perfectly interchangeable parts but of individual people. From practically the smallest job to the largest, it is plain that the person who fills it will determine to a greater or lesser extent how that job is done, will decide who benefits and who loses, on the basis of such variable factors as his or her values, perception of responsibilities, interpretation of circumstances, perhaps just mood. All of us are familiar with notorious exercises of discretion on the part of "street-level" bureaucrats such as the police officer who may decide to ticket one person but not another under precisely comparable circumstances.

Like individuals, groups which share, say, ideological views, will obviously see the roles of various agencies differently. Liberals in the Department of Housing and Urban Development (HUD) might see its mission, for example, as providing housing per se and hence promote grants to poor communities and easy loans to the neediest, while conservatives may use the same funds as seed money for corporations to lay cornerstones for economic development and lend money only to those who are safe bets to pay it back, much as the school loan program has worked. Particular bureaucracies, moreover, apart from their different missions and interests, have different traditions and styles. The Department of Defense has, not surprisingly, been aggressive; the Social Security Administration, equally expectedly, cautious; and the postwar State Department has been deemed so conservative as to "flirt with paralysis." It is this sort of organizational behavior that may occasion presidents, or Congress, wanting different policies implemented, to reorganize or create new agencies, as Roosevelt did in the thirties, or to turn to other agencies, as postwar presidents did in using, for example, the CIA instead of the State Department for foreign policy initiatives. This is just one example of how a democracy's politicians can exercise policy control over permanent bureaucrats.

"Knowledge is Power": Democratic Control of Bureaucratic Power

Max Weber himself didn't worry so much about individual or organizational inclinations. In mind of the axiom, "knowledge is power," he was more concerned about the power bureaucrats accumulated through their specialized knowledge and all the information they had—and often kept secret (echoing J. S. Mill, who feared government would gain a monopoly on such knowledge and its application and hence on the nation's "best and brightest"). This sort of concern was evinced in early 1988 by a group of leading university scientists who complained that the Reagan administration was keeping too much aerospace physics research secret and inaccessible to scientists outside of government. Secrecy of this sort of course chiefly retards the progress of science, but when it is exercised by agencies such as the FBI it may have wide civil rights implications as well.[8]

But while Mill worried that through this monopoly on knowledge bureaucracy would become a "power elite" (like Orwell's), Weber expected that bureaucracy's formality and impersonality would have a great "leveling" effect on society and produce mass democracy. While bureaucracy has not developed quite the way Weber envisioned, it has in one way promoted democracy. For, as some scholars argue, while our "representatives" in Congress (and in state legislatures and city councils) aren't really very representative of the population since they tend to be disproportionally wealthy and well educated, our bureaucracies do much more nearly reflect a cross-section of the population, since they employ people from practically all strata of society. This argument does not accommodate the fact that once people become bureaucrats in some agency they are more likely to identify with that agency or the government. Bureaucrats, however, also identify with professional or other groups, which offsets this tendency; Marty Feldman preferred to resign from President Reagan's Council of Economic Advisers and retain the respect of his professional peers at Harvard rather than promote "Reaganomics." Hence the threat of elitism and bureaucracy is likewise considerably diluted by such deconcentrating forces.

Another way this potential danger of a bureaucratic monopoly on expertise is controlled in our system is that, apart from the already competing plurality of organizations, Congress and the White House both have developed their own expert bureaucratic staffs to oversee the operation of *the* bureaucracy.[9] Then, too, interest groups have expertise in their areas, and a multitude of consulting firms make professional expertise available to those who can afford it. And surely it is not too sanguine to assume that bureaucrats themselves, as in our social agencies, look after the interests of their clients and constituents—those who have neither their own interest group nor the money for consultants—since that is, after all, in their own organizational and professional interest as well.

The Evolution of Bureaucracy In America

Among the many who complain about bureaucracy, there are those who claim that it really has no legitimate place in American government to begin with, no constitutional charter like the three branches, in other words. This argument can be diminished by another look at the Constitution and at the Declaration of Independence and its motivations.

It was, after all, British bureaucratic malfeasance that led the colonists to the Declaration and the Revolution to begin with; except for the political issue of taxation without representation, "almost all their complaints involved the abuse of *administrative* powers."[10] The Declaration of Independence charged, for example, that King George "has erected a multitude of new offices, and sent hither swarms of officers to harass our people and eat out their subsistence." More important, the founders' depressing experience with chaotic and inefficient management under the Continental Congress and the Articles of Confederation was a chief reason that they assembled in Philadelphia to create a more efficacious government.[11] In that Convention the founders were of course concerned with broad matters of constitutional design such as the distribution of power, but they did not altogether neglect this administrative side.

Constitutional Bureaucracy?

As we know from the Constitution, Article II, Section 1, "The executive Power shall be vested in a President of the United States of America." This president, in addition to being Commander in Chief of all the armed forces, according to Section 2, "may require the Opinion, in writing, of the principal Officer in each of the executive Departments, upon any Subject relating to the Duties of their respective offices." Section 2 goes on to say that "[the president] shall appoint . . . all other Officers of the United States, whose Appointments are not herein otherwise provided for, and which shall be established by Law." This, in that singularly concise document's lapidary fashion, firmly establishes the legitimate constitutional existence of the American bureaucracy. Like so much else only articulated in such axiomatic form in the Constitution, the matter of administration was more fully expounded in *The Federalist Papers:* Fully ten of them (68–77) are devoted to it and "are widely regarded as the first and perhaps the best treatise ever written on Public Administration."[12] That administration was indeed in the forefront of the founders' minds is, moreover, underscored by the fact that that term appears more often in *The Federalist* than the more expected terms, Congress, President, and Supreme Court.

Bureaucratic Responsibility

Then there are those who argue that bureaucrats only pursue their own ends, much as independent business people do, disregarding what their constitutional aims should be. This too is easily contradicted, not only by the evidence, but by the oath of office—the very one so insidiously violated by Oliver North, the exception that proves the rule. This is an oath, not to follow the leader or to carry out his expressed or presumed will, but to "support and defend the Constitution," to abide by that legal contract, so that it is every federal bureaucrat's responsibility to act not in his own, his leader's, or his bureaucracy's interests except insofar as these coincide with what is constitutional.[13]

The oath is a formal expression symbolic of a deeper personal and social obligation one takes on in accepting the "bureaucratic responsibility" of government employ. When one is hired in a bureaucratic position one does accept a formal responsibility to follow the dictates of one's higher authorities, the orders of one's bureaucratic or political superiors in the hierarchy, and to carry out the specific duties of the position. But beyond that American bureaucrats have obligations to the greater enterprise of which they have become part, and that is "the practice of democratic politics and the cause of effective public policy."[14] This means that, by taking a position in this government's bureaucracy one, in effect, makes a contractual "promise" not only to carry out one's prescribed duties but also to assure that the policies one carries out square with and promote the polity's democratic values, as embodied in the Constitution, and that their implementation is effective. This is one motivation of the occasional whistleblowers we hear of.

It is especially ironic, therefore, that, regardless of party, contemporary presidents—notably Nixon, Carter, and Reagan—have railed at the bureaucracy and, indeed, campaigned on anti-bureaucracy platforms. Given the popular views alluded to at the outset, this had doubtless garnered votes from those disenchanted, for reasons real or imaginary, with government in the form of "bureaucracy." Such anti-bureaucracy sentiment is really rooted in a strong American anti-government tradition generally; rejection of governmental repression was, after all, what moved those who first settled this land to begin with.

Bureaucracy Impeded

The American Revolutionaries violently objected to King George's "abuse of administrative power," particularly his excessive use of patronage to reward office-seekers at their expense. Their Articles of Confederation therefore rejected all forms of executive power as potentially tyrannical and vested all administrative powers in the Congress itself. Administration by congressional committees though resulted, not surprisingly, in "inefficiency and waste, if not downright peculation and corruption,"[15] and revealed an "inherent Principle of Delay," as General George Washington found when he was trying to win the war. At the same time, then-Congressman John Adams, who had initially liked his cousin Sam's idea of legislative administration, found that he was working eighteen-hour days to keep up with the tasks of his ninety committees.

Unworkable as this was, by the time of the Constitutional Convention departments separate from Congress, headed by single executives, had become well established, which likely explains the lack of further ado about them in the Constitution. (Who controls them, though, has remained somewhat ambiguous to this day. Being firmly bound neither to the Congress nor to the president, agencies found themselves on their own; this has led both to their comparative independence, playing one branch off against the other, and to their reliance on law per se.[16] This is one source of the pluralism that prevents

Orwellian bureaucracy.) This original "bureaucracy" was one of exceedingly small proportions: To begin with, there were only the Departments of State, War, and the Treasury. There was an attorney general, but he was simply a lawyer for whom the federal government was just another client. The "bureaucrats" in these departments were outnumbered by congressmen until the 1820s.

What kept more bureaucracy from developing were the vastly simpler governmental needs of the U.S., compared with European nations, through much of the nineteenth century. Three factors may be cited to explain this lack of a burgeoning bureaucracy—and the seemingly ingrained American antipathy to it.

Because of its geographical situation, the U.S. was long able to practice a policy of isolationism, which rendered unnecessary a strong national standing army and the large bureaucratic hierarchy that entails. Then, too, nine out of ten Americans were engaged in farming, self-sufficient and hence not dependent on trade and commerce, interstate or international, which made a domestic bureaucracy superfluous. Finally, what government tasks there remained were still quite simple, which meant that what government employees were needed, except on the highest level, could largely be hired on the principle of popular participation that Jefferson and subsequently Jackson espoused.

But the accelerated industrialization and concomitant urbanization, paralleled by commensurate growth in manufacturing, commerce, and the military expansion necessary to command markets, which occurred throughout the nineteenth century and positively mushroomed in its last decades necessarily placed extraordinary demands on government. As the society experienced such radical transformation from a rural, agricultural one to an urban, industrial one, the informal, local exercises of government administration ineluctably (if reluctantly) followed suit. Let us therefore have a brief look at the specific development of American civil service as it was shaped to meet these demands.

The Development of the American Civil Service

While heretofore the limited and simple responsibilities of government had largely been manageable by political amateurs, this new society and economy demanded the expertise of trained professionals all the way up to the national level. American administrative development is usually chronicled in six stages:

Government by Gentlemen, 1789–1829
Government by the Common Man, 1829–1883
Government by the Good, 1883–1906
Government by the Efficient, 1906–1937
Government by Managers, 1937–1957
Government by Professionals, 1957 to the Present[17]

Government by Gentlemen, 1789-1829

Just as the Constitution sought to reconcile conflicting demands for a strong centralized national government and autonomous states in a symbiosis of shared powers, American administration develped via a dialectic of (republican) representation and (democratic) participation which resulted eventually in a synthesis of the permanent civil service and its politically appointed leadership. Federalists like Hamilton and Washington, though clearly anti-monarchic, equally clearly did not favor genuinely popular democracy; to use a familiar phrase, they preferred government *for* the people to government *by* the people. Consequently, Washington hired officials for the new government on the basis of "fitness of character"—good family background, educational attainment, community esteem, and public honors. This amounted to a self-perpetuating elitism that more thoroughgoing democrats like Jefferson opposed.

Government by the Common Man, 1829-1883

A more Jeffersonian approach to administrative employment was ushered in with the election of Jackson, which itself was owed to the extension of the franchise well beyond the earlier property-owning elite, to the "common man" often without property. But more than just being enabled to vote, the common man was now also to participate in the work of government. How did this common man manage to get a job in government, which had hitherto been largely the preserve of the propertied classes? He got it through more of the same system that already prevailed in American government: patronage. Many traditionally associate the introduction of patronage—the spoils system—with the election and administration of Jackson, but this is a mistake. For the preceding administrations, be they Federalist or Democratic-Republican (even Jefferson's), had given over 90 percent of their higher civil service appointments to individuals of what we would consider the very upper class. Nepotism similarly was rampant and a goodly number of such appointees not only asserted a property right to their offices for themselves but a right of inheritance for their offspring as well. It was, in fact, precisely such pervasive exercise in administrative privilege that led the socially and economically diverse new voters of 1828 to help elect Jackson.

Jackson countered such elitist perpetuation of offices with the notion that a new administration should bring in new officers. The philosophical principle here, as articulated by Jeremy Bentham, was "rotation in office," but the political practice was better expressed in Senator William Marcy's famous phrase, "To the victor belong the spoils"—with the result that the initial "gentlemen's" patronage system was expanded to the "common man."

Ironically, though, this Jacksonian expansion of the spoils system laid the very foundations of the modern bureaucratic system in America. For while in principle purely political patronage should have made a federal job available to anyone who deserved one on the basis of his contribution to the party, in practice Jackson realized, of course, that while federal jobs might still be fairly simple they were hardly so simple that just any fresh-baked backwoods Democratic voter could fill one (or if they were so filled, the Democratic administration would quickly look rather incompetent). Since Jackson could obviously neither change these voters nor renege on the principle of popular participation, he set about to change the nature of federal jobs.

Jackson had told Congress that "The duties of all public officers are, or at least admit of being made, so plain and simple that men of intelligence may readily qualify themselves for their performance." Putting the emphasis on " 'admit of being made' so simple that any intelligent person could do them," the Jackson administration thus sought "to organize the executive department as a rationalized complex of offices, ordered by function, and defined by rules and regulations."[18] This amounted to the beginning in federal government of the classic bureaucratic division of labor with its functional job definitions, the organizational equivalent of the new machines with their interchangeable parts.

Nonetheless, spoils flourished and gave rise to two increasing, indeed often mutually exacerbating problems. For one thing, excessive rotation in office clearly prevented government officials from developing the necessary expertise demanded by an increasingly complex state; for another, corruption expanded exponentially as more and more officials were able to use their offices to enrich themselves, particularly in the notorious city machines.

Government by the Good, 1883–1906

Both those who had not benefited from spoils and those with a sincere interest in reform had long been advocating remedies. In 1853 the Senate actually moved to have department heads classify clerks and to arrange for their promotions on the basis of specific qualifications (implying the beginnings of a "merit" system of employment and promotion). That very year the same problems had come to a head in Britain, and the prime minister appointed an appropriately teamed pair—a politician and a public administrator—to devise a new civil service system to clean up patronage and corruption. The work of this team is pertinent to us because, in recommending "the abolition of patronage and the substitution of recruitment by open competitive examination under the supervision of a central examining board . . . and the filling of the higher posts by promotion from inside on the basis of merit rather than seniority," it directly shaped American civil service reform.[19]

Excursus: Making Policy in Democracy

That such reforms were not implemented in the U.S. for three decades can be easily understood if one recalls the issues that took political priority in that era, which culminated in the Civil War and Reconstruction. It was only well after that that Rutherford B. Hayes, who had been elected with a civil service reform plank in his platform, sent the former chairman of the nominal Civil Service Commission, Dorman Eaton, to Britain to study what had been done in the twenty-odd years since reform had begun there. Eaton's report on that system and its success provided the actual blueprint for the legislative founding of the modern American bureaucracy in the Pendleton Act of 1883.

Yet as with most American public policymaking precept and example did not suffice to lead to legislation; a crisis there was in American government, but the catalyst to action was lacking. This catalyst came in the form of the assassination of President Garfield by a "disappointed office-seeker," as the textbooks all have it. A brief look into this event will give us an instructive insight into our public policymaking process. Following Hayes, James Garfield ran for president in 1880, likewise with civil service reform on his agenda. But because of a factional split in the Republican party between reformers like Garfield (who wanted the Civil War wounds healed as well as the civil service cleaned up) and the so-called Stalwarts (who wanted neither), Garfield, like the proverbial northern presidential candidate who needs a southerner to balance the ticket, had to take on a Stalwart to get nominated.

That is why the reformist Garfield was shot by the "disappointed" office-seeker. This was one Charles J. Giteau who had been trying to get himself one of those cushy patronage posts—ambassador to Paris or consul to Vienna—but the spoils system had simply not been working for him. In the election of Garfield with the Stalwart Chester Arthur as vice president he saw his chance: He shot Garfield, shouting, "I am a Stalwart and now Arthur is president," and fancying that with a reputed spoilsman like Arthur in charge he should get his appointment. Shooting Garfield rather limited his eligibility, but it gave the necessary final impetus to legislative action which took the form of "An Act to Regulate and Improve the Civil Service of the United States," better known as the Pendleton Act of 1883. (Its passage was smoothed considerably by the fact that with it the Republican majority in Congress perpetuated the party faithful in the offices they had just awarded them through patronage.)

Government by the Good, Continued

The Pendelton Act, the charter of American bureaucracy, was based on a draft by Dorman Eaton and set forth, among others, the following familiar bureaucratic principles and practices: It stipulated that the president appoint a bipartisan three-member Civil Service Commission; it provided for examinations for applicants to the classified service (then still only the lowest levels such as clerical, comprising roughly 10 percent of the federal workforce; today the classified service comprises over 90 percent of it); it stipulated that those who did best on the examinations should be appointed; and there was to be a probationary period preceding permanent appointment.[20]

This was the beginning of the "Government by the Good" period. It was "good" because, following the abuses of spoils, such reform of the civil service had come nearly universally to be considered a "good," a moral imperative. It was good because it was based on "merit" rather than money or connections;

it was good because it was in principle open to all on the basis of that individual's merit; and it was good because it was politically neutral, since an individual's employ was based not on politics or payoffs but on neutral competence.

Shortly after the Pendleton Act, an Act to Regulate Commerce established the Interstate Commerce Commission, the first of the independent regulatory agencies. It confirmed the emergence of the bureaucratic state and conformed wholly with the principles of the progressive reformers, for an agency independent of the three political branches "was seen as the proper means of bringing scientific expertise to bear on problems and of shielding the experts from partisan—hence self-seeking—influence."[21] With these foundations of a professional system of public service in place, the further development of American bureaucracy was chiefly a matter of building the system up and enabling it to meet the exigencies of new times.

Government by the Efficient, 1906-1937

While "Government by the Good" brought reformers into the public service, being good alone did not suffice to meet the increasingly complex needs of government in this era. To do this government had, like business and industry, to be made efficient. In the same year as the establishment of the ICC, Woodrow Wilson, then a professor of political science, had already asserted that "a technically schooled civil service will presently have become indispensable" in order that government may carry out its tasks "with the utmost possible efficiency and at the least possible cost."[22] By roughly 1906 enough had been learned to inaugurate an era of "Government by the Efficient." As in the case of "government by the good," here too "efficient" came to be a moral imperative, a value that we still hold today and that persists in maligning bureaucracy.

The move towards "Government by the Efficient" received its impetus from Frederick Taylor's "scientific management" which applied modern science and technology and drew intellectual support from the social interpretation of Darwinism (i.e., that organisms evolved toward their greatest efficiency in order to survive). Scientific management succeeded with some of the new notions of specialization and technique and rendered government more capable of dealing with its routine tasks. But, as one might expect, it put too much emphasis on such technical factors and proved far from adequate to cope with more profound and pervasive problems such as those producing the Depression.

Government by Managers, 1937-1957

The bureaucracy had heretofore chiefly responded to prominent interests, such as those of trade and industry, by establishing the ICC and by subsidizing modern transportation. But to cope with the pervasive devastation of the Depression, it would have to shift its stance from such a "reactive" one to a "proactive" one. It was therefore this greatest modern American domestic crisis that led to the creation of the so-called positive state and hence the creation of a bureaucracy to meet the needs of a twentieth-century society and economy. Crises of such scope had previously come in the form of wars, and World War I had just palpably demonstrated the efficacy of bureaucratic organization.

A crisis such as this meant that government had itself to initiate policies and programs, what with the total bankruptcy of the business interests that had previously engendered most policy demands, and this in turn meant that government had to find individuals who could take the lead with new policy initiatives—policy entrepreneurs, as we have come to call them—and who could equally manage the effective implementation of these policies. It is worth noting that while we associate bureaucracy with government, businesses such as our corporations are every bit as much bureaucracies, and while from them we are familiar with the American business hero, the entrepreneur, entrepreneurs are to be found equally in government bureaucracy, especially beginning with this Roosevelt era of government expansion. Such public entrepreneurs include, among many others, Roosevelt's head of the TVA, David Lilienthal; J. Edgar Hoover, who built a small subsidiary bureau in the Justice Department into one of the most visible and familiar of federal government agencies; Robert Moses who built, for better or worse, the modern American city in the form of the New York megalopolitan area; and Hyman Rickover, familiar as the father of the nuclear navy. Hence this era of American administration, propagated by the recommendations of the "Brownlow Committee," (after its chairman, Louis Brownlow, the prominent public administrationist) in 1937, is termed "Government by Managers." New policies and programs on the domestic front required new organizations for their implementation, particularly in the still neglected social realm, and this gave us our familiar array of "alphabet agencies"—and, in fact, the concrete framework for our contemporary bureaucracy.

Following his most immediate emergency efforts to shore up Americans' pocketbooks and psyches, respectively, by declaring a bank holiday and legalizing 3.2 beer, Roosevelt proposed to Congress the creation of such agencies as the Public Works Administration, the Tennessee Valley Authority, the Federal Deposit Insurance Corporation, the Federal Security Agency, and the U.S. Housing Authority. Until then the federal bureaucracy had consisted chiefly of the original departments—State, War, Treasury; a handful of subsequently created ones—Interior, Justice, Agriculture, Commerce, Labor; and a few independent and legislative agencies such as the ICC and the GAO.

While the first three departments, as their creation hand in hand with the new government suggests, exist because they perform the most essential functions of government, the creation of subsequent ones reflects different evolutionary needs. The first two, Interior (1849) and Justice (1870), were simply responses to growth, in territory and in population. The next three departments to emerge were created not because of such express administrative needs of the government itself but rather in response to pressures from interest groups which had become nationally dominant. The first of these so-called clientele departments was, understandably, Agriculture (1862). Increasing industrialization produced Commerce (1903) and Labor (1913). The remaining departments, in contrast, were established in response to pressing national needs or to give priority recognition to certain problems, and many of these, such as HHS and HUD, grew out of the agencies created during the Roosevelt administration.[23]

Government by Professionals, 1957–the Present

The explosive growth of technology that began in this era, was accelerated by World War II, and became most signally marked by the space triumph of Sputnik in 1957, created an exponential demand for technical expertise in government. Administratively, the Sputnik crisis sparked President Eisenhower's installation of a White House special assistant on science which, in 1962, President Kennedy turned into a full-fledged Office of Science and Technology. This period, continuing into our own time, has been referred to as "Government by Professionals." The government is far and away the nation's largest employer of professionals, and this applies whether we think of researchers in the National Science Foundation, space scientists and engineers in NASA and DOD, nuclear physicists at Los Alamos, doctors in the Public Health Service, lawyers in the Justice Department, economists and other social scientists in Commerce, HUD, or the multitude of other specialists in other agencies.[24]

Bureaucracy and Democracy Today

If we review these periods, we see that there has been a continuous tension between two forces, between the professional (permanent civil service, merit system employment) side, which basically set in with the Pendleton Act, and the political (patronage and temporary appointment) side. We do want to have the best and most expert people doing our government's work for us, and hence have their employ based on their professional credentials and not on their political connections or their ability to "buy" offices, but we also want to maintain democratic control over what these bureaucrats do. These polar desires have, in principle, been reconciled in the structure of our bureaucracy, which can be envisioned as a pyramid composed nearly 95 percent of permanent civil service employees topped by 5 plus percent, roughly, of political officials appointed by the president and party in power. The underlying notion here is that the bureaucracy will thus indeed serve to carry out the voters' desires as expressed through the political representatives they elected.

Responsiveness and Representativeness

There is a good deal of skepticism as to whether bureaucrats actually follow the will of the electorate, as articulated by their politically appointed leaders, and actually change tack with shifting political winds or if they don't rather exclusively follow agendas of their own—the traditional view of the conflict of bureaucracy and democracy. While it is clear that bureaucrats, like all other people, will have their individual political preferences, their own professional priorities, and their own organizational and policy agendas, research and reflection both yield rather more reassuring results than bureaucracy bashers would make one suspect. Those who would say, for example, that it doesn't matter which party is in power, bureaucrats follow their own agendas anyway, are refuted by research that shows that policies implemented when one party was in power differ quite dramatically from those implemented under another part. They may not need any political help in developing policies. They decidedly must have political endorsement and support, not to mention fiscal support which is always ultimately a political question if they are to implement any given policy whatsoever.[25] This apart from their oath to serve the Constitution.

If we believe that we are ruled by a true bureaucracy which does what it will without regard for the wishes of the public as expressed at the polls, we need only consider the far-reaching policy changes that we ourselves have witnessed over recent administrations. Think simply of the vast social policy pushes achieved through the Great Society programs of the Johnson administration on the one hand and the similarly wide-ranging policy rollbacks attained by the Reagan administration—all done through essentially the same permanent bureaucracy. Perhaps bureaucracy is not, after all, the intractable bugbear it is so often made out to be.

Equity and Efficiency

Perhaps the most frequent of the accusations leveled at bureaucracy that were sampled at the outset is inefficiency. Inefficiency, or efficiency, is something that can really only be measured in comparative terms (i.e., delivering some good or service at a lesser cost), as among different firms providing the same good or service competitively. Government agencies, though, for the most part provide goods and services which no other organization can or will provide, such as national defense or environmental protection, because there is no profit in it, or which we, as a community, do not want organizations other than publicly controlled ones to provide, such as police protection. These we do not wish to be in the hands of private powers any more than, say, nuclear power. Where comparative measures can be used, however, such as in waste disposal, governmental agencies, all other factors being equal, have proven quite as capable of efficient performance as private ones.

Usually, too, we get the sense that bureaucracy is a disease afflicting government which private organizations are immune to. Those who are appalled at DOD disasters such as the Sergeant York gun might recall such models of private sector planning as the Ford Motor Company's Edsel; those who were upset when DOT decided that cars could not be started unless seatbelts were buckled might recollect the response that greeted Coca Cola's decision to change its "classic" formula.[27]

But then we must ask ourselves if efficiency is indeed the chief value we want from government. Not according to the Constitution. It warrants us equity and accountability, and to assure the bureaucracy subordinates considerations of pure efficiency to "bureaucratic" rules and regulations and to red tape. No student would like to be graded worse in class for the same performance as another or treated worse in a dean's office than another for the same accomplishments or difficulties; hence the rules and regulations the instructors and deans must apply. And to assure that these are applied equitably, instructors submit records of their actions to deans, and deans submit them to the administration. This renders them accountable to one another and ultimately to their "public," the student constituency, for their actions. It is thus that our very bureaucracies preserve and promote our democracy. For it is precisely through the hierarchic structure of bureaucracies that the rule of law is encouraged and that whole groups of people, whole organizations, can be directly devoted to uniformly carrying out the will of the democratic electorate.

So if you read another bureaucratic horror story of that perennial pensioner of newspaper notoriety who did not get her social security check, think of the 35,999,999 that month alone who not only got their checks on time but got their fair share as well.

Notes

1. Charles T. Goodsell, *The Case for Bureaucracy: A Public Administration Polemic,* 2nd Edition (Chatham, NJ: Chatham House, 1985), 2.
2. Ibid., 6–11.
3. Martin Albrow, *Bureaucracy* (New York: Praeger, 1970), 16–18.
4. Houston *Chronicle,* February 14, 1989.
5. Kenneth J. Meier, *Politics and the Bureaucracy: Policymaking in the Fourth Branch of Government,* 2nd Edition (Monterey, CA: Brooks/Cole, 1987), 30.
6. Goodsell, 113.
7. Max Weber, *The Theory of Social and Economic Organization,* trans. A. M. Henderson and Talcott Parsons (New York: Oxford, 1947), 333–334.
8. Our top bureaucrats, those appointed to head cabinet departments, are called "secretaries" precisely because the role of their original predecessors was administration of the government's "secrets" in confidential counsel to the king or other ruler.
9. Louis Galambos, "By Way of Introduction," in *The New American State: Bureaucracies and Policies since World War II,* edited by Louis Galambos (Baltimore: Johns Hopkins, 1987), 2.

10. James Q. Wilson, "The Rise of the Bureaucratic State," in *Bureaucratic Power in National Policy Making*, 4th Edition, edited by Francis E. Rourke (Boston: Little, Brown, 1986), 125.
11. Michael Nelson, "The Irony of American Bureaucracy," in *Bureaucratic Power in National Policy Making*, 4th Edition, edited by Francis E. Rourke (Boston: Little, Brown, 1986), 165.
12. John A. Rohr, *To Run A Constitution: The Legitimacy of the Administrative State* (Lawrence, KS: University Press of Kansas, 1986), 1.
13. Rohr, 187.
14. John P. Burke, *Bureaucratic Responsibility* (Baltimore: Johns Hopkins, 1986), 42.
15. Nelson, 166.
16. Ibid., 169.
17. Frederick C. Mosher, *Democracy and the Public Service*, 2nd Edition (New York: Oxford, 1982), 56–142.
18. Nelson, 172–174.
19. E. N. Gladden, *A History of Public Administration*, 2 vols. (London: Frank Cass, 1972), II, 312.
20. This civil service system stayed in place until the Carter administration's Civil Service Reform Act of 1978 which abolished the Civil Service Commission and split its conflicting functions into two agencies: the Office of Personnel Management which administers the civil service and the Merit Systems Protection Board which protects federal civil servants.
21. Galambos, 11.
22. Woodrow Wilson, "The Study of Administration," in *Classics of Public Administration*, edited by Jay M. Shafritz and Albert C. Hyde (Oak Park, IL: Moore, 1978), 3.
23. Meier, 21.
24. Matthew A. Crenson and Francis E. Rourke, "By Way of Conclusion: American Bureaucracy since World War II," in *The New American State: Bureaucracies and Policies since World War II*, edited by Louis Galambos (Baltimore: Johns Hopkins, 1987), 147.
25. Joel D. Aberbach, Robert D. Putnam, and Bert A. Rockman, *Bureaucrats and Politicians in Western Democracies*, (Cambridge, MA: Harvard, 1981), 248. The importance of political appointees in the achievement of federal government policy objectives has also been underlined by a new study of the National Academy of Public Administration which demonstrates how much more our system relies on such appointments than that of any other democratic country. Robert Pear, "Agencies Without Bosses Keep Going—But Where?," New York *Times*, March 5, 1989, Section 4, 1. But perhaps the single most instructive (and hilarious) account of the interaction of politicians and bureaucrats is to be found in *The Complete Yes Minister* by Jonathan Lynn and Antony Jay (New York: Harper & Row, 1988).
26. Meier, 5–6.

10 Democracy, Civil Liberties, and Political Tolerance*

JAMES L. GIBSON
AND JAMES P. WENZEL

Introduction

"Democracy" is one of the most basic concepts used by political scientists. Yet it is an elusive and controversial concept. It is elusive because political thinkers have defined it in a variety of different ways. It is controversial because the symbol of democracy has tremendous political importance and influence in the late 20th century. It is not surprising, therefore, that there is confusion and disagreement among those who study democracy.

By "democracy" we mean something that is neither elusive nor controversial, however. "Democracy" is a type of political system that allows all members of society to compete for political power. This open competition is important because it fosters political responsiveness: when leaders must account to the people for their decisions, there is a greater chance that they will be receptive to the preferences of the people. Such responsiveness is what is meant by the concept "majority rule." Robert Dahl states the matter more formally:

> . . . a key characteristic of a democracy is the continuing responsiveness of the government to the preferences of its citizens, considered as political equals . . . in order for a government to continue over a period of time to be responsive to the preferences of its citizens . . . all full citizens must have unimpaired opportunities:
> 1. to formulate their preferences
> 2. to signify their preferences to their fellow citizens and the government by individual and collective action
> 3. to have their preferences weighed equally in the conduct of the government, that is, weighted with no discrimination because of the content or source of the preference."[1]

This is what we mean by "democracy": democracies require that all citizens have an opportunity to compete for political power, individually, or in groups.

One of the greatest difficulties faced by democratic political systems is the tendency of those in power to want to maintain their positions of power. Ambition is not by itself necessarily threatening to democracy, but those in power frequently succumb to the temptation to try to control political competition

---

*This chapter is based in part on research supported by the National Science Foundation (SES 84–21037). NSF is not responsible for any interpretations or analysis.

by eliminating their political competitors. Thus, democracies must anticipate that leaders do not ordinarily want to share political power with their rivals and must try to build institutional mechanisms to maintain open political competition.

Political competition is enhanced to the extent that there are institutional mechanisms that attempt to insure certain rights and freedoms. These rights and freedoms include (1) freedom to form and join organizations; (2) freedom of expression; (3) the right to vote; (4) the right of political leaders to compete for support; (5) access to alternative sources of information; (6) eligibility for public office; (7) free and fair elections; and (8) institutions for making government policies that depend on voters and other expressions of preferences.[2] Where these rights and freedoms exist, political competition is more likely to be open and widespread. If these rights and freedoms are subject to the whim of the rulers, then they are precarious indeed.

Those desiring to create new democratic political systems have for centuries attempted to guarantee these rights and freedoms (as well as obligations) through constitutions. Constitutions are meant to be documents that set up the fundamental structure of the political institutions in a polity. In essence, they amount to a formal statement of the relationship between the people and the government. The United States constitution is a prominent example of such a document. It guarantees the right "of the people peaceably to assemble," as well as many other rights, freedoms, and obligations. The purpose of the constitution is to define the basic rights and structures of the political system. In a democracy, a constitution seeks to guarantee that everyone will have the opportunity to compete for political power.

"Guarantee" is a strong word. Just how does a constitution "guarantee" the right, for instance, to freedom of speech? Certainly, political institutions such as the United States Supreme Court are institutional means through which the United States seeks to guarantee rights. Yet those who write constitutions have often been accused of being too optimistic about the ability of laws alone to create a certain sort of reality. Indeed, rather than creating or sustaining a certain type of political system, constitutions tend to reflect the values of the people living in the system, and thus the values of the citizens are of utmost importance. Learned Hand, a distinguished jurist, made this argument several decades ago:

> I often wonder whether we do not rest our hopes too much upon constitutions, upon laws and upon courts. These are false hopes. Liberty lies in the hearts of men and women; when it dies there, no constitution, no laws, nor court can save it; no constitution, no laws, no court can even do much to save it.[3]

Hand is saying that the only effective guarantee of the right to compete for political power—"liberty"—can be found in the "hearts" of the citizens. Democracy, perhaps more than any other form of government, requires that a citizenry share a commitment to certain values.

When political scientists talk about the commitments of citizens to certain values, they frequently invoke the concept "political culture." The political culture of a polity is the sum of the beliefs, values, and attitudes of those living in the system. Citizens must subscribe to certain beliefs in order for democracies to survive.

What are the elements of a democratic political culture? It is perhaps impossible to provide an exhaustive list of beliefs, but there is widespread agreement that certain beliefs are important. One of the most important is political tolerance. Tolerance is the willingness to "put up with" that with which one disagrees and disapproves. Political tolerance is the preference that the state put up with even those political groups that are disagreeable. One who is politically tolerant is willing to have the political system allow all elements of the political opposition to compete for power.

But just what does *"put up with"* mean? In a democracy, it means to be willing to extend all rights of citizenship to one's political enemies. It means support for the rights of speech, assembly, association, etc., for all political groups, regardless of their ideologies. It also means that government will not discriminate among citizens, either in terms of conferring benefits, allocating rights or imposing sanctions, on the basis of their political preferences. Democracy, as a system of guaranteed opportunities for political competition, requires a citizenry that is willing to support the right of everyone to compete for political power. Democracies require a substantial degree of political tolerance, although it must be recognized that at the extremes too much tolerance may be inimical to democracy. For instance, tolerance of terrorist activity is not required by democratic theory. However, in modern political history, few democratic regimes have been toppled by excessive tolerance, while there are many instances (including Weimar Germany, for example) in which democracy has been lost due to too little tolerance.

We have so far seen that, according to theorists, democracies—systems of open political competition—are thought to depend upon a democratic political culture. One of the key elements of such a culture is political tolerance. It may be fruitful at this point to turn to American political history to see just how well the case of the United States conforms to this theory.

Political Repression in the United States

Americans today are frequently critical of newly-created regimes (e.g., Nicaragua) for their apparent failure to grant full democratic rights to all of their citizens. This criticism may be appropriate, but it is worth remembering that waves of political repression have recurred throughout the history of the United States. Perhaps the most infamous repressive statutes were the Alien and Sedition Acts, passed by Congress in 1798, within a decade of the ratification of the U.S. Constitution and the adoption of the Bill of Rights. This law made it illegal to write, publish, or speak anything "false, scandalous, and malicious" against the government or its officers, "with the intent to defame the . . . government, or either house of the . . . Congress, or the . . . President, or to bring them . . . into contempt or disrepute; or to excite against them . . . the hatred of the good people of the U.S. . . . or to stir up sedition within the United States." (Sedition Act of 1798, a Stat. 596) This law represented a broad assault on the rights of citizens to disagree openly with the policies of the government. It is common in newly-created regimes to find that political competition is so intense that groups try quite vigorously to eliminate their political opposition. Outbreaks of political repression also recur when political insecurity reasserts itself. American political history is replete with examples. Let us briefly consider a few such instances.

Red Scare I

In the twentieth century, there have been recurrent outbreaks of political repression in the United States. Repressive political policy may be defined as policy that places restrictions on oppositionist political activity (activities through which citizens, individually or in groups, compete for political power) by some competitors for power, but not all. The two most prominent examples are commonly referred to as the First Red Scare and the Second Red Scare. The First Red Scare began with World War I and was initially focused on those who opposed American involvement in the war. The legislative centerpieces of the repression of anti-war critics were the 1917 Espionage Act and the 1918 Sedition Act. The former forbade willfully making false statements with the intent to "interfere with the operation or success of the military or naval forces or to promote the success of its enemies," as well as attempts to cause "insubordination, disloyalty, mutiny or refusal of duty in the armed forces." Materials "advocating or urging treason, insurrection or *resistance to any law* of the U.S." were also banned from the U.S. Mail (emphasis added). The Sedition Act was even more repressive in that it outlawed nearly all criticism of the war or the government. As Goldstein has observed:

> Among the types of activities outlawed by it were making statements or performing acts favoring the cause of any country at war with the U.S. or opposing the cause of the U.S. therein; making false statements that would obstruct the sale of war bonds, incite disloyalty or obstruct enlistment; and uttering, printing or publishing any "disloyal, profane, scurrilous or abusive language about the form of the government of the U.S. or the constitution of the U.S., or the military or naval forces of the U.S. or the flag of the U.S. or the uniform of the army or navy" or any language intended to bring these institutions into "contempt, scorn, contumely or disrepute".[4]

These laws were used initially to silence critics of the American war effort. They were also used, however, to stifle a growing socialist movement in the United States. While thousands of individuals were silenced by these acts, perhaps their most significant impact is to be found in their effects on left-wing political organizations that were influential at the time. Organizations such as the Non-Partisan League (NPL), the Industrial Workers of the World

(IWW), the Socialist Party of America, the entire anarchist movement, along with many lesser groups, were broken by government repression during this period. The Democratic administration of Woodrow Wilson and its allies had successfully eliminated nearly all political competition from the left in the United States.

The First Red Scare continued unabated after the close of World War I. Post-war repression is commonly associated with the then U.S. Attorney General A. Mitchell Palmer. He led a concerted attack against miscellaneous leftists, socialists, and Communists, in part based on American fears of the successful Bolsheviks in the Soviet Union, and in part due to fear of the increasingly restive and aggressive labor union movement in the United States. In a sweep reminiscent of some recent drug raids, on January 2, 1920, Palmer led federal raids against radical organizations in over thirty cities across the country, resulting in the arrests of thousands. Shortly thereafter, however, political repression became so extreme that it undercut its own legitimacy: it simply went too far.

Most state governments enthusiastically joined in the attack on miscellaneous leftists by passing criminal syndicalism and sedition laws. "Criminal syndicalism" statutes are usually intended to limit the rights of groups and individuals who advocate the use of illegal means to effect political change. For example, the statute adopted by California shortly after World War I defined the crime as . . .

> any doctrine or precept advocating, teaching or aiding and abetting the commission of crime, sabotage (which word is hereby defined as meaning willful and malicious physical damage or injury to physical property), or unlawful acts of force and violence or unlawful methods of terrorism as a means of accomplishing a change in industrial ownership or control, or effecting any political change.[5]

Between 1917 and 1920, 24 states adopted criminal syndicalism statutes. By 1937, three states had repealed their statutes, although one of these—Arizona—apparently did so inadvertently during recodification. As recently as 1981, 7 of these states still had the statutes on their books, and one additional state—Mississippi—had passed such legislation. These laws were used to repress local leftists and radicals, and resulted in thousands of prosecutions.

One might well ask whether democracies are not entitled to repress those seeking the violent overthrow of the state. From the point of view of theories of democracy, the problem with these laws is that they forbade speech, not criminal behavior. Democracy does not require that criminal behavior be legalized; it does not require that the state allow or encourage its own violent overthrow and destruction. These criminal syndicalism laws, however, were directed against those with "bad ideas," not those engaging in illegal behavior. Democracies can legitimately prohibit revolutionary political behavior, though they cannot limit the right to advocate any political doctrine.

This tide of political repression receded as memories of World War I faded. Perhaps the repression lessened in part because it became so widespread and extreme that it finally mobilized opposition. Aside from more minor episodes, the next major wave of widespread political repression did not reach its crest until the period following World War II.

Red Scare II

The Second Red Scare is commonly associated with the name Joseph McCarthy, Republican Senator from Wisconsin. Most mark its inception with a speech McCarthy made in Wheeling, West Virginia, in February, 1950, claiming to have proof that Communists had infiltrated the American government. In fact, however, it is more appropriate to attribute the initiation of the Second Red Scare to President Truman, who, in March, 1947, announced a series of anti-Communist foreign and domestic policies and positions. Truman established a new government loyalty program, while his Secretary of Labor was calling for the outlawing of the Communist Party. This was only the beginning of a vendetta against leftists in the United States that all but destroyed opposition to the dominance of the Democratic and Republican parties in American politics.

A wide variety of repressive actions was taken by the national and state governments during this period. Two prominent pieces of federal legislation were the Internal Security Act and the Communist Control Act. The Internal Security Act of 1950 forbade efforts to establish a "totalitarian dictatorship" in the United States, and required "Communist-action" and "Communist-front" organizations to register with the Attorney General of the United States. Communists were barred from government employment or employment by private firms doing defense work for the government. Communists were prohibited from applying for or using a passport. Communist organizations were denied tax exemptions, making contributions no longer tax-deductible. The Act also severely penalized aliens who were Communists. (Generally, see Goldstein, 1978, pp. 322–23.) Goldstein calls the Internal Security Act "one of the most massive onslaughts against freedom of speech and association ever launched in American history."[6]

The Communist Control Act began by declaring that the Communist Party "should be outlawed." It asserted that the Communist Party was "not entitled to any of the rights, privileges and immunities attendant upon legal bodies created under the jurisdiction" of American law. The power to declare organizations, including labor unions, "Communist-infiltrated" (based on criteria such as whether the organization promoted the Communist movement and whether it was controlled by pro-Communists) was granted to the government. Once a labor union or other organization received the designation "Communist-infiltrated" it lost all of its rights and privileges, and its members were barred from employment in defense facilities, denied access to classified information, were ordered to register, and were ineligible for union office. The effect of the Communist Control Act was at once the persecution of Communists and the persecution of labor unions.

The state governments were also heavily involved in the persecution of Communists and other left-wing groups. Table 1 reports the various state laws directed at limiting the rights of Communists. Of the 50 American states, 25 took none of these actions against Communists. Two states—Arkansas and Texas—banned Communists from the ballot and from public employment, as well as banning the party and requiring that Communists register with the government. Another nine states took all three measures against Communists, but did not require that they register with the government. The remaining fourteen states took some, but not all of these, actions against Communists. These laws are only representative—they are not exhaustive—of the sorts of repression carried on by the states. Moreover, many cities and towns adopted their own ordinances. There were few safe havens in the United States for Communists during the heyday of the Truman/McCarthy era. This legislation was extremely effective at destroying the American Communist movement. Not only were top Communist leaders imprisoned, but the party itself was decimated. Membership in the Communist Party, U.S.A., dropped from over seventy thousand in 1946 to less than twenty-five thousand in 1954.

Table 1 Political Repression of Communists by American State Governments

State	Banned from Public Employment	Banned from Politics	Banned Outright	Scale Score
Arkansas	Yes	Yes	Yes	3.5
Texas	Yes	Yes	Yes	3.5
Arizona	Yes	Yes	Yes	3.0
Indiana	Yes	Yes	Yes	3.0
Massachusetts	Yes	Yes	Yes	3.0
Nebraska	Yes	Yes	Yes	3.0
Oklahoma	Yes	Yes	Yes	3.0
Pennsylvania	No	Yes	Yes	3.0
Tennessee	No	Yes	Yes	3.0
Washington	No	Yes	Yes	3.0
Alabama	Yes	Yes	No	2.5
Louisiana	Yes	Yes	No	2.5
Michigan	Yes	Yes	No	2.5
Wyoming	Yes	Yes	No	2.5
Florida	Yes	Yes	No	2.0
Georgia	Yes	Yes	No	2.0
Illinois	Yes	Yes	No	2.0
California	Yes	No	No	1.0
New York	Yes	No	No	1.0

Table 1 Political Repression of Communists by American State Governments—(*continued*)

State	Banned from Public Employment	Banned from Politics	Banned Outright	Scale Score
Delaware	No	No	No	0.5
Mississippi	No	No	No	0.5
New Mexico	No	No	No	0.5
Alaska	No	No	No	0.0
Colorado	No	No	No	0.0
Connecticut	No	No	No	0.0
Hawaii	No	No	No	0.0
Iowa	No	No	No	0.0
Idaho	No	No	No	0.0
Kentucky	No	No	No	0.0
Kansas	No	No	No	0.0
Maryland	No	No	No	0.0
Maine	No	No	No	0.0
Minnesota	No	No	No	0.0
Missouri	No	No	No	0.0
Montana	No	No	No	0.0
North Carolina	No	No	No	0.0
North Dakota	No	No	No	0.0
New Hampshire	No	No	No	0.0
New Jersey	No	No	No	0.0
Nevada	No	No	No	0.0
Ohio	No	No	No	0.0
Oregon	No	No	No	0.0
Rhode Island	No	No	No	0.0
South Carolina	No	No	No	0.0
South Dakota	No	No	No	0.0
Utah	No	No	No	0.0
Vermont	No	No	No	0.0
Virginia	No	No	No	0.0
West Virginia	No	No	No	0.0
Wisconsin	No	No	No	0.0

Note: A "bonus" of 0.5 was added to the scale score if the state also required that communists register with the government. See footnote 8 for details of the assignments of scores to each state.

Political Repression in Texas

Texas wasted little time in boarding the anti-Communist bandwagon, and it soon became one of the most repressive states in the Union (see Table 1, above). A variety of legislation was passed, although Governor Shivers never got his wish for a law establishing the death penalty for Communists. The Communist Control Act of 1951 is an example of one of the most repressive pieces of legislation written in the U.S. It states that a "'Communist' is a person who . . . commits or advocates the commission of any act reasonably calculated to further the overthrow of the Government of the United States of America, the government of the State of Texas, or the government of any political subdivision of either of them, by force or violence" (Vernon's Anno. Civ. Stat., Art. 6889–3, Sec. 1). This definition was passed as state law only six years after the United States had fought a war against Fascism, with Communists as allies. Ironically, it also makes white racists seeking to overthrow the government and establish a nation for whites only "Communists"! Nonresident Communists who visited Texas for five consecutive days were required to register with the Department of Public Safety, were to be fingerprinted, and were required to give "any . . . information requested by the department of public safety which is relevant to the purposes of this statute." (Sec. 4). Failure to comply was a felony, carrying a maximum prison term of ten years and a maximum fine of $10,000, or both (Sec. 4E). Three years later the Communist Party was outlawed altogether. Those who "assist in the formation of, or participate in the management of, or contribute to the support of, or become or remain a member of, or destroy any books or records of files of, or secrete any funds in this State of the Communist Party of the United States or any component or related part or organization thereof . . ." were subject to a fine of $20,000 and imprisonment for 20 years in a Texas prison. Moreover, those convicted were explicitly denied suspended or probated sentences (Vernon's Anno. Civ. Stat. Art. 6889–3A). Prosecution of these cases was given "priority over other cases in settings for hearing." Search warrants were authorized "for the purpose of searching for and seizing any books, records, pamphlets, cards, receipts, lists, memoranda, pictures, recordings, or any written instruments showing that a person or organization is violating or has violated any provision of this Act." In a move that truly distinguishes the Texas legislature from many other states, up to $75,000 was appropriated for enforcement of the law. It was not until 1965, in Stanford v. Texas (379 US 476), that the Communist Suppression Act was rendered ineffective by the United States Supreme Court.

In 1953, the state legislature forbade the payment of any state compensation for services performed by anyone who would not execute a loyalty oath. The oath attests to having never been a member of the Communist Party, as well as not having been a member of various "subversive organizations" in the preceding five years. The Act applied to compensation for services by doctors, lawyers, engineers, architects, skilled craftsmen, and laborers, and for special and under-cover services of law enforcement. No state or local jobs could be held by Communists. Jobs could be denied "where reasonable grounds exist, on all of the evidence, for the employer or other superior of [the potential employee] to believe that such person is a Communist or a knowing member of a Communist front organization" (Sec. 7). Another law required all students and teachers at Texas colleges and universities to execute the following oath:

I swear or affirm that I believe in and approve the Constitution of the United States and the principles of government therein contained, and will not in any manner aid or assist in any effort or movement to subvert or destroy the Government of the United States or of any State or of any political sub-division thereof by force, violence, or any other unlawful means. In the event of war with any foreign nation, I will not support or adhere to the government of such foreign nation.

I swear or affirm that I am not and have not during the past two (2) years been a member of or affiliated with any society or group of persons which teaches or advocates that the Government of the United States or of any State or of any political subdivision thereof should be overthrown or destroyed by force, violence, or any other unlawful means, or the adherence to the government of any foreign nation in the event of war between the United States and such foreign nation (Vernon's Anno. Civ. Stat., Art. 2908b, Sec. 1).

Communists were prohibited from becoming pharmacists. The State Board of Education was prohibited from purchasing textbooks for use in the public schools unless the author of the textbook filed an oath asserting that he or she was not a Communist or a member of another "subversive" organization (Vernon's Anno. Civ. Stat., Art. 6252–7, Sec. 3). Subversives were also denied property tax exemptions (Vernon's Anno. Civ. Stat., Art. 7150, Sec. 20). So pervasive was the repression of Communists that residents of Texas were probably "safer" from the Communist menace than any other people in the world.

The "Communist issue" in both the U.S. and in Texas was far from being limited to Communists. Indeed, there is very little relationship between the presence of Communists in a state and the adoption of legislation to repress communism. Instead, anti-Communist attacks were used to smear and undercut the legitimacy of left-wing and progressive organizations. For instance, racial desegregation in the South was, for many, a "Communist plot," instigated by "outside Communist agitators". Labor movements were, of course, routinely "infiltrated" and controlled by Communists. "Communist-front" organizations contaminated every sort of liberal and left-wing cause by their cooperation and participation. Even those favoring progressive types of education were charged with being "dupes" of anti-family, anti-children, and anti-god Communists. To label one's opponents as "Communists" was to declare their position to be "un-American" and outside the boundaries of legitimate political disagreement. Such labels were therefore very valuable political tools.

Just how great was the impact of Truman/McCarthyism on American politics? Though it is difficult to assess the full consequences, several facts are known. It has been estimated that of the work force of 65 million Americans, 13.5 million were affected by loyalty and security programs during the Truman/McCarthy era. Over 11,000 individuals were fired as a result of government and private loyalty programs. Over 100 people were convicted under the federal Smith Act, and 135 people were cited for contempt by the House Un-American Activities Committee. Nearly one-half of the social science professors teaching in universities at the time expressed medium or high apprehension about possible adverse repercussions to them as a result of their political beliefs and activities.[7] Perhaps the most chilling and long-term consequence of the era was the "Silent Generation" that emerged from Truman/McCarthyism. The resulting willingness of citizens to accept blindly the repression of the government may well have created a climate in which the debacles of Vietnam and Watergate could occur.

Were the two Red Scares of the twentieth century aberrations in American politics, or do they reflect a more fundamental antipathy toward political nonconformists? It is of course impossible to answer this question definitively, even if it might be extremely important to do so. Perhaps a useful way to pursue this problem further is to consider the degree to which intolerance is rooted in the more basic political culture of the United States. By doing so, perhaps we can draw some tentative conclusions about whether political repression reflects a temporary departure from basic democratic practices and beliefs, or whether the potential for political repression is a fundamental attribute of the American polity. It is to this task that we turn next.

American Political Culture

The political culture of a polity is a mixture of the beliefs, values, and attitudes of the citizens and leaders of the political system. When discussing democracy, an important element of the political culture is political tolerance. Just how tolerant is the culture of the United States?

We can only answer this question for more recent American political history because surveys, a basic source of our understanding of political culture, were not regularly conducted prior to World War II. The first major survey study of political tolerance in the U.S. was conducted in 1954 by the sociologist Samuel C. Stouffer.

Stouffer, personally concerned about the widespread political repression in the United States during the Truman/McCarthy era, sought to determine whether the repression was attributable, in a perverse sort of way, to democracy itself. That is, Stouffer wondered whether the repression of the era was an example of majority tyranny: the decision by the majority to withdraw political rights from the minority. Having witnessed mass-based tyranny during the 1930s and 1940s, many feared that the greatest threat to democracy was the people themselves. Many suspected that the political culture of the United States was not supportive of the rough and tumble political competition on which democracies thrive. Stouffer sought an answer to these questions through surveys of both ordinary citizens and political leaders.

Stouffer's findings were extraordinarily disconcerting for democrats. Most Americans were found to be extremely intolerant of the most important political minority at the time—political leftists. Table 2 reports some of the basic data from Stouffer's survey. Though there is some variability in the levels of support for political repression across the various groups and activities, these data give credence to the view that the American political culture is extremely intolerant.

Table 2 Tolerance in the United States, 1954

	Tolerance of Admitted Communists	
	Masses	Elites
Allow to speak	27	51
Allow a book in the library	27	42
Not fire high school teacher	5	9
Not fire college teacher	6	11
Not fire defense plant worker	6	5
Not fire store clerk	26	45
Not fire radio singer	29	48
Not boycott soap advertised by a communist	56	69

At the same time, Stouffer found that community leaders were vastly more tolerant than the ordinary citizens. These data are also reported in Table 2. For a variety of reasons, those able to achieve some degree of political power and influence in America are considerably more tolerant than the citizens whom they govern.

It is fair to ask, however, whether Stouffer's findings still characterize American political culture today. The answer is that they do, although there is an important caveat. Today, surveys reveal that the American people are far more tolerant of Communists and some other unpopular groups (see Table 3). At the same time, however, when survey respondents are asked about groups that they dislike a great deal—in contrast to being asked about groups preselected by the researchers—they are just as intolerant today as they were in the past. For example, though nearly two-thirds of the American people would allow a Communist to make a speech, only one-half would allow a group they dislike a great deal to make a speech. Only 16 percent of the American people would not ban members of their most disliked group from becoming president, and only 19 percent would allow members of the group to teach in public schools.[8] These data are testimony to the fact that the American people have not become more tolerant over the last several decades. While the American people may have become more tolerant of Communists, they have not become more tolerant in general.

It is not difficult to understand why tolerance of Communists and other left-wing groups has increased. Stouffer's survey was conducted during a period of widespread concern, if not hysteria, about the "Red Menace." Many feel that this concern was created by irresponsible political leaders seeking to make political capital out of the issue. The Korean War had just recently ended, and Senator McCarthy was in the process of conducting a congressional investigation (broadcast on television) of Communist influence in the United States Army. As the Communist "threat" has subsided in the United States—as domestic Communists were all but eliminated by government repression, as the United States established diplomatic relations with the People's Republic of China, as "detente" became popular—willingness to allow Communists basic political rights has increased. At the same time, however, people can still identify groups that they wish to repress, even though not everyone agrees that Communists represent the greatest menace. For instance, most of the black survey respondents name the Ku Klux Klan as the group they dislike the most. Thus, in only a limited sense is political tolerance more widespread today than it was in the 1950s.

There is an important sense in which political tolerance differs today, however. In the 1950s political intolerance was highly focused: that is, nearly everyone supported repressing left-wing groups. Today, political intolerance is more dispersed; there is less agreement on which political minorities to repress, even if nearly everyone favors the repression of some group. For instance, when asked to name a group they disliked the most, there is very little agreement even on whether these are groups on the left-wing or on the right-wing, and even less agreement on the specific groups.[9] Some have hypothesized that because there is no agreement on whom to repress, there are no concerted demands for the government to engage in political repression, with the result that there is more freedom available today. Some Americans want to repress the left-wing, some the right-wing, and because they cannot agree on whom to repress, there is less repression.

On the other hand, some believe that political tolerance in general has in fact increased recently. These scholars argue that larger changes in society have taken place that contribute to greater tolerance. The most obvious such change is in levels of education. In 1950, 66 percent of Americans over the age of 24 were not high school graduates; in 1979, the figure had dropped to 32 percent. Only six percent had completed college in 1950; in 1979, 16 percent had completed college. Since education is a major contributor to political tolerance, tolerance may have increased.

Other changes in society are believed to have had similar effects. For instance, as women increasingly join the workforce, they are exposed to a greater variety of social and political viewpoints. This exposure to diversity contributes to political tolerance. Similarly, geographic mobility increases tolerance, as does youth. As the population became more mobile, and as the average age dropped in the post-war years, greater tolerance would be expected. Thus, some believe that there is, or at least should be, more tolerance today than in the past.

Political Tolerance in Texas

Just how politically tolerant are Texans? Unfortunately, no statewide surveys on this topic have been conducted. Some limited evidence is available, however. Though we must be cautious about drawing conclusions about states on the basis of national surveys, a state-by-state analysis of the Stouffer survey data from 1954 reveals that Texas was among the more intolerant states in the Union. However, a very similar survey conducted in 1973 showed Texans to be only somewhat more intolerant than the national average and considerably more tolerant than in 1954. Perhaps increasing political tolerance in Texas reflects the growing political diversity resulting from the influx of immigrants and emigrants. In both surveys, the political leaders of Texas scored as among the most intolerant in the nation (although they were still more tolerant than ordinary residents of Texas).

Linking Political Repression with the Culture of Intolerance

The basic finding that elites are more tolerant than masses has given rise to the so-called "elitist theory of democracy." This theory seeks to account for the seeming inconsistency between relatively more intolerant opinion and relatively less repressive policy. It asserts that public policy is tolerant in the United States because the processes through which citizen preferences are linked to government action do not faithfully translate intolerant opinion inputs into repressive policy outputs. In general, it is uncommon to find a great deal of congruence between constituents' preferences and the actions of representatives, and so it not altogether surprising that public policy concerning the rights of political minorities fails to reflect the intolerant attitudes of the mass public. Instead, the extent that policy is protective of political minorities reflects the preferences of elites, preferences that tend to be more tolerant than those of the mass public.

For a variety of reasons, those who exert influence over the policy-making process in the United States are more willing to restrain the coercive power of the state in its dealings with political opposition groups. Thus, the elitist theory of democracy asserts that there is a linkage between policy and opinion, but that the linkage is to tolerant elite opinion, not to intolerant mass opinion. Mass opinion is ordinarily not of great significance; public policy reflects elite opinion and is consequently tolerant of political diversity. Ironically, the democratic character of the regime is enhanced through the political apathy and immobility of the masses, according to the elitist theory of democracy.

The elitist theory nonetheless asserts that outbreaks of political repression are attributable to the mass public. While the preferences of ordinary citizens typically have little influence over public policy—in part, perhaps, because citizens have no real preferences on most civil liberties issues—the intolerance of the mass public sometimes becomes mobilized. Under conditions of perceived threat to the status quo, for instance, members of the mass public may become politically active and demand political repression. When the masses are basically quiescent, elite preferences—in the main more tolerant than the masses—dominate public policy. Thus, the elitist theory of democracy seems to account for at least a portion of the political repression of the Truman/McCarthy era.

This view is surely too simplistic. First, a variety of institutional mechanisms tend to block even determined majorities. The powers of the federal judiciary are perhaps the most significant such institutional impediments. Federal judges (indeed, all judges) have the power of judicial review, the power to declare laws to be null and void if they are incompatible with the United States Constitution. For example, the village of Skokie, Illinois, passed three ordinances limiting freedom of assembly when the Nazi Party attempted to hold a demonstration there. One of the ordinances forbade dissemination of any material "which promotes and incites hatred against persons by reason of their race, national origin, or religion. . . ." Another ordinance prohibited people from engaging "in any march, walk or public demonstration as a member or on behalf of any political party while wearing a military-style uniform." These ordinances were overwhelmingly supported by the residents of Skokie. The village government tried to use the laws to block a demonstration by the Nazis. The Nazis sued in federal court and, ultimately, won a decision from a federal judge that the ordinances violated the rights to freedom of speech and assembly guaranteed to all Americans by the first amendment to the United States Constitution. Because the Skokie laws were incompatible with the Constitution, they were null and void. The right of the Nazis to demonstrate was thus secured by the federal judiciary, even in the face of a determined political majority seeking political repression.

The federal judiciary can be such an important limit on the intolerance of the majority because federal judges are appointed to life terms. That is, once appointed, they need not face the wrath of the majority through the electoral process. Though this lack of accountability has many critics, the framers of the American Constitution very specifically designed the judiciary this way in order to protect the rights of political minorities. This is not to say that the courts always stand as a bulwark of democracy. There are many instances of the federal judiciary ratifying the repression of political minorities. For instance, in 1944 the United States Supreme Court ruled that the forced incarceration of American citizens of Japanese descent, even though these Americans were neither convicted of nor even *charged* with any crime, was compatible with the Constitution. Indeed, there is evidence that the United States Supreme Court has been more active in protecting *privileged* minorities such as the wealthy than it has been in protecting *underprivileged* and unpopular political minorities. Nonetheless, the fact that federal judges need not face the majority and account for their decisions offers some opportunity to block the repressive desires of tyrannical majorities.

Other institutional mechanisms to neutralize tyrannical majorities were designed by the framers of the constitution. For instance, the framers believed that in a federal system—one in which there is a sharing of power between the national and state governments, with certain specific powers reserved for each level—the powerful national government could be kept in check by the competing interests of the various segments of society. Like the theory of pluralistic intolerance already discussed, it was expected that those pursuing repressive schemes at the national level would be blocked by those valuing liberty more highly. The structure of the national government—the difficulties in passing legislation imposed by bicameralism and separation of powers—insured that only the most determined of majorities would succeed in passing legislation.

At the same time that federalism describes the mechanism protecting liberty from the national government, however, it offers no remedy for abuses of political minorities at the state level. The pluralism of interests that may emerge at the national level may not emerge in many states due to their homogeneity. Without a diversity of interests, one "faction" is not counterbalanced by other "factions." Certainly, many states (e.g., California, Michigan, New York) are sufficiently diverse economically and politically to insure that political competition occurs. But in many states (e.g., Alabama, Oklahoma, Wyoming) political competition does not occur because there is no balancing of interests. Without state-level pluralism a major means for correcting the abuses of tyrannical majorities is not available.

Political repression and political intolerance in their more global formulations are often found at the local level as well. A good example of intolerance in action can be found in the politics of homosexuality in Houston, Texas. Houston has a fairly strong and politically active homosexual community. At the same time, the people of Houston are not very tolerant of gays. By looking at the ways in which this minority conflicts with the majority in Houston, we can get some sense of the importance of political intolerance in American politics.

Let us be clear about how an examination of the politics of homosexuality can elucidate our consideration of democracy and political tolerance. We are considering the right of homosexuals to be treated by the government in an even-handed fashion; that is, the right to be free from governmental discrimination. We are focusing on homosexuals here, but might just as well focus on any political or social minority that is unpopular with the majority. Homosexuality may well be an entirely private matter; however, the decision of a government to differentiate among citizens on the basis of sexual orientation lodges the issue squarely in the political arena. In this analysis it is unnecessary to consider the morality of homosexuality; we consider instead the politics of homosexual rights.

The Politics of Homosexual Rights in Houston

Homosexuals have become a salient and active force in Houston city politics. They have organized politically through the Gay Political Caucus (GPC).

The organization openly supports and endorses candidates for public office. Gays have some considerable political influence in Houston: the gay community is commonly given some degree of credit for the electoral success of Houston's mayor, as well as for several members of the city council.

Like many municipalities, Houston has an ordinance that prohibits employment discrimination based on sex, creed, age, color or national origin. In December, 1983, Councilman-at-large Anthony Hall proposed an amendment to this ordinance which would have added the term "sexual orientation" to the list of characteristics that were already banned as a basis for job discrimination. Although the matter was not at this point placed on the agenda, six months later an amendment to the existing ordinance and a resolution were brought before the city council for a vote. The amendment forbade discrimination on the basis of sexual orientation in city employment, while the resolution forbade affirmative action for homosexuals. In close ballots (8–6 and 8–7), with heated debate, both the amendment and the resolution were passed.

Proponents of the amendment adding "sexual orientation" to the city's nondiscrimination ordinance argued that this simply codified existing city practice (Mayor Whitmire had strong backing from Houston's gay community and her administration's formal policy was not to discriminate based on sexual orientation). However, there were some practical changes brought about as a consequence of the amendment. It allowed grievances to be brought under the civil service code in cases alleging discrimination, and it expressly forbade using sexual orientation as a criterion for hiring and promotion considerations.

Once the City Council passed the amendment, there was an immediate effort on the part of opponents to have the measures submitted to the voters in the form of a referendum. That submission would require 28,000 signatures (out of an electorate of 750,000) on a petition calling for a referendum. Within a two week period the anti-gay rights forces were able to gather 61,000 signatures. According to leaders of the petition drive, about one-half of these signatures were gathered in churches.[10] The election was set for January 19, 1985.

During the campaign the strategy of the Gay Political Caucus was to minimize public attention to the issue, hoping that a low turnout would reduce the size of the loss, or perhaps even lead to a victory. To the extent that the pro-gay rights forces campaigned, they emphasized that the issue was job discrimination, not gay rights. The bulk of their campaign effort was directed at quietly identifying their supporters and preparing to get the vote out. On the other hand, the opponents of the ordinance sought the widest possible public attention to the controversy. They attempted to associate the ordinance with issues touching sensitive nerves. They too were concerned about turnout, and sought to mobilize the electorate by appealing more to issues such as homosexual teachers in the public schools than to abstract discussions concerning equal protection of the laws. For instance, John Goodner—a councilman who spearheaded the anti-ordinance forces—observed: "Homosexuals are poor role models for children. Therefore gays should be shut out of such city jobs as recreation supervisors and police officers."[11] Occasionally there were reasoned arguments about the referendum being a political contest for power among groups with competing interests; however, the bulk of the campaign rhetoric tended to play on fears. The threat of AIDS was frequently raised, as were the dangers of homosexual lifestyles to public morality.

The most visible supporters of the ordinance were the Mayor and the councilmen who voted for the amendment and the resolution. Others voicing support included the League of Women Voters, former congresswoman Barbara Jordan, plus several local black elected officials and the Methodist and Episcopal bishops. The principal opponents were city councilman John Goodner, the Chamber of Commerce (in Houston, an organ of considerable power), the Harris county Republican party, and a host a religious leaders.

On January 19, 1985, Houstonians voted by a four to one margin to repeal the gay rights ordinance. Though it was expected that the ordinance would be repealed, the size of the vote was unpredicted. Before the election, many observers expressed doubt that as many as 10 percent of the electorate would turn out for the referendum. Only 13 percent had voted in the bond election held four months earlier, despite campaign expenditures of over a million and half dollars; in contrast, in the gay rights referendum the anti-gay forces spent $525,000 and the pro-gay forces spent $266,000. Nevertheless, turnout was 31 percent (compared to 34 percent in the previous contest for mayor). Generally, the referendum electorate appears to have been drawn from the more conservative sector of Houston, though the traditional impediments to voting—low information, low interest, low efficacy, etc.—demonstrated their usual effectiveness. Obviously, this issue touched the nerves of many Houstonians.

Another surprising aspect of the vote was the low turnout of blacks. Black turnout in mayoral elections usually equals white turnout. Even in the bond election, black turnout was only six percent lower than white turnout. However, only 13 percent of the blacks voted in the January 19th referendum compared to 41 percent of the whites. The most logical explanation is that blacks were cross-pressured; that is, they had reasons to support the gay rights side, but they also had reasons to oppose the issue. Because homosexuals clearly face discrimination, they would seem to be a natural ally of the black community. On the other hand, there is no reason to suspect that the practice of homosexuality is any more popular among blacks than among whites. The consequence of these cross-pressures was, apparently, nonvoting. Among whites, there were fewer cross-pressures, with the result that a larger proportion of white registered voters voted.

Liberals were also cross-pressured by the issue. An unusually large number of liberals claimed to have no opinion about the referendum and about homosexuals.[12] Though liberals have tended to support victimized minorities in general, they were very uneasy about supporting gay rights in the referendum. Conservative forces found the issue very easy—they do not like homosexuals, so they voted against gay rights. Many liberals, opposed to homosexuality as well, found it nonetheless impossible to vote against gay rights. Consequently, they did what many blacks did: they did not vote.

The voters of Houston made it plain that they did not support equal employment rights for homosexuals. But does this mean that they are willing to support more widespread political repression of homosexuals? We can best address this question by examining the opinions of Houstonians toward the political rights of gays. Table 4 reports the survey responses on several measures of willingness to support the denial of rights to homosexuals.

Only a minority of registered voters in Houston is willing to support any particular form of political repression against homosexuals. Even on the sensitive question of whether gays should be allowed to teach in the public schools, only slightly more than one-third would forbid homosexuals to be teachers. Though these data seem to reveal a great deal of tolerance on particular items, less than one-third of the respondents oppose any of the forms of repression against homosexuals. Even discounting the question of gays teaching in schools, less than a majority would allow homosexuals all of the political rights enjoyed by members of mainstream political organizations. These results reveal a substantial degree of political intolerance.

Table 4. Willingness to Repress Homosexuals—Houston Registered Voters

	Percent Supporting Political Repression Against Homosexual Political Organizations		
	Support	**Unsure**	**Oppose**
require to register with the government	19	21	61
prohibit from holding demonstrations	19	12	70
outlaw the organization	16	11	73
tap telephones	4	8	88
prohibit from running for public office	19	10	71
prohibit from teaching in public schools	37	16	47
support no repression		31	
support no repression except teaching in public schools		44	

More generally, Houstonians do not like homosexuals. Over two-thirds of those with an opinion believe that homosexual relationships are always wrong. While nearly one-third of the sample claims to have no opinion on whether they "like" homosexuals, among those with opinions, one-half dislike them a great deal. Approximately 17 percent view homosexuals as a great threat to

Houston; 41 percent perceive them as some threat; and 42 percent see them as no threat at all. Perceptions of the homosexual threat are roughly the same as perceptions of threats from Communists and from the Ku Klux Klan. Indeed, it is difficult to imagine a political minority that is more disliked in Houston than homosexuals. Thus, it appears quite likely that many of those who voted against equal employment rights for gays would be quite happy to have even more repressive legislation directed against the homosexual minority.

There are, however, limits to this intolerance. Within a year of the gay rights referendum, the voters of Houston had another opportunity to register their opinions on homosexuals. Encouraged by the overwhelming rejection of gay employment rights, a former Houston mayor challenged the incumbent. The challenger ran on a latent platform of opposition to gay rights. Midway through the campaign the challenger inadvertently succeeded in bringing the issue of homosexuality to the foreground. When asked off-the-air at a local television station what the challenger would do about the AIDS problem, he responded "Shoot the Queers!" Unfortunately for him, his microphone was in fact turned on, and the comment was broadcast. The challenger himself believes that the comment was fatal to his campaign, and many observers suggest that the gaffe may have served to make anti-gay sentiments less legitimate as an election issue. The incumbent won re-election easily.

This episode is useful because it reveals something about the limits of intolerance. While the American political culture has many significant elements of intolerance, it does not openly espouse the political repression of minorities. Just as with racial prejudice, there are few areas of the country in which it is socially acceptable to advocate anti-democratic views. Instead, these views are manifest only in subtle ways. While it may be rare to find those who openly advocate stripping homosexuals of their political rights, there are many who would couch their opposition in language rejecting "special privileges" for gays. It is legitimate to seek to limit the rights of political minorities in some fashions, while illegitimate to do so in other ways.

The gay rights referendum was misunderstood by many voters. Without doubt, the ordinance did not call for affirmative action for homosexuals in city hiring; indeed, it specifically forbade it. Nonetheless, it is much more socially acceptable to be against affirmative action for a group than to seek its political repression. Thus, many anti-gay rights voters actually believed that they were voting against affirmative action for homosexuals, because that was a more socially acceptable way of expressing anti-gay sentiment.

In the final analysis, the politics of homosexuality in Houston seems to fit well with the Elitist Theory of Democracy. It was political elites who took the initiative of seeking to institutionalize the rights of homosexuals via the ordinance. The issue caused a decidedly anti-democratic response from ordinary citizens, once they became aware of the ordinances. Ordinary people were mobilized by counter-elites. Just as predicted, the involvement of the mass public in an issue of minority rights resulted in a repressive outcome. At some point, however, the intolerance of the majority reached its limit and further repression became illegitimate. Thus, the issue subsided, and today homosexuals perceive little more repression in Houston than they did prior to the adoption of the referendum in 1984.

Conclusions

How then can democracy, by which we mean rule by majority preferences but without restraints on the opportunities of political minorities to become political majorities, be maintained? This question is certainly not an easy one in light of the fairly widespread political intolerance in the United States. We will conclude with some observations about the fate of democratic government within the context of an anti-democratic populace.

It may well be that under normal circumstances democracies do not require citizens who are committed to democratic values. So long as citizens are willing to defer to the more tolerant preferences of the ruling elites, democracies can function. Yet, as we have seen, the people ultimately have some impact on politics in democratic polities. Even if limited to times of crisis, mass political mobilizations do occur and democracies must develop some strategy for dealing with them. In the long term, mass political apathy is not a bulwark of democracy.

Perhaps in the end we must return to liberal democratic theorists such as J. S. Mill to understand democracy. Mill and others have argued that the value of democracy is to be found in its salutatory effects on citizens. As citizens take an active role in their self governance, they develop capabilities for governance, capabilities that at once make them better citizens and better individuals. In denying individuals the opportunity for meaningful political participation, democracies may be temporarily neutralizing the anti-democratic tendencies of their citizenry. But in the long run, democracy can only prevail when liberty "lives in the hearts of men and women." In the long run, democracy can only prevail when citizens learn to tolerate political differences with their fellow citizens.

References

Almond, Gabriel A., and Sidney Verba. *The Civic Culture: Political Attitudes and Democracy in Five Nations* (Princeton, N.J.: Princeton Up, 1963).

Bachrach, Peter., *The Theory of Democratic Elitism* (Boston: Little, Brown, 1967).

Brown, Ralph S., *Loyalty and Security* (New Haven: Yale UP, 1958).

Carleton, Donald E., *Red Scare!* Austin, TX: Texas Monthly Press, 1985.

Dahl, Robert A., *Polyarchy: Participation and Opposition* (New Haven: Yale Up, 1971).

Gibson, James L., and Richard D. Bingham, *Civil Liberties and Nazis: The Skokie Free Speech Controversy* (New York: Praeger, 1985).

Gibson, James L., and Kent L. Tedin, "Political Tolerance and the Rights of Homosexuals: A Contextual Analysis." Paper delivered at the 1986 Annual Meeting of the Midwest Political Science Association.

Goldstein, Robert Justin, *Political Repression in Modern America: From 1870 to the Present* (Cambridge: Schenkman Publishing Co., 1978).

Jenson, Carol E., *The Network of Control: State Supreme Courts and State Security Statutes, 1920–1970* (Westport, Conn.: Greenwood Press, 1982).

McClosky, Herbert, and Alida Brill, *Dimensions of Tolerance: What Americans Believe About Civil Liberties* (New York: Russell Sage Foundation, 1983).

Sullivan, John L., James Piereson, and George E. Marcus, *Political Tolerance and American Democracy* (Chicago: University of Chicago Press, 1982).

Stouffer, Samuel A., *Communism, Conformity, and Civil Liberties: A Cross-section of the Nation Speaks Its Mind* (New York: John Wiley & Sons, Inc., 1955).

Notes

1. Robert A. Dahl, *Polyarchy: Participation and Opposition* (New Haven: Yale Univeristy Press, 1971), pp. 1–2.
2. Dahl, p. 3.
3. Examples of such efforts are Almond and Verba, 1963; and Dahl, 1971 (especially chapter 8).
4. Robert Goldstein, *Political Repression in Modern America: From 1870 to the Present* (Cambridge: Schenkamn Publishing Co., 1978), p. 108.
5. California General Laws Annotated, Act 9428; quoted in Carol E. Jensen, *The Network of Control: State Supreme Court and State Security Statutes, 1920–1970* (Westport, Conn.: Greenwood Press, 1982), p. 25.
6. Goldstein, p. 323.
7. Paul Lazarsfeld and Wagner Thielens, *The Academic Mind* (Glencoe, Illinois: Free Press, 1958).
8. John L. Sullivan, James Piereson, and George E. Markus, *Political Tolerance and American Democracy* (Chicago: Univeristy of Chicago Press, 1982), p. 67.
9. Sullivan, Piereson, and Marcus.
10. The Houston *Post*, July 4, 1984, B-8.
11. The Houston *Post*, July 4, 1984, B-4.
12. James L. Gibson and Kent L. Tedin, "Political Tolerance and the Rights of Homosexuals: A Contextual Analysis" paper delivered at the 1986 annual meeting of the the Midwest Political Science Association.

11 The American Poor: Myths and Reality
HARRELL RODGERS

Poverty is one of those topics that is not often discussed in polite company, and when it is, like religion and politics, it tends to generate more heat than enlightenment. Many people believe that "the poor are always with us" because there is a certain percentage of any population who, whether for reasons of laziness, poor upbringing, or just plain bad luck, will be on the bottom rungs of the economic ladder. Others believe that most if not all poverty results from flaws in the economic, social, or political system and that most of the poor can be rescued from that condition and the relatively few unlucky sheltered from its consequences. Between these extremes is a wide variety of positions, including that of complete disinterest in the subject.

If for no other reason than that a significant percentage of the total federal budget and a considerable proportion of state and local dollars go toward social programs designed to alleviate or prevent poverty, it is an important topic that deserves consideration of a calmer and more extended nature than it often receives. Toward that end this chapter will provide basic information on poverty in an attempt to raise the general level of discourse on this complex issue. In keeping with its importance, poverty has been the target of so many studies that there is not space to summarize even the major studies here or to detail all of the complexities associated with poverty. Instead, we will provide basic data and some introductory concepts.

Counting The Poor

The United States is the only major western industrial nation that calculates an annual poverty standard. Beginning in 1959 the federal government has annually used an income standard which varies by family size to calculate how many Americans live in poverty. Table 1 provides an overview of the findings of the Bureau of the Census between 1959 and 1987.

The data in Table 1 reveal that poverty is a very serious problem in the United States. Even though poverty has declined from its high of almost 40 million poor (some 22% of the population) in the early 1960s, progress has not been steady. The number of poor declined to a low of 23 million (11.5% of the population) in 1973 but has risen to over 30 million during the years of the Reagan administration. Over thirty-two million Americans, or 13.5 percent of the population, lived in poverty in 1987.

Table 1 Poverty Schedule: Family of Four (Nonfarm): 1959–87

Year	Standard	Millions of Poor	% of Total Pop.
1959	$2,973	39.5	22.0
1960	3,022	39.9	22.0
1961	3,054	39.9	22.0
1962	3,089	38.6	21.0
1963	3,128	36.4	19.0
1964	3,169	36.1	19.0
1965	3,223	33.2	17.0
1966	3,317	30.4	16.0
1966*	3,317	28.5	15.0
1967	3,410	27.8	14.0
1968	3,553	25.4	13.0
1969	3,743	24.1	12.0
1970	3,968	25.4	13.0
1971	4,137	24.1	11.0
1972	4,275	25.4	12.0
1973	4,540	23.0	11.5
1974	5,038	24.3	12.0
1974*	5,038	24.3	11.5
1975	5,500	25.9	12.0
1976	5,815	25.0	12.0
1977	6,200	24.7	12.0
1978	6,662	24.7	11.4
1979	7,412	26.1	11.7
1980	8,414	29.3	13.0
1981	9,287	31.8	14.0
1982	9,862	34.4	15.0
1983	10,178	35.3	15.2
1984	10,609	33.7	14.4
1985	10,989	33.1	14.0
1986	11,203	32.4	13.6
1987	11,600	32.5	13.5

Source: Derived from U.S. Bureau of the Census, "Money Income and Poverty Status of Families in the United States." Series P-60, various years.
*Note: Revision in Census calculations.

The federal government's poverty standard is based on the calculation of the cost of an "adequate" diet for families of various sizes. The government assumes that food costs represent one-third of the total income of families of three or more, and 27 percent of the income needs of one and two-person households. Table 1 shows the poverty standard for an urban family of four between 1959 and 1987. In 1987 a family of four was classified as poor if it had a cash income of less than $11,600.

This official definition of poverty is not without its critics. Some liberals argue that the federal government's poverty standard does not take into account the kind of income it takes to produce healthy lives as opposed to merely staying alive at a subsistence level. Perhaps, more seriously, they argue, the official standard fails to take into account the millions of people who are barely above the minimum standard and thus are effectively poor but not considered. By this accounting the percentage of Americans in the poverty category is about 35 percent higher, on average, than is annually indicated. In 1987 this would translate into over forth—three million Americans living below the poverty level or within 125 percent of the poverty level.

Some conservatives, on the other hand, insist that the official definition tends to overstate the level of poverty in America. Many people underreport their income in order to qualify for aid, they argue, and many families with low incomes own their own homes, furniture, cars, etc. so that an apparently low income stretches quite far. Finally, and most important to these conservatives, the official standard does not take into account other in-kind (non-cash) government benefits such as food stamps, medical assistance such as Medicaid, public housing, and free or subsidized school meals. When the cash value of these benefits is taken into account, they contend, the percentage of the population below the poverty level is about forty percent lower than what is, on average, reported. By this calculation, in 1987, about eight percent of the American population falls below the poverty level.

Liberals respond that while in-kind programs certainly help low-income citizens, much of the aid is in the form of services such as health care which does not translate into disposable income. Most importantly, however, liberals claim that the poverty standard is unrealistically low. Liberals argue that if the poverty standard were revised to make it more realistic, even counting in-kind assistance would not alter the fact that some thirty to forty million Americans live in, or perilously close, to poverty.[1]

The complexity and controversy involved in something as apparently simple as the definition of poverty indicates how difficult it is to carry on a thoughtful discussion about poverty. It is for this reason that after reviewing some basic data on poverty, much of our attention will be devoted to laying to rest the common myths about poverty that get in the way of intelligent analysis.

Who are the Poor?

Table 2 provides an overview of the American poor in 1986. The data reveal a number of groups of Americans who have particularly high rates of poverty. Those most vulnerable to poverty include minorities, children, residents of central cities, households headed by a single woman, individuals living alone (especially minority widows), and residents of the South—particularly when they are minorities and/or members of a family headed by a single woman. Nationwide, minorities are approximately three times as likely to be poor as white Americans.

The poorest age group in America is children. One in five children lives below the poverty level. This statistic includes over 15 percent of all white children, 37 percent of all children of Spanish origin, and over 43 percent of all black children. Poverty among children has been getting worse, not better. In fact, the incidence of poverty among children increased by more than 50 percent from 1973 to 1986. Children have become a larger percentage of all the American poor in large part because of a huge increase in the number of American families headed by single women. The share of children in female-headed families more than doubled from 1959 to 1986. In 1986 women headed 16 percent of all families and 21 percent of all families with children. The two major reasons for the growth of female-headed families are marital dissolution and births to unwed mothers.[2]

Female-headed families have a rate of poverty that is almost six times higher than for two-parent families. More than half of all children living in a female-headed family are poor. Of the black children living in a female-headed family over two-thirds live in poverty. By all estimates this trend will continue. A Congressional committee recently estimated that the number of children under the age of ten living in female-headed families would increase by 48 percent between 1980 and 1990. If this estimate is correct, the number of children in such families would increase from 6 million to 8.9 million. This growth rate suggests that by 1990 one of every four children under ten would live in a family headed by a single woman.[3]

Although, almost half of all poor families are headed by a single woman, in recent years poverty among two-parent families has increased faster than among single-parent families. The primary reasons have been an increase in unemployment and a decline in real wages. In inflation-adjusted dollars, median family income has risen by only 1.5 percent since 1970.[4]

The majority of all the poor live in metropolitan areas, with large concentrations of poor people living in central cities. The poor black population is heavily concentrated in the poverty pockets of inner cities; poor whites tend to live in metropolitan areas but outside the central city. About forty percent of all the poor live outside metropolitan areas, with a considerable proportion living a good distance from a metropolitan area.[5]

On a regional basis poverty varies considerably. In 1986 40 percent of the poor lived in the South. The South's poor tend to be very poor, and they almost always receive very limited welfare benefits. About 16 percent of the poor live in the northeast, about 24 percent in the north central states, and about 20 percent in the West.

One group of Americans who have made great progress in escaping poverty over the last two decades is senior citizens. The poverty rate for Americans over 65 represent is currently about 12 percent. In the late 1950s over 30 percent of all aged Americans lived in poverty. However, because of increases in Social Security benefits and passage of the Medicaid and Medicare programs, the rate of poverty among the aged has dropped very considerably.

Poverty In Texas

Poverty in Texas typically averages about 2 percentage points above the national average. Between 1980 and 1986 approximately 16 percent of all Texans have lived below the poverty line. The 2 million plus Texans who live in poverty each year are very poor because welfare benefits within the state are very modest.

As we will detail below, welfare benefits vary greatly by state. Texas ranks near the bottom of all states in assistance to the poor. The major cash welfare program in the nation is Aid to Families with Dependent Children (AFDC). AFDC in Texas is limited to female-headed families with assets of less than $1,000 and little or no income. Families headed by an unemployed father cannot receive AFDC unless the father is disabled and all other asset and income requirements are met. Only a few thousand families a year meet this standard. If a family can meet the standards, benefits are very modest. The maximum AFDC benefits a penniless mother with two children could receive would be $171 a month, or $57 per family member. In March, 1986 137.9 thousand families received AFDC benefits in Texas. The average family received $174.21, compared to the national average of $354.36. Only four states pay lower AFDC benefits than Texas.

Most AFDC families also receive food stamps, but because AFDC benefits are so low, the combined programs still leave most welfare families in financial distress. For example, in January, 1985 combined AFDC/food stamp benefits averaged $375.00 in Texas. This represented only 54 percent of the poverty threshold for a family of three. In 1985 Texas ranked 45th among the states in combined AFDC/food stamp benefits.

Any family with assets of less than $1500 and income below the poverty threshold can receive food stamps. In Texas about 400,000 families (or 1.3 million persons) a month qualify for assistance. The average food stamp allotment per person is $44.00 per month, or about 50 cents per meal. Four of every five food stamp recipients in Texas are children, senior citizens, or disabled. Only about 40 percent of all Texans qualified for food stamps by income actually receive them.

Myths About Poor Americans

Poverty is a frustrating problem for most Americans. The public tends to believe that the poor should be assisted, but they also believe that welfare programs cost too much, that the programs are not very effective, and that a great deal of the poverty in our society results from personal deficiencies. The public believes that many of the poor are shortsighted, lazy, unmotivated, or physically, mentally, or emotionally ill. Such beliefs sometimes lead citizens and public officials to conclude that while the poor need help, little can be done.

The public, of course, often does recognize that many people become poor for reasons beyond their control. In fact, if an individual case of poverty is publicized, there is generally an outpouring of public support. The contrast between the public's attitude toward specific cases of poverty and the larger poverty population creates tension and perhaps some guilt. As a result of this guilt, and perhaps the complexity of the poverty issue, many strong beliefs about the poor have been popularized. Some of these beliefs are inaccurate—so inaccurate, in fact, that they qualify as myths. These myths impede both our understanding of the complexity of poverty and rational attempts to deal with the problem. Below we will discuss some of the most prominent misperceptions about the poor.

"The Poor Are Black"

Americans believe that poverty is a serious problem only among minorities. This belief is hardly surprising, given the concentrations of poor blacks and Hispanics in America's central cities and most media images of the poor. But, in fact, most of the poor are white, and this has always been true. The figures below reveal the racial breakdown of the poor in 1986.

As the figures show, 68.5 percent of all the poor in 1986 were white, and 27.7 percent were black. Of these two groups, 5.1 million, or 15.8 percent, were of Spanish origin.

Minorities do have a much greater chance of being poor. While only 11.0 percent of all whites were poor, 31.1 percent of all blacks and 27.3 percent of all citizens of Spanish origin were poor. Clearly, poverty is a greater hazard for minorities, but numerically whites are the most predominant group among the poor.

"The Poor Refuse to Work"

The public believes that the poor are not willing to work for a living. Employment problems definitely lie at the core of much poverty in America, but the problem is more complex than simple shiftlessness. A large percentage of the poor either cannot work or must depend on others for their support. As noted above, in 1986 over 52 percent of all the poor lived in a household headed by a single woman. Female-headed families have very high poverty rates because single mothers often cannot work, or they cannot find a job that pays enough to allow them to decently support themselves and their children. Generally, single mothers receive little financial help from the absent father.

Table 2 The Poverty Population, 1986*

Selected Characteristics	Below Poverty Level	Poverty Rate	% of All Poor
Race			
All	32,370	13.6	100.0
White	22,183	11.0	68.5
Black	8,983	31.1	27.7
Spanish Origin	5,117**	27.3	15.8
Age			
65 and over	3,477	12.4	10.7
Related children under 18	13,274	19.8	41.0
Urban vs. Rural			
In Metropolitan Area	22,657	12.3	70.0
In Central Cities	13,295	18.0	41.0
Outside Metropolitan Area	9,712	18.1	30.0
Family Structure			
Married-Couple Families	3,123	6.1	45.0
Male Household, No Wife Present	287	11.4	2.7
Female Household, No Husband Present	3,613	34.6	52.2
Unrelated Individual	6,846	21.6	21.0
Male	2,536	17.5	7.8
Female	4,311	25.1	13.3
Region			
Northeast	5,211	10.5	16.0
Midwest	7,641	13.0	24.0
South	13,106	16.1	40.0
West	6,412	13.2	20.0

Source: Bureau of The Census (1987) "Money Income and Poverty Status of Families and Persons in the United States." *Current Population Reports,* Series P-60, No. 157, pp. 5–6.
**Persons of Spanish-Origin may be of any race.

Many of the poor are dependents. In 1986, 52.0 percent of all the poor were either sixty-five or older or dependent children. Poor children alone numbered 13.3 million and constituted 41.0 percent of all poor Americans. One American child in five lived in poverty. The aged poor numbered 3.5 million, 10.7 percent of all poor Americans. Another 5 percent of all poor adults in 1986 were nonaged, handicapped persons.

Additionally, about half of all heads of poor families are in the work force. In 1986, 50.0 percent of all heads of poor families were employed, and 17 percent were employed full-time. Two million people, including 1.2 million heads of families, worked year-round at full time jobs but earned too little to escape poverty.[6] Fifty percent of all heads of poor families were not in the job market. The large number of family heads who were not in the work force reflects the fact that a considerable proportion of all poor family heads are mothers who care for their children.

"Welfare Recipients are Mostly Able-Bodied Men"

One of the most enduring myths about the poor is that most welfare recipients are healthy males who prefer to live off the dole rather than work. In fact, single males cannot qualify for the nation's major cash welfare program—Aid to Families with Dependent Children (AFDC)—and even fathers heading families have great difficulty in qualifying. Only twenty-eight states allow an unemployed father to receive AFDC benefits, regardless of the reason for his unemployment and poverty. Even in those states that allow some fathers to receive AFDC benefits, the restrictions are so severe that only a modest number of male-headed families ever manage to qualify.

Recent program figures are revealing. In 1986 some 3.7 million families (with 10.6 million recipients) received AFDC benefits. The monthly average of families headed by a male was only about 150,000. Women headed about 80 percent of all AFDC families in 1986, while relatives (mostly grandmothers) headed another 15 percent. Men headed only about 4 percent of all AFDC families.

"The Poor Get Rich off Welfare"

Many people imagine the poor using welfare payments to buy color TVs, Cadillacs, liquor, and luxury foods. In truth, most welfare families barely survive. Under current laws welfare benefits vary greatly by state. In the most generous states welfare benefits barely allow recipients to get by; in the least generous states welfare benefits keep families in a state of acute desperation. The figures below show the variation in average family AFDC benefits, by state, in March 1986.

The average AFDC family in March 1986 received $354.36 per month, or $120.34 per recipient. As the figures above reveal, however, there is a great deal of variation by state. Seven states provide average benefits of over $450.00 per month. Eight states provide average benefits of less than $200 per month. Even in the most generous states benefits are rather modest, and some states seem to make no serious attempt to aid their poor. In thirty states benefits are less than 50 percent of the poverty level.

Poor families qualifying for AFDC do generally receive other types of assistance. For example, in 1986, almost all AFDC families received some services under Medicaid. About 75 percent of all AFDC families also participated in the Food Stamp Program. Even among those families who can qualify for AFDC and other programs, such as food stamps or Medicaid, the cash income of the families ranges from extremely low to very modest. Even multiple benefits can leave recipients in acute poverty. In most of the states the combined value of AFDC and food stamps leaves recipient families far below the poverty level.

Table 3 AFDC Payments by State, March, 1986*

State	Monthly Benefit	State	Monthly Benefit
Alabama	$113.91	Missouri	$264.51
Alaska	630.13	Montana	329.13
Arizona	265.97	Nebraska	321.70
Arkansas	183.59	Nevada	241.25
California	532.29	New Hampshire	329.55
Colorado	303.43	New Jersey	376.66
Connecticut	478.75	New Mexico	233.96
Delaware	252.10	New York	461.90
District of Columbia	294.96	North Dakota	347.72
Florida	243.40	Ohio	303.99
Georgia	206.28	Oklahoma	283.44
Hawaii	402.95	Oregon	343.11
Idaho	271.62	Pennsylvania	341.77
Illinois	304.88	Rhode Island	444.90
Indiana	220.98	South Carolina	188.22
Iowa	353.03	South Dakota	264.54
Kansas	320.20	Tennessee	142.95
Kentucky	193.79	Texas	174.21
Louisiana	169.12	Utah	338.50
Maine	356.57	Vermont	409.55
Maryland	304.81	Virginia	253.75
Massachusetts	401.07	Washington	440.74
Michigan	477.29	West Virginia	244.72
Minnesota	483.09	Wisconsin	495.06
Mississippi	114.70	Wyoming	302.62

Source: Social Security Administration, Social Security Bulletin, Volume 49, number 11 (Washington, D.C.: U.S. Department of Health and Human Services, 1986), 70–71.

"The Poor Squander Their Money"

The prevailing belief is that poor people waste the assistance they receive. The evidence, however, indicates that the poor spend most of their money on essentials such as food, housing, and medical care. In 1985 HEW's studies showed that an average poor family spent 29 percent of its income on food, 34 percent on housing, and 9 percent on medical care. The figures below compare spending of poor families to those of affluent families:

These comparative figures show that poor people spend considerably more of their income on essentials than do the affluent.

"It Is Easy to Get on Welfare"

Many believe that anyone can get on welfare, and that all one has to do to start receiving a monthly check is go down to the local welfare office and fill

Table 4 A Comparison of Spending

Spending Category	Poor	Affluent
Food	29%	20%
Housing	34	29
Transportation	9	6
Medical Care	9	12
Clothing	7	5
Recreation	2	5
Tobacco	2	1
Alcohol	1	2
Other	7	10

Source: Social Security Administration, "Aid to Families with Dependent Children: 1985 Recipient Characteristics Study—Part II," U.S. Department of Health and Human Services, June 1986, p. 15.

out a form or two. As noted above, welfare programs are categorical, permitting benefits only to restricted groups of the poor. Nonaged males, single adults, and couples have great difficulty obtaining cash assistance, regardless of their need or the reason for their destitution. Most welfare goes to female-headed families and to the aged, disabled, and blind.

Second, getting on welfare and staying on welfare is complex even for those who qualify for aid. An applicant must fill out numerous forms and provide complete records on income (if any), bills, assets, and expenditures. These forms are usually long and complex. Additionally, each assistance program has separate and different forms, eligibility requirements, benefit schedules, regulations, and administrative policies and procedures.

Furthermore, an applicant who makes it through the paper blizzard must submit to an initial home visit and periodic home and/or office interviews while on welfare. During the period of benefit, all welfare recipients must submit to an ongoing audit of their income and expenditures.

An analysis of who obtains welfare assistance also reveals something about the difficulty of obtaining aid. Welfare recipients represent the poorest of the poor, but certainly not all the poor (even among the most destitute) receive aid. For example, unlike AFDC or Medicaid, poor nonaged males, single adults, and childless couples can receive food stamps if they meet the income and asset criteria. But their income must be below the poverty level, and they cannot have assets in excess of $1500. The income and asset barriers, plus the stigma associated with food-stamp use, perhaps explains why only about half the families and individuals qualified for the program receive benefits.

"The Poor Are Cheats"

The public generally believes that much welfare goes to people who are ineligible to receive it. The facts indicate that such charges are exaggerated. Many researchers have attempted to determine how many poor people are welfare cheaters, but none of the studies has ever reported finding that a significant percentage of all recipients are involved in fraud.7 For example, in 1975 a U.S. Department of Agriculture (USDA) study reported that food-stamp fraud equaled twenty-four thousandths of 1 percent of all participating households (Department of Agriculture, 1975). Other studies have found as much as 1 to 3 percent of program funds going to ineligible persons because of fraud or computational error.

Three points about incorrect expenditure of welfare funds should be noted. First, the poor sometime receive the wrong amount of aid because the welfare laws are so complex that even case workers cannot always keep the rules straight or learn all the rules that might apply to a particular case. In general, computational error is a bigger problem than fraud. Computational error is caused, of course, by strict laws designed to reduce fraud and restrict eligibility and by overworked caseworkers.

Second, it is extremely difficult to uncover many types of welfare cheating. If a recipient or applicant wants to cover up some small source of income, such as a few hours overtime, an extra half day of work, or a gift, it is not very hard to do. Studies of fraud, therefore, are unlikely to ever be very accurate. What the studies can do is detect serious fraud, such as ineligible people on the rolls.

Third, the cumulative evidence indicates that, on the average, the poor are neither particularly virtuous or particularly corrupt. They are much like the rest of the population. Some are honest, some are dishonest, and others can be tempted by a chance to increase their income by a little deception. This is similar to public cheating on tax reports, business cheating on government contracts, or dozens of other forms of dishonesty that a significant proportion of the population engages in.

"Once on Welfare, Always on Welfare"

The public tends to believe that families who obtain AFDC benefits stay in the program for a couple of decades. The official figures show that about 25 percent of all families leave the AFDC rolls within six months, half leave within two years, and three fifths are terminated within three years. In recent years, the average AFDC family stayed on the rolls for about thirty months.

Two points, however, are quite important. First, some AFDC families are repeaters. About one-third of all AFDC families have received assistance before. Second, of all the families who have obtained AFDC assistance over the last decade, most stayed on the rolls for a relatively short period. However, of current recipients, a majority have been on the rolls for five years or more. Young single mothers who become AFDC recipients tend to stay on the rolls for rather long periods. Mothers aged 25 or above who enter the AFDC program generally leave the rolls after a relatively short period.[8]

"Welfare Families Are Large"

The public imagines welfare families as being large because additional children may mean increased benefits. In fact, the size of welfare families is medial. In 1986 the average AFDC family had 2.2 children. Examining AFDC benefit figures reveals that having an additional child increases benefits too modestly to encourage childbearing. In most states the increase would average no more than $40 per month and would be much lower in the South, where over 40 percent of all AFDC recipients live.

Reforms

One thing that conservatives and liberals agree upon is that welfare programs need reform. In recent years there has been a growing consensus that the most promising way to reduce poverty is to help the able poor prosper in the job market. The reasoning is that welfare mothers can best escape poverty if they receive help in obtaining needed education or job training and assistance so that they can find and keep a job. In addition to financial assistance, the primary support welfare mothers require is decent child care at affordable prices. Currently most welfare mothers cannot enter job training programs or often even complete high school because they cannot obtain child care. If the mother can find a job, most often she cannot afford the average cost of $3,000 per year required to place one child in day care. In a few states innovative programs have been developed to train and place welfare mothers in jobs. During training and later on the job the mothers receive free or very inexpensive child care. These programs have produced very good results. In the state of Massachusetts over 31,000 welfare mothers have been trained and placed in jobs. After deducting the cost of the employment program, the state calculates that it has saved $100 million in AFDC expenditures.[9]

The National Conference of Governors and many state legislatures have endorsed the Massachusetts' plan as an alternative to AFDC for mothers with no children under age three. Poor mothers would enter into a contractual arrangement under which they would receive supported job training or job placement and in return they would agree to leave the welfare roles within a specified period. Child care would be included in the support services offered to the mothers. This would be a more positive and productive welfare policy than those currently in force. To be an optimum strategy, however, the child care provided must deal with the educational needs of the children. Child care which includes pre-school programs can be designed to allow the children to enter public schools on an equal footing with their more economically advantaged peers. The evidence on the favorable impact of the Head Start and other pre-school programs strongly supports the belief that pre-school programs can have a very positive impact on the educational achievement of children.[10] A version of a supported-work plan—the Family Welfare Act—will probably pass

Congress in late 1988. The plan before Congress would provide a modest program effecting only about 300,000 families a year, but it would be a base upon which the whole AFDC program could eventually be reformed.

In addition to supported-work, a number of nonwelfare policies with the potential of reducing poverty are currently receiving attention by policymakers. These include an increasing emphasis on child support enforcement, maternity and parental leaves to enable parents to balance their parenting and employee roles, sex education to reduce the number of unwanted and unintended pregnancies, expanded child care options for working parents, and tax reforms to improve the take home pay of low-income families. Combined with the reforms discussed above, these policies have the potential to substantially reduce the need for traditional welfare programs.

Conclusions

Poverty continues to be a persistent problem in America. Current welfare programs clearly relieve some of the most obvious suffering of the poor, but they do not prevent poverty or even remove those who receive assistance from poverty. In fact, our welfare programs are not designed to solve the problems that make people poor. They are basically designed to give modest, temporary relief while recipients figure out how to get back on their feet. The evidence indicates, however, that millions of welfare recipients stay on welfare for long periods, and that millions cannot escape poverty without assistance.

The increasing acceptance by both conservatives and liberals that our welfare programs do not work has focused increasing attention on supported-work as an alternative. Welfare recipients would be trained for employment and given supportive services so that they can stay in the work force. This alternative to the traditional welfare approach has potential, but jobs for the poor will have to be available. In the past the nation's high rate of unemployment has undermined many job-oriented programs.

Notes

1. Watts, H. W. 1986. "Have Our Measures of Poverty Become Poorer?" Focus. Institute For Research On Poverty, University of Wisconsin–Madison, 18–23.
2. Rodgers, H. R. 1985. "Youth and Poverty: An Empirical Test of the Impact of Family Demographics and Race." *Youth and Society.* Vol. 16. No. 4, 421–437;...............1986. *Poor Women, Poor Families: The Economic Plight of America's Female-Headed Families.* Armonk, New York: M. E. Sharpe, Inc;...............1986. "The Feminization of Poverty: Some Preliminary Empirical Explorations." *Western Sociological Review.* March, vol. 15, No. 1, 1–32.

3. Select Committee on Children, Youth and Families. 1983. "U.S. Children and Their Families: 1983: Current Conditions and Recent Trends." 98th Congress. 1st Session. Washington, D.C.: GPO.
4. Bureau of the Census. 1987. "Money Income and Poverty Status of Families and Persons in the United States: 1986." *Current Population Reports,* Series P-60, No. 157. Washington, D.C.: GPO.
5. Rodgers, H. R. and Gregory Weiher 1986. "The Rural Poor in America: A Statistical Overview." *Policy Studies Journal.* Vol. 15, No. 2, 279–289.
6. Bureau of the Census. 1987. "Money Income and Poverty Status of Families and Persons in the United States: 1986." *Current Population Reports,* Series P-60, No. 157. Washington, D.C.: GPO.
7. Joint Economic Committee, Subcommittee on Fiscal Policy. 1977. *Income Security for Americans: Recommendations of the Public Welfare Study.* Washington, D.C.: GPO, p. 75.
8. Bane, Mary Jo, and David T. Ellwood. 1983. "The Dynamics of Dependence: The Routes to Self-Sufficiency." Prepared for the U.S. Department of Health and Human Services, Office of the Assistant Secretary for Planning and Evaluation, Cambridge, Mass: Urban Research and Engineering, Inc.
9. Rodgers, H. R. 1986. *Poor Women, Poor Families,* pp. 132–133.
10. Schweinhart, L. J. and Weikart, D. P. 1980. "Effects of Early Childhood Intervention on Teenage Youth: The Perry Preschool Project, 1962–1980." *Monographs on the High/Scope Educational Research Foundation,* No. 7.

12

Federal-State Relations: New Federalism in Theory and Practice

MALCOLM L. GOGGIN

During Ronald Reagan's 1980 campaign for the presidency, he promised the American people that he would work for a policy of restricting the use of federal tax dollars for abortion. His position that each state should be free to determine for itself whether or not to fund abortions was prompted by a desire to preserve a state's right to define and protect its own community interests. The Republican presidential candidate justified his stand on the grounds that this traditional view represented the opinion of a majority of Americans. Jimmy Carter, Reagan's Democratic opponent in the 1980 presidential election, supported federal funding for abortion, thus upholding reproductive freedom as a minority right of the individual to be protected by the federal or national government.

While the 1980 election was neither won nor lost on this one issue, the clash between Reagan's emphasis on community autonomy as a way of advancing states' own interests versus Carter's preference for a more powerful presence for the central government in order to protect individual rights illustrates two conflicting views of how the nation's political institutions should share power to make and carry out public policies. These two views on the manner in which a nation should best organize—often called states' rights and national supremacy—divide Americans today, as they did Alexander Hamilton and Thomas Jefferson two hundred years ago.

To appreciate the main views or theories of federalism, or intergovernmental relations, and understand the debate surrounding federalism that has characterized recent presidential elections in general and the Reagan administration's two terms in office in particular, this chapter begins with highlights of the two hundred year history of how power among levels of government has been shared, a history which depicts the changes in the balance of power between national and subnational levels of government. This chapter then examines the theory and practice of the "New Federalism," which began as an experiment in the early 1970s and then was adopted as a major Reagan administration policy for the 1980s. New Federalism in the Reagan era is an attempt to make states' rights the effective policy of the land by reducing the role of the national government in state and local affairs, by slowing the flow of federal dollars to states and municipalities as part of a national strategy to discourage their dependency on the federal government, and by returning to state and local officials more control over how money should be spent. The concluding section of this chapter examines how the state of Texas has implemented and administered New Federalism policies in the 1980s.

I. History of Federal-State Relations

One of the most important issues in the political history of the United States has been the relative strength of the national versus state governments.[1] This section highlights three periods of history in which this issue was of paramount importance: the Founding Era, between 1781 and 1791; the Republican Era, which began with Thomas Jefferson's election as President in 1800 and ended when the Civil War did in 1865, and the New Deal and its aftermath, from the 1930s to the late 1960s.

The Founding Era

We begin with the period between 1781, when the Articles of Confederation were adopted, and 1791, the year in which the Bill of Rights was ratified. In these formative years, the Founders had a choice of three principal alternative arrangements for dividing the powers of government between the states and the national government. The Founders could adopt a unitary, federal, or confederal structure for the New Republic. In a *unitary* system the central government possesses all formal authority. A *federal* system, on the other hand, is one where formal authority is shared between at least two levels of government. In contrast to the unitary system, which may also have regional or local units of government to whom authority for formulating and implementing local laws may be delegated, subnational governments in a federal system have independent authority. A *confederation*—the third option available to America's nation builders—is a system where constituent units create the central government. In this last case, the subnational units of government determine how power will be shared between center and periphery. Hence, the member states, not the central government, have final authority.

It was not likely that the original thirteen states would have wanted to duplicate the British unitary system that they had come to despise. A federal system, on the other hand, would have been a political invention of the Founders—a novel political experiment without precedent. Because the Founders wanted to maintain the strength of the states as separate entities, with concomitant weak central authority, it was logical that they would look to some of the governments of ancient Greece and to the more contemporary example of United Netherlands as models of governance for this new nation in the late eighteenth century.

What the Founders initially chose for the nation was a "league of friendship"—a confederation. In adopting the Articles of Confederation in 1781, the first structure of government was a system of mutual assistance, where each state maintained its sovereignty. Under the Articles of Confederation, which could be amended only by a unanimous vote of the thirteen states, a national Congress was established with delegates chosen by each state's legislature. Real power rested with the states, not with the Continental Congress.

A host of governance problems plagued the new nation under the Articles of Confederation, not the least of which was the central government's inability to collect taxes and staff an army; nor could the Continental Congress formulate and implement foreign policy or agree on the terms of a peace treaty. In fact, the central government was severely handicapped because under the Articles it could neither prevent states from erecting trade barriers nor enforce laws affecting citizens in the states. Because states were unable or unwilling to fulfill their obligations, the confederal arrangement for governing America in the 1780s was simply not working well. Eventually, it became difficult even to get a quorum in Congress.

What ultimately led to the collapse of the Articles of Confederation were problems within the states. One incident that precipitated a crisis of governance was Shays' Rebellion, a fall 1786 uprising of Massachusetts debtors who, under the leadership of Daniel Shays, attacked state courthouses, thus preventing the courts from foreclosing on farmers' mortgages. When the governor of Massachusetts asked the Continental Congress for help in putting down the uprising, the central government could muster neither money nor army. Massachusetts authorities eventually hired a volunteer army to quell the rebellion, but in the face of an impending "tyranny of the majority," such as the Massachusetts rebels' demands for more democracy and for a levelling of inequalities through a redistribution of property, or the victory of the paper money party in the 1786 elections in the neighboring state of Rhode Island, in May of 1787 the framers of the Constitution scrapped the Articles of Confederation. In this context, the experiment with a weak central government can be viewed as a temporary device for governing that served as a stepping stone to the more permanent federal system of governance that was adopted as part of the U.S. Constitution.

When writing the Constitution, the framers opted for "compound federalism"—a convenient compromise that balanced the needs for elite autonomy and the protection of private property on the one hand, with the desire for greater equality through the establishment of the institutions of a popular government on the other hand. By choosing a federal system which combined checks and balances and the sharing of power among separate institutions of government with shared and dual powers among levels of government, the Founders avoided the concentration of power and ameliorated the evil effects of factions which, if unchecked, was to risk tyranny.

The Tenth Amendment to the U.S. Constitution, which was ratified by the states in 1791 as part of the Bill of Rights, codified the new arrangement and specified the division of labor between the states and the national government. As a practical matter, in defining the separation of powers among levels of government as "The powers not delegated to the United States by the Constitution, nor prohibited by it to the States, are reserved to the States, respectively, or to the people," the Tenth Amendment may have confused rather than clarified the issue. Today, these words mean national supremacy to some and states' rights to others.

The Republican Era (1800–1865)

The political debate between the Federalists, who wanted a strong central government, and the Anti-Federalists, who pressed for an arrangement that gave more power to the people, is well known from the exchanges that are recorded in *The Federalist,* a series of eighty-five pro-ratification essays and "anti-Federalist" writings that opposed ratification.[2] Thomas Jefferson, who challenged the Federalist administration of John Adams, became an ardent supporter of a policy that states alone were parties to the Constitution; but it was not until Jefferson's election to the presidency in 1800 that a United States President's policy of states' rights was so at odds with the Supreme Court Chief Justice's position in favor of national supremacy. The arguments for and against a federal structure were clearly articulated in the differences of opinion between statesmen like Chief Justice John Marshall and Thomas Jefferson—between Federalists and Anti-Federalists—and they have endured during the more than two hundred year history of the Republic.[3]

Over the years, federalism has had its proponents and opponents. Federalism has been praised because (1) it permits a flexible policy that can be adapted to individual circumstances, and, therefore, reduces conflict between levels of government; (2) it disperses power widely and, thus, in its pluralism minimizes the risk of tyranny; (3) it encourages public participation in governance, and, hence, makes office holders more accountable and more responsive to the needs of the people; (4) likewise, a more decentralized system tends to be more representative; thus, it can lead to a more equitable distribution of benefits and burdens; and (5) it improves efficiency (by reducing the delays and red tape usually associated with a central bureaucracy) and encourages experimentation and innovation at subnational levels of government.

On the other hand, federalism has been criticized because (1) it protects the interests of a local majority, often at the expense of racial and other minorities; (2) it permits states to thwart the efforts of the national government to achieve uniform standards, and equal treatment, across all the states, and, thus, leads to inequalities; and (3) in asking states and localities to rely more on themselves it gives advantages to rich states and disadvantages to poor states. These, then, are the most common arguments for and against a federal structure.

Even though this debate was settled temporarily when the North won the Civil War (fought in part over the issue of national supremacy v. states' rights), the war's outcome reinforced the idea of national supremacy in the sense that the Civil War resolved the issue of whether or not a state was free to secede from the union. In fact, though, the celebrated 1819 Supreme Court decision, *McCulloch v. Maryland*, had already delivered a serious blow to the cause of states' rights, because it helped to establish the scope of federal powers and national supremacy.

The case revolved around the ability of the state of Maryland to tax federal banks. The Supreme Court, headed by Chief Justice Marshall, sided with the national rather than the state government. In ruling that states may not tax a federal instrument, in this case a bank, the court established that the government of the U.S. was created not by the states but by the people. The federal government was supreme in the exercise of those powers conferred upon it. Thus, in interpreting the necessary and proper clause of the Constitution as it did, and by establishing the doctrine of implied national powers, the Supreme Court expanded the influence of the national government within the federal system. It was a victory for national supremacy over states' rights.

In spite of *McCulloch v. Maryland* and the outcome of the Civil War, however, some students of intergovernmental relations still describe the period between 1861 and 1930 as a "dual" federal system where autonomous national, subnational, and local governments all pursued their own interests independently. Each level of government maintained its own identity and autonomy, and each had direct authority over the same jurisdictions and citizens. If one accepts this "dual federalism" interpretation, then the New Deal marks the first time in U.S. history that powers in the system were widely shared between national and subnational governments. This redistribution of power recognized the growing functional interdependence of all levels of government and stressed cooperation rather than conflict in intergovernmental relations.[4]

The New Deal and the Great Society (1933-1968)

The New Deal has been viewed as a response to the cataclysmic events of the Great Depression, a period that witnessed major changes in the "public philosophy," or the set of principles that guide public policy.[5] Characteristics of the New Deal public philosophy were federal centralization and activism and a new kind of mass politics, one which encouraged widespread public participation in public affairs. There is no doubt that the New Deal of Franklin D. Roosevelt changed the face of federal-state relation by increasing the size and number of grants-in-aid programs, by enlarging federal government involvement in state and local functions, and by creating new areas of governmental responsibility, especially with respect to regulating and managing the economy and taking responsibility for the public's welfare.

In one sense, The Great Society, the seeds of which were sown during the Kennedy Administration and blossomed when Lyndon Johnson was President from November of 1963 until the end of 1968, extended the trend toward centralization. For example, the federal government expanded its role as a protector of workers to one of a guarantor of a decent income, job, education, health care, housing, and other goods and services that Americans had come to want and expect, as a right, from government. It was also during the 1960s that the federal government aggressively challenged the states' claim that because the state rather than the federal government was responsible for education in the state, it was the state's prerogative to establish a "separate but equal" educational system, even if it meant violating federal civil rights laws.

In another sense, however, the Great Society broke with the New Deal: the traditional influence of parties and pressure groups was displaced by the influence of experts and professionals, most of whom could be found in the federal bureaucracy, not in the states and localities. In fact, the increased responsibility of the federal government, sometimes described as the rise of the administrative state, during the New Deal and Great Society institutionalized the supremacy of national over state and local government.

It was also during the Great Society of the 1960s that a new twist was added to federal-state relations. The private sector was openly included as an active partner with national and subnational governments. In connection with this development, the Johnson administration also experimented with block grants. A block grant, a type of grant-in-aid, is federal money given to state or local agencies for general purposes. Other types of grants-in-aid are (1) the categorical grant, which specifies the category of services to be provided and sets conditions governing how much money the states have to raise to match the federal contribution, and when, how, and for whom states and localities can spend federal money; (2) the project grant, which allows federal agencies to assign grants for specific projects to governmental and nongovernmental agencies in the states on a competitive basis; and (4) revenue sharing, which sends money raised through taxes directly to states and to tens of thousands of local governments for purposes determined by state and local governments.

In 1966, as part of his administration's "creative federalism" plan to improve coordination and cooperation between levels of government and between the public and private sectors, a block grant was used as the instrument to provide comprehensive health services to poor people around the country. And the block grants experiment was expanded by the two Republican administrations that followed: in 1969, Richard Nixon proposed a "New Federalism," a variant of Cooperative Federalism; in 1972, the Nixon administration promoted "general revenue sharing" laws, a plan for collecting taxes and sending back the money directly to states and localities; and, in 1975 and 1976, Gerald Ford proposed an extension of these programs. In sum, in the eleven years between 1966 and 1976, five major block grants were enacted and implemented. How did these five grants operate in practice?

II. Previous Experience with Block Grants

With the rise of the welfare state also came a clear division between the level of government which was to be the primary provider and the primary financer for each type of policy. As Table 1 shows, elementary and secondary education and police and fire protection are local responsibilities whereas the

Table 1 Government Service Providers and Financers by Function, circa. 1982

Functions	Primary Provider	Primary Financer
Local Parks and Recreation	Local	Local
Libraries	Local	Local
Sewerage and Sanitation	Local	Local
Housing and Urban Renewal	Local	Federal
Education, Elem. and Sec.	Local	Local-State
Higher Education	State	State
Education, Other	Federal	Federal
Police Protection	Local	Local
Fire Protection	Local	Local
Corrections	State	State
Highways	State	State
Hospitals	Local-State	Local-State-Federal
Health Services	Local-State-Federal	Local-State-Federal
Public Welfare, Cash	Local-State-Federal	Federal
Public Welfare, Other	State	Federal
Natural Resources	Federal	Federal
Water Transportation	Federal	Federal
Air Transportation	Federal	Federal
All Functions, Combined	Local-State-Federal	Local-State-Federal

NOTE: A primary service provider is one that accounts for 50 percent or more of direct government expenditures, a measure generally accepted as an indication of the extent to which it provides that service. A primary service financer is one that accounts for 50 percent or more of the responsibility for financing the service, through direct government expenditures or intergovernmental assistance.

SOURCE: U.S. Advisory Commission on Intergovernmental Relations, *State and Local Roles in the Federal System* (Washington, D.C., 1982), pp. 7–8, and updates.

primary provider for water and air transporation and for natural resources is the federal government. On the other hand, health services and public welfare are joint federal-state-local responsibilities. Hence, federal-state relations vary by policy arena.

Many policies that are jointly sponsored are financed with block grants.[6] The first block grant, the Partnership for Health Act of 1966, collapsed, partly because the discretion that was granted local administrators was not used to achieve national goals, but rather to advance state and local governments' own internal agendas. Whereas significant policy and administrative discretion was achieved in this and several other block grants during the first year following their enactment, administrative discretion at the local level, over time, seemed to erode. In the Community Development Block Grant, for example, Federal officials tended to become more involved in local decision-making after the first years. But in spite of the slippage accompanying the implementation of the program, the question remained: Did decentralization lead to greater efficiency, flexibility, accountability, and increased citizen participation and thus greater client support, as the proponents of this brand of federalism had promised?

Apparently not. In one study, Nathan and Dommel report that they were surprised to find that only about half the officials they surveyed reported decrease in red tape, one of the indicators of efficiency. Ironically, state and local officials often ended up with even less flexibility.[7] Furthermore, when federal officials relinquished their control over resource allocation decisions, their fear of distributional inequities was heightened, and they took a "more threatening" position *vis-a-vis* state and local officials. They mandated stiff penalties for discrimination; and they asked for more auditing, monitoring, and evaluation.[8]

Not only has past performance fallen short of expectations on efficiency and flexibility criteria, but the decentralization that has accompanied the administration of the block grants has also been criticized because it has led to more muddled accountability. With the devolution of authority from federal agents to governors, mayors, and county executives in state and local government, decisions about who gets what at whose expense became politically charged. In fact, the pessimistic predictions that local autonomy would be undermined by powerful interest groups were not supported by the facts; political judgment about which interest group should benefit was probably more important in explaining why things happened the way they did. Contrary to expectations, early experience with these block grants show that the national goal of protecting minorities is not necessarily undermined by increased discretion in the hands of state and local officials.

But if the folding of categorical grants into a few block grants from the mid-1960s to the mid-1970s did not result in greater efficiency, flexibility, or accountability, surely decentralization stimulated more citizen participation. Here, the results are mixed. It is true that local decision-making programs, with public hearings, open meetings, and the like, were mandated by law; but Federal administrators virtually ignored these procedures, and the attitudes of local implementors and interest groups were determinant. Hence, in practice, the earliest attempts to achieve greater flexibility, efficiency, accountability, responsiveness, and citizen participation through the use of block grants failed, in large measure, to live up to their promises.

III. *The Crisis in Federalism*

The modernization that accompanied America's transformation from an agrarian economy of frontier freedoms to an advanced, technological society created many of the problems associated with federalism. The growth in the size and scope of the federal government and the rise of "national" problems like transportation, pollution, energy, and unemployment that became just too difficult for state and local governments to tackle on their own led to more centralized control and greater reliance on categorical aid.

Between Franklin D. Roosevelt's election as President in 1932 and 1978, public policy making and responsibility for its results became increasingly nationalized. One spurt in federal activity occurred in the early New Deal, and another occurred in the quarter century between 1954 and 1979, when the federal government tripled its share of total state-local general revenue from its own sources. The increases have been most dramatic in education, highways, public welfare, and housing and urban renewal.

Since the Great Depression, there has been a growing trend toward centralized control in Washington: the federal government made many state problems national problems; federal aid as a proportion of state and local revenues and expenditures grew at phenomenal rates; and new revenue sharing grants brought more aid from the federal government directly to cities.[9] The fifty years between the 1930s and the 1980s also witnessed a dramatic rise in the number of federal to state categorical grants-in-aid, with federal strings which set conditions for spending; and the federal courts also curbed the states' discretion over such activities as defining eligibility requirements for social programs. As Table 2 shows, federal aid peaked in Fy 1978, both as a percentage of state and local expenditures and as a percentage of Gross National Product (GNP). Although the spending in current dollars continued on an upward spiral, federal grants to state and local governments declined in absolute number and as a percentage of GNP and state and local expenditures. Increased centralization and a rapid rise in categorical aid created problems of planning, coordination, and accountability. Moreover, the proliferation of agencies and the fragmentation of authority has undoubtedly contributed to more conflict, inefficiency, disorder, and deadlock. In fact, some have wondered whether, under this system, it was still possible to govern at all.

In response to this ongoing crisis of federalism, each of the Republican Presidents who governed in the years immediately following the Great Society came up with his own version of how to ameliorate the crisis. However, the intergovernmental system of the 1970s was not the "old style" dual federalism of autonomous national, subnational, and local governments, each pursuing its own interests independently. What replaced dual federalism, however, is the subject of considerable discussion and debate. Is it a fragmented, chaotic system of every unit of government for itself? Or is it a "cooperative" federalism that stresses sharing of authority and responsibility among the different levels of government? In other words, as the United States prepares to enter the 1990s, is federalism dead? Is the existing system a unitary or a federal one?

The Reagan administration has tried to cope with this crisis of federalism by returning to a policy of dual federalism and states' rights. In theory, Reagan's "New Federalism" policies of consolidation, decentralization, and deregulation are designed to make government more efficient, more flexible, and

Table 2 Federal Grants to State and Local Governments, Selected Fiscal Years, 1929–85

Year	Billions of Current Dollars	Percent of GNP	Percent of State and Local Expenditures	Number[a]
1929	0.1	0.1	1.5	15
1939	1.0	1.1	10.3	30
1949	2.2	0.9	11.0	n.a
1954	2.9	0.8	9.7	n.a
1959	6.5	1.4	13.9	132
1964	10.1	1.6	14.7	212
1969	20.3	2.2	17.1	387
1974	43.4	3.1	21.2	n.a
1975	49.8	3.3	21.4	448
1976	59.1	3.5	23.5	n.a
1977	68.4	3.7	25.4	n.a
1978	77.9	3.7	26.2	n.a
1979	82.9	3.5	25.8	n.a
1980	91.5	3.5	25.7	539
1981	94.8	3.2	24.8	n.a
1982	88.2	2.9	21.6	441
1983	92.5	2.9	21.6	n.a
1984	97.6	2.7	21.2	404
1985 (est.)	107.0	2.8	n.a	n.a

Sources: Data for 1929–82 are from the Advisory Commission on Intergovernmental Relations, *Significant Features of Fiscal Federalism,* 1982–83 edition (Washington, D.C.: ACIR, 1984), tables 1,2,75; and ACIR, *Categorical Grants: Their Role and Design* (ACIR, 1978), tables I-7,I-9. Data for 1983–85 are from *Special Analyses, Budget of the United States Government, Fiscal Year 1986;* and ACIR, *A Catalog of Federal Grant-in-Aid Programs to State and Local Governments: Grants Funded Fiscal Year 1984* (ACIR, 1984).

n.a. Not available.

[a]For 1963 and earlier, the number in existence is based on those grants still in existence in 1968; however, the only grants known to have been terminated were fourteen associated with the Depression and temporary emergencies of world War II; for 1975 and earlier, the number is for the nearest available year.

more responsive and accountable to local needs. This states' rights policy is also supposed to result in greater participation by those most affected by the programs.[10]

Whether this actually is happening, at least in the state of Texas, is the empirical question that this chapter now addresses. In the next section, the theory and practice of the Reagan administration's "New Federalism" policies are reviewed. Then the findings of two recent studies of the implementation and administration of block grants in the state of Texas during the early- and mid-1980s are compared to these expected results.

III. Reagan's New Federalism in Theory

In the first weeks of his first term in office, Ronald Reagan proposed a major reform of the federal system. He asked Congress to consolidate dozens of categorical grants-in-aid into a few block grants. After months of internal bickering between members of the House of Representatives and Senators, a Conference Committee finally approved an acceptable compromise to include in the Omnibus Budget Reconciliation Act (OBRA) of 1981. Upon OBRA's enactment on October 1, 1981, fifty-seven categorical grants were folded into nine block grants, seven for immediate implementation, at the discretion of each of the fifty states, and two to go into effect twelve months later. The nine block grants are described in Table 3.

Table 3 Consolidation of Federal Aid Programs through Block Grants

New Block Grants, 1982	Old Categorical Grants Consolidated, 1981
Preventive health care and health services	Home health, rodent control, emergency medical services, fluoridation, rape crisis, hypertension control, health incentive, health education
Alcohol, drug abuse, and mental health services	Community Health Centers Act, Mental Health Systems Act, Comprehensive alcohol abuse and alcoholism prevention, drug abuse prevention
Social Services	Title XX of the Social Security Act
Maternal and child health	Maternal and child health grants, supplemental security income for children, lead poisoning prevention, genetic disease, sudden infant death, hemophilia screening, adolescent health services
Home energy assistance	Low-income energy assistance
Community services	Various programs of the Economic Opportunity Act of 1984, including senior opportunities and services, community food and nutrition, energy conservation and training
Community development	Small cities community development program (cities under 50,000 population); 701 planning grant; neighborhood self-help development; territories program
Primary health care	Community health centers; primary care research and demonstration grants
Education	37 elementary and secondary school categorical programs (such as desegregation aid; National Teachers Corp.; metric education; consumer education; education of the handicapped; migrant education; education of deprived, neglected or delinquent children; education of gifted children)

Has this latest attempt at restructuring power among levels of government gone the way of previous experiments in federalism reform? Or has performance lived up to the promise of the Reagan administration theory of federalism? To answer these questions, we will examine New Federalism theory and its practice in the state of Texas in the early- and mid-1980s.

In theory, the American people have been promised that if only the Federal government would turn much of its business over to state and local elected officials, government would no longer be part of the *problem*, but would become part of the *solution*. In his Inaugural Address of 1980, Ronald Reagan proposed giving states and cities more authority and responsibility, but fewer federal dollars. Under the banner of "New Federalism," President Reagan told the nation:

> . . . it is my intention to curb the size and influence of the Federal establishment and to demand recognition of the distinction between powers granted to the Federal Government and those reserved to the states or to the people. All of us need to be reminded that the Federal Government did not create the states; the states created the Federal Government.[11]

The underlying theory behind the New Federalism is deceptively simple: *if* the bulk of the 500 or so federal categorical aid grants now run by the Federal government were consolidated into a few block grants, *and* control over grants allocation and administration were turned over to state and local governments, *and* if this were accompanied by a reduction in the number of federal constraints on allocation, administration and reporting, *then,* compared to the period immediately before these New Federalism policies were enacted, the consolidated, decentralized, and deregulated programs would perform more efficiently, government would be more responsive, flexible, and accountable, grantees would participate more, and as a result of their increased involvement, grantees would be more supportive of government. From the perspective of the Reagan administration's conservative ideology, the "New Federalism" fit with the administration's goal of cutting domestic non-defense spending and its objective of getting government off the backs of the American people by reducing the number of Federal regulations and by granting state and local governments autonomy in the federal system.

IV. Reagan's New Federalism in Practice: The Case of Texas

If the New Federalism theory is valid, then compared to the 1970s, in the early 1980s we would expect to find both reductions in federal spending for the programs that are under the umbrella of the block grants as well as substantial changes in block grant program operations. As reported in one study of the practice of New Federalism in Texas,[12] there was virtually no change in overall funding levels, at least during those early years. Total federal assistance decreased by 14.7% in 1982, but in the following year funding increased by 17%. However, as a percentage of total state revenues, federal aid declined by 5.2%, more than double the national average. This decline was due more to changes in the state's economy, demography, and politics than to any specific New Federalism policies.

The funding situation was different when it came to the New Federalism block grants that are described in Table 3: grant funds were reduced from one year to the next and, within the block grant, money was shifted from program to program. With the exception of the Maternal and Child Health block grant, which because of demographic changes in the state increased by a healthy 38.1%, federal money for block grants showed a substantial decline between 1981 and 1983. Cutbacks ranged from a low of 7.1% in the case of the Community Services Block Grant to 23.7% in the case of the block grant for Alcohol, Drug Abuse, and Mental Health. The greatest cuts came in the first year; and where cuts were made, they were allocated on the basis of officials in Austin setting priorities among the various individual programs. In some instances, for example family care services, beneficiaries were shifted from the rolls of the block grant programs to other programs like Medicaid that provided similar services. In the community development programs, state officials "targeted" funds to those communities which were most in need, lending support to the theory that locally managed grants would be more responsive to the needs of the people. As was the case in other states, when cuts had to be made, they were allocated proportionately, according to allocation patterns of the pre-1981 period.

With respect to changes in program administration in the state of Texas, another, more comprehensive study of the implementation and administration of five of the block grants— the Maternal and Child Health (MCH), Community Development Small Cities (CDSC), Low Income Energy Assistance (LIEA), Social Services (SS), and Community Services (CS)—concluded that there were significant differences between pre- and post-1981 administrative behaviors.[13] What follows is a brief summary of the most important findings, based on an analysis of the subjective assessments of state and local officials who were interviewed as part of the study.

Seventy-six percent of the Texas officials who were interviewed reported a difference in the way grants were administered once the conversion to block grants was accomplished. The most frequently cited changes were that local officials now had more control over local priorities, state officials were more involved in program administration, and requirements for paperwork, monitoring, and technical assistance had increased in some cases and decreased in others.

Moreover, most state and local officials were satisfied with the new arrangement. While there was variability in level of satisfaction across the five block grants and from one part of the state to the next, more than eight of every ten of those interviewed said that they preferred block grants to the project or formula mode of federal funding.

Table 4 Percentage of Administrators Who Agree that Goals have Been Accomplished

Perceptions of Block Grant Performance Block Grant	MCH N = 16	CDBG N = 8	LIEA N = 10	SS N = 13	CS N = 9	All N = 56
Is Less Costly to Administer	100.0	50.0	88.9	46.7	57.1	71.1
Carries Fewer Strings to Spending	92.9	50.0	66.7	45.5	44.4	62.7
Results in Less Paperwork	75.0	25.0	44.4	40.0	25.0	44.7
Gives More Responsibility to State and Local Officials	84.6	100.0	90.0	81.8	75.0	86.0
Allows More Citizen Participation	75.0	50.0	88.9	60.0	22.2	60.4
Is Preferred by State and Local Officials	100.0	100.0	66.7	66.7	83.3	83.7
Mean	87.9	62.5	74.3	56.8	51.2	

Source: Malcolm L. Goggin, David Cownie, David Romero, Larry Gonsales and Susan Williams, "Block Grants and the New Federalism."

Using New Federalism in theory as a guide, the authors asked a representative sample of block grant administrators around the state whether they agreed or disagreed that certain programmatic objectives had been achieved. Administrator opinions are summarized in Table 4.

In general, the conversion from categorical to block grant was perceived as having greater success in some areas than in others. Table 4 illustrates the point: the change-over from categorical to block grants gave state and local officials more responsibility for program operations and increased administrative efficiency. But the conversion apparently did not reduce paperwork in all cases, nor did the change eliminate strings to funding or increase the level of citizen participation. Nevertheless, the overall assessment of the vast majority of those interviewed was that block grants were preferred to the more fragmented, Washington-directed categorical grants.

One of the effects of decentralizing decision-making by giving more responsibility to state and local officials is, *in some cases,* reduction in paperwork, especially monitoring and reporting. Surprisingly, paperwork seems to have increased in some cases and decreased in others. One possible explanation for increased paperwork is that state government merely filled the vacuum created when the federal government relinquished control and thus decreased its demands for reports and audits.

Previous experience with decentralized administration of grants suggest that once the targeting provisions that accompanied many of programs financed with categorical grants are removed, and federal strings to spending are eliminated, state and local officials will redirect funds to more affluent and more politically influential segments of the population. These same officials might also redirect the spending to more politically popular, distributive, pork barrel programs, undoubtedly at the expense of some of the less popular but needed redistributive programs that helped the poor. Did the New Federalism strategy of giving state and local officials more discretion over how to spend program funds result in less money for minorities?

With few exceptions, officials throughout the state thought minorities were not discriminated against in the administration of block grant programs. If this were true, then funding cuts must have been accomplished by redefining eligibility requirements for services so that middle income clients were no longer served by the program. State-wide changes in program requirements along these lines would be consistent with the Reagan administration's policies to provide government assistance to only the "truly needy," thus eliminating from the roles those who were not part of the "deserving" poor.

V. Summary and Conclusion

Beginning with the arguments in *The Federalist Papers* and Anti-Federalist writings and continuing throughout the first 200 years of United States political history, the manner in which political institutions share power to make and implement public policy has been continually debated. Throughout the nation's history, the pendulum has swung back and forth between national supremacy and states' rights. During Ronald Reagan's terms in office, the pendulum has swung once again toward a policy that is decidedly in favor of states' rights. The grants instrument for implementing this policy has been the block grant rather than the categorical grant or revenue sharing. As we learned from the recent experience with New Federalism in Texas, one likely result of decentralization is that the state will take on some of the responsibilities formerly performed by the federal government. In the face of declining federal support for activities covered by the block grants, Texas is faced with the hard choice of either cutting services or raising taxes. Faced with this option, virtually every state in the United States has raised state taxes and used the revenues to make up for cuts in federal spending.

The price of reducing the influence of the national government in favor of state and local elected and appointed officials and loosening the "strings" attached to federal grants—by converting many of them from categorical grants-in-aid to block grants and by doing away with federal "targeting" requirements—is the loss of hierarchical control. Rising federal deficits have meant that few major initiatives are likely to come from Washington, and as states become more self-reliant in the face of a paralysis of federal institutions that is created by a rising national debt, it will become increasingly difficult for elected and appointed officials in Washington to get subnational and local governments to accomplish national objectives, especially when those goals may not be as important to states and localities as they are to the federal government. By consolidating, decentralizing, and deregulating, the central government is now in a much weaker position to coerce governments in the periphery to do its bidding, with federal-state relations suffering as a consequence.

Thus, as the Reagan era comes to a close, its legacy may be a return to the "conflict" phase of intergovernmental relations,[14] with states increasingly challenging federal authority in those cases where both levels of government seek to establish control over the same or similar activities. In view of pressures for fiscal austerity brought upon by federal deficits and taxpayer revolts plus the sheer size of entitlement programs that leave little for discretionary spending, and in light of federal demands that states become more self-reliant, tensions are bound to rise at the center of the federation. One wonders how, as we enter the 1990s, these tensions will be overcome so that national objectives upon which the states place a low priority, or perhaps oppose, will ever be achieved.

Notes

1. According to Woodrow Wilson, the cardinal issue of the United States consitutional system is the nature of the relationship between the states and the federal government.
2. See J. R. Pool, ed., *The American Constitution: For and Against: The Federalist and Anti-Federalist Papers* (New York: Hill and Wang, 1987).
3. For an argument for centralization, see William Riker, *Federalism: Origin, Operation, Significance* (Boston: Little, Brown, 1964). For a defense of decentralization, see Daniel Elazar, *American Federalism: A View from the States* (New York: Harper and Row, 1984).
4. Scholars are divided on the question of how much vertical cooperation there had been among the levels of govenment before the New Deal. One school, represented by Morton Grodzins and Daniel Elazar, argues that there was never dual federalism. See, for example, Morton Grodzins, *The American System* (Chicago, Il.: Rand McNally and Co., 1958); and Daniel Elazar, "Federal-State Partnership in the Nineteenth Century United States," In *American Federalism in Perspective,* edited by Aaron Wildavsky (Boston, Ma.: Little, Brown, 1967). Another school, with Harry Scheiber and Samuel Beer as its spokespersons, maintains that there is little evidence of cooperative federalism before the New Deal. See, for example, U.S. Congress, Senate, Committee on Government Operations, *The Condition of American Federalism: An Historian's View,* Committee Print, 89th Cong., 2d sess., 1966.

5. Theodore J. Lowi, "The Public Philosophy: Interest Group Liberalism" *American Political Science Review* 61 (1967): 5–24. For a more detailed discussion of the public philosophy that has emerged sine the New Deal, see Malcolm L. Goggin, "Social Policy as Theory: Reagan's Public Philosophy," in *Public Policy and Social Institutions,* edited by Harrell Rodgers, Jr. (Greenwich, Conn.: Jai Press, 1984), pp. 55–96.
6. The following sections draw on portions of Malcolm L. Goggin, David Cownie, David Romero, Larry Gonzales, and Susan Williams, "Block Grants and the New Federalism: Theory and Practice," paper presented at the 1985 Annual Meeting of the Southwestern Social Science Association, Houston, TX., March, 1985.
7. Richard Nathan and Paul Dommel, "Federal-Local Relations under Block Grants," *Political Science Quarterly* 93 (1978): 41.
8. Carl E. Van Horn, *Policy Implementation in the Federal System* (Lexington, Mass.: D.C. Heath and Co., 1979), p. 154.
9. The rise of the administrative state—especially the federal bureaucracy—has been documented in William Riker, "Federalism" in *Handbook of Political Science* edited by Fred I. Greenstein and Nelson W. Polsby, (Reading, Mass.: Addison-Wesley, 1975, Vol. 5); and James Q. Wilson, "The Rise of the Bureaucratic State," *The Public Interest* 41 (1975):357–94. Congress's role in expanding categorical grants-in-aid is analyzed in John Chubb, "Federalism and the Bias for Centralization," in *The New Direction in American Politics,* edited by John E. Chubb and Paul E. Peterson Washington, D.C.: Brookings, 1985), pp. 281–86.
10. See Ronald Reagan's 1982 State of the Union Address for the outlines of the administration's policies in this regard. For a broader discussion of the origins, evolution, and effects of "New Federalism," see Michael Reagan and John Sanzone, *The New Federalism* (New York: Oxford University Press, 1981).
11. Text of Ronald Reagan's 1980 Inaugural Address on January 21, 1981, as reprinted in *Congressional Quarterly,* vol. 39, no. (January 29, 1981).
12. Susan A. McManus, Robert M. Stein, and V. Howard Savage, "The Texas Response to Reagan's New Federalism Program: The Early Years," in *Administering the New Federalism.* (Boulder, Colo. Westview Press, 1986). edited by Lewis G. Bender and James A. Stever. For a comparative perspective, see Marilyn Gittell, ed. *State Politics and the New Federalism* (New York: Longmans, 1986); and Richard P. Nathan and Fred C. Doolittle, *The Consequences of Cuts: The Effects of the Reagan Domestic Program on State and Local Governments.* (Princeton, N.J: Princeton University Press, 1983).
13. Goggin, et al., "Block Grants and the New Federalism: Theory and Practice."
14. Wright, *Understanding Intergovernmental Relations.*

Bibliography

Advisory Committee on Intergovernmental Relations. *The Federal Role in the Federal System: The Dynamics of Growth: The Conditions of Contemporary Federalism: Conflicting Theories and Collapsing Constraints.* (Washington, D.C.: Advisory Committee on Intergovernmental Relations, August, 1981).

Bender, Lewis G., and James A. Stever, eds. *Administering the New Federalism.* (Boulder, Colo. Westview Press, 1986).

Nathan, Richard P., and Fred C. Doolittle. *The Consequences of Cuts: The Effects of the Reagan Domestic Program on State and Local Governments.* (Princeton, N.J.: Princeton University Press, 1983).

Nice, David C. *Federalism: The Politics of Intergovernmental Relations.* (New York: St. Martin's Press, 1987).

O'Toole, Laurence J., Jr., ed. *American Intergovernmental Relations.* (Washington, D.C.: Congressional Quarterly Press, 1985).

Petersen, Paul E., Barry G. Rabe, and Kenneth K. Wong, *When Federalism Works.* (Washington, D.C.: Brookings, 1986).

Reagan, Michael, and John Sanzone. *The New Federalism.* (New York: Oxford University Press, 1981).

Riker, William H. "Federalism." In Fred I. Greenstein and Nelson W. Polsby, eds. *Handbook of Political Science.* (Reading, Mass.: Addison-Wesley, 1975), Vol. 5.

Walker, David B. *Toward Functioning Federalism.* (Cambridge, Mass.: Winthrop Press, 1981).

Wright, Deil. *Understanding Intergovernmental Relations.* 2d ed. (Monterey, Ca.: Brooks Cole, 1982).

13 The Texas Constitution
DONALD S. LUTZ

The Nature of a Constitution

The idea of a constitution goes back to the ancient Greeks. Aristotle collected and studied more than one hundred and fifty constitutions of Greek city-states and characterized a constitution as a plan for a way of life. As such, a constitution was composed of a description of the basic political institutions as well as the fundamental values and commitments shared by a people. Beginning with the Magna Carta in 1215 A.D., the English gradually developed over several hundred years the notion of a constitution as a limit on the power of the king, and eventually as a limit on the power of all government officials. But the modern written constitution was invented by English-speaking people in America during the seventeenth and eighteenth centuries. The first modern constitution, one not only characterized by its inclusion of the Greek ideas and the British notion of limited government but also written down in a single document, was probably the Pilgrim Code of Law written by the colonists of Plymouth, Massachusetts, in 1636, closely followed by the Fundamental Orders of Connecticut written in Hartford, Connecticut, in 1639.

Each of the first thirteen American states adopted written constitutions in 1776. Several important things need to be said about these documents. First, they look very much like our state constitutions today for the simple reason that they provided the models for later constitutions. Second, three states—Rhode Island, Connecticut, and Massachussetts—merely readopted colonial documents which they had been using as their constitutions since the previous century. The other ten states wrote new documents that essentially described their colonial institutions. Thus clearly the roots of American constitutionalism lay in the colonial era prior to independence. Third, these colonial institutions and documents were not copied from the English model. For one thing, England had no written constitution. For another, those in America had evolved a different, much more modern form of government than that which existed in England. Fourth, it is worth noting that the first constitutions were written not at the national level, but by states. When it came time to write a national constitution—first the Articles of Confederation, and then the Federalist Constitution of 1787 under which we still live—thirteen constitutional republics were already in existence. Americans chose to preserve the state constitutions under the umbrella of the national constitution and called the resulting form of government "federalism."

One interesting thing about the Texas Constitution, then, is that it is just as much a constitution as our national document and has a pedigree predating the national Constitution. Another interesting thing is that the Texas Constitution is part of a constitutional system called federalism. The easiest way to explain what this means is to note that Americans are citizens twice—a citizen simultaneously of the United States and of the state wherein they reside—"dual citizenship." All citizens legally residing in Texas are thus citizens of the United States and simultaneously citizens of Texas. The Texas legislature passes laws, and if a citizen of Texas breaks one of these laws he or she goes before a Texas court. The United States Congress passes laws, and if a citizen of the United States residing in Texas breaks one of these laws he or she goes before a national, or federal, court. In Texas courts the citizen has certain minimal rights guaranteed by the national Bill of Rights, but can and does have certain additional rights found in the Texas Bill of Rights. In federal courts, the citizen has only those rights found in the national Constitution. The rights of citizens of states will thus vary according to how many rights are found in their state constitution, always having a minimum "floor" of rights as described in the National Bill of Rights and applied against the states.

Federalism, then, is a political system in which there are two levels of government, each with its own powers. American federalism has evolved into a very complex system in which the national government has many more powers than it once did, and state power has been significantly reduced, but in which the state and national governments frequently work as partners in solving political problems, even though the partnership is as often marked by conflict as cooperation. State constitutions, and state governments, cannot be ignored in this partnership. The state governments defined by their respective constitutions still have considerable independent powers in addition to those shared with the national government. State constitutions still perform all those functions ascribed to any constitution worthy of the name.

What are these functions which a constitution is supposed to perform? *First of all, a constitution creates a form of government and describes its offices and institutions.* This description of the basic institutions for collective decision making is the heart of any constitution, for such a description provides the basic limits on government. Those with political power must reside in an office whose method of being filled, range of powers, manner of operation, and means for replacement are all spelled out in public. We take this deceptively simple aspect of politics so much for granted it is easy to forget that for most of human history until relatively recently, as is still true in many countries today, those in power ruled without the general population knowing for sure how and why decisions were made, let alone who made them.

We have already implied another major function of constitutions—to limit governmental power. A key aspect of a constitutional system is that the government cannot do whatever those who hold power want it to do, and what powers they do have are carefully circumscribed by procedures to prevent, or at least minimize, arbitrariness. Bills of rights are thus usually part of a modern written constitution to remove certain powers entirely from government, although as just noted the careful description of basic institutions and procedures is also an important way to limit governments.

The matter of limits is an especially interesting one when it comes to state constitutions because of one basic feature of the American constitutional system. In the United States Constitution, except for the powers explicitly given to the national government, or denied to the states, all other powers are given to the state governments. What are some of these powers? In addition to the police power, the power to regulate education, and the power to regulate intrastate commerce, the states may regulate the health, welfare, and morals of its people. For example, and just for example, in the 1780's various states regulated the height of fences, the price of bread, who could and could not make bricks, whether a single person could live alone, and what time people were supposed to go to bed. In other words, the power left to the states is potentially unlimited. As we will see, the framers of the Texas constitution were particularly sensitive to this problem.

Another function of a constitution is to define who is and who is not a citizen and then define the rights and duties of citizenship. This constitutional function was the basic one as far as the ancient Greeks were concerned. A constitution was, in effect, a plan for a way of life, and thus it was critical to determine who was and who was not to share in that way of life. Today we take for granted that everyone over eighteen, who has been either born or naturalized an American, is an equal as a citizen. The Texas Constitution lays out a definition of state citizenship in fulfilling this function.

Finally, a constitution, as just noted, lays out a plan for a way of life. In other words, a constitution lays out the fundamental values, hopes, and commitments of a people—what is known as a "political culture." It amounts to a description of the kind of people they are or that they hope to become. Most amendments to American state and national constitutions have to do with changing these fundamental values and commitments rather than altering the decision-making institutions.

A careful reading of a constitution provides a snapshot of a people—their shared values and commitments, the kind of lives they generally live, and the balance of political forces at the time the constitution was written. If there is a significant change in shared commitments and values, the general circumstances of their lives, or the balance of political forces, a people will amend or replace their constitution.

Background to the Texas Constitution

The people inhabiting Texas have at one time or another lived under one of eight constitutions. In each instance the shift to a new constitution was required by a significant change in values, circumstances, or political power—sometimes all three. In 1821 Mexico revolted from Spain and wrote a national constitution which included rule over Tejas as an interior province. By 1828 the northeast provinces had gained so much population that the combined state of Coahuila y Tejas wrote a state constitution that was in many respects a good, modern constitution. However, the rapidly increasing anglo-Texan population was not completely happy and agitated for more representation and a number of economic benefits. Political unrest finally led in 1836 to Texas' declaring its independence from Mexico, which required a constitution for the Republic of Texas. This new national constitution bore strong resemblance to American state constitutions of the time, especially the southern and border states from which most Anglo-Texans at that time came. Thus, when the Republic of Texas became another state of the United States, relatively few changes were required to turn its national constitution of 1836 into the Texas state Constitution of 1845.

In 1861 Texas wrote a constitution as part of the Confederacy, and the constitution's contents were expressive of that membership and the Confederacy's goals. The constitution of 1866 then had to provide for reentry into the union, and the Constitution of 1869 had to meet the demands of Reconstruction. Finally, in 1876, Texas was able to write a constitution free from the demands of broader political commitments or interference and thus more reflective of its own political culture. That is the constitution, much amended, under which we live today. Its many amendments (about 290 in all) are attempts to alter political culture to meet the drastic changes that have taken place since 1876.

The phrase "Texas' political culture" seems to imply that there is a single one when in fact it has always been a combination or an amalgam of several "ways of life." In particular, there were two major subcultures coexisting in Texas in 1876, sometimes competing, each of which called for somewhat different constitutional expression. The Texas Constitution of 1876 bears the marks of a compromise between the two subcultures—termed individualistic and traditionalistic.

The individualistic subculture is pragmatic and utilitarian and emphasizes private initiative with a minimum of government interference. If the government is supposed to do anything, it is to encourage a free market economy. Individualistically inclined people would tend to prefer 1) a constitution that strictly limits governmental power, especially in economic matters; 2) a weak legislature dominating an even weaker executive; 3) social and political relationships that are open, equal, and relatively unfettered—based more upon merit and accomplishment than upon tradition, family connections, or preferential treatment; and 4) a strong bill of rights that protects such social and political relationships.

The traditionalistic subculture reflects an older, pre-commercial society in which it is expected that those at the top of the social structure take a special and dominant role in government. Government has a positive role to perform and thus should be given some real power, but that role is primarily to protect and preserve the existing social order. To do so it tends to confine real political power to a relatively small and self-perpetuating group drawn from an established elite. In this rather organic view, with its strong elitist and paternalistic emphases, the marketplace is to be viewed with a certain ambivalence.

On the one hand the marketplace produces goods and services needed by the society, but at the same time it threatens the established social order not only by inducing unforeseen economic changes, but also by producing men of new wealth who tend to compete with the old elite. Also, the marketplace in its normal day-to-day operation makes use of, and glorifies, attitudes and values that threaten to undermine the core values of family, religion, stability, and tradition. Those inclined toward the traditionalistic subculture would be willing to give some significant power to government, but would wish to hem it in with restrictions that protect traditional values. They would value leadership and prefer action by offices filled by the "better sort" over a legislature, which means a preference for a reasonably strong executive branch. Paternalism would be expressed by constitutional provisions for taking care of "our own," and elitism would be expressed by provisions to restrict the suffrage and/or restrict office to a narrow range of the population.

The traditionalistic subculture had its roots in states like Virginia, Georgia, and South Carolina, and had spread westward to the other states of the Old South. East Texas and the upper Gulf coast were populated most heavily by immigrants from southern states, and before the Civil War had participated in the southern slave culture, although large plantations were rare in Texas. Map 1 shows the extent of this traditionalistic cultural area.

The 1850 census showed that such southern immigrants dominated Texas, comprising almost eighty-five percent of the white population. In turn, about two-thirds of the Texas population was white, a little over twenty-eight percent were black, and almost five percent had Spanish surnames. Between 1850 and 1876 the Texas population grew from around two hundred thousand to almost a million and a half. This explosive growth was fueled most heavily by immigrants from midwestern and border states like Tennessee, Indiana, Illinois, Missouri, and Arkansas. Texans drawn from these states brought with them the individualistic subculture that had originally developed in states like Pennsylvania, New York, Maryland, New Jersey, and Delaware. By 1876 the southern stock had declined from almost sixty percent of the Texas population to about forty percent; those from the midwestern and border states with their individualistic inclinations had increased from five percent to over twenty-five percent; another eight percent had come from Europe; the black percentage had declined to twenty-one percent (a decline that continued to 17% in 1910 and 12% in 1980); and those with Spanish surnames remained at about five percent (a percentage that remained more or less constant throughout the nineteenth century until mass migrations from south of the border began around World War I.)

Major cultural and ethnic areas in Texas circa 1876 by county

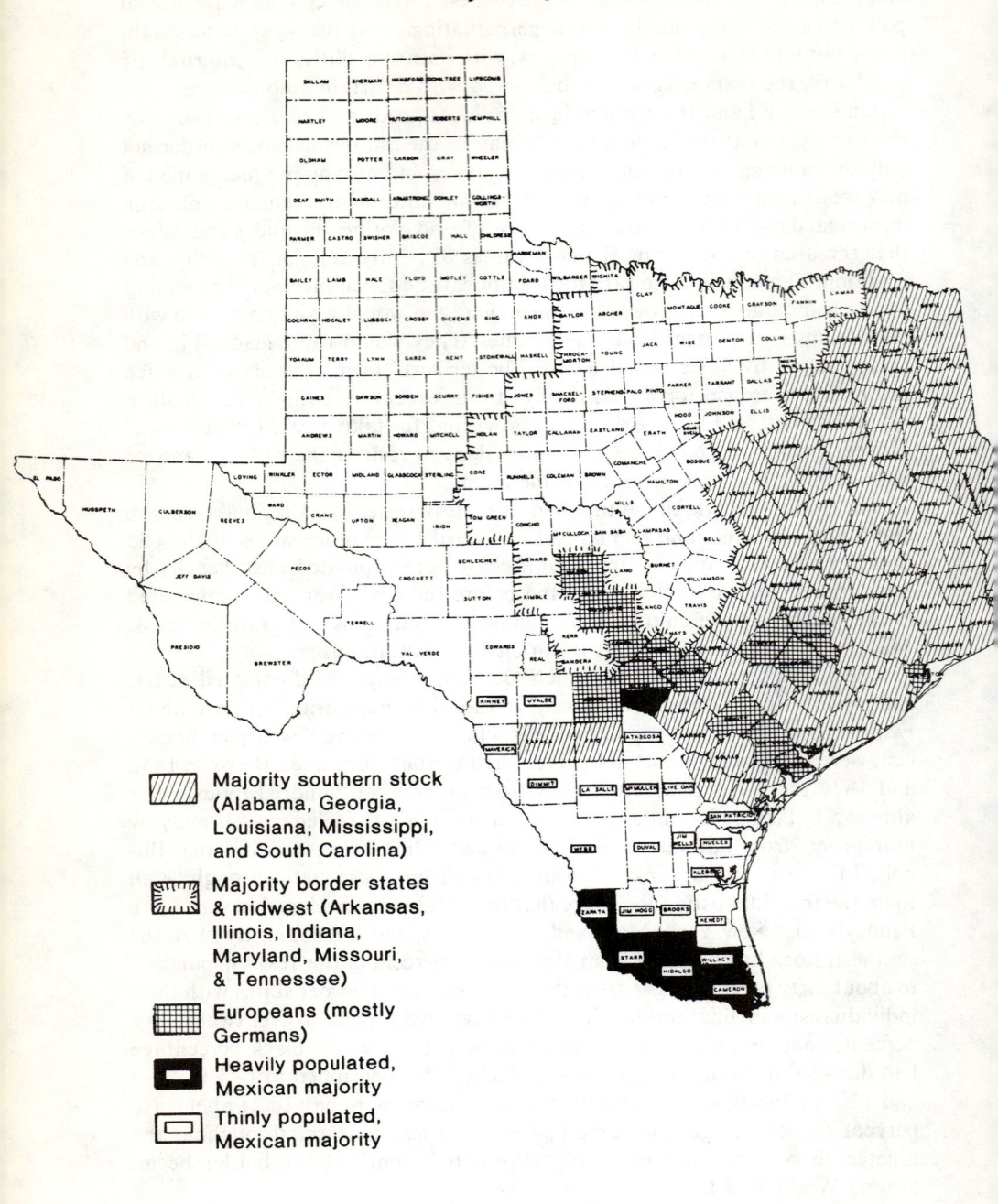

Most of the European stock were Germans, who moved westward from Galveston and northwest from Port O'Connor, meeting in Bexar County (San Antonio) and then spreading north and west into the hill country. The Germans, Czechs, Austrians, and Swiss, all of an individualistic bent, nicely complemented the individualists coming in from the north. Those of Mexican heritage were concentrated in the southern half of Bexar Country and along the lower Rio Grande. They were highly traditionalistic in their own way, but like the blacks were largely excluded from participation in politics.

Another way of showing the extent of the southern-derived traditionalistic culture is to examine the distribution of counties with the highest percentage of blacks. These would be the counties that most heavily participated in the slave culture, and thus in the southern social, economic, and political patterns. Map 2 shows that not all of East Texas belonged to the southern, traditionalistic cultural area. The counties east and south of Dallas (Dallas County) had large numbers of settlers from Tennessee, Missouri, and Arkansas who heavily diluted the traditionalistic culture. The counties most heavily settled by the Europeans stretching west from Galveston and north from Calhoun County also blocked development of a dominant traditionalistic culture. And in the southeast part of the state, those of French descent who migrated to Texas from Louisiana, while pursuing a traditionalist culture, did not take part in the southern American version of it based on a slave economy. They, too, introduced limits on a monolithic, traditionalistic cultural area in East Texas.

In 1876, then, Texas was in the process of moving from a southern, traditionalistic subculture, to one where traditionalism was more or less balanced in numbers by the individualistic subculture. In fact, despite their inferiority in numbers, those of the individualistic persuasion were more active politically and better organized. The rapid rise in importance of the individualistic subculture imported from the middle states was reflected in part by the strongest commercial and transportation links from Texas being with Kansas City and St. Louis, rather than with New Orleans and the south (although Galveston had ocean links with New Orleans, the East Coast, and Europe). It was also reflected in the 1876 Texas constitution where the traditionalistic/individualistic amalgam had a decided tilt toward individualism.

A third subculture, known as "moralistic," began in New England and followed the migration of New Englanders into the Northern tier of midwestern states like Michigan, Wisconsin, Minnesota, and all the way to Oregon. The moralistic subculture did not find its way into Texas, except in small pockets like the Quaker settlement at Friendswood south of Houston.

Circumstances in 1876 made it easier than usual for the two subcultures to agree on a constitution. Reconstruction had angered most Texans regardless of inclination. The traditionalists were most upset by the attempts to destroy the Old South's social patterns, while the individualists were deeply offended by the extravagance and wastefulness of the reconstruction government that

Texas counties in 1876 with highest concentrations of blacks

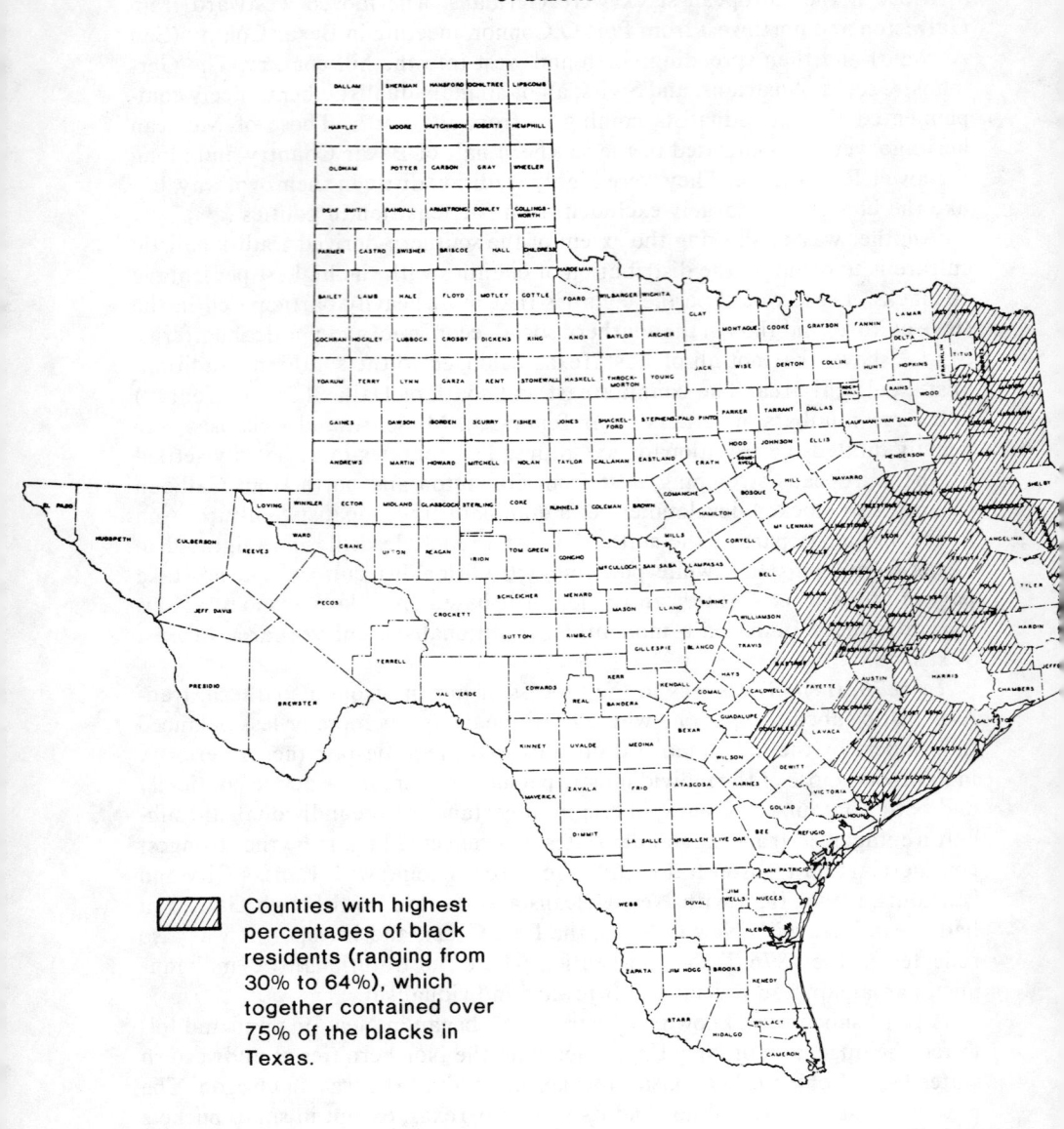

Counties with highest percentages of black residents (ranging from 30% to 64%), which together contained over 75% of the blacks in Texas.

had also been a relatively centralized one. Members of both groups could therefore agree on working for a new constitution that limited future government and carefully enforced governmental economy.

Furthermore, almost half of the ninety members elected to the constitutional convention were members of the Texas Grange. The Grange Movement was a loosely bound, agriculturally-based organization that was strongest in the midwest farming states. Originally organized for social and educational purposes, the local granges became vehicles for farmer protest against economic abuses, abuses they attempted to correct through cooperative efforts. One major concern was railroad monopolies that charged exorbitant shipping prices to get farm goods to market, as well as grain elevator owners who charged high storage fees. The latter problem was solved by setting up Grange-owned grain elevators, but solving the former meant passing laws to break up monopolies or regulating shipping charges. This necessity, in turn, meant reforming state governments that in many cases were being bribed by railroads to serve railroad interests. The creation of the Texas Railroad Commission, at first charged with setting fair shipping rates, later to regulate key parts of the Texas economy, reflects this Grange concern.

While such regulations might at first look contrary to individualistic concern for limited governmental intervention in the economy, they in fact reflect an attempt to break down monopolies in order to create a free market and thus are supportive of individualistic concerns. The Grange was an expression of individualistic farmers who banded together in cooperative enterprises to help make farmers independent and self-sufficient. The movement was born in Dallas, and its membership strength lay mostly within fifty or sixty miles on either side of a line running south-southwest from the Oklahoma border between Dallas and Fort Worth; through Waco, Killeen, and Austin, and on to San Antonio; and on either side of another line running from Austin to Galveston, thus encompassing the heart of the individualistic cultural area. Although the movement failed to achieve very much, and died off in 1896, its most lasting memorial is its impact on the 1876 Constitution.

The traditionalists could support many of the Grange aims, although often for different reasons. The railroads, centers of power run in most cases from the upper Midwest or the East, represented "foreign" intrusions upon control by the Texas elite. Traditionalists could support regulation of railroads, then, on the grounds of protecting control by Texas elites. While traditionalists were willing to support a reasonably powerful state government, they were also willing to support a highly restricted state government as long as to do so meant relative freedom for local government, and thus for local elites.

An unusual amount of discussion of local government in the Constitution of 1876 has the effect of emphasizing its importance. On the one hand county governments find themselves highly restricted by constitutional provisions, especially with regard to raising and spending money, but on the other hand they are also reasonably free from state government intervention. That is, because the state government itself is so weak and fragmented, it has difficulty imposing its will on city and county government. In effect, local governments are left to respond primarily to their respective local constituencies, and often they do so even though it means ignoring state law. For example, state law requires that counties collect personal taxes on automobiles; some counties do, some do not.

The blending of these two subcultures at a time in history when it was easiest to do so, for reasons that seemed compelling at the time, and which gained currency after 1876 simply because the constitution was in place and no new compelling coalition arose to challenge the synthesis for three quarters of a century, combined to produce a stable constitutional tradition which was amended piecemeal as needed rather than replaced. The constitution of 1876 defines a unique Texas political culture, a synthesis that has worked longer than that in all but a few states. Some view the continued use of this constitution as a reflection of a fundamental weakness in Texas politics, and most scholars are quick to criticize the document for its excessive length, confusing construction, and outdated provisions. Others, usually outside of universities, view the continued use of the constitution as a reflection of fundamental strength. It works well enough that no one can figure out how to replace a document that may still define the core of the Texas political culture, even if its institutions do not always seem appropriate for an urban, industrial state of the late twentieth century. Ironically, the Texas Constitution looks very much like one that supporters of President Reagan would like and thus is expressive, unintentionally and perhaps perversely, of a late twentieth century political movement.

A Weak Government Kept Close to the People

The 1866 Texas Constitution was very similar to the 1845 Constitution which had been suspended during the Civil War. It differed in the important respect that it gave equality to blacks and in general provided more security to the former slaves than did the new constitutions in the other former states of the Confederacy. However, in the November election of 1866 the United States Congress was won by the radical Republicans, who immediately began to impose upon the South a series of policies known collectively as Reconstruction.

For Texas the onset of Reconstruction took the most immediate form of Congress refusing to seat the two United States Senators and three members of the House of Representatives elected in November of 1866. The new Texas Constitution was set aside, and military officers replaced elected state officials. A new constitution was written and adopted in 1869 through elections supervised by the United States Army. In this setting radical Republicans gained control of the Texas Legislature and elected as governor E. J. Davis, a former Union army general.

The Constitution of 1869 was quite modern, but it was also very centralized compared with traditional Texas preferences. The Legislature met annually, the governor had a four year term, and judges were appointed by the governor rather than elected. Government officials had their salaries significantly increased. County courts were abolished. The net effect of the 1869 constitution was to centralize much more power in state government and thus greatly weaken local government.

This effect was enhanced by the way in which Governor Davis operated. Selectively using martial law and other methods of intimidation, between 1870 and 1874 Davis ran the most unpopular administration in Texas history. Extravagant public spending and enormous increases in taxes were coupled with blatant corruption. Even though the military continued to supervise elections, widespread anger among Texans led to the Democrats' regaining control of the legislature in the election of 1872. In 1874 Davis was defeated in what has been called the most fraudulent election in Texas history. The stage was set for drafting a new constitution free from outside interference.

Having managed to end the corruption of the Davis regime through fraud, Texans now set about to dismantle Reconstruction through more legal means. The constitutional convention was composed of ninety men, seventy-five Democrats and fifteen Republicans. Six of the Republicans were black. United in their resolve by the events of the previous ten years, the delegates had relatively little trouble deciding what to do. The despised Reconstruction government had been centralized, profligate, and intrusive. Decentralization, frugality, and limited power were the obvious antidotes. The goals of those delegates who were grangers simply served to strengthen their resolve in this direction. Any differences between delegates who preferred the traditionalistic as opposed to the individualistic subcultures were set aside in the pursuit of ends they did share. The Constitution of 1876 became an amalgam of both subcultures at the service of goals that swept over both sides of the division.

No institution escaped the drive to weaken state government. The term of the governor was lowered from four years to two, his salary was significantly reduced, and the power of the office was dispersed. Only in recent years has the governor been restored to a four year term. Aside from express limits on gubernatorial power, other means were used to weaken the office. The major executive offices that are usually appointed by the governor were made elective instead. Except for the secretary of state, whom the governor appointed, the lieutenant governor, comptroller, treasurer, land commissioner, and attorney general were all to be elected. Having the major executive officers elected rather than appointed left open the possibility that persons holding these offices could come from a different party than the governor, a situation that is even more likely today with the decline of Democratic party dominance in Texas politics. At the very least it guaranteed that those holding the major executive offices would each have an independent political base rather than be inclined to work with the governor. The traditional executive privilege of pardoning and parolling criminals was given instead to a board, only one of whose members was to be appointed by the governor, subject to approval by two-thirds of the Senate. The governor was even limited to reprieving no more than one death sentence in any thirty day period. Until 1954 it took a constitutional amendment to raise the governor's salary, a condition faced by other elected state officials as well.

Strangely, the governor was given one power that, in the absence of his other standard powers, looms larger than usual—the item veto. As with the United States President, the Texas governor can veto bills passed by the legislature, and the veto can be overriden by a two-thirds vote of both houses. An item veto permits the governor to reject specific portions of an appropriations bill while approving the rest. Experience has shown that it is much harder for a legislature to override such a partial veto because usually the interests affected are too narrow to muster two-thirds of the legislature in support. It is doubtful that the delegates to the 1876 Convention understood the full consequences of the item veto, or in their vengeful mood they would have denied this to the governor as well. Instead, the item veto appears to have been looked upon as a mechanism to enhance state frugality as it would permit the governor to check legislative tendencies to give a little something to everyone, thus inflating total expenditures beyond what good policy and fiscal prudence would dictate.

Having gutted the executive that Governor Davis made so unpopular, the delegates turned to the legislature. Perhaps under the theory that the less time the legislature met the less damage it could do, legislative sessions were limited to one every two years with a duration of one hundred and forty days. The Constitution even specifies that except for emergencies the legislature shall not pass any bills during the first sixty days of the session, an obvious attempt to restrict further the number of bills that can be passed and thus the amount of damage that the legislature can do. The governor may call the legislature together at other times for special sessions, but only to consider issues that must be specified before the session. The special session can only last thirty days.

In addition to limiting the legislature as to the days it can pass bills, twenty-one more sections in the Constitution of 1876 describe legislative procedures. For example, the title of a bill shall clearly indicate its contents, and anything in the bill not mentioned in the title is considered null and void. Obviously, the legislature is being told to inform the public in plain English what they were doing, no trickery allowed. Also, once a bill or resolution has been defeated, the matter may not be reintroduced during that session. There shall be no wasting of time at the public's expense. The expense to the public is kept low in any case by specifying in the constitution how much legislators can be paid. As of 1975, the most recent amendment in this matter, legislators are to be paid $600 per month when in session, and a per diem of $30 a day for expenses.

There are at least nine sections attempting to prevent legislative corruption. If a legislator has a private interest in the outcome of a bill, he or she is supposed to disclose that interest and not vote. Nor can a legislator accept any governmental position that was created by legislative vote during a term for which they were elected. Nor can a legislator hold any of a myriad of paying positions in national, state, or local government while serving in the legislature. Three sections deal explicitly with legislators accepting bribes and the penalties attached to such behavior. One cannot help but get the strong impression that those writing the Constitution did not trust those in government.

If all of this were not enough, numerous provisions limit what the legislature can or cannot do, especially with respect to finances. For example, Article 3, section 56 lists thirty specific things that the legislature cannot do because the powers belong to local government. Except in emergencies created by war or insurrection, the state is not to go into debt, and when such debt is justified it shall not exceed two hundred thousand dollars. The legislature cannot create lotteries, pledge the credit of the state for private ends, grant public money for private use (except to Confederate veterans or their widows), or operate contrary to any of the seventy-four provisions in the original Constitution regulating various aspects of taxation, spending state money, or affecting the use of private property. For example, the state is limited in the amount of money it can spend on public welfare. Amendments have added sixty-one more sections dealing with state finances. As a result, the initial urge by the framers of the Constitution to cut public expenditures to the bone has been carried forward to the present so that Texas is well known as a "low tax/low services" state. When it comes to protecting all forms of private property, making it difficult for the state legislature to tax, and regulating how and why state money is spent, Texas takes second place to no state.

Article two of the Constitution explicitly establishes separation of powers between the three branches, part of which is a prohibition on anyone's holding simultaneously positions in more than one branch. A number of prohibitions on the legislature in Article 3, Section 56 are designed to keep that body out of judicial matters. For example, the legislature is prohibited from changing the names of persons, changing the venue in civil or criminal cases, authorizing the adoption or legitimation of children, granting divorces, giving effect to informal wills or deeds, summoning or empanelling grand or petit juries, and changing the rules of evidence. These belong to the weakest branch, the judiciary, not the strongest branch, the legislature.

Having hemmed in the legislature on every side, the delegates to the Constitutional Convention of 1876 then turned to limiting the power of the state courts. All judges became popularly elected, and their terms of office were made relatively short instead of using the more standard practice of life tenure upon continued "good behavior." These provisions alone should have been sufficient to keep the courts "close to the people," but the framers of the 1876

Constitution were not satisfied. Going one step further, they divided the Texas judicial system so that there are in fact two top courts rather than one. The Texas Supreme Court has jurisdiction only over civil cases. Criminal cases are instead appealed to the Texas Court of Criminal Appeals, which in turn has only criminal jurisdiction. In effect, then, Texas has two supreme courts, each with one half of the jurisdiction normally placed in a single state supreme court.

Distrust of state government is also reflected in a number of provisions regarding the creation of special districts. Texas now has a large number of specialized districts to provide hospitals, water, fire prevention, mosquito control, noxious weed control, soil and water conservation, and, of course, there are over 1,000 school districts. Most have been created by an act of the legislature, but the constitution not only permits them, it encourages the creation of such districts as consistent with the constitutional intent to keep as much power as close to the people as possible. Not only are such districts more easily affected by local majorities, at least in theory, but the services provided by these districts are thereby removed from the state legislative agenda and thus diminish the range of state power.

Before moving on to a discussion of the bill of rights, how do we evaluate the constitution thus far? First of all, no one would mistake it for anything but an American constitution. Despite any differences one may note between subcultures, a common core runs through all American national and state constitutions that is recognizably American. Separation of powers, bicameralism, an independent judiciary, and a host of other characteristics are with rare exception found in American documents regardless of who writes them. At the same time, there are distinct variations on the common themes. It would appear that despite an approximately even split between the two subcultures both within Texas at large, and within the Constitutional Convention, the individualists managed to have the greater effect upon the document. A government that is decentralized, frugal and carefully limited in its power sounds like one designed mostly by individualists, but as we will see the traditionalists left their mark as well.

The Texas "Way of Life" and an Evolving Notion of Citizenship

Despite the many amendments to the Texas Constitution, there have been relatively few significant changes in the operation of the formal institutions of decision-making. The legislature, high executive offices, and judiciary operate very much as they were designed to operate in 1876. Local government has become, if anything, more independent, although it remains just as fragmented. The most important institutional changes have had to do with the growth of a state government bureaucracy, developments in the party system, and the proliferation of special districts and commissions.

Aside from these institutional changes, which have been reflected in various ways through constitutional amendment, the most important changes have had to do with shifting values and commitments, especially with regard to the notion of citizenship. By citizenship we mean the rights and duties associated with being a Texan. For example, even as originally written, the Texas constitution contains a comprehensive bill of rights. Everything found in the national Bill of Rights is found in the Texas document, plus a few more, often with an interesting twist.

Four sections in the Bill of Rights deal explicitly with freedom of religion. No religious test is required for holding office, says the first art of Section 4, but the last part says that an officeholder must "acknowledge the existence of a Supreme Being" to hold office. At the same time, a person who does not believe in a supreme being may still give evidence in court even though the oath to tell the truth has only civil, not religious sanctions attached to it. The state may not give money or property to any religious sect, but the state may "protect equally every religious denomination in the peaceable enjoyment of its own mode of worship." As long as no denominational preference is shown, the state is expected to protect religion. The Texas Constitution thus reflects the traditional American position of encouraging religion in general, but remaining neutral with respect to anything that represents sectarian differences. Still, all "reasonable" sectarian differences must be recognized, as reflected in Section 47 of Article 16 where pacifist sects like Quakers are exempted from bearing arms as long as they pay someone else to take their place. Provision for a pacifist minority apparently does not run contrary to traditional values, whereas the belief of the Church of Later Day Saints (Mormons) in polygamy does run counter and is not protected.

In the Bill of Rights we find expressed most obviously the blending of the traditionalistic and individualistic subcultures. The many individual rights reflect the strength of the individualistic faction at the Convention. Also, a number of these rights show specific concern with the goals of the Grange. The impairing of contracts by the legislature is prohibited. Section 26 prohibits the creation of monopolies. Primogeniture, the practice whereby property can be inherited only by the eldest son, is prohibited. These and other provisions support a commitment to individual equality and a free market.

On the other hand, a number of provisions in the Bill of Rights support the traditionalists. Section 1 declares Texas a free and independent state, subject only to the U.S. Constitution. This strong statement of state's rights, placed at the beginning of the entire document, is the most obvious reflection of traditionalism. The requirement that those holding office acknowledge a supreme being, and the provision that religion be protected, can now be seen as expressions of traditionalism in the blend with individualism. In a sense, since the protection of individual rights had been standard in American state constitutions for a century, the protection of these rights could also be seen as an expression of traditionalism, as reflecting what is traditional amongst us.

In any case, on balance, the Bill of Rights bears more the marks of individualism than traditionalism, just like the rest of the Constitution of 1876 as originally written. The traditionalist subculture was stronger in Texas when considering numbers of people carrying it, but those carrying the individualistic subculture were more organized and had a clearer sense of what they wanted. The individualists had the greater impact on the Constitution, but between 1876 and World War II the stronger traditionalistic element was able to move the Constitution more in their direction through amendment and informal practice.

Texas traditionalism in 1876 was expressed primarily in two ways. One was the strong concern for taking care of those members of the Texas community that best expressed its way of life. Thus, for example, the Constitution provides for pensions and other benefits for former confederate soldiers and their wives. Texas Rangers would also receive attention through public benefits. The other expression of traditionalism was a highly restricted electorate. Not directly expressed in the constitution, yet permitted by its silence, a high percentage of the potential electorate was excluded from voting.

Not only blacks, but an equally large number of whites were effectively discouraged from voting. A narrow electorate was part of the southern tradition designed to maintain control by traditional elites. Through the use of poll taxes, white primaries, and other practices Texas was one of the states most resistant to electoral reform. The overall effect of dispersing political power to the local level, fragmenting it even there, and then defining a restricted electorate, was to put local elites in charge almost everywhere in Texas, even in its cities.

The Texas Constitution contains in Sections 2 and 3 a strong statement of popular sovereignty. Whether traditionalist or individualist, Americans believed that ultimately their governments rested upon the consent of the people. Just how active that consent must be and how it is to be expressed, was not always clear. Still, these sections amount to a promise to future generations that however imperfect our system might be, this is our underlying premise. Sections 2 and 3 of the Constitution read as follows:

> Sec. 2. INHERENT POLITICAL POWER; REPUBLICAN FORM OF GOVERNMENT.
> All political power is inherent in the people, and all free governments are founded on their authority, and instituted for their benefit. The faith of the people of Texas stands pledged to the preservation of a republican form of government, and, subject to this limitation only, they have at all times the inalienable right to alter, reform or abolish their government in such manner as they may think expedient.
>
> Sec. 3. EQUAL RIGHTS. All free men, when they form a social compact, have equal rights, and no man, or set of men, is entitled to exclusive separate public emoluments, or privileges but in consideration of public services.

Note that the key words for citizenship in these two sections are "people" and "free man." Who is included among the people? Article 6, Section 1 excludes from citizenship "idiots and lunatics," paupers supported by a county, persons convicted of a felony, and persons under twenty-one years of age (the Constitution still says this even though the voting age was changed to eighteen).

There is also a residency requirement of one year in the state and six months in the county. On the face of it everyone else can vote and exercise their citizenship rights. In fact, women were excluded until 1919, and many blacks and whites were prevented from voting through a variety of means. By 1965 a little over fifty percent of the blacks in Texas, and a slightly higher percentage of whites were registered to vote. The Twenty-Fourth Amendment to the national Constitution outlawing the poll tax(ratified in 1964) and the effects of the 1965 Voting Rights Act passed by Congress removed most of the remaining restraints on voting. The extent to which Texas citizenship has been expanded and the extent to which the Texas political culture has evolved, were reflected by the addition of Section 3a to the Texas Bill of Rights in 1972, which includes equal rights for women and is thus a state E.R.A.

> Sec. 3a. Equality under the law shall not be denied or abridged because of sex, race, color, creed, or national origin. This amendment is self-operative.

The amendment may be self-operative, but it is not self-enforcing. We are still some distance from having in reality what the words describe. Still, the continued promise of the underlying commitment is there, and the commitment to popular sovereignty, political equality, and majority rule have continued to move Texas political culture away from the 1876 systhesis.

Conclusion

It is an axiom among students of constitutions that a constitution reflects and reveals who has political power (that is to say, who has full citizenship rights) and defines a way of life. When that way of life or definition of citizenship no longer reflect the underlying reality of politics, the constitution will be changed. There have been a great number of amendments to the Constitution of 1876 in the continuing attempt to make it reflect fundamental changes in how Texans live. Still, it is widely felt that whereas amendments have kept the document reasonably current with respect to a definition of citizenship, the formal institutions of decision-making are badly out of date. There is also criticism of the document's length, excessive number of amendments, and poor organization.

Let us consider the last charge first. The Texas Constitution has added more than ten times as many amendments as the United States Constitution in about half the number of years. State constitutions have all tended to be amended many times, and for a very good reason—state constitutions have more to do than a national constitution. States have been given responsibility for education, local government, and criminal law, to name just a few. Compared to the categories of power granted to the national Constitution, states just have more details to deal with in their constitutions. Some might say that these details do not belong in a constitution, but in fact they do at the state level. Give these powers to the national government, and its constitution would become messy as well.

One does not have to agree with those who wrote the 1876 Constitution to realize that their views required a detailed, restrictive constitution. Those who today advocate a simple, "clean" document are also advocating, of necessity, a state government with broad grants of power and many fewer restraints and restrictions. The Texas Constitution is too long, badly written, and poorly organized. It does, however, reflect the aims of the founders, and mere length is no test of a constitution's worth, good or bad. In a sense, the number of amendments may be viewed as a healthy sign—a sign that Texas takes its constitution seriously and is constantly and actively involved in popular, constitutional politics. A state with few amendments to its constitution may, on the other hand, be politically stagnant or else ignoring its constitution and taking political change out of the realm of popular politics.

Given what needs to be done at the state level, and thus given the number of amendments that state constitutions inevitably pile up, it would appear that state constitutions need to be periodically replaced to get rid of "dead wood" in the document and reflect social, economic, and political changes. Most states do in fact periodically adopt new constitutions. Texas has attempted to write a new constitution several times, most recently in 1976. While a number of reasons have been given for failure to adopt a new constitution, the most basic reason is that there has not been, and there is not yet, a coalition of sufficient size that agrees on what a new constitution should contain. Put another way, the political culture in Texas is either so deeply divided, or so essentially unchaged, that the 1876 systhesis cannot be replaced.

Regardless, there is an obvious need to reconsider institutions such as a legislature that meets only every two years, a judicial system that has grown like topsy and is overly fragmented and confusing, and a governor who lacks some of the tools needed to administer an industrial, urban state. Still, the prospects for writing a new constitution during the next ten years are not promising. A good deal of inertia must be overcome, and this is not an era of political reform. The Texas Constitution of 1876, the synthesis of an historically peculiar version of individualism drawn from the Grange, and of traditionalism drawn from an Old South that has largely faded, is likely to be with us for a good many more years.

Bibliography

H. Y. Benedict and John A. Lomax, *The Book of Texas* (New York: Doubleday, Page & Company, 1916).

George D. Braden, et. al., *The Constitution of the State of Texas: An Annotated and Comparative Analysis* (Texas Advisory Commission on Intergovernmental Relations, 1977).

Daniel J. Elazar, *American Federalism: A View from the States,* third edition (New York: Harper & Row, Publishers, 1984).

Joe E. Ericson, "The Delegates to the Convention of 1875: A Reappraisal," *Southwestern Historical Quarterly,* 62 (July, 1963):22–27.

Terry G. Jordan, "The Imprint of the Upper and Lower South on Mid-Nineteenth Century Texas," *Annals of the Association of American Geographers,* 57 (December, 1967):667–690.

A. J. Thomas, Jr. and Ann Van Wynen Thomas, "The Texas Constitution of 1876," *Texas Law Review,* 35 (October, 1957): the entire issue deals with the Texas Constitution.

14 The Transition of Electoral Politics in Texas: Voting for Governor in 1978–1986

KENT L. TEDIN

In 1978, with the election of Bill Clements, the Republican party captured the governorship of Texas for the first time since Reconstruction. The GOP lost the post in 1982 when attorney general Mark White upset governor Clements, but regained it once again in 1986 when Clements turned the tables on White and was elected chief executive for a second term. All three elections were close. Clements won by less than one percent in 1978 (17,000 votes). White defeated him by a margin of 53–47 percent in 1982, only to be defeated himself by an identical margin in 1986.

The 1978–1986 period merits close observation for at least two reasons. First, a Republican has won two of the last three elections in the largest state in the old Confederacy and the third most populous state in the nation. The dynamics accounting for the outcomes of these elections merit explanation if only because of the size and importance of Texas in the federal union, and the fact that three incumbent governors in a row have failed in their reelection attempts. Secondly, Republican gubernatorial success has fueled speculation that the state is undergoing a political realignment. A realignment is a shift in the aggregate partisan preferences of the electorate—in this case the electorate of Texas. In short, it is argued by some that the Lone Star state is on its way to becoming predominately Republican.

To understand the outcome of these elections it is important to appreciate the changing political environment in which they were held. Two changes merit particular attention. The first is the decline in importance of the Democratic primary. Until recently, state office holders were *de facto* chosen in the primary election—held in July until 1960 and in April or May thereafter. The November balloting was little more than a coronation. The second is the shift in party identification. Beginning in the mid-1970s, the Texas electorate has become increasing more Republican. This upsurge in Republicanism, as well as its underlying causes, has important implications for party competitiveness in the state.

Environmental Factors

The Decline of the Democratic Primary

It is clear from presidential elections that Texans have for some time been willing to vote Republican. By the early 1950s the post civil war anathema to the label "Republican" had passed. In 1952 Dwight Eisenhower carried the state with 53 percent of the vote. Republican presidential candidates went on to win in 1956, 1968, 1972, 1980 and 1984. But until the late 1970s, Texas Republicans had little potential for winning statewide political contests.

A principal reason for this lack of success was the institutionalization of the Democratic primary as the *de facto* structure for selecting statewide office holders. Ambitious and credible individuals aspiring for public office simply did not become Republicans. Prior to 1978, running statewide as a Republican in Texas was similar to running as a third party candidate in other parts of country. Contesting as a Republican might offer a platform to articulate an ideology, but from the standpoint of ever holding elective office it was a dead end. Rather, until as late as the 1980s, the Texas Republican party tended to be populated with "outsiders," unelectable ideologues and a few moderates mostly interested in receiving and dispensing federal patronage. There were exceptions of course. The affluent sections of Houston and Dallas had respectable Republican organizations, and occasionally Republicans would win local or Congressional elections. But even for conservatives, the action statewide was in the Democratic party.

A central feature of the primary election as the structure for final candidate choice was that it insulated contestants from the national short-term political forces that in some years favored the Democrats and in others the Republicans (an example of a short term force is Watergate which greatly damaged the Republicans in the 1974 election). Primary elections were held months before the crucial November elections, and were either fights between liberal and conservative factions within the Democratic party or were personality contests. Neither of these related easily to national political issues.[1] As a consequence, electoral decisions at the state level tended to be immunized from the interplay of national politics.

However, with the increasing success of Republican *presidential* candidates in Texas, many conservative Democrats became concerned that a strong national Republican tide in a presidential year might allow *statewide* Republican candidates to ride to victory on the coattails of the national ticket. In 1972, when George McGovern received the Democratic presidential nomination, this possibility almost became reality. Richard Nixon took over 66 percent of the Texas vote and Dolph Briscoe, the Democratic nominee for governor, managed to edge his Republican opponent by a scant three percent. Shortly thereafter the Texas legislature changed the two year term of Texas state officials to four years—with the elections being held in the off year (that is, the even numbered year without a contest for president). Elections with four year terms were first held in 1978. One hope, presumably, of those making the change was that national political forces affecting Texas elections would be weaker in the off-year than in presidential years. But as we shall see, statewide elections in the off-year are hardly immune to the national political climate.

When real electoral decisions were made in the primary, it was not surprising that by national standards voting in November tended to be low and voting in the primary election tended to be high. In 1950 almost three times as many people voted in the Democratic primary as voted in the November election. But in 1978 and following, there was a rapid drop in the primary vote relative to that in the general election. In that year voting in the Democratic primary was only 77 percent of that in the fall. Despite a hotly contested Democratic primary in 1982, turnout was only 35 percent of the fall turnout, and in 1986 it fell to 33 percent. These figures suggest that electoral politics in Texas are becoming nationalized. That is, elections in Texas are beginning to look more like elections in the rest of the nation and less like the pattern that characterized the old Confederacy prior to 1960.

The importance of this trend is that a large November turnout is potentially subject to the influence of national political factors as well as statewide campaign effects. Texas is a heterogeneous state. This population diversity inevitably means that people will differ in the way they see political issues. Partisanship, which plays no role in a primary (where everyone belongs to the same party), can play a major role in the general election. National forces were particularly strong in 1978 and 1982, and were an important factor in the election of the Bill Clements and his subsequent defeat by Mark White. On the other hand, 1986 seemed to have turned to a greater extent on state and local issues.

The Rise of Republican Party Identification

Many have observed that the political attitudes of white southerners are more in-tune with the national Republicans than with the national Democrats. White Texans in particular tend to be conservative on economic and racial issues, distrustful of the government in Washington, hawkish on foreign affairs, and enamored with the rhetoric of "free enterprise."[2] The natural home for these views is the Republican party.

As can be seen from Table 1, the Republicans have been making substantial gains in partisanship. Actual Texas Republican strength in 1986 is in fact even more robust than these data show. Many Independents when pressed will admit that they "lean" either to the Republicans or the Democrats. If we look only at the group that called themselves "Independent," our October, 1986 survey shows that 36 percent, when asked, admitted they leaned to the Republicans, while 24 percent leaned to the Democrats (with the remaining 40 percent being pure Independents). To draw the tale out even further, we asked the pure independents to rate the Republican and Democratic parties in either negative or positive terms. Fifty-four percent of the rated the Republicans favorably, but only 17 percent rated the Democrats favorably.

Table 1 Party Identification in Texas between 1955 and 1986

	1955	1968	1978	1980	1982	1984	1986
Democratic	66%	59%	48%	43%	42%	33%	33%
Independent	28	31	37	39	49	43	40
Republican	06	10	14	18	17	24	27
	100%	100%	100%	100%	100%	100%	100%

*SOURCES: The 1955 data are from the Belden Poll reported in Dyer et al. (1985); the 1968 data are from the Comparative State Election Study (Black, et al, 1974). The 1978 to 1986 data were collected by the Center for Public Policy at the University of Houston. The standard seven-point SRC question was used with "leaners" classed as Independents.

In 1986 there exists in Texas a bit of a partisan enigma. Even after making adjustments for "leaners," there are more Democrats than Republicans (42 to 38 percent). But the Republican party is better liked among Texans than is the majority Democratic party. Again, we can look at the question which asks respondents if they feel positive, neutral, or negative toward the major parties. A total of 71 percent of the Texas electorate give the Republicans a positive rating, but only 42 percent give the Democrats a positive rating. The importance of these data is that the psychological ties Texans have to the Democratic party seem to be substantially weakening. This weakening is one of the factors which has led to the rise of split ticket voting—that is, voting for some Democratic and some Republican candidates as opposed to voting a straight ticket. Self proclaimed Democrats are simply not as likely to vote a straight party ticket as they have been in the past.

One line of argument about Texas Republicanism is that it reflects little more than a short-term reaction to the Reagan electoral landslides. It can be argued that some people (in responding to survey questions) are confusing voting Republican in recent presidential elections with being a Republican partisan. There is clear evidence that levels of partisanship surge in the direction of the victorious political party shortly after a landslide presidential election. But partisanship levels in 1986 are not appreciably different from those in 1984. If there had been a temporary swell toward Republicanism as a consequence of the 1984 election, it should have subsided two years later. More likely, the change is real.

If it is real we should be able to identify its sources. At least three possibilities readily come to mind. First, some Texans may have simply changed their minds and abandoned the Democratic party in favor of the Republican. Second, generational replacement may favor the Republicans. Those who entered the electorate at 18 may be more Republican than those who left the electorate through death. Finally, the in-migration into the state might be biased in favor of the Republicans.

Table 2 Party Switchers and Their Original Party Preference

	Yes	No
Current *Democrats:* Were you ever a Republican	.09%	91%
Current *Independents:* Were you ever a Republican	07	93
Current *Independents:* Were you ever a Democrat	30	70
Current *Republicans:* Were you ever a Democrat?	43	57
		N = 713

Source: April, 1986 University of Houston Public Affairs Research Center Survey.

It is possible that people who used to think of themselves as Democrats or Independents have come to think of themselves as Republicans. Table 2 strikingly shows that the Republican party has been the big winner among those who have switched their party attachment. Forty-three percent of the current Republicans claim they were once Democrats, while only nine percent of the Democrats claim they were once Republicans. The Democrats also seem to be moving into the ranks of the Independents—perhaps as a temporary stopping point before making a complete switch.

One factor which differentiates those Democrats who shifted to Republicanism from those who did not is that the shifters are more likely by a 2 to 1 margin to call themselves conservatives. This conservatism may in part be tied to social mobility. Prior to World War II Texas was among the poorest states in the Union, a fact which may have kept many whites content within the confines of the Democratic party. But in the post-War era there have been ample opportunities, many of which were taken, for Texans to move into the solid middle and upper middle classes. That movement plus the tendency of the national Democratic party to nominate candidates more liberal than most white Texans are likely key sources of the trend we see in Table 2.

Generational replacement also seems to be working in favor of the Republicans. Forty-five percent of the Texas electorate over the age of sixty are Democrats, in contrast to 22 percent who claim to be Republicans (the remaining 33 percent are Independent). On the other hand, 35 percent of those under the age of 40 identify with the Republicans compared to 24 percent who identify with the Democrats (the remaining 41 percent are Independent).[3] If this pattern remains constant (and it may not, as the young have party attachments that are very unstable) the aggregate percentage of Republicans will creep upward as the older generation dies off and is replaced with those turning 18.

Texas has been one the fastest growing states in the union. Much of this growth as been a result of in-migration. There are more Republicans among these new arrivals than Democrats. Based on a series of survey results aggregated by Dyer et al. (1985), we can break the Texas electorate into the following groups based on length of residence in the state:[4]

>   Newcomers: 17%
> Long Term Residents: 23%
>   Natives: 60%

The most Republican of these groups at 41 percent are the newcomers (24 percent are Democrats and 35 percent Independents). The long term residents split about evenly (34 percent Republican, 35 percent Independent and 32 percent Democratic), with the natives still preferring the Democratic party by a lopsided margin (40 percent Democratic, 32 percent Independent, 28 percent Republican). Problems in the oil patch have sharply reduced the number of white collar professionals moving into the state. Nevertheless, the changed partisan complexion of the state is in part a result of past prosperity and the Republicanism of the new residents it brought into the state.

In summary, by 1978 (and perhaps earlier) there were real opportunities for Republicans to win statewide in November. Winning the Democratic primary did not automatically guarantee victory in the fall. There had been a gradual increase in the number of Republican party identifiers and a loosening of ties to the Democratic party. Under the right circumstances a Republican could be elected to statewide office.

The Divisive Democratic Primary and the 1978 Election of Bill Clements

In early 1978 there was little reason to think there would be any change in the Democratic control of the Texas governor's mansion. The incumbent governor, Dolph Briscoe, announced for reelection. For the Republicans, party chairman Ray Hutchinson announced he would seek the nomination.

However, Governor Briscoe was challenged in the Democratic primary by Attorney General John Hill. Briscoe represented the party's conservative wing and Hill the party's moderate/progressive wing—a typical battle often fought in the one-party south. But this contest was unique in that it pitted the state's two best-known office holders against each other. As might be expected, the contest was bitter and expensive. Hill fashioned a mild upset by winning without a run-off, taking 51 percent of the 1.8 million Democratic votes.

On the Republican side, political newcomer Bill Clements challenged party leader Hutchinson. While Clements was unknown, he had the major advantage of being sufficiently wealthy to fund his own campaign at whatever level necessary. Only 160,000 persons voted in the Republican primary compared to 1.8 million for the Democrats. Nevertheless, Clements contributed more to his campaign out of his personal pocketbook than Democratic primary winner

John Hill was able to raise from all sources. The investment paid off as the obscure businessman rolled up a three to one win over long-time party leader Hutchinson.

Few gave Clements much of a chance in November. However, many Democrats had not forgotten the primary and retained ill-feelings toward their nominee, John Hill. Clements effectively played on this animosity by repeatedly emphasizing that he was the "conservative" in the race and Hill was a "liberal/politician/lawyer."

It is now commonly appreciated that divisive primaries are harmful to the winner's November chances.[5] Supporters of the losing candidate will often remain bitter and some stay home in November or vote for the opposition party. The bitterest of these divisive primaries is when an incumbent officeholder is challenged by a member of his or her own party. Undoubtedly, Governor Biscoe and many of his supporters felt the Governor had a "right" to the nomination. He was, after all, the sitting governor. His administration was untouched by scandal. Was he not entitled to another term? Survey data from this election show a large scale party defection by those who voted for Governor Briscoe in the spring primary. Many switched parties and voted for Republican Bill Clements in the fall. Of those who voted for Briscoe in the primary, 47 percent voted for Clements in the fall. Even more graphic was the behavior of *conservative* Democrats. Of those who voted for Briscoe in the Democratic primary, fully 59 percent turned around and voted for Clements in the fall.[6]

The divisive Democratic primary was not the only reason Clements won. One lesson of the 1978 Republican primary and the later fall campaign concerns the importance of money and what it can buy politically when a candidate is unknown. He spent more than twice as much on the election as did John Hill. He had the resources to take advantage of an opportunity. Also, an unpopular Democratic, Jimmy Carter, was sitting in the White House. Studies of midterm congressional voting show that even under the best of conditions the president's party is electorally punished and loses seats. This tendency to punish the president's party in the off year was certainly a contributing factor in Hill's defeat. Carter's unpopularity might also have dampened the enthusiasm of some Democrats and contributed to their low turnout level. On the other hand, turnout in Republican precincts was high. Texas Democrats ceased being immune to national forces when the fall elections became competitive.

But the tradition of deciding things in the Democratic primary was the most important reason a Republican was able to capture the governorship. Combined with the changing partisan environment, the head-to-head clash between the state's highest ranking officeholders opened a door that had been firmly closed since the days of the Reconstruction. Clements, to his credit, was prepared to take advantage.

White Defeats Clements/Clements Defeats White: The Background

The Setting in 1982

Governor Clements was tagged very early as a heavy favorite for reelection. The governor's position as the odds-on favorite seems to have been based on several dubious assumptions by members of the press and others, plus taking at face value the early claims by Clements that statewide polls showed him ahead by up to 16 points.[7] These numbers were certainly too optimistic. A poll in May of 1982 by the Public Affairs Research Center at the University of Houston showed White leading Clements by a 47%–38% margin.

The common perception that Clements held the lead was based on several observations about the Governor's advantages that had only a tangential connection to the forces actually at work among the 1982 electorate. The first of these was a conviction by many who make the news that Texas was rapidly becoming a Republican state. Clements' 1978 victory was followed by Ronald Reagan's easy Texas victory over Jimmy Carter, leading to an inference by some of Republican ascendancy. But presidential Republicanism had been a feature of Texas politics since the 1950s, and it might well be argued that Clements' 1978 victory was somewhat of a fluke, as much a function of Democratic mistakes as anything else. Second, Clements was the incumbent and his administration had been untouched by scandal (as had Governor Briscoe's before him). Third, Clements had amassed a very large financial warchest (14 million dollars)—larger than any Democrat could hope to match. And fourth, the Clements campaign had a reputation for being highly professional and tightly organized. Most conceded it had done an excellent job in getting out the vote in 1978.

Less attention was given forces operating to disadvantage the Governor's reelection. First, in 1982 Democrats still outnumbered Republicans by a 2–1 margin. Second, with a divisive Democratic primary and low turnout in Democratic precincts, Clements had in 1978 only won by 17,000 votes. The 1982 Democratic primary had three contestants, but it was nondivisive.[8]

Third, political money was worth more to Clements as an unknown in 1978 than it was to Governor Clements in 1982. Clements was now a highly visible public figure with an image as a bad tempered curmudgeon firmly established in the minds of many Texans. Large expenditures of political money proved unable to soften the Governor's roughhewn image. Third, while Clements raised over fourteen million dollars in 1982, that money was unlikely to be as effective as the seven million he spent in 1978 when he was virtually unknown. After a point, political money has a sharply declining value. The eight million dollars Mark White raised was enough to insure that he would not be denied the essentials that money can provide for campaigns. The large revenues that Clements raised could not all be effectively spent. One lesson of the 1982 election is that political office cannot be bought by money alone. The fourth factor working against Clements was that the national economy had been in a recession since 1981. With a Republican in the White House, the national forces almost certainly favored the Democrats. Then the Texas economy, once immune to the national economic downturn, went into a sharp downturn late in the election year. In March of 1982 unemployment in Texas was 6.2 percent and the subject of little comment. In September it was 8.6 percent and a major news item. Unprecedented economic prosperity had graced Texas during the first three and one-half years of the Clements administration. However, three months prior to election, the Texas economy went into a nose-dive, and Clements faced the voters with economic problems at both the state and national level very much on their minds.

The Setting in 1986

Contrary to 1982, in 1986 the defeat of the incumbent governor was widely expected. A poll sponsored by the *Houston Chronicle* showed in April (before the Republican primary which Clements won easily) that the former governor led Mark White by a margin of 57 to 34 percent (with nine percent undecided).[9] Nevertheless, there was reason to think that 1986 might be a good Democratic year. Historically, the "out" party has done very well in the sixth year of a president's term. And, to a certain extent, this pattern repeated itself in 1986. The Democrats picked up six seats in the U.S. House of Representatives and took away control of the U. S. Senate from the Republicans. White's defeat ran counter to the national trend (although Republican candidates for governor generally did well in 1986). An election whose outcome is counter to the national climate alerts one to the possibility that local issues, or more likely personality factors, played a major role in determining vote choice.

Given the early polls, White was in trouble before the campaign started. Certainly an important factor was the state of the economy. Texas was mired in a long recession which began with the decline in the price of oil. This decline in turn had ripple effects throughout the economy (e.g., as oil prices declined, so did the amount of construction). Oil, which had been as high as $30.00 a barrel in 1982, fell to as low as $10.00 a barrel in 1986. Getting less statewide media attention, but also important, was the recession in the state's second major industry—agriculture. The foreclosures and hard times that hit the midwestern farm states affected Texas as well. Farm income dropped noticeably, and in a number of dramatic cases farms were foreclosed. With the recession, state income plunged and the state comptroller estimated that Texas in 1986 was facing a five billion dollar deficit. Debate ensued over raising taxes vs. cutting services. Although Mark White could do nothing about oil prices or farm prices, hard economic times are almost inevitably bad electoral news for a state's most visible officeholder.

White had also embarked upon a controversial set of educational reforms which included competency tests for teachers and six week suspensions from extracurricular activities for any student who failed one or more subjects. Teachers were particularly bitter about the requirement that they be tested for their academic competency. Having been certified once, they felt insulted that their skills should be called into question. The "no pass-no play" provision was attacked by many as being too harsh. A six week suspension often meant the major part of football or basketball season would be missed by students who had received a failing grade.

Finally, there was the nebulous issue of personality and leadership. White was accused of being unable to provide the leadership necessary to diversify the Texas economy given the states's decreasing reliance on oil. Critics referred to the governor as "Media Mark," whose long suit was a slick public appearance, but whose short suit was ideas and action concerning the state's financial problems. While many lauded his accomplishments on educational reform, many others felt the governor had simply not grasped the reins of economic leadership. In hard economic times the governor seemed in particular to neglect his minority and working class constituency.

It should be remembered, however, that White represented the conservative wing of the Texas Democratic party. He had a fundraising edge in 15 of 19 major professional and business groups (oil and high tech were the major exceptions). White collected $1,523,507 from the real estate developers compared to $364,993 for Clements; $224,769 from the bankers compared to $135,278 for Clements, and $87,750 from insurance executives to Clements' $53,000. White was also endorsed by every major newspaper in the state (if an endorsement was made) with the exception of The Dallas Morning News. It was White, not Clements, who was the preferred candidate of establishment Texas elite.[10]

The Aggregate Vote Returns

An analysis of voting patterns reveals distinct differences between 1982 and 1986. The 1982 election was a high turnout contest, the 1986 election a low turnout contest. A total of 2.3 million voted in 1978. That figured jumped to 3.1 million in 1982, but increased only to 3.4 million in 1986. High turnout elections like that of 1982 usually benefit Democrats while low turnout elections like that of 1986 tend to benefit Republicans. In high turnout elections, the influx of new voters tends to come predominantly from minorities and the working class. For example, a sample of black precincts from Harris county showed that the turnout of 46 percent in 1982 dropped to 37 percent in 1986. Similarly, working class whites were down from 41 percent in 1982 to 37 percent in 1986. On the other hand, middle class and affluent white turned out at about the same rate in both elections.

The Swing in the Vote

In an attempt to determine "where the votes came from" we can compute the "swing" in the vote. The swing is the net gain in votes received by the winning candidate from one election to the next. In 1986 Mark White received 113,449 fewer votes than in 1982. Bill Clements received 348,851 more votes in 1986 than in 1982. The swing between 1982 and 1986 is thus 462,300 votes (113,449 + 348,851). The swing between 1978 and 1982 was 230,638 in favor of the Democrat.

What parts of Texas contributed most to the swing? To answer that question the state can be divided by county into four groups: (1) those counties casting more than 100,000 votes (Harris, Bexar, Dallas, Tarrant and Travis), (2) those casting between 40,000 and 100,000, (3) those casting between 15,000 and 39,999 and (4) those casting fewer than 15,000 votes.

The majority of the swing between 1978 and 1982 came from the rural areas. Of the 230,000 vote swing, 129,000 came from counties casting less than 15,000 votes. The big urban counties contributed 66,000 votes to the swing. The remaining counties contributed substantially less.

These numbers suggest that White's 1982 victory came primarily from rural voters who were disenchanted with the Democratic nominee in 1978, but who came back to the fold in 1982; and secondarily from a turnout increase among blacks and blue collar workers in the large urban counties. These data fit well with the events of the time. Rural voters in Texas are traditionally conservative. When Governor Briscoe, a conservative Democrat, was defeated in the primary by moderate John Hill, many rural conservatives voted Republican. When conservative Democrat Mark White was nominated in 1982, rural Democrats came back to the party. In urban areas, minorities and blue collar workers responded to the hard economic times, and to the fact of there being a Republican in the White House, and turned out in record numbers. For many, a vote against Bill Clements was a way of sending a message to Ronald Reagan.

In 1986 the rural vote deserted Mark White with a vengeance. The more rural the county, the greater the swing toward Clements. Of the 462,300 vote swing to Bill Clements, the rural counties contributed 283,657 votes. The five most urban counties contributed only 21,424 votes to the swing. We can partially summarize this pattern for the 1978–1986 elections by looking at the percent vote for Clements in all three elections. These figures are easy to understand but a bit misleading since they summarize only the change in the two party division of the vote, not the change in turnout. The Clements victory in 1986 came essentially from the same areas that had given victory to Mark White four years earlier. The two most plausible reasons are the House Bill 72 (educational) reforms, and the severe economic problems in rural areas.

Table 3 Percent Clements by County Size (votes cast) for Three Elections

Counties Total Votes Cast	% Clements 1978	% Clements 1982	% Clements 1986
under 15,000	47%	41%	57%
15,000–39,999	53	49	58
40,000–99,999	47	44	49
100,000 plus	53	50	51

The aggregate data reveal state voting patterns to be in a state of flux, a condition thought by many to be associated with political realignment. Prior to 1986, Texas Democrats had been strongest in rural areas and weakest in the midsized to large cities. The 1986 election reversed this pattern. In 1986 Clements' strongest base was in rural Texas. White, on the other hand, carried Harris county by nearly 30,000 votes. In fact, in many white, middle class areas of Harris County, Mark White actually improved his showing over 1982. A sample of middle class white precincts showed White with 27 percent of the vote in 1982, improving to 46 percent in 1986. In a sample of affluent white precincts he moved from 16 percent in 1982 to 28 percent in 1986. These patterns are something other than "politics as normal" in Texas.

Individual Level Analysis: A Look at the Surveys

Party Identification

The Democratic party has held a partisan advantage in Texas since the end of Reconstruction. However, the GOP can win in Texas because (1) Republicans are more loyal to their nominees than are the Democrats, and (2) many Independents are really "closet" Republicans. Table 4 presents a cross tabulation between party and vote choice for 1982 and 1986. Note the similarities in the relationship despite the fact a Democrat won in 1982 and a Republican in 1986. Even in 1982, when events favored the Democrats, a majority of the Independents (54 percent) voted for Clements. In 1986 the percentage is, of course, even greater. Also, look at the categories "Independent Democrat" and "Independent Republican." These are people who initially responded "Independent," but were asked if they "leaned" toward either the Republicans or the Democrats. The Independent Republicans are about as "party loyal" as those who called themselves Republicans, but not strong, at the outset. The Democrats were much more likely to defect in all categories save the "strong" Democrats. Given the remarkable similarity in the 1982 and 1986 party vote, why did White win one year and Clements in another? Among the reasons are (1) turnout among Democrats was higher in 1982 than in 1986, and (2) by 1986 there were more Republicans.

Table 4 Relationship Between Party Identification and the Vote: 1982–1986

	Party Identification						
Vote Choice 1982	Strong Dem	Not Stg Dem	Ind Dem	Pure Ind	Ind Rep	Not Stg Rep	Strong Rep
Clements	08%	28%	24%	54%	88%	86%	95%
White	92	72	76	46	12	14	05
	(25%)	(16%)	(10%)	(17%)	(13%)	(09%)	(10%)
							N = 511
Vote Choice 1986	Strong Dem	Not Stg Dem	Ind Dem	Pure Ind	Ind Rep	Not Stg Rep	Strong Rep
Clements	12%	36%	38%	61%	80%	81%	93%
White	88	66	63	39	20	19	07
	(19%)	(16%)	(08%)	(15%)	(18%)	(11%)	(16%)
							N = 467

Demographics

The key demographic variables behaved much the same in 1986 as they did in 1982. In Texas, race and income are the major predictors of the partisan division of the vote. In 1982, Clements had a 54%–46% advantage among whites, but lost the blacks 94% to 6% and the Hispanics 75% to 25%. In 1986 Clements improved his showing among whites to 67%–33%. The most likely reason was his stronger showing in rural areas than in 1982. Blacks again voted overwhelmingly for White 94%–6%, but of course, fewer of them voted in 1986. Clements also did a bit better among Hispanics at 61%–39%.

Income demonstrated a strong linear pattern; as income increased the vote percentage for Clements increased. In 1982 those making less than $20,000 gave only 32 percent of their vote to Clements, while those making more than $40,000 gave 64 percent of their votes to Clements. Clements did a bit better among the lower income groups in 1986, getting 43 percent of those making less than $20,000, but a bit worse among the affluent, getting 61% of the vote among those making over $40,000. While these differences are not large, they reflect a strange turn of events where a very conservative Republican, every bit as conservative in 1986 as in 1982, avenged an earlier defeat against the same Democratic opponent by losing support among the wealthy and gaining support from the lower end of the income spectrum.

In recent years there has been much talk about the women's vote and the gender gap. The gap was first noticed in 1980 when men voted overwhelmingly for Reagan by a 56%–36% margin, while women gave him only a 47%–45% plurality. If the 1982 election had been held before 1920 (when only men could vote) Bill Clements would have won. He received 51 percent of the male vote, but only 40 percent of the female vote. In 1986, if women only could vote,

White would have won. Clements received only 49 percent of the female vote, but 59 percent of the males. Thus the magnitude of the gender gap (the difference between male and female candidate preferences) did not change between elections, but White got fewer females votes in 1986 (51% in 1986 vs. 59% in 1982).

Issues

The economic problems the state faced seemed to harm Bill Clements in 1982 more than they harmed Mark White in 1986—at least in a direct fashion. Of course, in 1982 Clements faced a double whammy. There was a recession in both Texas and the nation. In the 1982 and 1986 surveys respondents were asked to the name the most important problem facing the state. In 1982 the first five responses concerned the economy. In only one category (inflation) did Clements have an advantage over the challenger. White rolled up big margins among those mentioning unemployment and high utility rates. The 1986 data are not exactly comparable, as all mentions of the economy were grouped into one category comprising 70 percent of all respondents. Among this group Clements led White by a 52% to 48% margin.

But for the most part Texans in 1986 did not hold White responsible for the state's economic problems. In the October, 1986 survey we asked respondents who they thought was to blame for these problems. Seventeen percent thought White was "very much to blame," 11 percent thought the Reagan administration was "very much to blame." Twenty percent blamed the Texas oil and gas industry. Most of the blame went to the Middle East oil producers and OPEC, with 50% saying they were very much to blame and another 30 percent saying they were somewhat to blame.

However, projecting down the road, 44 percent thought the Texas Republicans could better solve the state's financial problems compared to 32 percent who felt the Democrats would do a better job. Thus White may have been hurt by the perception that Republican leadership could, in the future, better deal with Texas' economic problems, even though few thought he was personally to blame.

One immediate consequence of the bad economy was a projected five billion dollar deficit, and because the Texas constitution requires a balanced budget an issue in the 1986 campaign was whether to fund the debt through cuts in services or by raising taxes. We asked respondents in April what approach they would favor in solving the budget problem—raise taxes and fees, reduce services and programs provided by the state, or a combination of both. Fifty-eight percent preferred a combination with 23 percent wanting to reduce services and only eight percent wanting to raise taxes. Those preferring a combination split their vote 52% Clements, 48% White. Those few that preferred a tax raise overwhelmingly supported White (70%–30%), and the one-fifth or so who favored severely cutting services even more overwhelmingly favored Clements (77%–23%). The tax issue seems to have hurt Mark White. In a post-election survey by Tarrance and Associates, 63 percent of respondents felt Clements would do a better job of holding down taxes, while only 20 percent said White would do a better job in this area.[11]

While most respondents mentioned the economy as the number one problem facing Texas, 12 percent mentioned the educational reforms, particularly "no pass-no play." Of these, 70 percent favored Clements over White. The correct interpretation of these data is that for those who profoundly cared about the educational reforms (more so than even the depressed economy) the vast majority opposed them. One should not, however, lose sight of the fact that 62% of the Texas electorate "strongly approved" of the controversial "no pass-no play" provision, and 53 percent were opposed to any easing of the six week "no play" penalty. As expected, the major opposition to no pass-no play came from the rural areas. Almost 60 percent of the respondents from predominately rural West Texas favored an easing of the no play penalty. On the other hand, only 33 percent favored easing the penalty in the more urbanized Gulf Coast Region.

Personality

A common criticism of the voting public is that decisions are frequently based on candidate image and personality rather than on issues. We have a variety of personality indicators that we can contrast in 1982 and 1986. We shall first examine positive, negative, and neutral candidate evaluations. The 1982 data indicate that one reason White won was the unpopularity of Governor Clements. Note from Table 5 that there was almost no movement in Clements' popularity between May and November. He is no more or less popular earlier than later.

White declines in popularity between May and November. This movement would seem to reflect the effects of the Clements' campaign. White was simply not as well known as the incumbent governor. In May 34 percent said they knew "a lot" about Bill Clements, vs. 22 percent who said they knew "a lot" about Mark White. There was, therefore, room to affect the challenger's image. By election day White and Clements were equally known, and some of what the electorate learned about White (perhaps through the Clements' ads) was

Table 5 Evaluations of Clements and White: 1982–1986

	May: 1982			November: 1982		
	Negative	Neutral	Positive	Negative	Neutral	Positive
Clements	33%	16%	51%	33%	15%	52%
White	17%	19%	64%	27%	15%	58%

	May: 1986			November: 1986		
	Negative	Neutral	Positive	Negative	Neutral	Positive
Clements	23%	12%	65%	27%	19%	54%
White	40%	19%	41%	37%	18%	45%

not favorable. But the Clements campaign was unable to reduce the governor's own negatives (or raise his positives) despite spending 14 million dollars. To reiterate, there are limits to what money can buy in politics.

Turning to candidate evaluations in 1986, Clements was considerably more popular in May of 1986 than in November, as in May it appears voters remembered the Clements administration with a certain nostalgia. Some of that nostalgia was wiped away during the course of the campaign. By November of 1986 Clements was only slightly more popular in his winning effort than he had been four years earlier in a losing cause. Losing in 1982, Governor Clements was viewed positively by 52 percent of the Electorate. Winning in 1986 increased his positives to only 54 percent.

While personal unpopularity contributed to Clements' 1982 loss, it was a major contributing factor to White's loss in 1986. Note how much more unpopular losing Governor White was in 1986 than was losing governor Clements in 1982. White had 10 percent more negatives in 1986 than Clements had in 1982. As losers go, Clements was better liked, and by a nontrivial margin.

Also observe that after four years out of office, the voters *did not* fundamentally reassess Clements. He gained only two percent in positives, although his negatives were not as high. However, after four years the voters *did* change their assessment of White, which was much more negative in 1986 than in 1982. The Republican's victory seems due more to a dislike of White than a nostalgic desire to return Clements to the governor's mansion. This point is reinforced in a post-election survey done by Tarrance and Associates. In 1982 they found that 15 percent of those who voted for Clements claimed they were really voting against Mark White. In 1986, 41 percent of the Clements voters claimed they were really voting against Mark White.[12]

Next we shall examine what specific personality traits voters liked and disliked about Clements and White in 1982 and 1986. In post-election surveys we asked respondents to what extent the following traits described Bill Clements and Mark White: honest, compassionate, inspiring, a problem solver, fair to all, and providing strong leadership. The responses to these items are presented in Table 6. They seem to confirm the thesis that White's major shortcoming was an inability to convince the public he could provide the needed leadership. Images of the candidates as "honest" or "compassionate" do not change much between 1982 and 1986. On the question of "fair to all" White drops substantially, but part of this drop is due to the fact that "fairness" (or lack thereof by Clements) was a major part of the White campaign in 1982. It was also a message that got across as 70 percent felt White was fair. He dropped in 1986, but was still garnered a respectable 49%.

Table 6 Assessment of Traits of Clements and White: 1982–1986

	1982 Describes Clements	1982 Describes White	1986 Describes Clements	1986 Describes White
Honest	64%	68%	63%	56%
Compassionate	41%	62%	50%	60%
Inspiring	37%	55%	51%	38%
Problem Solver	54%	57%	64%	36%
Fair to all	50%	70%	59%	49%
A strong leader	NA	NA	64%	41%

*The question asked if the trait described Clements/White: Extremely well, quite well, not too well, or not well at all. Extremely well and quite well were combined for statistics presented in the table.

On the other hand, White drops precipitously into the 30 percent range on questions relating to his being inspiring and a problem solver, where he had been in the 50 percent range in 1982. Clements improves on these items. He did well both years as a problem solver. Even in defeat, 54 percent thought the term "problem solver" described Clements. In 1986 the figure rose to 64 percent. In bad economic times, this "can do" image left over from his earlier administration was an asset to the Clements campaign. He also was thought to be more inspiring in 1986, with 51 percent applying this descriptor compared to 37 percent in 1982. Finally, we added the phrase "provides strong leadership" in the 1986 survey. Clements came out considerably ahead of White by a margin of 64% a 41%. The analysis of traits indicates that many Texans felt Mark White had not (and by implication probably would not) provide the inspiration and leadership the state would need in the next four years.

Conclusion

Elections in Texas are coming into the American electoral mainstream. That does not mean state politics have been completely nationalized. Only three Republicans have won statewide races (Tower, Clements and Gramm). The remaining statewide officeholders are all Democrats. But the reason for this Democratic dominance does not seem to be an unwillingness on the part of the electorate to elect Republicans. Rather, it is a lack of credible GOP candidates. One lingering after-effect of one-party Texas is that few Republicans have an opportunity to get the necessary statewide exposure required to mount a successful campaign. However, being a Republican in Texas is now quite respectable. In future years the party should be able to recruit increasingly better candidates. In doing so, Republicans will likely enjoy additional electoral successes, and meaningful two party competition may not be limited simply to presidential elections and to the most visible statewide offices.

Bibliography

Paul R. Abramson, et al, *Change and Continuity in the 1984 Elections* (Washington: Congressional Quarterly Press, 1985).

James A. Dyer, David B. Hill and Arnodl Vedlitz, "The Partisan Transformation of Texas," paper presented at the American Political Science Association Meetings, September, 1985.

Gary C. Jacobson, *Money in the Congressional Elections* (New Haven: Yale Univeristy Press, 1980).

Malcolm Jewel, *Parties and Primaries* (New York: Praeger, 1984).

Alan Rosenthal and Maureen Moakley (eds), *The Political Life of the American States* (New York: Praeger, 1984).

James R. Soukup, *Party and Factional Division in Texas* (Austin: University of Texas Press, 1962).

Notes

1. Richard W. Murray, "The 1982 Texas Election in Perspective," *Texas Journal of Politics,* 2 (Spring/Summer, 1983), p. 49.
2. Although, as is usually the case, it depends on the circumstances at hand. When the price of oil exceeded $28.00 a barrel calls for the deregulation of gas and oil were very frequent in Texas. When oil fell below $15.00 a barrel the broadsides against government regulation abruptly ceased and there were calls for various forms of government intervention such as import quotas.
3. These data are from the April, 1986 UH Public Affairs Research Center survey.
4. Newcomers are those who have lived in the state less than ten years. Long term residents have lived in Texas more than ten years, and natives were born in the state.
5. The latest work on this subject is Patrick J. Kenney and Tom Rice, "The Relationship between Divisive Primaries and General Election Outcomes," *American Journal of Political Science,* Vol 31 (February, 1987).
6. Kent L. Tedin and Richard W. Murray, "The Dynamics of Candidate Choice in a State Election," *Journal of Politics,* Vol 31 (May, 1981).
7. Jack L. Smith, "Clements loses Hold in Survey," Fort Worth Star Telegram (August 8, 1982), p. 1.
8. Mark White received 45 percent of the vote, Buddy Temple 30 percent and Bob Armstrong 18 percent. Since no one received more than 50 percent a runnoff was required. However, Temple dropped out and left the nomination to White.
9. The poll was conducted by the Public Affairs Research Center at the University of Houston.
10. David Denison, "The Defeat of Mark White Sends a Message to the Democrats," *The Texas Observor* (November 21, 1986), p. 3.
11. Press release by Tarrance, Hill, Newport and Ryan (undated).
12. Ibid.

15 The Politics of Judicial Selection in Texas
RICHARD MURRAY

I. General Patterns of Judicial Selection in Texas

The fifty American states differ greatly in patterns of judicial selection. Only three states (Maine, New Jersey, and Rhode Island) follow the federal pattern where the chief executive nominates and the senate confirms a judicial candidate. In New Hampshire the governor nominates judges but they are confirmed by a special five member elected council. Three other states (Connecticut, South Carolina, and Virginia) provide for legislative appointment of judges. About a dozen states use some variant of the "Missouri Plan" wherein a blue ribbon commission prepares a short list of prospective candidates from which the governor must designate an appointee. That person must then be periodically confirmed in a retention election (voters can only remove or sustain a particular judge—they cannot directly elect another candidate). California reverses the Missouri Plan process. There the governor designates a prospective nominee who can then be vetoed by a special judicial commission.

The majority of states provide for the direct election of judges. In thirteen states this is by partisan election which means serious candidates must secure the nomination of the Democratic or Republican party. Another seventeen states choose judges in non-partisan elections. Texas, like most southern states, uses a partisan election system.

The Texas selection system, like many other structural aspects of state government, reflects the political climate in the mid-1870s when Texas adopted its present constitution. The previous constitution, enacted in 1869 during the Reconstruction Period after the Civil War, granted vast appointive powers to the governor, including all judicial positions. Republican Governor E. J. Davis made aggressive use of these appointments to dominate state and local government. When conservative white Democrats regained control of the state in 1875 they quickly moved to rewrite the Texas Constitution. Intent on preventing abuse by the chief executive, the Texas framers greatly reduced the appointive powers of the governor. After 1876 governors could still fill all vacant judicial positions, but judges had to stand for election every four or six years (for appellate courts). Anger at the Republicans was reflected in the constitutional requirement that judicial elections be partisan affairs, a decision based on the expectation that virtually all persons elected would be from the resurgent Democratic party.

For nearly a century the partisan element of judicial selection worked as expected. Republicans rarely sought and almost never won Texas judgeships. Whatever electoral activity occurred was confined to the Democratic primary.

What the framers did not anticipate, however, was the tremendous importance of the governor's remaining power to fill judicial vacancies. In the more than 110 years since enactment of the 1876 constitution, the majority of Texas judges have first come to the bench via gubernatorial appointment. Henderson and Sinclair found, for example, that 66 percent of all the judges who served during the period from 1940 to 1962 were appointed initially.[1] Once on the bench, appointees were rarely challenged and almost never defeated. In 1956, for example, 86 percent of the judicial elections had only one candidate—typically the incumbent judge. Just 1.4 percent of the incumbent judges seeking reelection around the state were defeated that year.[2]

In practice Texas thus had something approaching a Missouri Plan system of selecting judges rather than a competitive election process. Most judges were appointed by the governor and then routinely elected by voters in subsequent elections. The electoral process was confined to the Democratic primary where all serious candidates filed. Contests were unusual unless there was an "open" bench where no incumbent was seeking reelection.

Governors made appointments based on advice from political supporters and friends in the State Bar. Generally, they chose qualified people; the governor's image could be damaged if nominees were incompetent or incapable of winning the next general election. From the 1930s to the 1970s, Texas governors were conservative Democrats, and the judicial appointments usually went to white males in their 40s or 50s, from prominent backgrounds, who had attended the more prestigious law schools in Texas (University of Texas, SMU, Baylor), and who had been active in conservative Democratic politics. Obviously, this pattern excluded women, blacks, Hispanics, Republicans, and most persons from lower socioeconomic backgrounds. However, it did produce a judiciary that was reasonably qualified and experienced.

And the election system, though seldom used, was somewhat effective as a constraint. Judges knew they *could* be challenged and defeated under certain circumstances. That possibility doubtlessly made them more sensitive to the general public than would have been the case under a pure appointive system.

Through the late 1970s, the Texas court system was a quiet backwater in state politics. With few election contests, little money was raised and spent campaigning, and the press paid only modest attention to judicial developments. This changed quite suddenly in the late 1970s and early 1980s. Partly this resulted from the rise of the Republican party in Texas, which ended the dominance of the Democratic primary in electoral politics. A second contributing factor was the increasing intervention of interest groups in the selection process. Taken together, these developments have resulted in many more contested judicial elections, increasingly expensive campaigns, and growing controversy about the court system. We begin our analysis of the modern court system by focusing on the impact of organized group activity, then look at how party politics has changed judicial selection. Finally, we consider some of the controversies that have engulfed the courts and the prospects for reform.

II. Interest Group Intervention in Judicial Elections

The courts in Texas were not only a white, male preserve, they were also bastions of political conservatism. In the civil courts this meant that decisions tended to favor defendant groups like insurance companies and large corporations as opposed to plaintiffs who sued these interests. In 1949 a group of plaintiff attorneys, unhappy with their lot in state courts, organized the Texas Trial Lawyers Association. Most of their political efforts in the 1950s and 1960s were directed at the legislative process but they were occasionally active in state or local judicial contests. In the 1970s, the group began to urge their individual members to get involved in judicial elections, especially for the Texas Supreme Court, a nine member body to which judges are elected to six-year terms. The Supreme Court is particularly important because as the highest civil court in the state, its decisions define the guidelines under which all non-criminal trials are conducted.

The trial lawyers had a major success in 1978 when they backed Franklin Spears, a liberal former state senator from San Antonio, and Robert Campbell, a plaintiff lawyer, for Supreme Court seats. In 1980 they helped elect Jim Wallace, a liberal state senator from Houston, and C. L. Ray, a local judge from East Texas, to the high court. In 1982 they strongly supported Bill Kilgarlin and Ted Robertson and both were elected. Thus, in just four years, the trial lawyers group was able to replace six conservative judges with individuals likely to be more friendly to plaintiff lawyer interests.

The results were evident in a series of decisions from 1983 to 1987 that expanded the opportunities for plaintiffs to recover damages. As liability rules were expanded and larger judgments were assessed against insurance companies, corporations, doctors, and other defendants, a strong political reaction occurred. The corporate lawyers' organization, the Texas Association for Defense Attorneys, also began to urge its members to get involved in judicial elections and the group began to recruit and support candidates to oppose judges thought too pro-plaintiff. In 1982 they successfully backed the re-election of James Denton in the Democratic primary, only to have his victory negated by his death (Kilgarlin eventually won the seat). In 1986 they were strongly behind Supreme Court Justice Raul Gonzalez's victory, but the other two candidates they supported were defeated.

As contests became more and more common when seats came up on the Supreme Court, other groups like the Texas Medical Association have begun backing candidates. The principal result of these various group efforts is a dramatic increase in the amount of money spent in getting elected or reelected to the bench. In the 1960s the occasional statewide judicial race might cost

$100,000. By the early 1980s major candidates were raising and spending over one million dollars. And in the 1988 contest for Chief Justice of the Texas Supreme Court, Ted Robertson and Tom Phillips spent about two million dollars each (this election is discussed in detail later).

III. Party Politics and Judicial Selection

As we noted, Texas is one of 13 states that elect judges on a partisan ballot along with candidates for the presidency, Congress, major state offices, and county positions. Traditionally, few judge candidates ran as Republicans so the only meaningful election contests were in the Democratic primary. However, as Republican strength steadily increased in Texas, it was just a matter of time until party politics would reach the judicial arena. The specific event that brought this change on was the election of Bill Clements as governor in 1978 and again in 1986. We examine how Clements' election fostered two party politics in the judiciary; first in Harris County (Houston) and then on the Supreme Court of Texas.

Judicial Elections in Harris County

Until the 1980s, judicial contests were rare in Harris County. Occasionally, more than one candidate would file for the Democratic nomination, typically when a new bench was created or an incumbent did not seek reelection. The absence of Republican challengers in the general election meant that Houston, like the rest of Texas, effectively had a non-partisan system of judicial elections in which most judges were initially appointed and ran unopposed thereafter.

The confinement of judicial politics to the Democratic primary shielded the local judiciary from the shifting winds of party politics that started blowing across Texas in the 1950s and 1960s. Local voters could move back and forth between Democratic and Republican candidates for the presidency or congressional office, but this had no impact on judicial elections because of the absence of GOP candidates.

Table 1 documents the patterns of party voting in Harris County elections from 1948 to 1978. Through the 1960s, no Republicans were candidates for judicial office. In 1972 when Republican President Richard Nixon was swamping Democrat George McGovern in Houston and the nation, two Republicans lost badly in bids for local judgeships. The pattern was repeated in 1976. Republican President Gerald Ford carried Harris County, but two local GOP judicial candidates (including a county judge recently appointed by Harris County Commissioners Court) were defeated. In 1978, two Republicans again filed, but this time they were defeated by narrow margins. One got over 47 percent, the other over 49 percent.

Table 1 Voting Patterns in Harris County General Elections: 1948–1978

Year	Republican % of 2 Party Pres. Vote	Republican % of 2 Party Cong. Vote	GOP Performance in Local Judicial Races Number Contested	Number Won	Mean GOP % of Jud. Vote
1948	42.4	14.5	0	0	—
1952	57.6	—	0	0	—
1956	61.1	38.6	0	0	—
1960	53.1	34.5	0	0	—
1964	40.4	35.1	0	0	—
1968	52.5	48.0	0	0	—
1972	62.9	49.0	2	0	37.1
1976	52.6	52.5	2	0	43.0
1978	(no election)	54.5	2	0	48.7

From the data in Table 1, some basic trends can be identified. First, Harris County voters began to give strong support to Republican presidential candidates in the 1950s (Eisenhower easily carried the area). Local Republicans running for congressional seats ran far behind the presidential ticket, but the gap steadily narrowed in the 1960s. Since 1968, GOP candidates for Congress have been competing on an equal footing with local Democrats. The impact of these partisan shifts did not trickle down to the judiciary for several more years, but by 1978 it was clear that traditional voting patterns were changing at this level as well. All that was needed to complete the transition to competitive partisan elections for the judiciary was for a significant number of candidates to file as Republicans. That happened in 1980 and has been the case in each general election since. [See Table 2]

The sharp break between 1978 and 1980 is indicated by the fact that in the latter year 17 local judge races featured Republicans squaring off against Democrats. The principal reason for the increase was that Governor Clements had appointed several new judges and they chose to stand for election as Republicans. And, with Ronald Reagan leading the GOP presidential ticket, many local candidates concluded 1980 was a good year to run for office as a Republican. That guess turned out to be correct, as Republican judicial candidates got slightly more votes than Democrats in contested races and won 9 of the 17 contests.

The success of Republican candidates in 1980 encouraged more competition in 1982 when 32 local judicial races (out of about 50) were contested in the general election. But 1982 turned out to be a good year for the Democrats as Governor Clements was unseated by Democrat Mark White, and only six Republicans won compared to 26 Democrats. In 1984, the tables turned as President Ronald Reagan crushed Walter Mondale by more than 200,000 votes in Harris County and carried every local Republican judicial candidate to victory.

Table 2 Vote Patterns in Local Judicial Elections in Harris County, Texas: 1980–1988

Year	No. of Contested Races	Mean Party Vote Republican	Mean Party Vote Democratic	Mean Party % Rep.	Mean Party % Dem.	Races Won Rep.	Races Won Dem.
1980	17	297,162	291,754	51.3	48.7	9	8
1982	32	191,108	204,581	48.3	51.7	6	26
1984	16	406,970	355,245	53.4	46.6	16	0
1986	38	207,049	223,952	48.0	52.0	12	26
1988	26	368,816	342,517	51.8	48.2	18	8
Total	129	—	—	49.9	50.1	61	68

Source: Official Returns, Office of County Clerk, Harris County.

In 1986, a record number of local judge races were contested in the county (38), and Democratic candidates won the majority (26) behind a strong local performance of Governor Michael White. Then, in 1988 a strong victory by George Bush over Michael Dukakis in the presidential race gave Republicans an advantage as they won 18 of 26 contests.

The Harris County data in Table 2 establish the following patterns. Many local judicial contests are now contested—a total of 129 in the last five elections. Overall, there is no partisan advantage in the county. The mean vote for Democratic and Republican candidates has been split almost exactly 50% for each, with Democrats winning slightly more seats (68 to 61). Republicans have done well in presidential years (1980–1984–1988) when their national candidates have piled up big leads in Texas and the Houston area. Democrats have had more success in the off-years (1982–1986) when their state candidates have run well against GOP nominees.

In looking at the patterns of judicial voting, one notes that about 15–20% of the local voters simply skip all the judicial races. In 1988, for example, 833,000 people voted in the general election, but only about 700,000 voted in the typical judicial race. Among those who do vote in judicial contests, it seems clear that the largest number (80–85%) vote for all the candidates of one party or the other. Every Democratic candidate and every Republican candidate thus gets by far their greatest number of votes simply by being their party's nominee. In years when the party tide is running strongly, as it was for the Democrats in 1982 and the Republicans in 1984, many judges were elected in Harris County because of straight-ticket voting. This high degree of party voting reflects the inability of most voters to keep track of individual candidates when the ballot has 30 or 40 local contests as is often now the case in Harris County.

Unfortunately, the parties' have little control over who runs under their label (any lawyer with four years' experience can file in either the Democratic or Republican primary by paying a filing fee and submitting a petition with a modest number of signatures of registered voters). This has meant some rather poorly qualified individuals have gotten on the general election ballot, often opposing respected incumbent judges, and have won. Twenty-eight sitting judges, including several with long tenure and high ratings from local lawyers, have been defeated in the 1980s. This has brought a substantial "potluck" element to judicial contests in Harris County, as the varying fortunes of top-of-the-ticket races for president and governor influence party voting patterns in unpredictable ways.

More often than not, however, there have been enought "ticket-splitters" to determine the outcome of local judicial elections. These voters have gone down the ballot and crossed back and forth, voting for some Democrats and some Republicans. In order to appeal to these ticket-splitters, who tend to be middle-aged, well educated Anglos, judicial candidates try to organize effective campaigns to reach these local voters. These efforts almost always require money, so those who want to be a judge, or stay on the bench, now must spend a considerable amount of time raising money. A competitive judicial race in Harris County now costs about $100,000, and the combined expenditure on such races is in the $2–3 million range. Almost all these monies are raised from lawyers practicing in the specific courts contested, which has occasioned considerable criticism in recent years, a point we will return to later.

Partisan Elections and the Texas Supreme Court

During his first term in office (1979–1983), Governor Clements was able to appoint only one Republican to a vacancy on the Supreme Court, and that candidate was narrowly defeated in the 1980 general election. The state's highest court thus remained in Democratic hands with most electoral action occurring in the party primary. After Clements' second election in 1986, however, things changed greatly. The Chief Justice, John Hill, resigned halfway through his six-year term, as did two other justices. This gave Governor Clements the opportunity to name three new Republican judges in 1987–1988. Coupled with the regular expiring terms of three members, this meant six of the nine justices had to stand for election in 1988. The state Republican party made a major commitment to support their newly appointed judges and capture another seat or two on the bench. For the first time in the state's history, a battle royal for control of the Supreme Court was fought out along party lines.

The results of the six Supreme Court races are summarized in Table 3. In the most visible and hard-fought race, Republican Tom Phillips turned back a challenge from Associate Justice Ted Robertson to hold the Chief Justice position. Clements' appointee Eugene Cook also bested Democrat Karl Bayer, and GOP challenger Nathan Hecht unseated Democrat Bill Kilgarlin. But one of Clements' choices, Barbara Culver, lost to Democrat Jack Hightower, and the Democrats won a contest for an open seat (Doggett defeating Murphy). Finally, the court's only minority member, Democrat Raul Gonzalez easily defeated maverick Republican Charles Ben Howell, who was not supported by the GOP establishment.

Table 3 General Election Results for Texas Supreme Court: November 1988

Position	Republican Candidate—Vote—%		Democratic Candidate—Vote—%	
Chief Justice	*Tom Phillips*	2,881,140 56.6%	Ted Robertson	2,206,480 43.4%
Place 1	Paul Murphy	2,302,619 45.1%	Lloyd Doggett	2,807,114 54.9%
Place 2	Nathan Hecht	2,506,293 50.3%	Bill Kilgarlin	2,479,864 49.7%
Place 3	Charles Howell	2,064,511 42.1%	Raul Gonzalez	2,844,744 57.9%
Place 4	*Barbara Culver*	2,243,502 44.5%	Jack Hightower	2,799,838 55.5%
Place 5	*Eugene Cook*	2,537,129 51.7%	Karl Bayer	2,368,634 48.3%

Note: Incumbents are underlined. Associate Justice Robertson sought to move into the Chief Justice position, so both he and Judge Phillips were sitting on the Supreme Court in 1988.

In sum, the 1988 Supreme Court results were a split decision. Republicans won three, Democrats three, and the overall party vote seemed to be about even. Unless the election rules are changed, it seems likely the state's highest court will continue to be a partisan battleground, given the inconclusive results in 1988.

IV. Is Justice for Sale in Texas? Some Problems with Electing Judges and Prospects for Reform

In 1985 a Houston jury awarded Pennzoil $10 billion in a breach of contract lawsuit against Texaco. This controversial verdict, the largest award ever rendered in an American civil court, brought immediate and often critical national attention to the Texas judicial system. This interest did not lessen when a Court of Appeals and the Texas Supreme Court upheld the jury verdict and Texaco was forced into bankruptcy before agreeing to a $3 billion settlement with Pennzoil.

One element of controversy centered on the fact that the original trial judge in Harris County, Anthony J. P. Farris, had received a $10,000 campaign contribution from Pennzoil's lead lawyer, Joe Jamail, a few months before the trial commenced. [Jamail also served as Farris's finance chairman and solicited funds from other sources for the judge.] Challenged by the Texaco attorneys, Farris would not recluse himself from the case, arguing it was legal, common, and accepted practice for judges in Texas to accept sizeable campaign contributions from lawyers with cases before their courts. Farris's position was sustained on appeal, but the episode called public attention to a widespread practice fraught with possible conflicts of interest.

In 1987, the well-known CBS television program Sixty Minutes filmed a segment on the Texas courts entitled "Is Justice for Sale in Texas." Focusing on attorney Joe Jamail, who received a $300 million legal fee for his services in the Pennzoil-Texaco case, Sixty Minutes presented a decidedly critical view of judicial election practices in the state. The program documented a pattern wherein attorneys with important cases pending in state courts, and especially before the Supreme Court, were expected or pressured to make sizeable contributions to the election warchests of the judges who would pass on their cases. Jamail's close ties to Supreme Court Justices Ted Z. Robertson and Bill Kilgarlin were cited as prominent examples of the pattern.

While Sixty Minutes did not directly answer the question they posed, the segment left little doubt that something was rotten in the Texas courts. The program caused considerable reaction in the state, with Governor Clements and the Republican party joining the critical chorus as the potential for breaking the Democratic lock on the Supreme Court became apparent. Sixty Minutes rebroadcast the piece in mid-1988 as the campaigns were getting under way for the Supreme Court and the Phillips-Robertson race for the chief justice post centered around the charges raised by CBS. Both Phillips and Robertson made commercials utilizing footage from the Sixty Minutes story, with each claiming they were the "reform" candidate who would clean up the mess. Phillips obviously got the better of the argument, as indicated by his 57% to 43% victory in November 1988.

Phillip's success, and the replacement of the pro-plaintiff majority on the Supreme Court have eased pressures from conservative business interests, the defense bar, and some Republicans for reforming judicial selection in Texas, but the basic problem documented by Sixty Minutes remains. If Texas is going to elect judges in partisan contests, judicial candidates must mount campaigns, and such campaigns are increasingly expensive. Aside from personal wealth, the only reliable sources of campaign funds for judges are lawyers or their clients with cases before the judges' courts. Judges simply cannot be expected to refuse all such contributions, but the acceptance of large sums from such interested parties inevitably creates the image if not reality of bias.

Is this system of judicial selection in Texas likely to be changed? Various proposals have been advanced for legislative action in Texas, with the most common focus on restricting the size of individual contributions, and making at least the appellate courts appointive with retention elections after several years of service. The Texas legislature has been reluctant to endorse major changes, especially of a "Missouri Plan." Opposition stems from a widespread public preference for electing public officials including judges, coupled with the legislature's traditional distaste for giving more formal powers to the governor's office.

At this time (March 1989), the prospects for reforming judicial selection are difficult to assess. One reason for this uncertainty is the existence of a major new challenge to the Texas system of selecting judges. We noted earlier that traditionally the bench in Texas was largely a white male perserve. That has changed slowly over the years as women, Blacks and Mexican Americans have won some judicial positions. In Harris County, for example, Blacks won five of the 129 contested races in the local courts between 1980 and 1988, and Mexican Americans were successful in an equal number of cases. But this success rate of less than 8 percent in a county about 40% Black of Mexican American has led to charges that the existing election system discriminates against minorities in Texas. In 1988 a lawsuit was filed in federal court (LULAC v. Clements) challenging the judicial selection system in most urban areas of Texas under provisions of the Voting Rights Act (VRA). A victory by the plaintiffs might force massive changes in the way judges are selected in the state. Until the lawsuit is resolved, the future of Texas judicial selection system is in limbo.

Notes

1. Bancroft C. Henderson and T.C. Sinclair, *The Selection of Judges in Texas: An Exploratory Study* (Houston: Public Affairs Research Center, University of Houston, 1965), p. 21.
2. *Ibid.,* p. 20.

16 The Politics of Educational Reform in Texas

GREGORY R. WEIHER AND THE GRADUATE STUDENT PUBLIC POLICY RESEARCH GROUP[1]

Americans are inveterate reformers, particularly in the area of public education. Perhaps it is the central importance that is given to education in the American ideology of opportunity and success; but, whatever the cause, it is difficult to remember a period in American history when some reform of education was not being either proposed or implemented.

Again, probably because of the central importance of education, it has been among the most "local" of public policy areas. Educational policies are implemented by teachers and administrators in thousands of local school districts. The funding of public education has always been a state and local matter. Federal funds to the public schools have never amounted to more than ten percent of all public school funding, and under the Reagan administration the percentage has been much lower. The state of Texas spends approximately eleven billion dollars on public elementary and secondary schools, making education by far the largest area of state expenditure. Perhaps the best indication of the "localness" of public education is the frequency with which educational issues become community controversies. Busing, prayer in classrooms, sex education, the content of textbooks—few issues can polarize communities and dominate the public agenda as quickly as educational issues.

Since the 1960s, reform and local control of schools have been rather at odds with each other. Critics argue that local control, and the compartmentalization of resources that goes along with it, causes inequality in the educational opportunities available to American children. The quality of the education that a child receives, they say, depends primarily upon the wealth of his or her school district. They argue that these in-equalities in educational opportunity are unjust.

Educational Governance in the United States

One of the principal causes for the ongoing educational reform movement is the structure of educational governance in the United States. American school politics gives testimony to the importance of local government in the American political mythos.

Owing to its liberal antecedents, American political thought has always been skeptical of centralized political power. Madison showed great ingenuity in finding ways to fragment power, and his initiatives in this area were reinforced by Thomas Jefferson's preoccupation with strong local government. Local government is valued on a number of grounds—that it is more responsive and more accountable, and that it provides opportunities for the people to become practiced in democracy.

There are 83,341 discrete units of government in the United States according to the Bureau of the Census. Of these, 82,291 are local governments. Over fourteen thousand of these local governments are school districts. This figure does not include school districts that are operated by city governments, of which there are about 1500.

One of the consequences of this decentralization of school governance is that education in the United States is financed through about 16,000 separate financial systems. The autonomy of these systems varies from state to state. Some states, like California, finance public education almost entirely. In other states, however, the finance of public education is predominantly a local matter. The local source for educational funding is the property tax.

School districts vary a great deal with respect to their endowments of taxable property. Some school districts are blessed by having shopping centers, or large manufacturing plants, or—in the case of Texas—vast oil fields within their boundaries. In such cases, the ratio of resources to students is likely to be favorable. Property rich districts are typically able to spend large amounts on each student without having to levy particularly heavy taxes.

Other school districts, however, not blessed with large concentrations of taxable property, struggle constantly to provide adequate educational programs. It is common for property-poor school districts to tax local properties very heavily, yet find themselves unable to spend minimally adequate sums for the education of their students.

The American system of educational governance and finance creates inequalities in the delivery of educational services by isolating resources within geographic compartments. Though an elementary school may be located across the street from a shopping center, the school will not benefit at all from the substantial tax revenues that the shopping center generates if a school district boundary runs between them.

The American Conception of Equality

Equality is one of the fundamental tenets of the "American creed," but Americans believe in a particular type of equality. They do not believe in equality of outcome. That is, the American conception of equality does not require that we all share the same level of material reward. Suppose one individual has three cars, a boat, and two large houses, and another has a small house, no boat, and relies upon public transportation. Nothing in this comparison is inherently offensive to the American sense of equality. Peculiarly enough, Americans can remain steadfastly dedicated to the concept of equality while being entirely uninterested in the relative material conditions of citizens.

The concept of equality to which Americans adhere is equality of opportunity. The American idea of justice requires that individuals have equal chances rather than equal rewards. Drawing upon the liberal tradition fathered by John Locke, Americans have insisted that the way to acquire property is to work for it—to claim it through labor and ingenuity. Some men and women, will be willing to work harder and will work more skillfully. They, in turn, will receive greater rewards. The majority of Americans agree that this outcome is just. Injustice arises when barriers are imposed upon those who are willing to work. When some are prevented from going as far as their talents would otherwise have taken them, the American sense of equality is offended.

It is this peculiarly American sense of equality which gives salience to the pattern which characterizes the finance of American public education. For education is the first rung on the ladder of opportunity in the American system. Americans believe in education as the great equalizer. The poor-but-virtuous young person, working at part-time jobs while obtaining a college degree, is a folk hero in American culture. Furthermore, it is demonstrably true that higher educational attainment correlates with greater economic success. Inequality in the provision of education sits uneasily upon the American conscience because education is such an important arbiter of opportunity in American life.

School Finance Litigation

Reformers have pursued change in the structure of American educational governance through a number of channels including the courts. The case which tested this structure in the federal courts was *San Antonio Independent School District v. Rodriquez*. Rodriquez, whose children attended school in the property-poor San Antonio District, claimed that they were being denied the equal protection of the laws guaranteed by the Fourteenth Amendment. Had the Supreme Court agreed, the property-based system of school finance would have been declared unconstitutional. The Supreme Court, however, decided that the Constitution did not guarantee an equal education to all children.

Although the argument for reform was defeated at the federal level, it has been more successful at the state level. The constitutions of most of the states declare that education is a state function. The unequal provision of education has been found to be a violation of a state constitution in a number of cases (New Jersey, California, West Virginia, Arkansas, and Michigan). In these states, local systems of finance have been invalidated, and school funding has become a state function. In Texas, poor school districts have recently brought suit in state district court (Edgewood v. Kirby) in hopes of gaining the relief that was denied them in *Rodriquez*.

Reform Programs in the States

Most states are sensitive to the problem of interdistrict financial equity. They have usually adopted one of two measures, or a combination of both, to address the problem.

The first is called a "foundation" program. Under such a program the state arrives at a minimal dollar amount—a foundation—which is required to fund an adequate academic program. It may determine, for instance, that a district must spend $1,350 per student to provide a basic education. The state then guarantees that each district will spend that amount for each student, even if some districts cannot raise enough money through local taxes. The local district shortfall will be supplied from state funds.

Additionally, states frequently adopt "power-equalizing" programs. These programs focus on local tax effort. They stipulate that districts taxing at a certain level should be able to provide a certain amount of money for each student. Districts which tax at the state-mandated rate, yet fall short of the stipulated dollar figure per student, receive state aid to raise them to the predetermined expenditure level.

Even with these programs, which are meant to raise the level of spending for poor districts and to bring them closer to the wealthy ones, the levels of spending that states are willing to guarantee are usually low.

For a number of reasons, the results of such programs have been disappointing. Shifting additional funds to poor districts can be accomplished in two ways. One is to increase taxes and use the proceeds to increase the amount of state aid to poor school districts. It is politically difficult to pass tax increases that benefit only poor districts, however, since other districts and their residents have no reason to support them. The price of passage for funding programs that benefit poor districts is frequently the inclusion of spending provisions that benefit wealthy districts also. Obviously, using such a tactic limits the degree to which rich and poor districts are equalized.

A second way of generating additional funds for poor districts is to take state aid away from richer districts. This method has all of the political liabilities of the first. Additionally, even when such a program is adopted, wealthier school districts compensate for the loss of state funds by increasing local taxes slightly. As a result, expenditures per student in wealthy districts increase along with expenditures in poor districts. Again, the result is that little equalizing takes place.

Educational Governance in Texas

The localistic and fragmented pattern of governance that characterizes American education generally is reproduced in Texas. In the 1985/86 school year, there were 1069 school districts in the state. They range in size from mega-districts like the Houston Independent School District (average daily attendance: 166,867) to very small districts with enrollments of less than one hundred. Some are predominantly rural. Others are suburban, and others serve central cities of large metropolitan areas.

These school districts also display great demographic diversity. Some school districts are predominantly white, while there are others that are entirely black or Hispanic. Most large metropolitan districts have substantial enrollments of whites, blacks, and Hispanics; and, in many school districts, Asians have now become a significant minority.

There is also great socioeconomic diversity. Alamo Heights Independent School District enrolls students that come for the most part from upper- middle class homes. North Forest Independent School District educates the children of the urban working-class. Patterns of class all-too-frequently mirror patterns of race and ethnicity. Alamo Heights is a white school district, while North Forest is overwhelmingly black.

The point is that conditions which have been said to characterize public education nationally also characterize public education in the state of Texas. Educational governance is fragmented, and the units of government display great variety on a number of dimensions. Furthermore, because of the autonomy that the Texas system gives to local units, diversity often translates into inequity.

School districts in Texas which preside over land which is not highly valued for any use are handicapped in their ability to generate revenue. Without commercial or industrial development, or high-value residential development, school districts with relatively large enrollments must spend much less on their students than do more favored districts. Moreover, residents of property-poor school districts are likely to have to pay burdensome taxes for school programs that are, still, inferior.

House Bill 72: Educational Reform in Texas

In 1984, the Texas legislature passed House Bill 72 to reform the structure of public education in the state. House Bill 72 was meant to accomplish a number of things. It was meant to improve education statewide by increasing funding. It was meant to make students, teachers, and administrators more accountable. It was also meant to make school finance more equitable.

The state has always maintained that students should receive an adequate education regardless of the wealth of the particular school district within which they happen to live. The Texas School Code, for instance, states:

> It is the policy of the State of Texas that the provision of public education is a state responsibility . . . so that each student enrolled in the public school system shall have access to programs and services are appropriate to his or her educational needs . . . and that are substantially equal to those available to any similar student *notwithstanding varying local economic factors.*

Regardless of the rhetorical flourish with which this passage supports near absolute equality in the distribution of educational resources, House Bill 72 did not attempt to achieve absolutely equal outcomes for students. No reform which stops short of dismantling the property-based system of school funding can hope to approximate such a goal.

Yet House Bill 72 did try to reduce the range between the wealthy and poor school districts. It established a foundation of $1,350 to be spent on each student in the public schools in the state, regardless of the wealth of the local district. More importantly, the basic allotment was to be increased for students in high-cost educational categories. Higher allotments are to be granted for disadvantaged (read poor) students, and for students who require bilingual education. These provisions tend to increase the money received by poor school districts since they have higher proportions of disadvantaged and bilingual students.

Additionally, the Foundation Schools Program includes enrichment funds which are distributed as a supplement to the basic allotment. These funds, meant for the enrichment of curricula, are distributed to poor school districts which cannot generate significant enrichment funds by themselves.

Finally, funding of the basic allotment is divided between the state and local school districts. That is, of the basic amount of $1,350, part must be supplied by the state and part by the local district. The local share is determined on the basis of district wealth. The wealthiest districts provide eighty percent of the basic allotment, while the poorest districts are responsible for only eight percent.

These elements of House Bill 72 are clearly designed to put public education on a more equal financial footing. They require that wealth and the nature of the students that districts must educate be taken into account in the distribution of state funds, and that poor school districts which face difficult educational tasks get more state money than wealthy ones.

The Failure to Achieve Equity

It is relevant, then, to ask "To what degree has the goal of financial equalization been realized?"

This question is most simply answered by examining the ranges in spending per student between the district that spent the most and the district that spent the least both just prior to the implementation of House Bill 72 and just after its implementation. If these ranges are reduced for the years following implementation, there is reason to conclude that equalization has been accomplished.

Table 1 presents figures on high and low expenditures for the 1983/84, 1984/85, and 1985/86 school years. It also presents the high-low ranges for these years, and the ratios of high expenditures to low expenditures.

Table 1 District Expenditures per Student: Maxima and Minima, Ranges, and Ratios

		Unrestricted	Restricted
1983/84	Minimum	$ 1,444	$ 1,678
	Maximum	$20,415	$14,010
1984/85	Minimum	$ 2,220	$ 2,260
	Maximum	$19,057	$13,002
1985/86	Minimum	$ 2,344	$ 2,344
	Maximum	$20,312	$13,554
1983/84	Range	$18,971	$12,332
	Ratio	14:1	8.3:1
1984/85	Range	$16,837	$10,742
	Ratio	8.6:1	5.8:1
1985/86	Range	$17,968	$11,210
	Ratio	8.7:1	5.8:1

These figures are divided into two groups. Figures for the "unrestricted range" include all school districts in the state. The "restricted range" figures, however, are computed after the wealthiest five percent of districts and the poorest five percent have been excluded. The argument is made that the very wealthiest districts and the very poorest are, in a sense, "freaks." They are not representative of the circumstances in which most school districts find themselves. Most school districts, for instance, cannot draw upon vast oil fields to finance their programs. Nor are they as hard pressed as school districts in the Valley which must educate large numbers of the most educationally handicapped Hispanic students using modest local resources. To include such "outliers," this argument goes, would be to distort the picture of interdistrict financial relationships. As the counter-argument can be made that it is precisely these extremes of wealth and poverty that are most in need of correction, it is best simply to include both sets of figures.

A look at the pattern in high-low ratios indicates substantial progress in reducing spending inequalities in the wake of HB 72. For instance, the ratio of expenditures by the highest expenditure district in the state to the lowest expenditure district was reduced from 14.1:1 to 8.6:1 after House Bill 72 took effect.

This impression is slightly altered if one concentrates on the ranges in expenditures from high to low, however. Over the three year period, these ranges are somewhat reduced, but not in the dramatic sense in which expenditure ratios were reduced. The unrestricted range for 1985/86 is still 95% of the range for 1983/84, just before HB 72 was enacted. The restricted range in 1985/86 is about 91% of the earlier range.

These two observations combined suggest that the principal impact of HB 72 has been to shift the level of expenditure upward for all districts. This shift has resulted in a reduction in expenditure ratios, but it should not be confused with a large reduction in the size of the disparities between high- spending and low-spending districts. The chief outcome of HB 72, then, has been to improve the lot of poorer districts, not to bring them considerably closer to the spending levels of the wealthier districts.

Finally, a multivariate statistical analysis of pre- and post-HB 72 district financial data reveals which factors are most strongly related to school district expenditures per student. This analysis indicates that district property wealth is far and away the best predictor of a district's ability to spend. The most important determinants of district expenditure are, in descending order:

Assessed Valuation/Student
Tax Levy
Other Receipts/Student
Other Resources/Student
Average Daily Attendance (negative)
Intermediate Receipts/Student
Proportion State Aid

The statistical analysis indicates that local school district wealth is about fourteen times as important in determining expenditures per student as is state aid. The import of this ordering of variables is straightforward: wealthy districts will continue to spend more on their students than will poor districts. Put differently, the predominance of property wealth means that the curricula, the facilities, and the quality of teachers provided to students will be determined by the ability of districts to generate revenues locally.

The mention of local revenue generating ability recalls the extreme differences between districts in this area. Even after House Bill 72, the disparities in revenue potential among Texas school districts are impressive. For instance, the yearly school taxes paid upon an $80,000 home in the Iraan- Sheffield ISD amount to $33.00.[2] On a home of the same value in the North Forest ISD, the annual tax bill is over $900.00. Nevertheless, Iraan- Sheffield outspends North Forest by a considerable margin ($6890.97 in current operating expenditures per student to $3097.89). Or, we can compare the 500,000 students in the wealthiest Texas school districts to the 500,000 students in the poorest districts.[3] If the tax levy in the wealthy districts is increased by one cent per hundred dollars assessed evaluation, the result will be an increase in expenditures per student for the fortunate 500,000 of over four hundred dollars. A similar increase in tax levy in the poor districts will produce increased expenditures for the unfortunate 500,000 of about seven dollars per student. If the state permits its level of support for public education to decline, and districts are thrown back upon local resources, disparities such as these will quickly result in larger interdistrict fiscal inequities.

Causes of Persistent Inequity

Why have the results of educational reform been so disappointing with respect to equalizing district finances? There are a number of reasons. The first is that House Bill 72 mandates payments to wealthier school districts which are losing state funding. Over a period of two years after implementation of the bill, these payments cushion the blow of diminished revenues for property rich districts. In the 1985/86 school year, these payments reinforce existing inequities. They will be entirely phased out by the 1986/87 year, however.

A second, more enduring reason for persistent fiscal inequity is that reforms of state school finance which take state aid from wealthy districts to supply more to poor districts encourage the wealthy districts to replace state funds by increasing taxes. Wealthy school districts tend, in a sense, to be undertaxed. Increasing local taxrates in these districts by one or two cents is relatively painless. The impact of equalizing reforms at the state level is offset by local revenue increases in the wealthy districts.

House Bill 72 increased state funding for public education by a billion dollars. In the two years after HB 72 was implemented, however, the school districts increased local tax revenues by an equal amount—a record rate of tax increase for school districts in Texas.[4] The increased state funds were distributed using redistributive mechanisms, but local revenue increases are not redistributive in their impact.

Indeed, the taxing power of wealthy districts would cause one to suspect that they would benefit most when a large increase in local taxrates occurs in the aggregate. Figures for the last two years confirm this suspicion (Table 2). Texas school districts were divided in quintiles (groups of twenty percent each) by wealth (assessed valuation per student). The average change in local receipts per student from 1983/84 to 1985/86 for each quintile was then computed. In the poorest twenty percent of districts, local receipts increased on average by $56.31 per student. In the wealthiest twenty percent of school districts, the increase per student was $792.55. Clearly, much of the equalizing that would have been accomplished by House Bill 72 was negated by increasing local revenues in the wealthy school districts.

Table 2 Mean Increase in Local Revenue per Student by Quintile by District Wealth

Quintile:	1	2	3	4	5
	56.31	143.66	210.32	371.15	792.55
N =	(213)	(213)	(213)	(212)	(209)

Average District Increase: 312.94

The Future

House Bill 72 has made important advances toward the goal of interdistrict fiscal equity, but that goal is still a considerable distance away. Local districts are finding it very difficult to meet state mandated standards for class size and for the career ladder for teachers. Proposals are now before the legislature to weaken these standards. If the allowance for maximum class size is increased and the provisions for the career ladder are relaxed, what is likely to be the interdistrict impact? Clearly it will be that poorer districts will have larger classes and less well-paid teachers. The wealthy districts, after all, are not the ones having trouble meeting these standards.

There will be a similar impact if present levels of state formula funding are allowed to slip. (Even if nominal-dollar amounts are carried over into the next biennium, that will represent a slip in funding in real-dollar terms.) Of all the determinants of district spending listed above, only state funding has a redistributive impact. All of the other factors hinge upon local revenue generating ability. Any slippage in state funding, therefore, will magnify the importance of local property wealth and increase the inequities between wealthy and poor districts. In a period of increasing educational costs, a reduction in proportions of receipts from state funding will shift the burden to the local tax base. Wealthy districts will be able to shoulder the increased burden by increasing local taxes. Poor districts, on the other hand, are likely to be faced with deterioration in programs.

Notes

1. The Policy Workshop for Fall, 1986 is comprised of Thelma Bell, Larry Damrell, Mary Clayton, Bernadette Mckinney, Marjorie Elkins, Timothy Pulz, Howard Smiga, Stephen Bodnarchuk, Suzanna Spruill, Lynn Smith, Dionne Bagsby, and Carla Baltagi.
2. These figures are taken from the Texas Research League Publication, *Bench Marks for 1986–87 School District Budgets in Texas* (Austin, Texas, Texas Research League, 1986.)
3. These figures are taken from the article, "The Shame of the Schools," *The Texas Observer,* January 23, 1987.
4. Texas Research League, 1986. *Bench Marks for 1986–87 School District Budgets in Texas.* Austin, TX: Texas Research League.

17 City Charters and Their Political Implications
ROBERT THOMAS

American politics occurs within three arenas of government—national, state, and local. Just as there is a national constitution and a state constitution many cities have charters which effectively function as constitutions for local government. Constitutions provide a framework for politics which includes limits on what government can do. These limits, and the political structure defined by a constitution, are often viewed as too restrictive or inappropriate for the times by members of the community as well as by elected and appointed officials. Political struggles ensue in which political actors attempt to achieve their goals within the defined structure or attempt to alter that structure.

In American history three basic forms of city charters have evolved—the commission form, the council-manager form, and the mayor-council form. The commission form was invented in Galveston, Texas after the hurricane of 1900 completely disrupted normal politics. Each of the major services of a city, such as water, police, and fire protection, is run by a single individual called a commissioner. The commissioners get together from time to time in a commissioners' council, which sometimes includes a mayor, to coordinate their efforts, but each runs his area largely free of control by the council or other commissioners.

In the council-manager form of government, an elected city council hires a professional administrator who oversees all of the city services. As long as the manager's performance is satisfactory to the council there is no problem, but the council can fire this city manager whenever it wishes. If there is a mayor in this system, he or she is largely a figurehead. In a mayor-council form an elected council serves as a legislature; an elected mayor serves as the executive. The relationship between the two is very similar to that between the governor and legislature of a state, or the president and congress at the national level.

Since Houston was granted a charter by the Texas legislature on March 18, 1905, it has used all three forms of local government at one time or another. The charter in effect at a given time both reflected the political reality of the city and helped shape that reality. An historical overview of Houston politics since 1905 thus provides a nice "laboratory" for studying the relationship of formal political structures to political behavior. That history will have four major phases. Beginning with a commission form of government

(1905–1941), and moving through a relatively brief period where the council-manager form was used (1942–46), Houston since 1947 has used a council-mayor form, first with a strong-mayor, eight-member council (1947–1978), and then a strong-mayor fourteen-member council (1979 to the present).

The Beginnings: Commission Government

The 1905 Charter embodied different, and seemingly contradictory, models of local government. Its central feature was based on what turn-of-the century municipal reformers considered the "best" form of city government: the commission-style of government which had originated in nearby Galveston, Texas. The centerpiece of the new government was a city council composed of a mayor and four aldermen.

The document also reflected legacies of nineteenth century Jacksonian principles aimed at democratizing city government. Since each council member was elected every two years and received the annual sum of $2,000, city business was conducted by part-time, grass-roots amateurs. Furthermore, both legislative and administrative decision-making resulted from council bargaining. The mayor was weak, yet the charter did give him several authorities that reform advocates later suggested were necessary for governmental efficiency: a veto power, appointment power (with council approval), power to remove department heads at his own discretion, and budget preparation authority.

Finally, the 1905 Charter followed British precepts that local government should be removed from popular control.[1] The document did not have a recall article; thus the citizenry had no oversight over their officials' conduct in office until the next election. And, without an initiative and referendum article, the charter provided no formal citizen input into policy making.

From Legislative to Local Charter Development

A Home Rule Amendment was added to the Texas Constitution in 1912. Thereafter, charter changes were debated in the local arena rather than in the halls of the state legislature. When the development of city governance was directly subject to legislative scrunity, local structures and processes had to be acceptable to a legislative consensus. Home rule redirected the charter development process to city leaders who were allowed to fill in the details of city governance so long as those details did not conflict with state law. Under these circumstances, the Texas Constitution, not the legislature, provided the whole cloth from which local leaders could design their own locally generated patterns. Since 1912, Houston's Charter has been constructed almost exclusively as a local document reflecting community compromises that emerged from the socio-economic and political habits, customs, and peculiarities of the community.

Houston's leadership and citizens quickly put an indelible local imprint on the city's charter. A package of charter changes were ratified in 1913. Many of these remain part of the charter today, or they have provided the foundation on which subsequent changes have been developed.

The 1913 changes were grouped into several specific areas. First, powers were enhanced or added to allow the city to stimulate community growth and progress by having autonomy to annex on a simple council vote; to buy and sell utilities; to do harbor and waterfront work; and, to establish improvement districts. Second, city officials could protect the public interests through enhanced regulatory authority over private activities such as electrical utilities that provided a community-wide need. Third, charter provisions were added to increase professionalism and fiscal efficiency in city government. A civil service commission was created and charged with making administrative rules and regulations and offering a grievance process for city workers. Also, the city controller's fiscal oversight responsibilities were redefined. Finally, territorial democracy was firmly implanted in the document in several diverse ways. Aldermanic positions were redefined so that each alderman stood for election in one of four designated commissioner positions: Tax and Land, Fire, Streets and Bridges, and Water. Recall, initiative, and referendum articles were added to make city officials more accountable to the citizenry.

Difficulties in Commission Government

The commissioners' administration of city government was beset with difficulties inherent in governments that combine legislative and administrative functions in a single body. Formally, the mayor was a semi-autonomous executive. His political and administrative leadership was limited even though he could appoint and remove ordinance-created department heads, prepare their budgets, and veto council actions. The city's major administrative functions, however, were directly under individual commissioners making the mayor less than one among equals in city administration. While the mayor's budget authority extended only to departments created by ordinance, the four commissioner-headed departments consumed the bulk of city expenditures.

The veto power, which extended some mayoral control over policy, also had its limitations. The veto is a reactive policy tool, not an agenda-building one. Nonetheless, even its negative attributes were hampered by the commission government, since a council majority could override the mayor's veto. As a council member, the mayor could participate in the vote, apparently an advantage for the mayor. However, in practice, aldermen did not tolerate a mayor's meddling in a commissioner's administrative area. The alderman's turf was sacrosanct, which created a protectionist dictum for each commissioner: "Thou shall preserve the sacredness of a fellow commissioner's authority, lest I might lose my own!" The mayor occupied a position that was structurally weak. What power he exercised came from force of personality and persuasion rather than formal authority. As one might well imagine, the mayor's position changed from one personality to the next.

Houston's commission-style of government, subsequently, suffered from the same pitfalls that other such governments encountered. Commissioners staked out an administrative domain. Comprehensive decision-making could not be achieved because commissioners defended the interests of their particular departments during council meetings. City business was thus conducted by logrolling. On budget matters, for example, alliances were established. A commissioner unable to make a deal for his department got budgetary leftovers. Under this system, executive leadership was virtually non-existent.

By the 1930s, city administration was completely politicized and fragmented. Commissioners staffed their individual departments with persons loyal to their needs and interests. Not to be outdone, mayors used their power to appoint staff to ordinance-created departments to develop a spoils system of their own. Thus, a patronage-laden bureaucracy emerged in Houston under the commission form of government. This spoils system occurred even though the city had a civil service commission.

The 1913 charter revisions, along with amendments through the 1920s, placed the Civil Service Commission (CSC) formally at the center of city personnel action. The CSC was empowered (1) to make rules and regulations for the conduct of business; (2) to provide for classification of all city officers and appointees, including police and fire, except department heads; (3) to establish an open, competitive, free examination for classification; and (4) to render decisions in employee firings and grievances.

The CSC operated with some definite disadvantages in "taking politics out of administration." It was composed of three members appointed by the mayor, with council approval. Their term of office coincided with the mayor's and council's two-year tenure. Moreover, one member of the CSC had to be a commissioner. While the CSC could make employee rules and regulations, they were subject to council approval and change. Under these circumstances, the CSC was politically subservient to the mayor and council and became a microcosm of commission politics.

While the shortcomings of commission government led to its downfall, some mayors thrived under this fragmented, patronage-ladened system. For example, three mayors worked against the 1933 charter changes that would have enhanced the mayor's administrative authority by eliminating the election of aldermen as department heads. The amendment stated: "[aldermen] . . . shall perform as a body, without reference to designation, all the duties provided for in this charter to be performed by an alderman or commissioner." By implication, this change would have strengthened the mayor's executive powers by placing the major city departments under his control. Other charter amendments, designed to consolidate and strengthen executive functions (e.g., a finance department) were also approved in 1933. Combined, this package of amendments effectively eliminated a council-dominated administration.

Mayor Walter E. Monteith spearheaded the campaign to pass the 1933 amendments. Ironically, although Monteith's efforts succeeded in getting the changes ratified, he lost his reelection bid to Oscar Holcombe. Monteith's defeat kept the strong-mayor provisions from being implemented, as the mayors who served between 1933 and 1942 (Holcombe, R.H. Fonville, and C.A. Pickett) simply did not implement the charter revisions. Aldermen continued to act as department heads, just as they had since 1913. For the next decade commission-style government remained in force.

Why were the 1933 provisions not implemented? It would seem that Holcombe, Fonville, and Pickett would have tried to use the 1933 changes to enhance their control over city administration. The explanation for their successful resistance to change is found in Oscar Holcombe's political base. For some 45 years between 1921 and 1957, Holcombe was on-and-off the official city scene. During these years, he ran for mayor sixteen times and was elected eleven times. Holcombe was undoubtedly popular, but he was also a fixture on the Houston scene for so many years because of his alignment with conservative business interests who benefited from a fragmented city government with a council-led bureaucracy. Holcombe was, in effect, part of the business establishment that advocated a pro-business city government.

In recapturing the mayor's office in 1933, Holcombe resurrected a coalition that he had built in his previous years as mayor from 1921 to 1929. That coalition had three components. Its core was centered around city employees whom Holcombe had placed in office during his earlier tenure as mayor. Its resources came from contributions by construction firms and key downtown business leaders. It was solidified by the commissioners, who supported Holcombe's opposition to a strong-mayor arrangement. Formal charter changes were thus overridden by "acknowledged collective benefits of stability" among Holcombe's supporters.[2] City government as usual, meaning commission government, benefitted key interests both inside and outside city hall. Holcombe simply managed an "opposition to change" that was already firmly implanted in the community.[3]

The City Manager Interlude

As demonstrated by the ability of three mayors to ignore charter changes in the 1930s, the barriers to change are formidable. The defenders of "things as they are" can usually place obstacles in the reformers' path, especially when reforms are comprehensive. When the character and intensity of each side's position is essentially equal, then the *status quo* is almost always preserved. Reformers, typically, need some extraordinary community conditions to make their case for change. Change proposals are usually not successful when there is not a perceived "crisis" to necessitate altering the *status quo*. What also appears helpful for state and local governmental reforms are examples of successes elsewhere. These circumstances during the early 1940s dramatically turned Houston government away from commission control to embrace a council-manager government.

The seeds of these changes were planted in a package of charter recommendations offered in 1938. These proposals, rejected under the conditions of the late 1930s, called for a council-appointed business manager, a council with only legislative powers, and other changes designed to professionalize city government. In slightly different form, these proposals were resurrected in the early 1940's when the city was gripped with a public health crisis during a series of polio and diphtheria epidemics. When citizens became disenchanted with the government's ability to respond, the crisis was blamed on an overstaffed, patronaged-filled city bureaucracy. The health problems merely brought out in the open what had been festering for sometime: the desire for a more responsive, efficient, and effective city government. The more immediate problem gave way to more enduring dissatisfactions.

Government reformers were in their heyday in the 1930s and 1940s. A professionally organized and managed bureaucracy, they argued, could cure almost all of society's ills. Administration would be freed from politics to carry out the mandates of the legislative branch efficiently and economically. The opponents of commission government embraced this reform model and campaigned vigorously for its adoption in Houston.

Charter reforms placed before the voters in 1942 significantly altered city government. A professionally-managed administration, with the manager as the key executive, was the core ingredient. The manager was to have almost exclusive power over departmental policies, personnel, and budgeting. The council would act as a board of directors by appointing the manager and by having authority to remove him. Other than this oversight, the charter reform proposals decidedly limited the mayor's and council's administrative powers, and of the two the mayor's most notably.

An eight-member council was advocated, all to be elected at-large, but with five required to reside in geographic districts. Preferential balloting was to be used to nominate district council members, with the three at-large seats filled by candidates with the largest number of votes. Council members were prohibited from exercising any administrative powers or heading any city departments. The mayor was to be the weak sister of city government. Removal of the mayor's veto was the most telling divestment of his authority.

Monteith spearheaded the 1942 campaign for the city manager system, being joined by four former mayors and a host of "good government" reformers. They persuasively argued that a city manager would run the city in a more efficient and business-like manner. Abolishing the commission government with its council-led bureaucracy, they argued, would take city administration out of the doldrums of fragmentation and patronage. Another factor also motivated the reformers' efforts: underlying the "good government" campaign was an "anti-Holcombe" campaign. Holcombe had not only thwarted Monteith's earlier 1933 efforts to reform the city, but he was also instrumental in opposing the 1938 proposals.

In 1942, Holcombe unsuccessfully tried to use his political acuity to offset the city management plan. Along with council, he tried to sidetrack the move to adopt city management government. First, the council simply refused to order an election, forcing the reform advocates to circulate an initiative and referendum petition to the electorate. After the petition campaign succeeded, the council assumed that a low voter turnout would certainly defeat the plan. Accordingly, the council scheduled the election for August 15, 1942, a date that fell between two primary elections. The tactic failed, as turnout was considerably heavier than anticipated, and the city management plan was approved. Next, as he had done before, Holcombe tried for reelection as mayor, presumably to stop the plan from being implemented as he had done in 1933. However, in the November, 1942 election Holcombe was defeated by Otis Massey, who supported the city manager plan.

Houston's five-year experiment with a professionally managed government did not succeed. After the war, influential entrepreneurs and many civic and public leaders alike wanted a government that reflected, not directed, growth and development. Influential citizens wanted a *laissez-faire* approach wherein government facilitated and supported private economic activities by doing what was minimally required to keep the peace and provide for the health and safety of the citizenry. Government could be tolerated so long as it performed this "proper" role.

The private sector's opposition to the city manager system was articulated publicly by Oscar Holcombe. He reemerged in 1946 to capture the mayor's office once again. His campaign concentrated on two alleged failures of the city manager system: inadequate services and extravagant fiscal management. Holcombe's unsuccessful opponent, Holger Jeppensen, supported the city manager system. Jeppensen accused Holcombe of ward heeling, political blacklisting, and fostering a spoils system.

The Strong-Mayor System

The city manager system was relegated to the scrap heap with Holcombe back at the city's helm. Yet, the city's experience with a manager was a necessary prelude to a strong-mayor. It is doubtful that a strong-mayor system could have emerged from the commission-style government. The city manager interlude offered a formal model for an aggressive executive directing city affairs. It also provided a focal point for the opposition to blame all the city's ills on the manager, a target not available in the commissioner government. The significance of the manager system, therefore, was to provide a framework for a strong executive and weak council.

The 1947 Charter amendments abolished the city manager position but essentially retained the other structures of city government that had been instituted in 1942: an eight-member council (all elected at-large, with five required to reside in districts) and a vetoless mayor. The effect of abolishing the manager position, though, was to make the mayor the central figure in city government. The extensive managerial authorities given to the manager in the 1942 charter were simply transferred to the mayor, but without council oversight attached.

The path of administrative responsibility and power in city government was dramatically changed. The commission-run government had fragmented administrative responsibility and power. A commissioner could always avoid responsibility for an administrative function, except his own, by shifting blame to another commissioner. The mayor, likewise, could avoid public scrutiny by hiding behind the skirts of the council. The manager system had centralized administrative functions, but still obliquely shifted responsibility. The manager was directly answerable to the council, who appointed him and could remove him at its discretion. But council could avoid criticism by shifting responsibility back to the manager or, simply, by firing him. The strong-mayor system, for the first time in the city's history, provided a direct link between the administration and the electorate. By the same token, selected interests could channel their demands to the mayor's office. The focal point of city governance and politics in the post-World War II years, thus, has been on mayoral politics.

Council Challenge

Moving from councilmanic to mayoral control in 1947 left some ambiguities about mayor-council powers and responsibilities. The council was at the pinnacle of control over city affairs, first, as departmental administrators for 37 years in the commission government, then as the board of directors for five years in the manager government. That tradition of authority lingered into the 1950s leaving questions about council authority. Just how much authority, if any, did council have (or could it assume) over city administration? Should mayoral appointees such as the city attorney serve the mayor only or both the mayor and council? There were also questions about the best electoral methods to use in selecting city officials. The use of preferential ballots and at-large elections were both criticized as grossly unfair and inadequate. Should district council members be selected by district or city-wide voters? At-large voting for district-designated council members could (and did) result in the election of members who received a majority of the city-wide vote, but finished second or even third in the district vote.

These issues were subdued during most of Holcombe's two-terms as strong-mayor. Holcombe's leadership philosophy was the same in the strong-mayor system as it had been in the commission system: he was a quiet consensus-builder. In his relationship with council, he nurtured members' support and allowed them to share power. Holcombe and the council were also allies in pursuing a policy of economic growth through low taxes and no interference in private sector activities, other than to support and facilitate them.

In contrast, the election of Roy Hofheinz in 1953 brought a new perspective and leadership style to the mayor's office. Hofheinz aggressively asserted his leadership over council and likewise over the business establishment. "Hofheinz believed that problems ought to be solved by making them public issues and if the city council didn't support the mayor then the mayor should use his formal power and public support to overcome council opposition."[4]

Mayor-council relationships steadily deteriorated during Hofheinz's first term. By the outset of his second term, the city was ensnarled in a major crisis of governance. A number of mayor-council skirmishes erupted into a full-scale conflict when Hofheinz's called for a twenty percent tax hike which, he contended, was necessary to keep services in line with needs. Council and most business leaders were emphatically opposed. The downtown business establishment would be hardest hit by new tax reassessments. Hofheinz had stirred up a hornet's nest of opposition.

A movement began immediately to decrease the mayor's powers. First, the council attempted to abolish several mayoral staff positions and at least one department head position. When Hofheinz successfully countered this action by mustering public support, council proposed a complex package of eighteen charter amendments designed to make the mayor little more than a ceremonial head of government with a charter-designated council administrator running city departments and an elected attorney overseeing the city's legal affairs. A city election was called for August 16, 1955.

Hofheinz reacted by proposing a nineteenth amendment which, if ratified, would effectively negate the council's proposals. Hofheinz advocated having runoff elections rather than preferential ballots, having all eight council members elected at-large (retaining the requirement that five reside in designated districts), and having a strong-mayor provision giving absolute mayoral control over executive functions while expressly prohibiting any council interference in administration. Hofheinz's proposals were designed to bury the last remaining vestiges of council authority over city administration.

The mayor-council impasse finally resulted in an outright council mutiny when, on July 15, 1955, all eight council members voted to suspend Hofheinz for one month pending the outcome of an impeachment hearing, that hearing scheduled for August 4, 1955, just eleven days before the charter vote. The council leveled a variety of charges against Hofheinz ranging from seemingly minor improprieties to out-and-out illegalities. Hofheinz was accused of improperly trying to persuade the City Controller, Roy Oakes, to refuse to issue vouchers for payment of city salaries. The council also said that Hofheinz ordered the Public Works Director not to collect or dispose of garbage and to have sewage disposal plants shut down. Council contended that Hofheinz took each of these actions to stress the need for more tax dollars and, thus, force the council to accept the tax increase. Finally, Hofheinz was accused of illegally allowing the sale of public lands to developers.

When council members voted to suspend Hofheinz, they tried to install the mayor pro tem as acting mayor. Hofheinz refused to move aside and obtained a court injunction against the council's action. He also rallied public support. The mayor pro tem had already taken steps to assume control of city government. He informed all department heads he was acting mayor and ordered the city attorney to enforce that edict. The city attorney, Will Sears, as well as city department heads simply ignored the mayor pro tem's directive. They felt on solid ground holding that Hofheinz was still in charge.

When the impeachment hearing was held, only two witnesses appeared to testify against Hofheinz: a disgruntled, recently fired, department head and Roy Oakes, the city controller. All other summoned witnesses felt secure in not testifying after the Sheriff—on direction from the state district court—refused to serve the warrants. To save face, council ended the fracas by voting simply to reprimand Hofheinz.

Hofheinz's nineteenth amendment was ratified in the August 16th vote. Although he had successfully fended off the council's impeachment efforts, Hofheinz's opponents did not give up. They persuaded Oscar Holcombe to run again for mayor. Holcombe easily defeated Hofheinz with 57 percent of the vote.

The outcome of the Hofheinz-council clash solidified the mayor's control over city government and relegated the council to a secondary position in city governance. As might be expected, the antagonism between the two branches of government did not disappear. There were efforts to change the composition of council in the late 1960s and through most of the 1970s. These proposals focused mainly on some mixture of district and at-large representation on council. While these changes were initiated from community groups and some city officials, they did not become a reality until 1979.

The Charter Changes of 1979

The most recent major changes in Houston's charter resulted from the interaction of two seemingly unrelated political processes—Houston's annexation policy and the Voting Rights Act passed by the United States Congress in 1965.

From the 1940's through the 1970's Houston's economy underwent sustained growth, which in turn fueled a population that almost doubled every ten years. As this population grew and continually spilled over beyond the city limits, Houston used permissive state annexation laws to annex aggressively the areas surrounding it. These annexations prevented Houston from being surrounded and locked in by suburbs, and they also resulted in the city being one of the largest in the nation in land area.

The Voting Rights Act was designed to prevent discrimination against minorities in elections. Texas was not originally included in the provisions of this act or its 1970 extension, but in 1975 Congresswoman Barbara Jordan and

U.S. Senator Lloyd Bentson led a successful effort to extend the Voting Rights Act to Texas over the strong opposition of Governor Dolph Briscoe and other Texas officials. Because Texas has two large minority populations, blacks and Hispanics, because there has been a strong tradition in Texas of minority litigation, and because there are so many local governments in Texas to generate such cases, Texas quickly came under disproportionate scrutiny from national authorities with respect to the Voting Rights Act.

Residents of an area around Clear Lake annexed in 1978 did not wish to be so annexed and sued for deannexation. Part of the grounds for the suit was that annexation disproportionately annexed white voters to the city and diluted the black vote, thus insuring their continued exclusion from effective participation in city politics. A closer look at this controversy and the changes it produced is deeply instructive concerning Houston politics.

Racial and Ethnic Voting Patterns

For most of its history, Houston fit the pattern of southern politics described by V.O. Key who found that "the peculiarities of southern politics come from the impact of the black race [because] . . . the predominant consideration in the architecture of southern political institutions has been to assure locally a subordination of the Negro population and, externally, to block threatened interference from the outside with these local arrangements."[5] In Texas generally and Houston specifically white primaries, poll taxes, difficult registration laws, and informal pressures worked to exclude or dilute black electoral influence. The evidence of the effectiveness of these mechanisms is shown in racial voting patterns over the years.

Just becoming part of the electorate has been a slow and arduous process for Houston's minorities. Prior to the 1940s, black voting in City of Houston elections was almost non-existent. Significant black participation did not come until 1944 when the US Supreme Court, in *Smith v. Allwright,* effectively struck down the white-primary system that had operated to exclude blacks from most elections in Texas as well as the entire South. Since the *Smith* case originated in Houston, it took on added importance for the city's black population. Afterwards there was a steady increase in black voter registration, which by the 1970s compromised nearly the percentage of the city electorate that the black population warranted. Houston's Mexican-American community also steadily increased its voter rolls (albeit at a relatively slower pace than blacks). While Mexican-American are the fastest-growing population group in Houston, they lag behind both whites and blacks in their registration and voting levels. By 1980, the combined voter strength of blacks and Mexican-Americans was approximately one-third (32 percent) of Houston's electorate.

Against the background of a relatively small number of minority voters until recent years, it is not surprising that Houston's voting has been polarized along racial lines. Like other southern cities, race makes a difference to Houston voters. Richard W. Murray and Arnold Vedlitz found, for example, in five southern cities (including Houston) that candidates supported by blacks were usually opposed by a majority of whites. When blacks ran for office, racial voting was even more pronounced.[6]

Prior to council redistricting in 1979, Houston's charter required the at-large election of all eight council members. (Five, however, had to live in and "represent" geographic areas.) Minorities, thus, had to compete against a citywide, white-dominated, electorate with a history of racial voting with regard to minority candidates. Not surprisingly, minority candidates fared poorly. In 96 council elections between 1956 and 1977, only four were won by a black (Judson Robinson, Jr. won a seat in 1971 and was reelected three times). No Hispanics were elected. Except for Robinson, minority candidates did not come close to winning a citywide council election. The twenty minority candidates, other than Robinson, who contested council seats between 1971 and 1977 averaged less than 10 percent of the white vote. The most successful black candidate garnered only 36 percent of the citywide vote, while no Hispanic attained as much as 30 per cent of the city-wide vote.

Initial Attempts to Alter the City Council

The first step to have council members elected by districts began in federal court. The impetus came with Mayor Fred Hofheinz's election in 1973 which was attained with black support. That, coupled with his avowed support for council reform, led a coalition of Houstonians to file a federal court suit against the city's at-large council system. The initiative came from a coalition of local individuals and groups. The legal avenue available to the coalition at the time were the principles of equal protection of the law as defined by the US Supreme Court's decisions in *Westbury v. Sanders* (376 U.S. 1, 1964) and *Reynolds v. Sims* (377 U.S. 533, 1964). There is no question that a legal avenue, outside the locality, was available to the coalition, but it was not "big brother" initiating or mandating the suit. Rather, it came from local political activists. But that avenue was temporarily closed through the individual discretion of the trial judge, Allen G. Hanney, who as a conservative on racial matters simply delayed hearing the case for three years.

The second step was influenced by the interrelationship of political actions in the federal system. While local efforts were on hold in Judge Hanney's court, in 1975 the US Congress extended the provisions of the Voting Rights Act to Texas and a number of other jurisdictions that had not been covered by the original 1965 Act or its 1970 amendments. Section Five of the original Act required that changes in a local government's electoral system that altered minority voting strength must be precleared either by the US Attorney General or by a declaratory judgment from the District Court for the District of Columbia. When Congress amended the Voting Rights Act in 1975 to include language minorities—defined as persons constituting at least five percent of the voting population whose dominant language is other than English—the preclearance requirement took on added significance for Houston which had used large-scale annexation to spur growth and development.

With the 1975 changes, an entirely new set of extra-community legal arrangements—not available in 1973—were opened to advocates for council reform. With Texas now covered by the Voting Rights Act, and with specific federal legal provisions protecting minority voting strength under circumstances of municipal boundary expansions, the rules under which future annexations in Houston would occur had been irrevocably altered. Moreover, with Houston's substantial Mexican-American population, the reformers could solicit a sizable number of citizens to their ranks.

The effects of these new federal legal arrangements allowed the plaintiffs in the still-pending 1973 lawsuit to file a second suit charging that the City of Houston violated the Voting Rights Act by not seeking Department of Justice approval for various annexations undertaken since 1972.

The City of Houston survived the original court challenge. Judge Hanney finally set the trial for late 1976. In a five-week proceeding the city's attorneys countered charges that the at-large system was inherently discriminatory. It was the city's position that while few minorities were elected under the at-large system, that did not diminish city services to these groups because all members of the council had to be responsive to black and brown voters since they constituted a sizable part of the electorate. The city prevailed when Judge Hanney found that the plaintiffs had "failed to prove that the city discriminates against minorities in providing city services or that minorities are denied access to the process of city government." (Houston Chronicle, March 8, 1977: 1). While the proponents of council reform had been rejected in their initial foray outside the community, they were shortly provided with new opportunities to advocate change.

1977 and 1978 Annexations

Annexation was a central element in Houston's massive economic and demographic growth after 1945. It had allowed the city to prevent suburban encirclement, spread the tax base over a broad territory to remain a low tax city, as well as spread out the racial distribution of the population. Annexation had been so successful for Houston that by the late 1970s, it did not resemble most other large US cities. For example, among other factors, it was not surrounded by suburban cities and it was fiscally sound. Continued annexation, however, was deemed a vital part of Houston's continued progress, especially given the rapid development occurring in unincorporated areas where the prospect of new cities was rearing its ugly face to Houston officials.

Rapid suburban development and suburban incorporation initiatives compelled Houston officials to act. The potential of suburban encirclement anywhere on Houston's borders, loss of the city's future tax base, and increased minority numbers in the inner city—all perceived to be avoidable through annexations of unincorporated areas—led to a series of annexation proposals at the end of 1977 by outgoing Mayor Fred Hofheinz and continued in 1978 by his successor, Jim McConn. These mayoral actions were strongly supported by the Chamber of Commerce. The council approved the mayor's annexation plan and annexed about 75 square-miles of territory that contained more than 150,000 people, most of whom were middle-income whites. These annexed areas sued the City of Houston to be deannexed, using every argument they could muster.

The opportunity was ripe for the proponents of single-member districts to seek a solution through the court. In the summer of 1978, encouraged by the Clear Lake suit the plaintiffs in the earlier suit on appeal in the US Fifth Circuit Court, urged the Department of Justice to block Houston's annexations under the Voting Rights Act. One week later, the Department of Justice filed suit against the city for failing to secure approval for the 1977 and 1978 annexations and then blocked all municipal elections until the issue was settled.

At this point, Houston officials could defend the city's annexations and the at-large council system, or—as San Antonio had done—reach a settlement with the Department of Justice. Houston chose to contest the suit by attempting to show that the at-large system did not dilute minority voting strength and that the 1977 and 1978 annexations had only slightly reduced minority vote percentages. These arguments were countered by the plaintiffs with evidence of racial voting in city elections that centered mainly on the population estimates used by the city to arrive at its conclusions. The Department of Justice informed Houston officials that they would consider withdrawing its objection if the city adopted a system in which blacks and Mexican Americans are afforded representation reasonably equivalent to their political strength. Such representation "would include the election of some (not all) city council members from single member districts, if the districts are fairly drawn and if the number of districts is sufficient to enable both blacks and Mexican Americans to elect candidates of their choice."[7] Houston was prevented from holding any elections until an acceptable system of representation was adopted. While the issue had been debated in political institutions outside the local arena (with all concerned local interests participating), the final resolution was now left to local negotiation and bargaining. The initial reaction from both sides was understandably hostile. From Mayor McConn, the council, and business leaders came a harsh attack on the Department of Justice for an unwarranted intrusion into local affairs. On the other side, black and Mexican-American leaders along with their supporters, while pleased to get a formal objection, were dismayed by the willingness of the Department of Justice to accept a mixed plan retaining some at-large seats.

Adoption of the Nine-Five Council Plan

There then began a process of local negotiations to change Houston's council. The solution emerged from the traditional power brokers in the city. Understanding that change was inevitable, they tried to devise the best solution. What they came up with was a plan for a mixed council of nine elected from districts and five elected at-large. (The mayor was to remain a voting member of council.) Butwhile they understood that change had to come, they did not give up trying to hold onto the status quo. When the city council scheduled an August 11, 1979, vote on the 9–5 plan, it also attempted to put another proposition on the same ballot to retain the existing system. Acting as the referee, the Department of Justice refused to allow voting on anything except the 9–5 plan, thus tacitly putting its stamp of approval on the 9–5 plan.

In a strange twist of circumstances, the long established opponents to council change lined up to campaign vigorously *for* the proposed change. These champions of the 9–5 plan included such earlier supporters of no-change as private business leaders, the Houston Chamber of Commerce, Mayor McConn, and practically all long-time supporters of traditional city hall activities. Those who had worked long and hard to come to this point now found themselves opposed to the council change. Blacks and Mexican-Americans—joined by labor leaders, neighborhood activists, and recently annexed suburbanities—wanted a twenty-member council with at least sixteen seats elected by districts.

In the campaign that ensued, local political clout, not federal intervention, was the decisive factor. On the one hand, the 9–5 opponents were at a severe disadvantage, as they had been historically, when they attempted to contest citywide elections. For example, they hastily put together a "Citizens Coalition for Responsive Government," but could raise only $4,595. With this sum they could not even buy a 30–second TV commercial during prime time. On the other hand, a blue-ribbon group of Houston's most prominent business leaders quickly raised almost $200,000 to put together a media campaign supporting the charter change. These efforts were supported by many large business firms which urged their employees to vote for the proposal.

The die was cast. On election day, with only 11 percent of city's voters going to the polls, the 9–5 plan passed almost two to one. It was a case of simply too much voter power for the traditional power brokers. The margin of victory was attributable to the far heavier turnout in affluent and middle-class white areas (22 and 13 percent) than elsewhere in the city. Moreover, despite the favorable vote, the electorate voted along racial lines. Ninety-one percent of blacks and 77 percent of Mexican-Americans voting opposed the plan. Whites strongly voted for the plan. The only exceptions were whites in two newly annexed areas: Clear Lake where 92 percent opposed and Alief where 53 percent opposed.

The last remaining step was to draw district lines. Again the Department of Justice left the decision largely to the city's traditional power brokers, although it retained its position as rules interpreter. With the aid of three outside consultants, Houston drew various district plans, each based on population estimates for 1979, rather than official 1970 census counts, which had the effect of shifting representation to fast-growing suburban areas. Although strong objections came from the other side, the Department of Justice approved the city's district plan. It was one that did not maximize black political influence.

The Current Charter

The most recent charter alterations amounted to a change in the constitution of Houston's government. Did the constitutional change make any difference? First of all, since the move to a 9–5 council approximately a third of its members are black or Hispanic. Furthermore, there have been several women elected to the council whereas before the change there had been none. Although charter reform did not meet minority expectations, the Houston political system has been significantly more open and representative than it had been earlier.

Also, there has been a shift in the kind of person elected to City Council. From 1945 until 1977 members of the city council were not only white, middle aged males who usually operated small businesses; they were also political amateurs with only a marginal interest in politics. As a result, they tended to be relatively inactive during council meetings and not inclined to involve themselves in developing or advocating major policies. Since 1980, not only are council members more representative of racial and gender diversity, but the average council member is now much more of a political creature, on average younger, more educated, and much more experienced politically. As one might expect, this kind of council member is more politically astute, and much more inclined to be activist, consequently the council is more inclined to exercise oversight over the mayor and bureaucracy and more inclined to propose or take stands on major policies.

However, the assertiveness of the new council is a matter of degree rather than a fundamental alteration in Houston politics. During the quarter of a century prior to the most recent charter changes Houston institutionalized a classic strong-mayor form of government. By most objective standards the mayor's powers are dominant over those of the council. Comparing the powers of the two is instructive. Houston's mayor is endowed with most of the legal powers to direct council action; consequently, the mayor initiates policy direction for the city and the council reacts. For example, the mayor organizes the legislative agenda, recommends policy, and casts a vote as a member of the council.

Even when the council is authorized to exercise "control" or "oversight" over the mayor, this power is limited. The council may approve all mayoral appointments to city departments and to boards and commissions, but if the mayor chooses to remove any of these officials the council cannot interfere. Without council approval the mayor can create and fill a number of high-paying executive staff jobs in the mayor's office, which effectively allows him to maintain policy control and direction not only over the city's business and its programs but also over outside state and national programs that the city administers.

The council can alter any item recommended in the mayor's budget by increasing, decreasing, or omitting it. Under the city's eight-member council this budget veto was not used. The mayor prepared the budget, and with almost absolute control over the city's bureaucracy, the mayor shaped budget recommendations to suit his priorities and thus established council reactions. Since the election of the 14-member council in 1980, the council has more closely reviewed the mayor's budget.

In addition to being the legislative leader, the mayor is the city's chief executive and administrator, standing at the apex of the bureaucracy, essentially without peer. The mayor performs the administrative functions of a strong city manager: hiring, firing, making personnel decisions, and being generally in charge of the conduct of city business.

The mayor's office has been expanded to match the increased administrative demands of the job. Thus Mayor Welch had two executive assistants; Mayor Roy Hofheinz Jr. had five; and Mayor Jim McConn had a senior executive assistance plus seven executive assistants. Mayor Kathy Whitmire departed form the practice of using executive assistants, but she still maintains a staff of close advisers.

The growth of the mayor-office bureaucracy is largely attributable to three principal factors. First, the sheer complexity of administering an ever-increasing city bureaucracy has made a larger mayor staff essential. Thus, Mayor McConn appointed executive assistants to oversee each general area of city government. Second, the growth of national grant programs in the 1970s has required an effective city administrative machinery in or closely associated with the mayor's office. Third, mayoral staff appointments have become patronage plums, given to minorities in recognition for their electoral support.

· The mayor's powers are far from unlimited, however, being constrained to varying degrees by an elected controller, the city civil service system, and the bureaucracy. Also, the city council exercises "oversight," and while in the past it was of minor importance, the most recent charter changes have resulted in a more activist council that now must be counted as a significant restraint on the mayor. The mayor must now be more responsive to minority concerns than in the past, more sensitive to how major policies affect various interests in the city, a set of interests that is now significantly broader than before. Put most succinctly, the mayor and council, both with respect to each other and their respective constituents, must operate more politically and less administratively than in the past. The most recent city charter changes, like those in the past, reflect broader developments in Houston. Houston, now the fourth largest city in the nation with the economic, social, and political diversity that such status implies, is once again in the process of evolving its political system to match its changed circumstances.

Notes

1. Anwar Syed, *The Political Theory of American Local Governments* (New York: Random House, 1966), p. 3.
2. Herbert Kaufman, *The Limits of Organizational Change* (University, Alabama: University of Alabama Press, 1971), chapter 1.
3. Herbert Kaufman, *The Limits of Organizational Change,* p. 8.
4. Kenneth E. Gray, *A Report on the Politics of Houston* (Cambridge: Mass.: Joint Center for Urban Studies, 1960), p. 14.
5. V. O. Key, *Southern Politics in State and Nation* (New York: Knopf, 1949), p. 665.
6. Richard W. Murray and Arnold Vedlitz, "Racial Voting Patterns in the South: An Analysis of Major Elections from 1960 to 1977 in Five Cities," *Annals of the American Academy of Political and Social Science,* Vol. 439 (September, 1978), pp. 29–39.
7. Letter of Attorney Genereal Edward H. Levy, 2 April 1976, p. 24.

18 Power in the City: Patterns of Political Influence in Houston, Texas
RICHARD MURRAY

I. Introduction

Since the publication of Floyd Hunter's *Community Power Structure*, a study of decision-making in Atlanta in the early 1950s, social scientists have focused considerable attention to the question of who runs American cities. Their attention reflects several factors. First, there are many cities, and they are convenient and accessible, especially to scholars whose institutions are often based in urban areas. Since most Americans live in or near cities, the question of who makes urban decisions engages broad public interest. And cities, as relatively self-contained economic and political units, present useful opportunities to study the interactive effects of private economic power and public decision-making processes.

Most students of community power agree that when it comes to the urban rulers and the ruled, there are few of the former and many of the latter. Lasswell and Learner note that "government is always government by the few, whether in the name of the few, the one or the many."[1] Beyond this numeric consensus, there is strong disagreement as to the nature of the ruling few. An *elitist* tradition, stretching from Floyd Hunter and C. Wright Mills in the 1950s to Thomas Dye in the 1980s, emphasizes the institutional and class bases of the leadership corps.[2] Elitists stress the similarity in familial and educational backgrounds of leaders, the interlocking nature of public and private institutions, and the ability of elites to dominate public policy making processes by virtue of the institutional power they wield. Their *pluralist* opponents, led by Robert Dahl of Yale University,[3] argue that political leadership in cities is far more fragmented than elitists suggest. Pluralists argue that a close analysis of specific public decisions shows no single group dominates across a range of policies and that elected public officials—not private economic elites—most often decide key political issues.

Some urban scholars have sought to move beyond the elitist v. pluralist arguments, suggesting that power patterns vary from one community to another and within specific cities over time. Atlanta in the 1950s may well have had strong elitist tendencies, but that does not mean San Francisco in the early 1970s could not be decidedly pluralistic. If cities can be placed on some sort of elitist-pluralist continuum, what defines where they fall? Terry Clark, Robert Lineberry, and Ira Sharkansky suggest a decisive role for the demographic patterns of cities, their governmental structures, and political cultures.

Following the Clark, Lineberry, Sharkansky approach, we begin our analysis of political power in Houston by focusing on the demographic, structural, and cultural characteristics of the community. We then look at "intermediating" power structures—political parties, interest groups, labor unions, the public bureaucracies—that are relevant to decision-making in Houston. Finally, we look at the specific leadership patterns in Houston. How have these changed over time? Who are the most powerful people in the city in the 1980s? What is the basis of their power? And who are likely to be Houston's leaders of the future?

Immediately, two methodological problems arise when one focuses on "community power." Specifically, what community is referred to, and how is power defined? As to the first question, our focus is on the City of Houston, the incorporated municipality of 1.6 million people, as opposed to the Houston metropolitan area with its 3 million or so inhabitants. By power, we simply mean the ability to control and direct important events, decisions, or behaviors. Since our concern is primarily with political power, we are more concerned about public decisions (i.e., should taxes be raised) than private sector choices (should Exxon USA move its corporate headquarters to the suburbs) although one remains alert to possible interconnections (Exxon's decision might turn on Houston's tax policy).

II. Demographic Characteristics of Houston

For cities, demography is destiny in a most fundamental sense. The nature of urban decisions in a poor, largely black city like Newark is going to be substantially different from the patterns in a relatively affluent, mostly white community like San Diego. Mayors and private business leaders may come and go in each city, but basic demographic realities define the general patterns of governance in each city. The specific importance of demographics can be demonstrated in many ways. For example, the race of a city's mayor is largely predicted by the racial composition of the city in question. Cities with black majorities (Newark, Atlanta, New Orleans, Detroit) almost always elect black mayors. Cities with white majorities (San Diego, San Francisco) usually elect white mayors. Cities that are closely divided racially (e.g., Chicago) feature mayoral battles fought along racial lines.

If demographics matter, what specific patterns are most important? We suggest five aspects are particularly important for large American cities in general and Houston in particular: (1) the employment base of the community; (2) the population and areal growth patterns; (3) the racial and ethnic diversity of the city; (4) the general class patterns; and (5) the residential patterns of the community.

Houston's Economic and Employment Base

City growth or decline is largely based on whether local jobs are being created or lost. That is especially true for Houston, which attracts few residents because of its cool breezes, mountain vistas, or retirement amenities.

From its founding in 1836 until 1900 Houston was a *mercantile* city connecting an agricultural hinterland with domestic and foreign markets. The city's small port and railroad connections facilitated the collection and exporting of raw materials like cotton and timber and the importation of finished goods for the local area. This modest economic base expanded significantly after the Spindletop oil discovery in 1901 just 90 miles east of Houston. The availability of sizable oil deposits in the area soon led to development of a sizable refining base and, in time, the development of a major petrochemical manufacturing complex. World War II accelerated the development of Houston as a refining/petrochemical center and supported development of one of the nation's largest ports. In the 1970s and early 1980s higher oil prices supported a dramatic expansion of the oil service manufacturing sector as new drilling rings, offshore platforms, and bits were in sudden demand.

The energy dependent nature of Houston's economy was also increased by the concentration of managerial and technical staffs for the oil and gas industry in Houston. During the 1960s, 1970s, and early 1980s tens of thousands of new white-collar jobs were transferred to Houston or created here to serve the energy industry. The local economy also grew due to the emergence of the Texas Medical Center as a world renown research and treatment center and the federal government's siting of the Manned Space Center in the Clear Lake area. Nevertheless, the key engine pulling the Houston economy was the energy industry.

The critical dependence of Houston on the energy sector was demonstrated in 1982–83 and 1986 when falling oil prices led to a severe slump in the oil and gas business. The Houston area lost about 150,000 jobs in 1982–83, or about 10 percent of its employment base. Losses in 1986 were somewhat lower, but local unemployment rates reached 10 percent in the 1980s or about three times the level of the 1970s.

Population and Areal Growth

The first U.S. census in Texas counted 2,396 Houston residents in 1850. By 1880 the city had reached 16,513 inhabitants and had more than doubled again by 1900 when the population was 44,633. The growth of the city and its land area since 1900 is detailed in Table 1. Obviously, Houston has enjoyed tremendous population growth throughout the 20th century. The increasing job opportunities associated with the energy industry supported huge population gains in every census count. In percentage terms growth has varied from 29.4% in 1970–1980 to 111.4% in the 1920–1930 period. By 1980, the city was just short of 1.6 million residents, rating fourth in the nation behind New York, Chicago, and Los Angeles.

Table 1 Houston Population and Land Area Trends: 1900 to 1980

Year	Houston Population	Percent Increase	Land Area (sq. mi.)	Pop. Density (per sq. mi.)
1900	44,633	62.0	9.0	4,959
1910	78,800	76.0	15.8	4,987
1920	138,276	75.5	39.0	3,545
1930	292,352	111.4	72.3	4,044
1940	384,514	31.5	73.1	5,260
1950	596,163	55.0	160.1	3,724
1960	938,219	57.4	349.4	2,685
1970	1,232,802	31.4	445.7	2,766
1980	1,595,138	29.4	557.8	2,860

Source: Houston City Planning and Development Department.

Much of this growth occurred as a result of annexations of adjacent areas. Table 1 shows the population growth of the city being accompanied by additions of new land areas to the cities. Liberal annexation laws permitted Houston to avoid the suburban encirclement common to most American cities, a pattern that stopped population growth for most of the nation's large cities. In fact, as the population density figures show, all of Houston's growth is accounted for by annexations since 1900—the population density of the city per square mile has decline since the early 1900s, but the huge gains in territory have more than compensated for the dispersion. If Houston's size had been fixed in 1940 (about the time many cities ceased annexations), the 1980 population would have been just 375,467, or 9,000 less than it was 40 years earlier.[4]

Racial and Ethnic Diversity

Nationally, most large cities have seen a dramatic increase in their minority populations as whites move out of the older central cities into suburban communities. In Houston, with the city's annexation powers, this tendency has been restrained. The minority populations in the city have been growing (See Table 2) since 1940, but blacks still constituted only 27.4% of Houston residents in 1980, compared to 16.8% Hispanics. The small but growing Asian population numbered 32,944 in 1980 or 2.1%, and American Indians accounted for just 0.2% of area residents. By combining the various minority populations, we can see that the non-Hispanic whites (or Anglos) are still by far the largest ethnic group in Houston, with over 52 percent of the total population.

Table 2 Growth of Black and Hispanic Populations in Houston

Year	City Population	Black Population	Black %	Hispanic Population	Hispanic %
1940	384,514	86,555	22.5	N/A	N/A
1950	596,163	125,660	21.1	31,004	5.2
1960	938,219	215,037	22.9	63,372	6.8
1970	1,232,802	316,551	25.7	149,689	12.1
1980	1,595,138	436,359	27.4	281,321	17.6

Source: Houston Department of Planning and Development, Research Section.

General Class Patterns

In 1900 Houston and Texas were among the poorest cities and states of the nation. Per capita income in the southwestern U.S. was only about 60 percent of the national average. As the city industrialized and gained corporate workers, the local patterns gradually changed. After 1950 per capita incomes in Houston were generally above the national average. By 1979, at the height of the oil boom, median family income in the Houston urban area was 120 percent of the national figure, or fifth among the 41 urban areas with populations over one million.[5]

These income gains reflect the growth of a very large middle and upper middle class population in the Houston area. Much of this new affluence was concentrated in the Anglo population, but local black and Hispanic populations also enjoyed sizable income gains in the 1970s and developed larger middle class bases.

In many urban areas the most affluent neighborhoods are outside the central city. That is generally not true in Houston. The most affluent neighborhoods in the Houston area, including River Oaks, are within the incorporated city. This housing pattern means that the most powerful economic "movers and shakers" are city residents, not suburbanites.

Residential Patterns

Houston, like most cities, is marked by a high degree of residential segregation by race. Over 85 percent of the local black population is concentrated in a broad belt running from northeast to south central Houston. Hispanics are more dispersed, but large concentrations are southeast and northwest of downtown Houston.

East of the predominantly minority areas is a relatively small area of blue collar and lower middle class whites, centered along the Gulf Freeway in southeast Houston. Most of Houston's white population, however, lives in the middle and upper class areas on the west side of the city. Since 1975 there has been a significant movement of minorities into the Anglo west side, especially into older apartment complexes. Homeowner neighborhoods remain overwhelmingly non-minority.

To sum up the most important demographic aspects, Houston has continued to experience significant population and areal growth long after most central cities have stabilized or begun losing population. Minority populations have increased in the city, but Anglos remain by far the largest population group, with Hispanics the most rapidly growing. The oil boom lifted Houston's population to a high level of affluence, some of which has been lost with the slumps of the 1980s. Still, the white population in the city is largely middle and upper middle class and is concentrated in the western half of the incorporated area. Minority residents remain heavily concentrated in a broad swath of neighborhoods running from north to south through the city's center.

III. Political Structures

Political rules are never neutral. They enhance the power and position of some groups and lessen the impact of others. Historically, the operative political rules in Houston enhanced the position of the Anglo middle class voters. From the late 19th century minority voters in Texas and Houston were prevented or discouraged from registering and voting by a variety of mechanism such as the white primary, annual poll tax payments, and a short registration period that closed nearly a year before the city elections were held. Federal court rulings and legislation eventually forced state and local authorities to abandon these rules so that, at least since the mid-1960s, the voter lists have been relatively open to all citizen residents of the city.

The City of Houston, like most municipalities in Texas, elects its officials in non-partisan elections held every two years. This nonpartisan approach effectively excludes political parties from the electoral processes and forces candidates to run individual campaigns. In a city as large as Houston, such campaigns are necessarily expensive for serious candidates, so the cost of elections in Houston is very high. A typical mayoral campaign now costs about $2 million and is escalating rapidly. The short term of office (24 months) forces city officials to devote a large proportion of their term to raising funds and campaigning. The fact that there are no limits on the size of individual contributions or campaign expenditures means that most city elections are funded by wealthy individuals and/or persons doing business with or regulated by city hall.

From 1955 to 1979 all 10 elected city officials—the mayor, controller, and eight council members—were elected at-large by voters throughout the city. This electoral scheme operated to minimize minority political power in a city where Anglos constituted over 50% of the population and 60% of the registered voters. During this period, only one minority candidate, Judson Robinson, Jr., was elected to city office (a councilman position). In 1979, the U.S. Justice Department forced the city to expand its council to 14 members with nine elected from districts and five at-large. Since then the previously white-male dominance of city government has lessened considerably. In 1989 four blacks were serving on council, one Hispanic, and two Anglo women. Experience shows that candidates can compete effectively for district council positions without huge financial resources. However, the more important positions of mayor, controller, and at-large council seats require larger and larger warchests.

The mayoral position is especially important in Houston. The executive post combines the powers usually given a city manager with those of mayor. The result is Houston has the strongest "strong mayor" system of municipal government in the country. The mayor prepares the budget, hires and fires all department heads, oversees the municipal judiciary, and votes on council decisions. This tremendous concentration of power in a single post helps explain why such huge sums of money are required to secure and hold the office.

IV. Houston's Political Culture

The term *political culture* refers to the basic beliefs, values, and attitudes about politics and the political order that characterize a given culture. The foremost student of American political cultural variations, Daniel Elazar, argues that three different cultural streams spread across the United States, dominating different communities and regions. He labeled these the moralistic, individualistic, and traditionistic political cultures.[6]

The moralistic culture emerged in New England and was carried by migrants across the upper Midwest and on to the West Coast. It views the political system as a "commonwealth" and politics as a means of bettering society. The moralistic culture fosters a concern for public issues, is directed toward the welfare of the common man in his search for the good society, and sees government as playing a positive role in this effort. Much of the Progressive movement in the early 20th century was rooted in this stream.

The individualistic culture originated in the Middle Atlantic states and spread into virtually all areas of the nation, becoming the dominant element in the American political tradition. This culture views the democratic process as a "marketplace" where individuals advance their personal interests. Government should be relatively passive, intervening in the private sector only to promote the success of business enterprises. Issue-based politics is of secondary importance.

The traditionalistic culture, dominant in the South Atlantic slave states, was carried westward into the lower Mississippi Valley and the Southwest as the frontier advanced in the 1800s. In this view the main purpose of government is preservation of established values and institutions. Politics centers around factions headed by notable individuals whose family ties are often important determinants of their role and position. Since traditionalistic culture discourages mass participation, political decision making is left to small, self-perpetuating elements who inherit their right to govern through family connections and/or social position.

Elazar's scheme placed Texas and Houston in a subculture that was predominantly traditionalistic and secondarily individualistic. A close inspection of Houston, however, suggests the local culture is now more of a hybrid, drawing on all three of the major American streams.

In a number of ways, Houston fits the individualistic mold, with the political world viewed primarily as an extension of the marketplace and the appropriate role of government seen as assisting private economic needs. Growth and development have long been highly prized goals among Houston's leaders, and the city has stood ready to support programs that would enhance private economic expansion. In other respects, however, Houston has traditionalistic qualities. The structure of local government has encouraged elite control. Mass participation has not been encouraged, and electoral laws were framed to minimize the challenges "outsider" groups like blacks could pose to elite control.

The elite that Houston relied on for political direction, however, has been very different from that described by Elazar in a traditionalistic culture. In Houston, old family ties and social position have counted for virtually nothing. The political elite has been traditionally defined by the economic marketplace, as successful business leaders were expected to exercise great influence in local decision making. Most of these successful businessmen, born in small towns or rural areas, came to Houston as young men to make their fortunes. These self-made entrepreneurs were then drawn into the relatively small circle of established business leaders who operated behind the political scenes with great effectiveness. The apex of this covert elite activity centered on Suite 8F in Houston's Lamar Hotel. Leon Jaworski, a junior member of the group in the 1950s, recalled some 20 years later how it operated: ". . . Jesse Jones, for instance, would meet Gus Wortham, Herman Brown, and maybe one or two others and pretty well determine what the course of events would be in Houston, politically, particularly, and economically to some degree."[7]

The 8F group have passed from the Houston scene. Even the hotel has been demolished. But local business leaders still exercise considerable influence in the political process. But they must compete in a much more complex arena than existed in the 1950s and 1960s.

V. *The Organization of Political Power in Houston*

One of the reasons economic elites were so effective in Houston was a lack of competition from other organized power sources. Through at least the 1950s there were simply no alternative political institutions in Houston that could counter the activities of growth-oriented business leaders.

The Absence of Machine Politics in Houston

In many American cities political machines emerged in the 19th century. These organizations, based on the patronage derived from controlling local government, dominated politics in Boston, New York, Chicago, and San Francisco for decades. Although machines were less common in the smaller southern cities, New Orleans and Memphis did develop strong patronage organizations, but machine politics never took hold in Houston. Several reasons can be cited, starting with the absence of a large European immigrant base that provided the votes for most machine organizations. The reform oriented "good government" forces were usually in the ascendancy in Houston, and any attempt to establish a political organization based on public jobs and the dispersal of public favors drew strong criticism. Local government was relatively small, so the supply of jobs and potential favors was not great. And established business leaders were strongly opposed to any rival force based on the mobilization of the electorate.

Weak Political Parties

Related to the absence of machine politics in Houston was the absence of meaningful partisan politics for most of the 20th century. The Republican party, crushed by the Democrats in the 1890s, virtually disappeared as a force in state and local politics. Under these conditions, one-party politics soon degenerated into "no-party" politics in Houston in that all political players considered themselves to be Democrats, so party identification had little practical meaning. Since voters were not offered choices between Republicans and Democrats, party organization atrophied, and elections centered on individual candidates and the organizations they could create. The absence of competition between parties and party organization activity almost certainly contributed to the low levels of electoral involvement Houston experienced in the period from 1900 to 1950.

The Republican party gradually began rebuilding a base in Harris County after 1952, but almost all its efforts and attention were focused on national and then state political issues. Increasing Republican activity and electoral successes have forced local Democrats to become more organized, but their interests have also been on federal and state contests.

The ineffectiveness of party organizations in city politics is partly a result, of course, of the non-partisan ballot used in city elections. Candidates for city office can run under a "slate" name on the ballot, but not under a political party label. The occasional effort by party activists to mobilize Democrats or Republicans in city elections has not borne fruit. In 1981, for example, Republican Louis Macey sought the support of the GOP organization in his mayoral race. Despite help from many Republican leaders, polls showed Macey ran third among voters who considered themselves to be Republicans.

A Small Organized Labor Movement

In many cities organized labor is a major power, but not in Houston. Although organized labor established a beachhead in Harris County in the 1930s and 1940s, it never gained the level of membership it reached in Northeastern, Midwestern, and West Coast cities. No more than 15% of the local workforce was ever unionized, compared to over 50% in many cities. Union strength was greatest in East Harris County, near the refineries and plants along the Houston Ship Channel, which meant that the most heavily union precincts were outside the city limits of Houston.

The small labor movement has been politically active since World War II, but most of its efforts have been directed at national and state-level contests with little attention given to Houston municipal races.

A Relatively Small and Political Divided City Work Force

As urban governments expanded in the 20th century, huge public bureaucracies emerged in New York, Boston, San Francisco, and other cities. In time, these work forces, often mobilized by municipal unions, became major powers at the polls and in the policy making process. Houston has not followed that pattern. City employment has stayed relatively low, not reaching the 20,000 level until the mid-1980s. With a local workforce of nearly one million, city workers are not a major factor in either the employment base or the electoral process.

The ineffectiveness of city workers in the electoral process partly results from their inability to support common objectives. Police organizations and the local firefighters union are often at odds, and neither works closely with other municipal employees. Such fragmented efforts, coupled with a lack of numbers, condemn city workers to a secondary role in shaping policy decisions.

Houston Blacks: A Late Start and Organizational Fragmentation

Although state and local electoral rules minimized the political potential of Houston's huge black population until the 1950s, blacks have made impressive gains in the political arena since then and have become a major force in city elections. Black voter registration is relatively high in Houston (close to 30% of the registered voters were black in 1989); blacks have a history of voting fairly heavily in city elections; and blacks usually unite behind favored candidates in city elections which increases their effectiveness. Consequently, no mayor has been elected in Houston without strong black support since 1971.

But the electoral power of blacks has still left them with only moderate power over city politics. Blacks can usually decide which of two white candidates should win the mayor's position, but they are not in a position to elect a black to the top office themselves or even to support the election of a white or Hispanic clearly identified with the political priorities of the black community.

Much of the political difficulty blacks face stems from the arithmetic; three of every ten city voters are black, seven are not. And the bottom line in Houston is that it is very difficult to get Anglo or Hispanic voters to support a black for the powerful mayor position. When Curtis Graves, a black state representative, challenged Louie Welch in the 1969 mayoral contest, Graves got over 90% of the black vote, about 20% of the Hispanic vote, and less than 10% of the Anglo vote. No serious black challenger has run for mayor since Graves failed (he got about 33% of the total vote cast).

Part of the political problems blacks face can be traced to the absence of effective political organizations in the black community. The old-line civil rights groups like the NAACP have lost members and momentum now that the battles against legal discrimination are largely over. And political groups that were effective in the 1960s, especially the Harris County Council of Organizations, have little impact in the 1980s. In an election the black vote usually firms up behind particular candidates, but between elections there are few organizational resources pushing black issues.

Hispanics: Potential But Little Realization

Hispanics, as noted in Table 2, are the most rapidly growing segment of Houston's population, yet their political influence lags far behind their population share. A major problem is low levels of political participation. Hispanics constitute 20% of Houston's population in 1989, but less than 10% of the registered voters. In addition, of those registered, the Hispanic turnout is typically far below that of Anglos or blacks. Hispanic voters also show little inclination to vote together, in contrast to the black electorate.

No effective community-wide organizations exist capable of mobilizing the Hispanic voters in city elections or on pressing community issues at other times. Councilman Ben Reyes, who represents the sole district with a Hispanic majority, is the most prominent Mexican-American leader in Houston, but Reyes is a controversial figure within the community. The deep division between pro-Reyes and anti-Reyes factions seems to assure the Hispanic vote will remain divided and largely impotent, as it was in the 1985 mayoral election between incumbent Kathy Whitmire (a bitter foe of Reyes) and former mayor Louie Welch.

Hispanics and blacks have generally not been able to form effective coalitions in city politics that would enhance their clout. Hispanic voters show little inclination to support black candidates, and black voters have been only moderately supportive of Hispanics seeking citywide office.

In time, the simple numerical presence of Houston's Hispanic community will undoubtedly result in growing political power, but that day is not at hand.

The Gay Political Coalition

The importance of political organization and targeted participation is emphasized by the success of the Gay Political Coalition (GPC) in Houston politics. A visible homosexual community emerged in Houston in the 1960s, centered in the Montrose-Westheimer area southwest of downtown. The GPC was formed in the 1970s, largely in response to police harassment. Over the last 10 years the GPC has emerged as a major player in city politics. In 1979 the GPC was instrumental in defeating long-time council member Frank Mann, who had been a vocal critic of "queers and oddwads" in his last years in office. Two years later the GPC strongly supported Kathy Whitmire's initial and successful campaign for mayor.

The organized gay community is small, and a major force in only 10 or 12 of the 400 voting precincts in the city, and probably influence no more than 20,000 to 25,000 of the city's 700,000 registered voters. Their political effectiveness comes from a demonstrated ability to raise money for candidates, generate significant volunteer support, and deliver a small but occasional decisive vote on election day. Most of Houston elections end up with the 97% or so of the non-gay vote closely divided, which gives the GPC an opportunity to deliver the pivotal margin to winners.

The limitations of GPC influence were starkly demonstrated in a 1985 city referendum on two ordinances including homosexuals in anti-discrimination legislation. Passed with the support of Mayor Whitmire and a majority of council members who had enjoyed GPC electoral support, a public petition drive forced a vote on both issues in January 1985. Despite vigorous efforts by GPC and their council allies, the propositions were defeated by an enormous margin—82% to 18%—in an election marked by extremely heavy turnout. Since the 1985 referendum, the GPC has adopted a much lower profile in city politics. Mayor Whitmire did not openly seek the group's endorsement in her 1985 race against Louie Welch, although she received overwhelming support from gay voters in the contest. The furor over Aids and its uncertain political fallout has also left the GPC unsure of future strategies.

Evangelical Christians

Houston is generally not considered a "Bible Belt" city, and religious leaders have not been active in most local elections. The uproar over council approval of the GPC supported ordinances changed that pattern. Ministers from a wide range of Christian congregations supported the petition drive requiring an election and worked to get the vote out when balloting occurred. Having defeated "the forces of darkness," most of the city's religious leaders withdrew from the fray and took no position in the regular city elections in November 1985. A group of fundamentalist and evangelical Christians, however, continued their efforts to cleanse the city of sin, or at least of sinful leaders. They organized a "Campaign Houston" to defeat Mayor Whitmire and the council majority that had supported the anti-discrimination ordinances. This new group backed Louie Welch against Whitmire and recruited five candidates to run on a slate against incumbent council members. The Campaign Houston effort had modest success. Two black councilmen were forced into run-offs for at-large seats, but won the final election by substantial margins. And Mayor Whitmire, helped by her opponent's inept campaign, clobbered Welch by a 59% to 41% margin.

The evangelical leaders have indicated they will remain active in future campaigns, but their effectiveness in city elections is much in question.

Business Organizations

As earlier noted, business leaders, especially those involved in growth and development (bankers, contractors, home builders, engineers) wield great influence in Houston. Much of this activity has simply been undertaken by individuals or specific firms, particularly in support of candidates for local office. Many firms like Tenneco and Texas Eastern have also developed political action committees, or PACs, to channel funds from their managerial employees into the political process. Aside from these individual and company efforts, the major general business group in Houston is the Chamber of Commerce.

The Houston Chamber of Commerce, organized in 1912, is far more than the booster group found in most cities. With a professional staff of over 150, an annual budget of more than three million dollars, and access to the expertise of many members, the chamber has great influence in local governance. That influence rests on several sources.

(1) The chamber's directors are typically high-ranking executive officers from the biggest local firms. Its membership brings together local bankers, lawyers, real estate, manufacturing, and marketing elites. While their business interests obviously differ, the chamber's leaders, strongly committed to continued economic growth, support public policies consistent with that objective.

(2) The chamber's leaders have exceptional access to decision-makers in county, city, and other local government. In the case of the City of Houston, this access has been facilitated by a "revolving door" policy that allows upper level business leaders to move in and out of the public sector.

(3) From 1974 to 1985 Louie Welch was the council president. Drawing on his 20 years in elective city office, Welch was a skillful and resourceful political insider who made effective use of his knowledge of local business and politics.

(4) During the Welch years, the chamber mobilized its resources to exclude potential challengers. Welch and other chamber leaders undermined potential financial support for the Houston Metropolitan Organization—a grassroots activist organization that has tried to mobilize residents of inner-city neighborhoods.[8] And in 1978, Welch personally scuttled "Houston United," an effort to bring business leaders together with local ethnic, religious, and civic leaders.

Since Welch left the chamber to run for mayor in 1985, the organization has taken the lead in supporting public policies to revitalize the Houston economy, the number one political problem in the city for most people. The Houston Economic Development commission (HEDC), a multimillion dollar group funded with both public and private support—largely a chamber creation—continues to have close ties with the older group.

VI. Current Leadership Patterns in Houston

Reexamining the Elitist v. Pluralist Argument

At the beginning of this article we discussed the dispute between those who argue big cities are dominated by a few powerful leaders, rooted in the private economic sector, and those who contend that political leadership in cities is actually quite fragmented and that elected public officials—not private economic elites—decide most key urban policy questions. Who seems to have the better case in Houston? Is the Bayou City basically elitist or pluralist when it comes to patterns of governance?

Our analysis suggests no simple answer is possible. Historically, Houston displayed strong elitist tendencies. The 8F crowd fit closely the profile of powerful, behind-the-scenes players Hunter found in Atlanta 30 years ago. And a close look at more recent decisions show continuing elitist tendencies. In the 1970s, for example, the City of Houston came under great pressure from the federal Environmental Protection Agency (EPA) to clean up its sewer treatment facilities. The EPA threatened to shut down all new construction in the city until the problems were solved, a very grave threat in a city experiencing one of the greatest building booms in the history of American cities. How was this major public policy problem addressed? The elected city leaders allowed Public Works Director E. B. Cape to negotiate quietly a deal with the EPA whereby the city agreed to a moratorium on new construction in most residential areas of the city in return for continued development in the central business district where projects worth hundreds of millions of dollars were on the drawing boards. This major public policy decision was made with virtually no debate or discussion; indeed it seems likely few voters ever realized such a deal was struck.

But other cases can be cited where the desires of "insiders" were overridden by broad community pressures. In the early 1970s the Houston Chamber of Commerce and other local business leaders were instrumental in getting the Texas Legislature to approve a bill allowing organization of the Houston Area Rapid Transit Authority (HARTA). Growth and development oriented elites strongly backed HARTA, fearing that traffic congestion would eventually strangle Houston unless a major public transit program was initiated. But the voters of the area, who were required to approve a funding mechanism for HARTA, decisively rejected the proposal supported by the downtown business community. Houston did not establish a public transit authority until 1979, when METRO was created with the support of a general public now much more concerned about mobility problems.

Another important case of elites being reversed occurred in 1983 when METRO, with the strong backing of the chamber and downtown business leaders, tried to secure public approval to build a "heavy rail" transit system. Despite an expensive, slick campaign promoting METRO's plan, a hastily organized coalition of opposition groups, with little money, convinced 60% of the voters in a special election to reject the rail proposal.

The limits of business elite power in Houston are evident in other areas. If one had to designate one business leader in Houston as most influential, the choice would likely be Walter Mischer, owner of numerous local businesses. Mischer is a quiet, low-profile individual who enjoys wide respect in the business community. His forte is fund-raising. Some of the events he has organized have generated up to three million dollars for presidential or gubernatorial candidates. Mischer has also been a consistent player in city politics and elections, and has raised substantial sums for these battles. Nevertheless, in recent years he has mostly ended up on the *losing* side. Even in defeat, Mischer is a force to be reckoned with in city politics, but his inability to elect or defeat mayors is testimony to the limits of his power.

The reality is that Houston has become more pluralistic over time. One reason is simply that the city has grown. There are 1.6 million people here in 1989, not 600,000 as was the case in 1950. And the population has become more diverse. The black population is larger, the Hispanics are increasing, and sizable number of Yankees have moved in. In such a diverse modern city it is not possible for an 8F crowd to wield the influence it had 30 years ago. Power now must be shared with more and more participants. This diversity means political power in the city is largely *coalitional* in nature, because no single ethnic, ideological, or economic group dominates the city. Successful leaders have to pull together diverse coalitions to back their policies. The career of Mayor Kathy Whitmire illustrates this political necessity.

When Kathy Whitmire first ran for mayor in 1981, her political base was the younger, professional people in Houston—the Yuppies. In a multicandidate field she received about 30% of the total vote in the November 1981 general election—enough to lead, but far short of the majority required for victory. Whitmire won the runoff against Sheriff Jack Heard by expanding her coalition to include the great majority of black voters (most of whom had backed neither Heard or Whitmire in the first round) and some of the downtown business community had that supported incumbent Mayor Jim McConn in the first round.

Once elected, Whitmire solidified her position in the black community by her surprise appointment of Lee Brown, a professional black police administrator from Atlanta, as the new police chief. The Brown appointment was doubly helpful because he turned out to be popular with most original elements of the mayor's coalition (Yuppies, gays, professionals) as well as her new friends in the downtown business community. Whitmire's political base was threatened when her support for the "gay rights" ordinance split away her business supporters who backed the repeal effort. But despite suffering a crushing defeat on the referendum in January 1985, Whitmire was able to pull most of her electoral coalition together by the following November when she defeated former mayor Welch by 59% to 41%.

Whitmire's political success largely reflects her ability to hold a diverse coalition together rather than any great personal popularity with city voters. Unlike Mayor Henry Cisneros of San Antonio, whose tremendous personal popularity with local voters made him virtually unbeatable, Whitmire wins because once the choice is narrowed to two contenders, more voters invariably prefer her to the alternative. Her position near the middle of the city's political spectrum facilitates this coalitional strategy. Whitmire is close to the black community, but not too close. She works with most elements of the downtown business community, but does not take directions from that quarter. And while many liberals, feminists, and gays feel she is far too cautious on their issues, these voters simply refuse to accept more socially conservative candidates like Heard or Welch. The Achilles heel of the Mayor's coalition is the black community, whose votes normally account for about 50% of Whitmire's total. Any appreciable defection of black voters (say on the order of 25–30%) would make Mayor Whitmire extremely vulnerable to a white opponent who would likely inherit the substantial anti-Whitmire vote from older, more conservative Anglos.

VII. Future Political Leadership

Prophecy, someone once said, makes fools of us all. Predicting the future of a complex entity like Houston is likely to demonstrate the truth of that saying. Big cities are simply subject to far too many unpredictable forces and influences to allow specific judgments about the course of coming events. Will the local economy bounce back in the 1990s? Will the new immigration law slow down or speed up immigration from Mexico and Central America? Will Congress authorize a manned space station to be directed from the Johnson Center in Clear Lake? Dozens of such questions cannot presently be answered, but taken together they will have tremendous impact on what happens in Houston in the next decades.

Ruling out specific predictions does not, however, prevent us from identifying some general patterns that are likely to continue or emerge in Houston.

(1) Political power is likely to become more fragmented, more pluralistic. The diversity of the local population has been accelerating since the 1960s and there seems little reason to expect a reversal. By 1990 or so Anglos will no longer constitute a majority in the city (although they will remain the largest single ethnic group and will have a majority of the voting population).

(2) Political power, reflecting the realities of the voting population, will remain largely in Anglo hands. a black mayor could be elected before the year 2000 in Houston, but the odds are against this happening. The basic problem is a black can only win with significant support from whites (25–30%), and there are few black leaders on the scene that can draw such support. Black leaders like Barbara Jordan, who developed a strong base among Anglo and Hispanic voters are the exception, not the rule, in urban politics. And votes

aside, the economic establishment in Houston remains overwhelmingly dominated by male Anglos. Short of a Maoist revolution, that pattern will change very slowly over the years.

(3) In the tug-of-war between elected public leaders and private economic elites, the elected officials will retain the advantage as Whitmire has been able to do in the 1980s. A major reason for this advantage is superior access to the mass public via local media. Elected officials are known, newsworthy figures who can get their case across much easier than much less known business leaders. Behind the scenes, access at city hall is still important, but power in a modern city requires the ability to mobilize support from mass publics; elected leaders are simply in a much better position to do that.

(4) Finally, while occasional efforts will be made to restructure city government, the odds are against any major reforms. The reason is simple. Substantive reform would almost certainly reduce the tremendous powers now held by the mayor, and the very power of that official makes it unlikely that charter changes could be pushed through over the objections of the city's chief executive. Political leaders do not often voluntarily surrender formal powers, and mayors of Houston show little inclination to reverse that pattern.

Notes

1. Harold D. Lasswell and D. Lerner, *The Comparative Study of Elites* (Stanford: Stanford University Press, 1952), p. 7.
2. See Floyd Hunter, *Community Power Structure* (Chapel Hill: University of North Carolina Press, 1953); Thomas R. Dye, *Who's Running America: The Conservative Years,* 4th ed., (Englewood Cliffs: Prentice Hall, 1986).
3. See Robert A. Dahl, "Critique of the Ruling Elite Model," *American Political Science Review,* 52 (June 1958).
4. These data are from "Implementing Equality: The Voting Rights Act and Its Impact on Municipal Government," paper presented at Southwestern Political Science Association meeting, 1987, by Margaret K. Purser and Mary P. Beeman.
5. See *1980 Census of Population and Housing: Provisional Estimates of Social, Economic and Housing Characteristics: States and Selected SMSAs* (Washington: Government Printing Office, 1982), Table P-4.
6. Daniel J. Elazar, *American Federalism: a View From the States* (New York: Crowell, 1972), pp. 93–126.
7. Craig Smyser, "Houston's Power," *The Houston Chronicle,* June 27, 1977.
8. See "Upper Class Mobilization of Bias in Houston," a paper presented at the Southwestern Social Science Association meeting, 1978, by Chandler Davidson and Stephen J. Reilly.

19 The Grand Jury: Texas as a Case Study
ROBERT A. CARP

I. Introduction

The Fifth Amendment to the United States Constitution begins "No person shall be held to answer for a capital or otherwise infamous crime, unless on a presentment or indictment of a Grand jury. . . ." This, the requirement that a person be first indicted by a grand jury before he can be brought to trial for a serious crime, is a fundamental right of American citizens in federal courts. That is, since the national Bill of Rights protects only citizens of the United States in this regard, the Fifth Amendment does not protect us in state courts unless the state constitution also protects the right to a grand jury proceeding.

In 1787 almost all state constitutions protected this right, but today only twenty states have some form of grand jury system. Texas is one of these states. Section 10 of the Bill of Rights at the beginning of the Texas Constitution says in part, ". . . and no person shall be held to answer for a criminal offense, unless on an indictment of a grand jury. . . ." Texans are thus protected by the right whether in state court or in federal court.

Despite the importance of grand juries for Texans, they, like most Americans, know very little about the operation of grand juries. Unlike the trial proceeding itself, no movies or television programs are built around grand jury proceedings. In all the years he was on television, only twice did Perry Mason deal with a grand jury, and neither time was it made clear that he was not in front of a trial jury. In other words, in the presentation of legal proceedings in our media and literature the story invariably moves from the arrest to the trial, and the operation of the grand jury is taken for granted.

Also, while hard figures are not available, it is safe to say that the average Texan never serves on a grand jury and does not know anyone who has. In some states as many as a fourth of the population will do jury duty during their lifetime, yet it is doubtful that as many as one half of one percent of the adult population in that same state will ever serve on a grand jury.

The situation is made worse by the rules under which the grand jury usually operates. Even in those places where notetaking by grand jurors is permitted, the proceedings move too quickly and are too complicated for jurors to provide systematic information after the proceedings are over. And then the standard practice is for grand jurors to be bound by oath not to discuss cases outside of the actual proceedings. The result is that not even political scientists and legal experts know very much about how grand juries operate. There is almost no literature on the subject. This chapter, then, in providing hard and systematic information on the operation of grand juries in Houston is almost unique in the light it sheds on one of our important political institutions.

Data for this study derive from three principal sources. First, as a participant-observer on the 177th District Court Grand Jury, which met in Houston, Texas between November, 1971, and February, 1972, the author had the opportunity to perform a case-by-case content analysis of the 918 cases considered by that grand jury. This analysis includes a complete record of all votes taken, the amount of time spent deliberating on the various cases, and extensive notes on the discussions among the grand jurors and between members of the grand jury and the district attorneys. Because of the oath of grand jury secrecy to which the author is bound, the information provided must deal with the cases in the aggregate, not individually, and great care has been taken not to divulge specific information about sensitive or confidential subject matter.

Second, in-depth interviews were conducted with former members of Harris County grand juries. The interviewees were not selected at random but were selected from a group of recent grand jury members and jury foremen. Twenty-three such persons in all were contacted (including six jury foremen), and all of them agreed to be interviewed. The primary purpose of these interviews was to compare the grand jury experiences of this author with those of others to determine if the performance of the 177th Grand Jury, from which the hard data were drawn, was typical. No attempt was made to quantify the results of the in-depth interviews; thus the information they provide is anecdotal although frequently interesting and insightful.

Third, the study contains data from a questionnaire mailed to all persons who served on Harris County grand juries between 1969 and 1972. Of the 271 questionnaires mailed to the grand jurors, 156 (58 percent) were returned and included in the analysis. The questionnaire solicited information about the socioeconomic characteristics of the grand jurors and about the nature of their grand jury deliberations and experiences. The results are used throughout the article to supplement the other sources of research data and to provide a comparison and contrast between the data of the 177th Grand Jury and their other grand juries that immediately preceded and followed it.

Finally, a word should be said about Harris County itself and about the degree to which one may generalize the conclusions of this case study for application to grand juries in general. Harris County, with its population of approximately 1.9 million, is one of the largest, most cosmopolitan urban centers in the United States. Because it is located in a state that is both "southern" and "western" and has a sizable minority-group population with a large influx of citizens from the east and the midwest, it seems reasonable to suggest that Harris County is fairly representative of modern American society. In addition, the Texas laws that outline the functions, duties, and powers of the grand jury, while unique in some ways, are not too dissimilar from those that govern grand juries in other states. For these reasons the author believes that the conclusions of this study may well apply to grand juries in general throughout the United States.

II. The Selection and Socialization of the Grand Jury

A. Selection and Composition of the Grand Jury

The process of selecting grand jurors in Texas is as intricate as it is arbitrary. Unlike many of its sister states that nondiscriminately select the names of grand jurors from a lottery wheel containing the names of hundreds of potential jurors, Texas grants jury commissioners almost unlimited discretion to compile a small list of names from which the grand jury is impaneled. The local district judges select not less than three nor more than five qualified persons from different parts of the county to serve as jury commissioners. After taking a comprehensive oath and receiving a set of instructions from the district judges, the commissioners secure from the district clerk the last tax assessment roll of the county and a list of those who are either exempt or disqualified from service on the grand jury (for example, persons previously convicted of a felony). With this information, the commissioners are free to select sixteen prospective grand jurors who meet broadly defined statutory standards. The names of those selected are written down in numerical sequence, placed in a sealed envelope, and delivered to the district judge in open court. When the list is opened, the judge conducts an inquiry as to their qualifications, and the first twelve who are qualified are impaneled as the grand jury for a term of three months.

Very little is known about the actual criteria by which jury commissioners select prospective grand jurors. Interviews with former grand jury members suggest that most jurors were selected either because of their personal friendship with the commissioners or because they were associates of the commissioners' friends. The following two statements by former grand jurors appear to be representative of the process by which most jurors are selected. One grand juror recounted:

> One of Judge [X]'s jury commissioners goes to our church, and I am good friends with his wife, I mentioned one or two times that I'd kind of like to serve on the grand jury, and I guess she mentioned this fact to her husband because one day he called me and asked if I would like to serve. I talked it over with my husband and then called him right back and said that I'd be happy to be on the jury.

Another grand juror explained:

> I teach in the School of Social Work at the University. One day our department chairman came into my office and said that he had had a call from Dean [X] of the Law School who is one of Judge [Y]'s jury commissioners. The Dean had asked our department chairman if there was anyone in the department who would like to serve on the grand jury, and for some reason or other the chairman approached me about this. I told the chairman that if he didn't mind my missing a few of my classes now and then, I would be happy to serve. The chairman said he thought it would be good experience for me, and he then called back the Dean and had me put on the list.

Historically, most jurists have argued and the courts have officially determined that grand juries, like trial juries, should be representative of the population of the community as a whole. Although there is still considerable uncertainty about how this goal is to be achieved, the United States Court of

Appeals for the Fifth Circuit has determined that the Constitution requires that members of Texas grand juries represent a fair cross section of the community. In light of this judicial determination it is fair then to ask: How representative are Texas grand juries of the county populations from which they are selected? This is largely an empirical question, and for a partial answer we may compare the results of the questionnaire sent to former grand jurors in Harris County with the 1970 census figures for this same county.

Thus, the typical Harris County grand juror is an Anglo-Saxon male college graduate about fifty-one years of age who is quite likely to earn about $25,000 per year while working either as a business executive or as a professional. How does this profile compare with what the 1970 census indicates about the "typical" citizen of the county? a brief summary of the data reveals the following information about the residents of Harris County: 49 percent are male and 51 percent are female; the median adult age is thirty-nine; 69 percent are Anglo-Saxon, 20 percent are black, and 11 percent are Mexican-American; the median education is twelve years (a high school diploma); and the median family income is $10,348. These figures clearly demonstrate that even by rudimentary standards Harris County grand juries do not meet the judicial criterion of a fair cross section of the community's human resources. Grossly underrepresented are women, young people, Blacks, Mexican-Americans, the poor, and those with less extensive educational backgrounds.

What does this information suggest about the relationship between grand jury composition and the substantive decisions of the grand jury? A typical civil libertarian might ask how are the young people, the minority groups, the poor, and the oppressed to be accorded due process of law when they are not proportionally represented among those who administer the laws. Such a critic would do well, however, to consider what numerous investigations reveal about the attitudes of high-status persons toward dissident and minority factions in American society. Studies reveal that higher-status people (those with at least a college degree and who are in the professions or who are business executives) are significantly more likely to be solicitous toward the rights of ethnic minorities and social dissidents than are those who come from the lower end of the social and economic spectrum.

On a more specific level, the interview data suggest strongly that the better educated grand jurors who work in an executive or professional capacity are more likely to possess the social efficacy to confront the district attorneys when they believe the attorneys have intentionally confused or misled them. It is often the social and economic elite who possess the intellectual capacity and sensitivity to probe into the complexities of the judicial labyrinth and to insist on due process and fair play. Many grand jurors readily stated that they were often confused and intimidated by the technical language and the complexities of the judicial process and that they looked to the more mature members of

Table 1 Socioeconomic Characteristics of Harris County Grand Jurors Compared with 1970 Census Figures (N = 156 for the Questionnaire Sample)

	Percentage of Grand Juries	Percentage of County
Sex		
Male	78	49
Female	22	51
Age		
21–35	10	23
36–50	43	18
51–65	37	8
Over 65	10	5
Median juror age, 51	Median adult age, 39	
Income		
Under $5,000	1	16
$5,000–$10,000	3	31
$10,000–$15,000	25	29
$15,000–$20,000	16	9
Over $20,000	55	15
Median juror income, $25,000	Median family income in county, $10,348	
Race		
Anglo	82	69
Black	15	20
Mexican-American	3	11
Education		
Less than high school	0	24
Some high school	3	23
High school degree	8	25
Some college	34	13
College degree	32	Comparable data not available
Graduate degree	23	
Median juror education, 16 years	Median county resident education, 12 years	
Employment		
Business executive	35	
Proprietor	7	
Professional	20	Comparable data not available
Employed worker	13	
Retired	13	
Housewife	11	
Other	1	

the grand jury to represent them in their confrontations with the district attorney. Such older leaders are almost invariably the better educated professionals and executives on the grand jury. The following quotation by a very young member of a former Harris County grand jury provides a typical and insightful illustration:

> I remember one day we were all pretty depressed about what was going on with a particular case. We were all saying to each other [when the assistant district attorney had left the grand jury room], "We're just pawns of the district attorney with this case. One minute he tells us one thing about what our powers are with this case and the next minute he tells us something else about what we can do." I felt like they all did, too, but I was pretty young, and the D.A. seemed pretty cool and experienced, and I knew I didn't want to tangle with him. Finally, when he [the assistant district attorney] came back in, old Mr. [X] stood up and really let him have it. Mr. [X] ran a big real estate firm and was a real conservative when it came to welfare and government spending and things like that, but he was pretty much of a liberal when it came to civil liberties. Well, Mr. [X] said to the D.A., "Look, I just don't have to take this. If one of my employees gave me all this doubletalk, I'd fire him on the spot. Now I want you to level with us on this thing, and I want you to put it in writing so we can show it to Carol Vance [the Harris County District Attorney] in case you're not telling us the truth." From then on the D.A. treated us with kid gloves. None of us would have dared to talk to the D.A. like that, but Mr. [X] was a big shot and I guess he is used to pushing until he gets a straight answer from people.

Thus one consequence of the grand jury selection process may be that it recruits those individuals in society who are not only most supportive of civil liberties but also most likely to possess the intelligence, personal self-confidence, and social efficacy to translate their instincts for fair play into substantive reality.

B. Training and Socialization of the Grand Jury

The grand jury begins to hear cases the very day it is impaneled. How well prepared is the average grand juror to perform his important and responsible function of determining whether there is probable cause for a citizen to be formally indicted for a felony and to be put on trial? In Harris County all new grand jurors are provided with a training program that entails three different aspects: a voluntary one-day training seminar conducted primarily by police and sheriff's department officials; two booklets pertaining to grand jury procedures and instructions, one composed by the District Attorney and the other prepared by the Harris County Grand Jury Association; and, finally, an in-depth, give-and-take discussion between the grand jury and an experienced member of the District Attorney's staff.

How adequately does this training program prepare the grand jurors for their work? First, the series of lectures by law enforcement officials seems to be of limited utility for the novice grand juror. Not only are these lectures given several days after the formal work of the grand jury has begun, but most grand jurors tend to agree with an evaluation that was included in a recent grand jury report: "The day-long training session was interesting, but for the most part the lectures were irrelevant to the primary functions of a Grand Jury, and many of us noted some rather unsubtle political overtones in the formal presentations." Interviews with more than a score of former grand jurors and a content analysis of grand jury reports reveal that the primary function of the law enforcement lectures is to explain and to "plug" the work of the respective departments rather than to provide the grand juror with substantive insights into what his grand jury duties entail.

The pamphlets prepared separately by the county grand jury association and by the District Attorney are well written and provide a good summary of the formal duties and functions of the grand jury. Since these booklets are not provided until the first day of jury service, however, they cannot be read until after the grand jury has put in one full day of work, which usually consists of hearing at least fifty cases. More importantly, however, interviews with former grand jurors indicate that very few jurors read and study these booklets. This comment by one former grand juror is typical:

> Yes, I took the books home with me that first night and I glanced through them, but I can't say I really read them. I figured that we'd meet our problems as we came to them, and that's about what happened. If we had a question during our deliberations, one of us would usually say, "Let's see if the booklet says anything about this." That's how we used the books when I was on the jury. I don't think any of us actually read them as such.

The give-and-take discussion between the grand jury and an assistant district attorney is usually scheduled for the first working session, and it is the final aspect of the grand juror's formal on-the-job training. When such a discussion does indeed occur, it appears to be of some use in acquainting grand jurors with their new duties. This comment by a recent member of a grand jury, however, was typical:

> Yes, we were supposed to meet with one of the D.A.'s at the end of the first day, and he was supposed to explain to us what the hell was going on. But can you believe this? They [the assistant district attorneys] presented us with so many cases on our first day, it got to be five o'clock and we didn't have time for anyone to explain to us what we were supposed to be doing. We heard dozens of cases that first day, and when I got home that night I was just sick. I told my wife, "I sure would hate to be one of those guys who had his case brought before us today."

How long does it take for the average grand juror to understand the duties, powers, and functions of a grand jury? The results of the questionnaire survey reveal that the typical grand juror does not claim to fully understand his basic purpose and function until well into the third full working session of the grand jury.

III. Grand Jury Deliberations

This part of the chapter will examine the amount of time the grand jury spends deliberating on each case, the degree of evidence required for an indictment, the role of the grand jury foreman in the deliberation process, and the rate and nature of internal dissension among grand jurors.

A. Time Allotted Per Case and Evidence Required for "Probable Cause"

How much time does the average grand jury spend with each case to determine whether there is enough evidence to place a man on trial for a felony offense? Although the data suggest considerable variation in the amount of time spent deliberating on the various categories of cases, the evidence reveals that the typical grand jury spends only five minutes per case. (In 1971 twelve Harris County grand juries spent an estimated 1344 hours deliberating on 15,930 cases.) This average time of five minutes includes the assistant district attorney's summary of the case and his recommendation as to how the case should be decided (about sixty seconds per case), the hearing of testimony, and the actual secret deliberations by the grand jury. By anyone's standards, justice is indeed swift.

Well over half of the grand jurors claim that their grand jury brought true bills only when every item of evidence sufficient to convict could be demonstrated to the grand jury. The question arises how is this possible when only five minutes is allotted to each case. Several explanations are possible: that the memories of the grand jurors are poor; that the questionnaire respondents intentionally misrepresented their experience so as not to make their grand jury "look bad" in the eyes of the researcher; or that even after three months of grand jury service most grand jurors are ignorant of basic rules of evidence and of the meaning of "probable cause." It is the conclusion of this researcher, based on his own experience and the contents of the in-depth interviews, that the third explanation is the correct one. Given the inadequate training and preparation of grand jurors for their judicial service and the continued reluctance of the assistant district attorneys to provide any more information than is absolutely necessary for the disposition of each case, it is not surprising that nearly two-thirds of the grand jurors felt that after five minutes they were adequately informed to decide the fate of the accused.

Does the grand jury become more efficient as its term progresses; that is, is it able to deal with a larger number of cases per hour toward the end of its term than at the beinning? Eighty-four percent of the questionnaire respondents indicated that this was their impression, and such was the case with the 177th Grand Jury. The 177th Grand Jury spent an average of 7.4 minutes per case during its first six working sessions while spending only 5.9 minutes per case during the final six working days.

Other questions concerning the deliberation process are how many and what types of cases are actually discussed by the grand jury and how many are simply voted on without any discussion after the district attorney's sixty second summary of the facts of the case. For the 177th Grand Jury 80 percent of the cases were voted on with no discussion whatsoever.[1] This percentage is probably even greater for most other Harris County grand juries, since the 177th Grand Jury spent a mean time of seven minutes per case, whereas the average figure for the other grand juries between 1969 and 1971 was five minutes.

The percentage of cases discussed by the grand jury tends to decrease as the term progresses. For instance, during its first nine sessions (November 3 through December 6) the 177th Grand Jury discussed 27 percent of its cases. During its last nine sessions (January a through January 31), however, it discussed only 12 percent of its cases. A former grand jury foreman perhaps gave the best explanation for the decreasing percentage of cases discussed:

> As time went on fewer and fewer of the cases were actually discussed. Toward the end of the term someone would say he wanted to discuss a particular case, and then someone else would pop up and say, "What's the point of discussing this case? We had a case just like it a couple weeks ago. You know where I stand on cases like this, and I know where you stand. Why discuss this all over again? Let's just vote on it and get on to the next case." And more often than not, nothing more would be said. We would just vote without discussing the case.

The phenomenon of discussing fewer cases as the term progresses probably explains the increasing grand jury "efficiency."

Evidence from this study also suggests that grand juries do discriminate in the amount of time allotted to various types of cases. For instance, while a grand jury might spend several hours investigating and discussing a prominent murder or rape case, it might spend less than a minute on a robbery or drunken driving case. The following table, summarizes the pattern of discussion for the 177th Grand Jury.

Table 2 Percentage and Types of Cases Discussed by the 177th Grand Jury

Type of Case	Number of Cases	Percentage of Total Cases	Number of Cases Discussed	Percentage of Cases Discussed
Victimless Sex Crimes	15	2	10	67
Crimes of Passion	66	8	24	36
Drug Crimes	47	5	16	34
Theft	288	33	80	28
Burglary	136	16	26	19
Robbery	93	11	8	9
Forgery and Embezzlement	110	13	7	6
Driving While Intoxicated	110	13	6	5

There are fifty-three miscellaneous cases not included in any of these types.

Table 2 reveals that the 177th Grand Jury discussed two-thirds of all victimless sex crimes (which are comprised mostly of prostitution cases—rape is listed as a crime of passion) but discussed only one out of twenty driving-while-intoxicated cases.

B. The Role of the Grand Jury Foreman

According to the grand-jury handbook prepared by the Harris County District Attorney,

> The principal duties of the foreman are to preside over all sessions and to conduct its business in an orderly manner. . . . Generally, the foreman is the spokesman and liaison member of the grand jury to the press, the Court, or any other agency. Any mail addressed to the grand jury will be given unopened to the foreman. . . . The foreman should designate one of the grand jurors to as secretary to the jury.

Aside from these brief guidelines there are no instructions about how the foreman should conduct himself on a day-to-day basis, nor is the foreman given any advance training or advice on the role he might play in the grand-jury deliberations. Presumably, the precise role of the foreman is something he must develop with his fellow grand jurors as the working sessions get under way.

The foreman is designated by the judge who impanels the jury; the grand jurors have no part in the foreman's selection. This system enables the grand jury to begin its work immediately without having to "waste" any of its time or energy selecting from among its ranks the person whom they most respect and believe to be an effective leader and spokesman. It also means, of course, that the prestige and effectiveness of the foreman may be diminished, first, because the judge has very little idea beforehand who will make the most effective foreman for the particular grand jury, and second, because the designated foreman might not be the choice of the jury members themselves. The interviewees almost unanimously asserted resentment because they could not select their own foreman. This statement by one former grand juror was typical:

> We all thought that we got to pick our own foreman. I don't know if I got that idea from the movies or Perry Mason or what, but some of us kind of resented the judge telling us who our leader would be. As it turned out, he [the foreman] did a pretty good job, but I doubt if our jury would have chosen him if we could have voted on it.

Despite whatever initial setback the foreman's leadership may suffer because of the "undemocratic" selection process, most grand-jury foremen appear to emerge as moderately effective leaders in their own right as the jury sessions develop. The following table indicates how questionnaire respondents described the leadership role of their respective grand-jury foremen.

Table 3 Grand Jurors' Opinions of the Role Played by Their Jury Foremen (N = 152)

Opinion	Percentage of Jurors
He played a major role in our discussions and acted as a forceful leader.	42
He simply moderated our discussions and had about the same influence as the average grand juror.	52
He was not a forceful and effective leader and in fact did not play as significant a role as did other members of the grand jury.	6

Thus, 42 percent of the grand jurors regarded their foremen as forceful leaders; about half viewed them as being no more than first among equals; and only 6 percent reported that their foremen played less than average leadership roles in the deliberations. This recollection by one former grandjury member perhaps best exemplifies the role played by the average jury foreman:

> Our foreman played a very unauthoritarian role-very low keyed. He frequently said that he didn't wish to be domineering and this was indeed the case. However, he would frequently redirect the discussions and make procedural recommendations which we followed. I think he did an effective job because I don't think we would have worked well with an authoritative foreman.

Aside from personal leadership characteristics that the designated foreman may possess, the only factor contributing to his leadership potential is that, in a morass of confusion and uncertainty about the jury's duties and functions, most grand jurors look to their foreman for guidance and instruction and expect him to perform. As one former foreman put it,

> I didn't know any more about what we were supposed to be doing than anybody else, but everyone kept asking me, "Can we do this? Are we supposed to do that?" I finally got so I really studied our [grand jury] handbook every night, and I used to stop by the D.A.'s office [actually the office of Assistant District Attorney in charge of the Grand Jury Division] every now and then and asked them for advice. In time I was able to keep one step ahead of the other grand jurors, and I guess that way I earned some of their respect as a leader. But most of the time I didn't know about what was coming off any more than they did, and I doubt whether I fooled them very much.

C. The Extent and Nature of Internal Dissension

What types of cases cause the greatest amount of internal dissension among Texas grand juries? That is, in which cases is there most likely to be a less-than-unanimous vote among grand jurors?[2] Before responding to this query perhaps it should first be noted that there is a rather high degree of unanimity in the voting behavior of most Harris County grand juries. This phenomenon is confirmed by interviewing former grand-jury members and by examining the voting record of the 177th Grand Jury: out of 918 cases decided by this Grand Jury, a nonunanimous vote occurred in a mere forty-two cases (5 percent).

The evidence also indicates that as the grand-jury term progresses, there is a tendency toward increased unanimity in voting patterns.

During its first eight working days the 177th Grand Jury cast less-than-unanimous votes in 9 percent of its decisions, whereas during its last eight sessions there was a divided vote in only 1 percent of its decisions. This excerpt from a journal kept by one former grand-jury member is significant:

> In general there is a fairly unified spirit among us, and I think we all feel the pressure to "dissent only when absolutely necessary," as Chief Justice Taft used to urge. I myself today felt inclined to bring a T.B. [true bill] in a case this afternoon, but I could see no one else agreed with my position, and so when the vote was taken I held my peace.

With respect to cases in which internal disagreement did occur, Table a reveals a remarkable degree of uniformity with only two exceptions: the 177th Grand Jury reached no divided votes on cases dealing with forgery and embezzlement and split its vote on one-third of all victimless sex-crime cases.

Table 4 Cases in Which the 177th Grand Jury Reached a Divided Vote

Crime	Number of Cases	Number of Divided Votes	Percentage of Divided Votes
Victimless Sex Crimes	15	5	33
Crimes of Passion	66	4	6
Drug Crimes	47	3	6
Theft	288	15	5
Burglary	136	5	4
Robbery	93	4	4
Driving While Intoxicated	110	4	4
Forgery and Embezzlement	110	0	0

There are fifty-three miscellaneous cases not included in any of these categories.

Table 5 Grand Jurors' Estimates of Cases in Which the Grand Juries Had the Largest Amount of Internal Dissension (N = 243)

Type of Case	Percentage of Total
Drug Crimes	40
Crimes of Passion	25
Victimless Sex Crimes	9
Forgery and Embezzlement	7
Driving While Intoxicated	7
Theft	5
Burglary	4
Robbery	2

Because questionnaire respondents were permitted to identify more than one category, N exceeds 156.

Table 5 analyzes the types of cases in which the grand juries represented by the questionnaire respondents experienced the most internal dissension.

Table 5 indicates that grand jurors most frequently divide on drug cases, crimes of passion, and on victimless sex crimes, but are more unified on cases of theft, burglary, and robbery. Such findings are not surprising, since cases in the first three categories are likely to be the most serious and complex. They are also the cases on which society in general seems to be most divided, questioning whether these offenses are really crimes at all or whether they are merely actions of social dissidents and psychopaths.

IV. Grand Jury Relations with the District Attorney

The attitude of most grand jurors toward the district attorney and members of his staff is best characterized as ambivalent. On one hand, the district attorney and his staff are regarded as competent, dedicated professionals whose noble task is bringing criminals to justice. In this sense they are the "men in the white hats" whose advice should be respected and whose recommendations should be followed. On the other hand, these officials are regarded as persons who want to secure as many indictments and convictions as possible simply for the sake of prosecution alone, as men who care more about "keeping the cases moving" than about a fair and careful evaluation of each case, and as individuals who view the grand jury as a nuisance or impediment to the expeditious performance of their official duties. While all of the interviewees in this study generally praised the District Attorney's Office, they also asserted that their respective grand juries were conscious of a need "to remain independent of the D.A." and "to keep from becoming a rubber stamp."

The evidence suggests that grand jurors have three general types of complaints against the assistant district attorneys who present their daily caseloads and that these criticisms serve as continuing sources of irritation between the district attorney's staff and the grand juries throughout the three-month term. First, grand jurors tend to complain that the assistant district attorneys present them with too many cases each day and that as a consequence the grand jury does not have time to consider each case carefully enough. Most grand jurors feel compelled by the district attorneys to deal with an enormous number of cases in a considerably short period of time. One former grand juror explained:

> They [the assistant district attorneys] kept telling us, "You're not turning out as many cases as the other grand juries. You know, if you get behind, you might be keeping some poor fellow in jail waiting for his case to be brought to trial. Now you wouldn't want to be responsible for that, would you?" Of course, none of us wanted to keep anyone in jail needlessly because of a delay on our part, but we did resent all the pressure they put on us to crank out those cases.

The following excerpt from one of Harris County's local newspaper stories provides an interesting insight into how the district attorneys evaluate the quality of grand juries:

> The Harris County grand jury which is investigating the Raymond G. Novelli matter has been described as an extremely effective group.
>
> "This is one of the most efficient and effective grand juries I've ever been connected with," Gene Miles, an assistant district attorney, said.
>
> In regard to the number of matters the group handled, Miles said, "Their term total, 2121, is one of the biggest numbers ever heard of." This is almost double the number of cases handled by most grand juries. On their final day of the first term, Miles said he could account for at least 112 matters on which they took action. . . .
>
> "This grand jury represents classic Texans," Miles said, explaining that they "have a philosophical Texas viewpoint. If you're a Texan, you know what's way good, and what's way bad. This group is down the middle, square, extremely attentive, and very fair," Miles said. He added, "If I got in a jam, this is the group I would want to get in a jam with."[3]

A second criticism of the district attorney's staff is that, hardened by their work, these attorneys are insensitive to the rights of the accused and blind to the inequities of our system of law enforcement. Whether such a criticism is valid may be less important than the fact that many grand jurors believe it to be true. One former grand juror (a conservative, middle-class mother whose son had long hair) became so incensed at a statement made by one of the district attorneys during a grand-jury session that she copied it verbatim to show to her husband:

> A policeman can smell a crook a mile off. That's why he stops carloads of "longhairs" and checks for dope. There's just a good chance that when you see a group of them hippies, there's marijuana present. That's just a fact. Now you may call that harrassment, but I say that's good police work.

This type of statement by the district attorneys arguably alienates fair-play-conscious members of middle-class grand juries.

Finally, grand jurors are frequently critical of the careless and incomplete way in which many persons on the district attorney's staff prepare and present cases to the grand jury. One former grand juror gave an example of what he considered the carelessness of an assistant district attorney:

> In one case the accused claimed he was on active military duty when the auto theft occurred. The police and the D.A. never even bothered to telephone the National Guard to check his story before bringing this case to us. The Grand Jury asked that the D.A. do this, and eventually we learned that the defendant's story was correct, and we voted a no bill. I think this is an example of the Grand Jury at its best because we saved the defendant a lot of time and expenses, but it's really something that the police or the D.A. should have done on their own.

Another grand juror once noted in the daily journal of his grand jury work, "This afternoon Mr. [X], one of the D.A.'s, apologized to us for so poorly preparing his cases today. We all concluded after he left that this is the Grand Jury acting at its best, i.e., serving as a check on a sloppy prosecutor." The results of the mailed questionnaire contain additional support for this third criticism. When the respondents were asked whether they thought their respective grand juries served any other function besides simply indicting or refusing to indict persons accused of crimes, 66 percent (seventy-six of the 116 persons responding affirmatively) responded that they had caused the district attorney to investigate cases more carefully.

Despite all of these criticisms, however, the evidence suggests that most grand juries tend (or are forced by circumstances) to rely heavily on the skill and integrity of the assistant district attorneys in deciding whether to bring an indictment.

Over half of the grand juries represented usually indicted only after investigating beyond the district attorney's representations of the evidence in the files. Given the average time of five minutes per case, such claims could not possibly have been the usual practice of any of the grand juries. What is perhaps most significant, however, is that nearly half of all grand juries (the author believes this to be a highly conservative figure) usually take action on cases solely on the basis of what the district attorney says the defendant's file contains without even bothering to examine the file or to require full demonstration by the district attorney.

Table 6 Cases in Which the 177th Grand Jury Refused to Follow the Recommendations of the District Attorney

Types of Cases	Number of Cases	Number of Disagreements with District Attorney	Percentage of Disagreements
Drug Cases	47	13	28
Victimless Sex Crimes	15	4	27
Crimes of Passion	66	11	17
Theft	288	20	7
Burglary	136	7	5
Forgery and Embezzlement	110	2	2
Robbery	93	1	1
Driving While Intoxicated	110	1	1

There are fifty-three miscellaneous cases not included in any of these categories.

The 177th Grand Jury refused to follow the district attorney's recommendations in only 6 percent of all its cases, but disagreed with the district attorneys in 28 percent of the drug cases, 27 percent of the victimless sex crime cases, and 17 percent of the crimes of passion.[4]

The longer the grand jury is in session the more its decisions appear to be in accord with the district attorney's recommendations. More careful analysis reveals, however, that this is not necessarily the case. For the 177th Grand Jury, the evidence suggests that the district attorneys became less likely to present to the grand jury cases in which they believed the jury would vote contrary to their recommendations. For example, of the first 137 cases presented to the grand jury, twenty-five (18 percent) were drug cases, whereas only three (2 percent) of the following 123 cases dealt with drug crimes. Apparently, the district attorneys had determined after a few weeks that they would be more successful by taking their drug cases to one of the other two grand juries sitting at the same time. In fact, this determination was conceded by one of the district attorneys during a working session when a grand juror asked, "Why aren't you giving us any more drug cases?" The attorney replied candidly, "Well, you folks are requiring so much [proof] of us with those cases that we've had to take them to the other grand juries or we're going to get way behind." Therefore, a phenomenon that may well occur in Harris County is for the district attorneys to "size up" the grand juries during their first several working sessions and then to present cases to the grand jury that is most likely to act in accordance with the district attorneys' wishes. To what extent this occurs is unknown, but that it does occur to some degree is beyond doubt.

V. Some General Conclusions and Suggestions

There are several impressions about the composition, inter-workings, and functions of the grand jury that bear emphasis. First, the data strongly indicate that the make-up of the grand jury is not truly representative of the community at large, since there is a marked bias in favor of the upper social and economic elements of society. The evidence also suggests, however, that higher status persons are not only more likely to be solicitous of the rights of the accused than are lower status citizens but are also more likely to possess the intelligence and social efficacy to demand full due process from hardened, work-weary district attorneys. Thus, the grand juries' potential to contribute to civil libertarianism is credited directly to their nonrepresentative character rather than limited by this character.

Second, one may well conclude that whatever their potential for according full due process to the accused, grand juries fall woefully short of the mark, and, as a consequence, the very purpose and utility of the grand-jury system itself must be called into question. There are a variety of reasons why the grand jury does not fulfill its ideal function of carefully screening and evaluating the prosecutor's evidence to determine probable cause that a crime was committed. One reason stems from the patently inadequate training program for newly selected grand jurors. Since grand jurors do not learn systematically from an independent source the full measure of their duties, functions, and prerogatives, there exists the strong possibility that they will become "rubber stamps" of the district attorney's staff. This is not to suggest that all grand juries become mere tools of the district attorney, but the potential for this result is by no means minimal. Jurors who do not fully understand their basic functions, who do not comprehend the meaning of "probable cause," and who do not know how to conduct careful, complete investigations of each case are prime candidates to be manipulated by artful and experienced public prosecutors. Moreover, the evidence indicates that the district attorneys do indeed take advantage of ignorant grand juries by withholding significant pieces of information from grand jury purview and by deliberately routing cases to the grand jury that they expect will act most favorably.

In addition, the never-ending flow of cases with which grand juries are daily bombarded places another obstacle in the path of a full and fair hearing for all those accused of felonies. Given the generally vague and inaccurate nature of the police reports and of the district attorney's file on the accused, five minutes per case is certainly not enough time to spend on the determination of probable cause.

Besides the fact that only a small percentage of cases (probably no more than 5 percent) are examined with any care at all by the grand jury, the evidence suggests that even the selection of that percent is an arbitrary process reflecting the bias of the upper-middle-class grand jury composition. The evidence reveals that the vast majority of these cases includes the bizarre, unusual, or "important" cases that are covered by the news media and that frequently involve the names of well-known local personages, businesses, and organizations. Murder of a prominent socialite, corruption in the local fire department, and alleged immoral conduct by professors at a local state university have all been subjects of extensive grand-jury investigations in Harris County. Such cases are regarded as significant by upper-middle-class grand juries, because the subject matter has a special appeal to the moral, ethical, or even salacious instincts of the middle-class mentality. On the other hand, the robbery of a liquor store, the stabbing death of a derelict in a ghetto bar, and the forgery of a credit card tend to be regarded as routine, boring cases by most grand jurors. As one grand juror said in candid jest,

> We kind of looked forward to the rape and sodomy cases and stuff like that because they broke the routine. I mean if you've heard one bad check case, you've heard them all. But the unusual cases were a little more interesting, and we kind of took our time with them.

The result of this bias may be that the more bizarre, infamous, or salacious the case, the greater the likelihood that it will be among the small percentage of cases in which the grand jury carefully performs the investigation. Conversely, the more routine and uninteresting the case, the greater the likelihood that it will be hastily concluded in reliance on the district attorney's advice that any mistakes will be corrected at trial. Since 46 percent of all Harris County grand-jury indictments since 1950 have ended in either dismissals or acquittals, one may well assume that many mistakes are indeed passed over by bored, unresponsive, and overworked grand juries.

Finally, the data reveal that some of the complex social problems that divide society as a whole, such as marijuana and hard drug laws, the possible pathology of the murderer and the rapist, and the permissibility of "abnormal" sexual relations between consenting adults cause disagreement not only among individual members of the grand jury but also between the grand jury and the district attorney's staff. Moreover, the inordinate amount of time the grand jury spends deliberating on these cases and the level of dissension that these discussions evoke also reflect the upper-middle-class composition of the grand jury. A large number of public opinion polls leads social scientists to conclude that concern with reform of the narcotic laws and revision of the criminal code pertaining to sexual mores is almost exclusively a middle and upper-middle-class phenomenon.

Before the internal dynamics and characteristics of the grand jury can be fully discovered, additional data on several aspects of the institution must be compiled. First, much more information must be discovered about the selection of grand jurors. Research must produce specific answers to questions such as these: Who are the jury commissioners and on what basis are they selected?

What criteria do they use in selecting prospective grand jurors? What standards does the judge use in designating grand-jury foremen? Second, students must acquire more knowledge about the grand jurors themselves. What are their values and what are their attitudes toward the police, the judicial system, and those arrested for a variety of crimes? The additional use of questionnaires and in-depth interviews with a large cross-section of grand jurors is necessary before an accurate profile of the typical grand juror can be drawn.

More evidence on grand-jury deliberations is also needed. Which types of grand jurors are likely to have more influence in the deliberations than others? Some evidence in this study suggests that grand jurors may give deference to a juror whose race or profession relates to the subject matter of a particular case. For example, the members of the 177th Grand Jury listened attentively to the only black on the jury in cases involving a black defendant charged with police harrassment. They also gave considerable deference to the only lawyer on the jury in cases that hinged on highly technical legal questions. Do grand juries develop standard ways of dealing with similar cases (clearly a practice of the 177th Grand Jury) as their terms progress? Is the grand-jury foreman more likely to be on the winning side of divided votes than other grand jurors?

Finally, more data are needed on the influence and role of the assistant district attorneys in relation to the grand jury. Are some district attorneys more successful than others in obtaining desired results from the grand jury? What tactics do district attorneys employ in preparing and presenting cases to grand juries? To what extent do district attorneys present specific cases (or types of cases) to a grand jury that is considered most likely to resolve the cases in accordance with the district attorneys' wishes? If answers to these questions are found, we will gain a clearer understanding of an institution that at this time remains largely unexplored by students of the judicial process.

Bibliography

Abraham, Henry J. (1986) The Judicial Process 5th ed. (New York: Oxford University Press), pp. 105–11.

Cain, Anthony A. (1978) Jury Reform: A Selected Bibliography (Rockville, Md.: National Criminal Justice Reference Service).

Carp, Robert A. (1977) "The Commissioner Method of Selecting Grand Jurors: A Case of a Closed and Unconstitutional System," 14 Houston Law Review 371.

Carp, Robert A. (1982) "Federal Grand Juries: How True 'a Cross Section of the Community,' 7 Justice System Journal 257.

Notes

1. Records of Robert A. Carp, member of Grand Jury impaneled by the 177th District Court, November 1971, in Harris County, Texas.

    The usual procedure in Harris County is for the assistant district attorney to present his cases for the day and then to leave the jury room. Then the foreman asks each grand juror which cases he feels should be discussed. With the 177th Grand Jury, even if only one of the jurors wished to discuss a particular case, discussion occurred. The interviews suggested that other grand juries follow a similar practice.
2. Texas law requires that nine out of the twelve Grand Jurors must vote for a true bill before there is a indictment.
3. The New Citizen, Feb. 4, 1972, at 10.
4. Disagreement with the district attorney was defined as a case where at least one of the following conditions occurs: district attorney recommends true bill and grand jury votes no bill; district attorney seeks no bill and grand jury brings true bill; grand jury indicts for a crime other than the one recommended by district attorney; grand jury requires district attorney to collect additional evidence for a particular case before they will consider it.

20 Politics and the Texas Economy: The Market for Texas

ALAN STONE

Introduction—The Collapse

During the 1970s and early 1980s most Texans thought that oil, their major product, made the state recession proof. Bumper stickers proposed "Let the Yankees freeze in the dark." Unemployment rates were consistently under the national average. At the beginning of 1981, for example, Texas' unemployment rate was more than 2 percentage points under the national average. Accordingly, workers in depressed regions flocked to Houston and other Texas cities in search of jobs. Smug radio commercials proclaimed that Houston would supplant New York as the financial capital of the United States. In short, the heady view during the 1970s and at least through 1981 was that the Texas boom would go on forever.

And then it happened. The collapse did not occur all at once, although to many Texans it appeared that way. Rather, energy-dependent base employment peaked in early 1982 and then began a precipitous slide that continued throughout mid-1987. The state, although far from a tropical monoculture economy, was clearly energy driven. Accordingly, the petroleum collapse triggered major adverse impacts elsewhere. For example, the overall unemployment rate rose from 5.3 percent in 1981 to 6.9 percent in 1982 and then 8.0 percent in 1983. Although the figure declined to 5.9 percent in 1984, it skyrocketed to 8.9 percent in 1986 and through 1988 never was below 7.4 percent. These figures should be compared to rates slightly more than 5 percent in 1980 and 1981. One should recall that, in contrast, the *national* unemployment figures declined sharply from 1983 through 1986.[1]

The oil declined rippled throughout the Texas economy, with the financial and real estate sectors particularly hard hit. Some of the damage to the state's infrastructure may have been permanent, or at least, long lasting. A *New York Times* reporter summarized: "Once Texas banks aspired to be great powers; now virtually all the major banks in the state are owned outside it. The state's savings and loan industry, which made huge and probably uncollectable loans to real estate and energy entrepreneurs who then went bankrupt is a disaster awaiting Federal relief".[2] At the same time, the oil bust imposed a great deal of pressure on the state's tax base, as well as on the state's major communities. Thus, oil and gas' share of total tax revenue dropped from about 28 percent in 1981 to approximately 8 percent in 1988.

The resulting pressure on the ability of state and local governments to spend on services, including the upgrading of infrastructure,[3] must be measured against a national perception of the south, generally, and Texas, particularly. The states of the Old Confederacy were burdened with the twin images of economic backwardness and intense racial strife. To many non-southerners, the images conjured by the South included police dogs snarling at civil rights demonstrators in Montgomery, Alabama or poor sharecroppers living in wooden shacks. Texas' images included not only racism and grinding poverty, but also the urban and rural cowboys as well as the gaudy rich typified in the television show "Dallas". Cutting across all of these images, whether in the highbrow literature of William Faulkner, the middlebrow epic *Giant* or the lowbrow film *Urban Cowboy* was the theme of backwardness.

Images are important, even when they are false or partially true. For businesses contemplating relocating or opening in the first instance do not always undertake a meticulous investigation of a potential location's culture. Sometimes a negative image may rule out a prospective location. One must be careful, however, to appreciate that there are contrary images that reflect the mixed picture of the real world. Yes, there are urban cowboys, but there are also, in Dallas and Houston, two of the greatest medical centers in the world as well as several major megauniversities in which breakthrough research in such new fields as superconductivity has been undertaken. Texas, in brief, has a mixed reputation and most firms considering locating there will be attuned to probing the direction the state and its communities will take in the post-energy economy. The task of political and economic leaders is to anticipate what prospective entrants seek and to act accordingly.

Political Strategy and Location Decisions

States and local governments compete to attract business that will advance their economies. States compete with other states while cities, even those within one state, compete with each other. Houston, Dallas, Austin and San Antonio may compete with each other as well as against cities in many other states. Sometimes the bidding for new businesses can reach striking proportions. Twenty-five states and numerous localities within each of them offered various packages of tax abatements, infrastructure improvements and other inducements to attract General Motors' vast Saturn auto plant. State governors personally visited General Motors corporate headquarters. In another instance, Illinois offered a package valued at $80 million to land the Chrysler/Mitsubishi Diamond-Star automobile plant in the Bloomington-Normal area.[4]

States and communities can be very innovative in attracting and supporting new businesses through financial and other inducements. Consider Michigan, a state with one of the most flexible sets of economic development programs. As the Michigan program illustrates, the problem of attracting—and holding—new enterprise is far more complex than simply throwing money at prospective entrants and hoping that the dollar value of your package is larger than those of your competitors. The decisions from the perspective of public policymakers is clearly economic, but in a far more complex sense than an immediate measurement and comparison of the dollar value of tax inducements and the like. It also involves, from the perspective of state and local policymakers, a strategy for attracting business coupled with a keen sense of an area's advantages and disadvantages. Let us begin with the strategic element, using Michigan as an example.

Michigan is, of course, the automobile capital of the United States, and the state's traditional association has been with manufacturing. Because of the decline in manufacturing, especially in automobiles, the state veered toward insolvency in the early 1980s, and suffered the highest unemployment rate of any state four years in a row. In the four years ending 1983, the state had lost 283,000 jobs in manufacturing alone. In that year James Blanchard, a former congressman from suburban Detroit became governor. Blanchard is widely credited with designing the strategy that turned Michigan around. Assessing the state's labor pool, Blanchard rejected the fashionable stategy of emphasizing the attraction of high tech industries; blue collar factory workers are not readily transformed into softwear designers. Rather, Blanchard and his economic development team decided that it would emphasize manufacturing, Michigan's traditional strength. Accordingly, Blanchard's group designed a package to promote blue collar job growth.

Among the economic development instruments the state has employed is, first, venture capital loaned to new enterprises. State funds come, in part, from public employee pension funds. Second, Michigan Modernization Service, a state agency, provides free advice and technological help to existing enterprises seeking to modernize. Third, another state agency, the Strategic Fund, contributes to a loan-loss reserve fund that provides an incentive to banks to make risky loans. It also backs new products in return for royalties. The Strategic Fund is also creating a statewide network of public-private finance companies that make loans to start new companies. While not entirely responsible for Michigan's remarkable recovery—non agricultural employment jumped from about 3.2 million in 1982 to almost 3.8 million in 1988—these programs clearly contributed importantly.[5]

Michigan is, of course, not one of this nation's "glamour" states that enjoy major advantages in attracting new business. Yet its experience illustrates the importance of the political element in economic development. States and communities need not sit still awaiting changes in their economic fortunes. They can adopt an active political strategy to turn things around. But no political strategy will work unless it is wedded to economic incentives. Prospective business entrants are, in the final analysis, concerned with the "bottom line"—how a new location will contribute to the firm's profitability. Nevertheless, it is necessary to think of economic incentives in the proper way, and not in the limited sense in which the phrase is often used. Economic considerations include far more than direct business costs.

The Economics of Location Decisions

Most of us sharply differentiate what we think of as "economic" considerations from social ones. In the former category we generally include such factors as prices or rates, availability of a product or service and the price-quality tradeoff. In the realm of economic legislation we traditionally think of such diverse things as fiscal and monetary policies, subsidies to agricultural industries and the regulation of telephone rates. Social legislation is usually conceived as pertaining to the quality of life and work. Thus, the conservation of wilderness areas, environmental controls and rules directed against cigarette smoking are conceived as social legislation. While there is general public awareness that the attainment of many social goods involves the expenditure of public and private funds, only rarely do we place a price tag on matters of health, safety or aesthetics. Indeed, many of us think that it is almost obscene to think in economic terms when matters of safety, health or scenery are concerned. Yet, if we reflect on the matter, it is precisely in economic terms that we should think of such matters, especially as they affect location decisions.

The central problem in our thinking is that while we are used to placing a value on traded goods, such as onions, automobiles and houses, we are unused to doing so for untraded "goods", such as life, health and scenery. Yet it can be done, and, indeed is done in a variety of settings. For example, juries place values in negligence cases on such things as loss of a limb or a disfiguring injury. The sums are, to a considerable extent, judgmental. Yet in an approximate manner we do engage in calculations involving such losses. Similarly, aesthetic considerations play major roles in the price of homes. When one "moves" the same home from a high crime area to a low crime area it will usually be more expensive in the latter. Similarly, the same home overlooking the Pacific Ocean in California will be more expensive than if it is located 25 miles inland. The market for homes will almost always incorporate asethetic considerations. Again, employment decisions and the market for labor will usually take into account such factors as the noise level, safety, the degree of emotional stress associated with the job, and so on. That we cannot place *precise* figures on such considerations in the same way that we can precisely calculate the cost of tomatoes does not mean that these considerations are not incorporated into economic calculations. They clearly are.

Now let us consider this conclusion in our discussion of location decisions. One would initially think that a comparison of the *direct* costs of doing business—labor costs, taxes, rent and so on—will determine a location decision. Under this view, if such direct costs are lower in Fargo, North Dakota than in Los Angeles, California, a firm contemplating relocation will select the former above the latter. If that were all there was to it, Fargo's strategy would be easy. Lower the direct cost that can be controlled such as taxes and point to the comparisons adverse to your rival. Since such costs are, in fact, lower in North Dakota than in Southern California one could expect under this reasoning a larger number of businesses to relocate in North Dakota than in California. But that has not been happening. In fact, high direct cost locations, such as Southern California and the New York City metropolitan area continue to lead other locations in attracting new business. Such decisions can be understood when we consider that "economic" decisions take into account far more than the direct costs of doing business. Such factors as weather, crime rates, quality of the labor pool, infrastructural conditions, and cultural amenities are also taken into account.

And, of course, relative weights and assessments vary from industry to industry and even from firm to firm. For example, a company contemplating opening a biotechnology company will place greater weight on the availability of skilled researchers than a shoe manufacturer will. The biotechnology company will be attracted to areas with universities that train and graduate large numbers of good researchers. Moreover, that company must be alert to the issue of cultural amenities since Ph.Ds in biology and biochemistry will be generally far more concerned than factory workers about the quality of museums, symphony orchestras and so on. In contrast, the company contemplating opening the shoe factory will be concerned with the wage levels of unskilled labor, labor availability and the quality of primary and secondary education. The latter factor is often overlooked, but labor intensive firms do require that many of their employees attain reasonable levels of proficiency in reading instructions and simple mathematics.

When one takes into account the diversity of reasons to locate in one place rather than another and the variations from one kind of business to another, it is clear that the political economy of relocation is a far more complex matter than simply designing tax incentives to encourage movement to your area. Nevertheless, as the Michigan experience shows, it is possible to design a political strategy to encourage the selection of one area rather than another. Political leaders need not sit back and wait for improvements to occur. They can make things happen.

Chasing Smokestacks with Tax Concessions

Two schools of thought have emerged on government's role in economic redevelopment. The first of these emphasizes reducing taxes as the principal mechanism for attracting outside business. The second emphasizes various spending programs as the best way to attract new firms. Of course, these are matters of emphasis, not mutually exclusive categories. People who emphasize tax reduction will spend public money to attract new business while those who advocate spending policies are alert to the fact that firms making location decisions consider tax rates. Moreover, both schools, which, for the sake of brevity we will call the tax reducers and the spenders, concur on certain kinds of activity, such as public relations, that brings an area's favorable features to the attention of outsiders.

Within both frameworks location decisions involve practical problems, are subject to negotiations, and are measured by results. That is, inducing firms to locate in a community involves far more than presenting a sales pitch. It entails operating through the processes of government to attain results. In one careful study of the process, Calhoun County, Texas, which suffered a 15.8 percent unemployment rate in 1986 sought to attract a new plastics plant that would employ approximately 2,700 workers and cost $3.2 billion to construct. Formosa Plastics, the Taiwanese corporation contemplating the move, wanted not promises, but a variety of political decisions that would reduce or suspend taxes, relax environmental controls and ease entry restrictions for Taiwanese managers and professionals. Agencies as diverse as the federal Environmental Protection Agency, the Texas Air Control Board, the Texas Water Commission, Calhoun County Commissioners and local school boards had to make decisions that would facilitate the new plant coming online.[6]

All of this necessary activity as well as the increasing professionalization of those involved in economic development sometimes obscures the fact that there are real choices in strategy. Professionals at the highly respected Economic Development Institute at the University of Oklahoma, local chambers of commerce and state and local governments as well as the journalists at such trade magazines as *Plant Location* are concerned with details, specifics and experiences. Our concern here is with the evaluation of broad political strategies. We will look at the tax reducers in this section and then will consider the spenders in the next one.

Both the tax reducers and the spenders are bound by the limitations and advantages of locations. For example, certain regions and cities are located in major markets while others are located in smaller ones. Any firm will realize that east coast and California cities are situated in areas with high population density and excellent trade facilities. That is, locating a new plant in Los Angeles not only puts one in easy proximity to a major market, but makes available port facilities that provide access to Asian markets as well. For the same reason, locating in Baltimore puts one in the midst of what has been termed the "Megalopolis" stretching from Boston, Massachusetts to Washington, D.C. Baltimore also provides good trade access to markets in Western and Eastern Europe. These are natural advantages that decision makers in North Dakota or Texas must take into account. No amount of public relations about the "quality of life" can hide the relative disadvantages of Texas locations, and to a much greater extent, North Dakota ones.

One implication should come immediately to mind. A city or region should highlight its natural advantages. This casts considerable doubt on an exclusive or predominant tax reduction strategy. These considerations are easier to state than apply. But 2 Ohio cities illustrate the point. Columbus became a midwestern success story because it combined existing manufacturing strength with educational and research strengths—it is the home of Ohio State University, one of the nation's premier institutions—to attract service companies linked to its traditional bases.[7] Similarly, a study of Cleveland showed that its salvation lay more in building upon its manufacturing sector rather than in writing off that sector and focusing largely on businesses unrelated to Cleveland's traditional economy.[8]

The lesson for Texas, generally, and the Houston metropolitan area is clear. Do not write off the energy and petrochemical industries that have traditionally been great strengths of the region simply because the fall in petroleum prices triggered much of Texas' decline in economic well-being. True, relying upon one product can be terribly dangerous. But Texas never was a monoculture almost wholly dependent on oil. It has had traditional agricultural strengths and, more recently, its major medical centers in Dallas and Houston are unparalleled in the world. Nevertheless, an emphasis should be on attempting to attract business to which energy prices and availability are very important. One major econometric study, for example, concluded, on the basis of data supplied by individual firms, that low energy costs and an available pool of technically proficient workers were far more important factors in location decisions than tax concessions designed to attract new business.[9]

This raises generally the issue of tax reduction as a *primary* focus of government policy in attracting new business. Obviously, firms, like people, would rather pay less in taxes than more. But people do not gravitate to the low tax states from the high tax ones without incorporating many other factors in their economic judgments. Indeed, many factors play more important roles than state and local taxes in individual and family considerations. For example, California's 1986 per capita state and local taxes were $1,144, Arizona's was $975, Nebraska's was $700 and South Dakota's was $570.[10] Yet, people did not flock from Arizona and California to Nebraska and South Dakota. Rather with respect to those states the movement was very much in the other direction, indicating that lower taxes were not a critical factor in personal location decisions.

Of course, firms contemplating a move will attempt to use the lower taxes chip if they are involved in negotiating with 2 or more locations. Why should a firm not attempt to reduce its tax burden as it weighs moving to a new location? Sound negotiating strategy suggests that such a firm should overstate the importance of taxes, by making statements that tax concessions are crucial in its decision. Any poker player is familiar with the strategy. But such public statements should not be confused with the serious balancing of advantages and disadvantages in which most relocating firms are engaged. To take a parallel situation GTE, the nation's largest independent telephone company, compared the action of Texas telephone regulators adversely to Florida regulators as it weighed Tampa and Dallas as alternative sites. A GTE official, attempting to influence a pending Texas rate decision, complained about its shareholders' anger if it moved offices to an unenlightened state.[11] Yet within a short period after this proclamation, GTE announced its decision to move to Dallas.

The superficial appeal of principally relying on tax incentives to lure new business is questionable for several reasons. First, we must distinguish between selective tax inducements to attract *specific* firms or kinds of facilities and the state's general tax structure. Selective tax concessions to attract particular firms are particularly insidious and often are counterproductive. Shifting a fixed tax burden from new arrivals to older established firms can cause sufficient resentment to lead older firms to relocate. Moreover, the precedent, once established of granting a selective tax concession to a newcomer guarantees that all other potential entrants will demand the same or greater concessions. Firms already in an area will have an incentive to threaten that they will depart—unless they, too, are provided with tax abatements and other concessions. For example, a manufacturer of hydraulic equipment in Columbus, Ohio announced that it would close its local facility in response to the City Council providing a generous tax concession to a West German competitor that agreed to locate in Columbus.[12] Selective tax concessions almost inevitably guarantee demands for further concessions and can lead to an overall decline in tax revenues sufficient to undermine the community's ability to finance the necessary infrastructural improvements to attract new business. In short, selective tax concessions can be very counterproductive.

This leads to another major criticism of tax reduction policy in both its selective and general tax reduction forms. Simply put, costs may outweigh benefits. In their zeal to attract new businesses communities may offer a package of concessions that outweigh the benefits in jobs added, retail business generated and so on. Garland County's concessions to Formosa Plastics have been criticized in this respect. Consider the following important example of concessions being too large relative to the benefits. Kentucky is providing $125 million in tax concessions and other special incentives to Toyota Motor Corp. for a facility that could employ no more than 3,000 people. Among the special concessions, the state agreed to educate the children of Japanese workers in Japanese at a special school 6 days a week for 20 years.[13] While the benefits may eventually be assessed at a greater value than the costs—or may not—rarely do the proponents of tax concession policy carefully engage in such calculations before or during the bidding wars with their opponents. Rather, they tend to get caught up in the struggle to lure the newcomers and are able to portray those who would exercise caution as enemies of adding new jobs to the state and community.

Most importantly, many, although not all, of the studies concerned with the relocation issue have found that local and state tax levels and concessions play relatively insignificant roles in the eventual decision on where to locate. The fear of firms moving to more hospitable tax environments is not new, and, as long ago as 1958, a highly respected study discovered that the hypothesis was not correct in most cases.[14] A 1986 historical review of the literature on the topic again found that corporate tax reductions played little role in relocation decisions, although the myth of their centrality persists.[15]

Tax breaks can be translated into specific sums. In that sense they are homogeneous, unlike other inducements. One state can readily offer a set of tax inducements that will match or beat other states bidding for an enterprise. At which point, the first state has a strong incentive to match the second bidder. And like sales of fungible commercial products (such as wheat) "prices" of all suppliers tend to reach the same market level. For this reason, when General Motors was considering various locations for its Saturn Division, it reported that tax concessions and rates played little role in the site choice because the inductments offered by every community was virtually the same.[16]

One should not conclude from this discussion that tax levels and tax concessions play *no* role in the site selection process. Rather, the point is to place tax policies in perspective by showing their limited roles. Too much political rhetoric on the subject of local and regional development is based upon the incorrect premise that tax concessions, and low tax rates are primarily responsible for luring new enterprises. Such thinking has a superficial appeal since all of us would rather pay lower taxes than higher ones. But much more is involved in luring enterprises as the Michigan experience shows. Redevelopment expert Roger W. Schmenner has summarized the policies advocated by the tax reducers perceptively: "Taxes and financial inducements seem to be, at best, tie breakers acting between otherwise equal towns or sites. These traditional linchpins of state and local industrial development efforts simply cannot be relied on, by themselves, to attract new plants that would otherwise locate somewhere else. The fact that the tax and financial results . . . are so weak suggests that the traditional tax and financial incentives—tax reductions, moratoriums, roll backs, assessment breaks, industrial revenue bonding *et al*— may not be worth the cost".[17]

Political Entrepreneurship

There is no quick fix for attracting new business to a state or locality any more than there is a guaranteed way to make $1 million in a short time. The entrepreneur in business hoping to become rich must have a plan based upon his or her skills and talents, must have a novel product or service in mind or a new way to produce or offer an older product to the public, and must be prepared to incur risks to succeed. The business entrepreneur must be willing to outlay substantial sums long before he or she reaps any profit. Political leaders seeking to attract new business firms must develop some of the same attributes. They must plan, undertake risks, incur costs, and follow through, in order to succeed. Political leaders must be prepared to fail as well as to succeed. They must, in short, be entrepreneurs. While the history of state and local politics in this country should leave one pessimistic about whether entrepreneurial talent is drawn into government when the rewards are greater in the private sector, it has occasionally happened. More importantly, public officials concerned with economic development should be judged on how effectively they design public policies to attract new business. They should not get away with a commitment to nothing more than tax reductions and public relations.

The first steps in designing policies are to recognize certain essential facts about potential business entrants and the factors that attract businesses to an area. This, in turn, leads to the appreciation that different kinds of firms weigh differently the various inducements offered. As we saw earlier, states and cities are advised to play to their strengths as well as to move in new directions in making their offers to potential entrants. They must realize that the task is an arduous as well as a potentially creative one. This is because most of the new jobs offered in the American economy come from small and medium sized firms, and not the few large ones. This, of course, does not mean that a city should spurn the possibility of landing a major new General Motors plant. Such possibilities should obviously be pursued, but development policy must be based upon incentives designed to attract and sustain the large numbers of small and medium sized firms.

David Birch, one of the most important figures in redevelopment studies, was one of the first to recognize the importance of smaller enterprises in job creation. Between 1969 and 1976 approximately two-thirds of the net new jobs were created by firms with fewer than 20 employees, and 81 percent by firms with fewer thatn 100 employees. This trend persisted during the 1980–1982 economic downturn and continued during the boom that developed thereafter in the Reagan Presidency and continued into the Bush Presidency. Moreover, much of the growth during the Reagan boom was in new enterprises, rather than in the expansion of older small businesses. There are many implications that follow from these trends, but several are critical from the perspective of economic development policy.

First, state and local efforts should be guided toward assisting prospective entrepreneurs in reducing the risks normally associated with founding a new business. Thus, providing venture capital through state pension funds to reduce the capital needs of new entrepreneurs, as Michigan and several other states have done, can be an inportant tool in redevelopment. Other forms of assistance, such as job training for employees, including production, distribution and management skills can be equally useful in both luring existing firms into an area and encouraging would-be entrepreneurs to start up new firms. Based upon North Carolina's experience, Alvah Ward, that state's Director of Business and Industrial Development of the state Department of Commerce, concluded that the free job training program is "overwhelmingly our best and most used incentive."[18] Interestingly, the state's access road program in which North Carolina builds such roads to places of work was ranked as the second most important incentive.

The list of possible innovative programs that a state could undertake is very large. but more important than the details is the strategy. The lesson is clear. Areas that now seek firms should not retrench in the face of adversity and ruthlessly cut the provision of services, possibly destroying infrastructure in the process. Like a well-managed business firm, government must invest—and that might mean raising taxes—in order to attract and stimulate new businesses and the employment that will eventually compensate for the investment. Doug Ross, the director of the Michigan Commerce Department, put it succinctly: "The premium is on building a better public infrastructure to serve the private sector. The new idea is that the state becomes the broker and the seed investor for change in the private sector."[19]

There are innumerable industries and services in the United States, and every state and community, although it emphasizes some of them, is diverse. There are many ways of categorizing these industries and services. One useful way for our purposes is to divide them into labor intensive and capital intensive business. One can also categorize industries by the kind of labor dominantly employed into low, medium and high depending on the extent of training and skill required. Each state and community must make its own decision on the kinds of industries and services that it will emphasize. But running through most of the range of industries and services in the American economy and each category there are a few constants in desirable public policy. David Allen and Victor Levine surveyed 301 firms and asked the decision-makers in these firms to rank in order of importance the factors that determine location decisions. The list included 31 items, of which taxes on personal income and property ranked 31st. The top twelve factors ranked ordered are: proximity to market, proximity to family, labor availability, commuting distance, cost of property, skill level of labor, interaction with other firms, availability of business services, wage and salary levels, cost of living, proximity to research services and good schools for children.[20]

Obviously, state and local government cannot do anything about proximity of family, and their ability to affect other variables is certainly limited. But the emphasis on labor availability, the skill level of labor, good schools, proximity to research services (such as research oriented universities), the transportation infrastructure does clearly suggest major policy directives for Texas. Nothing could more clearly undermine the economic recovery that Texas began to experience in the late 1980s than cuts in infrastructural and educational expenditures. If anything, the evidence adduced here supports the view that the state should be spending more on education, research, job training, sewers, water, transportation and other infrastructural development than it now does, even if that means tax increases. Coupled with the low housing costs and costs of business that prevail throughout the state and together with an industrial development policy of the Michigan type, the gradual recovery that began in the late 1980s can move forward—or at least not be reversed. As the oil bust demonstrated, regional advantage can be short lived.[21] Government policies can play a major role in preventing a recurrence of the Texas' dreadful fall.

Notes

1. Peter Applebome, "Texas After the Oil Collapse: Back if Not Quite Swaggering", *New York Times* (December 5, 1988): 8.
2. *Ibid*, p. 8.
3. Infrastructure is "those structural elements of an economy which facilitate the flow of goods and services between buyers and sellers. Examples of these structural elements are communications and transport (roads, railways, harbours, airports, telephones, etc.) housing, sewerage, power systems, etc." David W. Pearce, (ed.) *The MIT Dictionary of Modern Economics,* 3rd Edn. (Cambridge, Mass.: MIT Press, 1986), p. 204.
4. William A. Testa and David R. Allardice, "Bidding for Business", *Chicago Fed Letter* (December, 1988), p. 1.
5. Rose Gutfeld and Eugene Carlson "Made in Michigan", *Wall Street Journal* (August 11, 1988): 1, 10.
6. Peter Elkind, "The Wooing of Chairman Wang", *Texas Monthly* (February, 1989): 77–78, 124–127.
7. See, generally, Thomas M. Stanback, Jr. and Thierry J. Noyelle, *Cities In Transition* (Totowa, N.J.: Littlefield, 1982).
8. Aaron Gurwitz and Kingsley G. Thomas, *The Cleveland Metropolitan Economy: An Initial Assessment* (Santa Monica, Ca.: Rand Corporation, 1982).
9. Dennis W. Carlton, "The Location and Employment Choices of New Firms: An Econometric Model With Discrete and Continuous Endogenous Variables" *Review of Economics and Statistics,* 65 (1983): 440–449.
10. *The World Almanac and Book of Facts, 1989* (New York: World Almanac, 1988), p. 141.
11. "GTE Official Pans Texas Regulation", *Houston Chronicle* (October 29, 1988): 4C.
12. Testa and Allardice, p. 3.
13. Greg Meyers "Bidding Wars", *Business & Economic Review* (March, 1987): 10.
14. Alan K. Campbell, "Taxes and Industrial Location in the New York Metropolitan Region", *National Tax Journal,* 11 (1958): 195–218.
15. David N. Allen and Victor Levine, *Nurturing Advanced Technology Enterprises* (New York: Praeger, 1986), pp. 11,12.

16. *Ibid,* p. 26.
17. Roger W. Schmenner, *Making Business Location Decisions* (Englewood Cliffs, N.J.: Prentice Hall, 1982), p. 51.
18. Quoted in Myers, p. 12.
19. William E. Schmidt, "What the States Are Doing for Industry", *New York Times* (February 5, 1989): E2.
20. David N. Allen and Victor Levine, *Nurturing Advanced Technological Enterprises* (New York: Praeger, 1986), p. 74.
21. See Philip L. Rones, "An Analysis of Regional Employment Growth 1973–1985," *Monthly Labor Review* (July, 1986): pp. 3–14.